THE EARLY STEWART KINGS

The Stewart Dynasty in Scotland Series
Series Editor: Norman Macdougall
Senior Lecturer in the Department of Scottish History
University of St Andrews

1. *The Early Stewart Kings:*
Robert II and Robert III, 1371–1406
Stephen I. Boardman

2. *James I* (1406–37)
Michael Brown

The Stewart Dynasty in Scotland

THE EARLY STEWART KINGS: ROBERT II AND ROBERT III
1371–1406

STEPHEN I. BOARDMAN

TUCKWELL PRESS

First published in 1996 in Great Britain by
Tuckwell Press Ltd
The Mill House
Phantassie
East Linton East Lothian EH40 3DG
Scotland

ISBN 1 898410 43 7

The publisher gratefully acknowledges subsidy
of the Scottish Arts Council for the publication
of this book.

British Library Cataloguing-in-Publication Data.
A catalogue record for this book is available on
request from the British Library.

Typeset by Hewer Text Composition Services, Edinburgh
Printed and bound by
Cromwell Press, Broughton Gifford, Melksham, Wiltshire

Contents

Acknowledgements   vi

List of Illustrations, Maps and Genealogical tables   vii

Foreword   ix

Preface   xiii

1. A New Dawn for Yesterday's Man   1

2. The Foundation of a Dynasty: Politics, Power
   and Propaganda   39

3. Unleashing the Hounds: The Stewart
   Settlement in the North   71

4. Anglo-Scottish Relations, 1371–84   108

5. Broken Promise: The Carrick Guardianship,
   1384–88   130

6. Brothers Divided: The Guardianship of the
   Earl of Fife and Menteith, 1388–93   159

7. Ghosts of the Past, Visions of the Future:
   Robert III, 1390–98   194

8. Comets and Shooting Stars: The Lieutenancy
   of the Duke of Rothesay, 1398–1402   223

9. Contempt of Court   255

10. Endgame: King, Bishop, Castle, Knight   278

    Conclusion: The Kindly King   302

Bibliography   315

Index   327

ACKNOWLEDGEMENTS

I should like to acknowledge the financial assistance provided to me, through the Glenfiddich Fellowship, by Dr Alexander Grant Gordon of William Grant and Sons Ltd. The final stages of the project were completed with the help of a British Academy Postdoctoral Fellowship. I should also like to thank the staff of the Scottish Record Office, the National Library of Scotland and St Andrews University Library for all their assistance during the course of my research.

I owe a great debt of gratitude to a number of my colleagues and friends who have helped me in a variety of ways. Dr Athol Murray of the Scottish Record Office and Dr Alexander Grant of the Department of History at the University of Lancaster generously supplied me with material collected by them for a forthcoming edition of the Acts of Robert II and Robert III. In addition, Dr Grant offered many helpful ideas and suggestions based on his own extensive research on late fourteenth-century Scotland. I have also benefited from the specific advice and general encouragement of my friends in the Department of Scottish History at St Andrews, notably Dr Roger Mason, Dr Carol Edington, who introduced me to my computer, and Dr Michael Brown. Long and animated discussions with Dr Brown on his own research into the reign of Robert III's son and successor, James I, have honed many of the arguments advanced in this book.

My greatest academic debt remains that to my former thesis supervisor and current editor Dr Norman Macdougall, who has performed both roles with care, patience and good humour. His contribution to the completion of this book has been immense, ranging from the discussion of the issues raised by the text to the rather more mundane and grisly business of reuniting split infinitives.

Outwith the world of Scottish History my wife Sheila has been a constant source of support and encouragement through trying times, while my eldest daughter, Kirsty, has kept up a regular supply of impressionist portraits of cranes and foxes to brighten my office. Finally, I would like to thank my father and mother for all their help over many years. This book is dedicated to them both.

ILLUSTRATIONS (between pages 142 and 143)

1. 'Syr valtir the bald leslye'
2. Doune Castle
3. Henry Percy's captured pennon is displayed
4. Urquhart Castle
5. Rothesay Castle
6. The tombs of Sir Duncan Campbell of Loch Awe and his second wife
7. The episcopal castle at St. Andrews
8. The tomb of Alexander Stewart, earl of Buchan and lord of Badenoch
9. Dumbarton Castle
10. The Bass Rock
11. The insignia of the Stewart earls of Ross, Carrick, Fife and Strathearn

	Facing page
MAPS	1
1. Stewart Earldoms, Lordships and Castles	1
2. The Wolf's Lair	87
3. Locations of Royal Acts: Robert II (1371–1390)	92
4. Locations of Royal Acts: Robert III (1390–1406)	284

TABLES

1. The Stewart Claim	2
2. Sons and Daughters: The family of Robert II	41
3. Brothers-in-Arms: The Lindsay-Leslie Affinity	80
4. The Douglas Inheritance	165
5. Highland Connection: Albany and the Lordship of the Isles	210

Foreword

The early Stewart kings, perhaps understandably, have lacked biographers, but they have never been short of detractors. Most modern writers have taken their cue from Jean Froissart's unflattering description of Robert II in his seventieth year, 1384, the year in which the king, in Professor Duncan's memorable phrase, 'was given statutory notice of redundancy', rather than from Abbot Bower's comments that Robert II was 'most highly regarded', and that Robert III had 'a sound conscience . . . and love of justice'. Part of the problem may be that neither of these roles appears to merit the praise of those twentieth-century historians who equate effective government with masterful kingship, the domination of a turbulent nobility by a ruthless monarch.

Thus the early Stewarts, according to Professor Dickinson, were 'both old and of little force of character'; Professor Donaldson caustically remarked that the famous dynasty had made 'a somewhat pedestrian beginning'; and Professor Nicholson went so far as to group the accession of the Stewarts together with 'other afflictions' of the late medieval period. Nicholson was, of course, working to his own agenda. His praise of David II, Robert II's predecessor — much lauded for his 'intensive government' — required the corollary of a rapid Stewart decline in order to set off King David's presumed virtues in high relief. Alone amongst recent writers, Dr Alexander Grant pointed to the peace and stability of Robert II's reign, and to the king's even-handedness in the distribution of patronage.

When historians sit in judgment on key figures from a period of the past which is still to be studied in depth, we may be forgiven for feeling more than a little sceptical. Dr Boardman's study of Robert II and Robert III is not however an attempt to register special pleading for the early Stewarts, still less an effort to replace yesterday's historical prejudices with those which are currently fashionable. Rather the book, the first scholarly study of the early Stewart kings, seeks to understand the nature of their kingship, the forces which shaped their style of government, the constraints which were placed upon it, and the policies attempted or effectively pursued by both rulers. It is a remarkable story in its own right, covering the first two generations of what was to become one of Europe's most famous royal dynasties.

Even a casual glance at the facts reveals that Robert II and his successor espoused a different governmental style to that of David II. Firstly, there are striking differences in geographical orientation, with Robert II to be found conducting royal business most frequently in Perth, or nearby Methven or Scone, rather than Edinburgh, the location of the great majority of David II's *Acta* (though not those of David's father, the hero king Robert I, whose principal centres of business were Berwick and Scone, with Edinburgh a poor third). The change undoubtedly reflects the Stewarts' origins as west-coast magnates, their domination (by the early 1380s) of Scotland north of Forth, and their enthusiasm for a mixture of business and pleasure in Highland Perthshire.

Secondly — and more significantly — as Dr Boardman shows, in the crucially important area of crown-magnate relations there emerged a highly decentralised style of kingship, with extensive delegation of royal authority to the great regional families, above all to the king's Stewart kinsmen. Stewart power lay partly in the territorial strength of the family 'firm', but also in Robert II's skill in defusing trouble from the very outset in 1371, when he faced a challenge from William, earl of Douglas, supported by some of those with close ties to the former king, David II. Robert II's response to this threat, as Dr Boardman shows, was to make deals and alliances, leaving his major opponents with their regional influence intact, or even enhanced. Such policies reflect 'the techniques of a man long schooled in the practicalities of baronial politics'. Dr Nicholson has a different view; when he comments that 'opposition was bought off; loyalty was not taken for granted but was richly rewarded', he means it as a damaging criticism of the early Stewarts. But perhaps most rulers, and certainly successful ones, behave in this way to a greater or lesser degree; and Robert II was not after all the creator of the great MacDonald and Douglas territorial lordships with whose leaders he had to deal as king.

Furthermore, King Robert's succession in 1371 was a surprise only in the sense that David II's death was unexpected. Robert Stewart had been waiting in the wings for half-a-century, he had spent his manhood in ruthless pursuit of his wide-ranging territorial interests in the west and north, and he succeeded in terms of an act of succession as old as 1318. It is difficult to equate the usual view of Robert, the mediocre, prematurely aged, and decrepit king, with that of Robert, the ruthless expansionist magnate in pursuit of the crown. And it may be added that Robert II, at fifty-five, was hardly on the verge of senility. His second son Robert, earl of Fife and duke of Albany, first the *éminence grise* and latterly the uncrowned ruler of Scotland for more than a generation, made his most ruthless political coups in his early sixties and died aged eighty.

It would be difficult to make a convincing case for Robert II's heir, John, earl of Carrick, who took the crown as Robert III, as an effective ruler. His failure may however be accounted for largely by internecine feuds and palace revolutions which afflicted the royal Stewart family, and in which he played a central role, during the 1380s. Having ousted his father from government in 1384, the future Robert III was replaced in his turn by his forceful younger brother, Robert, earl of Fife, in 1388. It is undoubtedly a commentary on the nature of Stewart politics at this time that the most significant turning point of the period was not the succession of a new king, Robert III, but rather that of a new royal lieutenant, Fife, together with the third earl of Douglas, Archibald 'the Grim', in 1388. The ensuing two years, graphically described by Dr Boardman, in effect witnessed the political marginalisation of the future Robert III and made him, in the early 1390s, little more than an observer of Scottish politics.

Supporters of masterful kingship may however take comfort from Robert III's most enduring legacy, namely the political aspirations of his sons David and James, who both possessed a much more exalted view of Stewart monarchy than that of their father. The old king lived long enough to see his elder son David, duke of Rothesay, take control of government as lieutenant-general at the age of 21, only to perish at the hands of his uncle and rival, Robert, duke of Albany, three years later. Writing in the early sixteenth century, Hector Boece commented that Rothesay had died a martyr, and that miracles were performed at his tomb until his younger brother, James I, took revenge on the entire Albany family, at which point the miracles ceased. Subsequently James I himself was assassinated, a martyr, as Dr Michael Brown has shown, for the power and prestige of the Stewart dynasty. In their different ways, both these sons of Robert III set the agenda for a more dominant and aggressive style of kingship; but it was also a style which the Scots were reluctant to accept, and indeed prone to resist, until the 1450s.

A generation ago, Professor Donaldson pronounced judgment on the early Stewart kings before the case had come to court. 'Admittedly', he remarked, 'no attempt has yet been made to bring the resources of modern historical research to bear on Robert II and Robert III . . . but it is beyond the bounds of probability that, even if this is done, either of them will emerge as a man who did much positively to shape Scottish history.' The attempt has now been made. Readers may judge for themselves.

Norman Macdougall
Series Editor

Preface

A s the author of the most recent general history of Scotland has observed: 'Less is known about Robert II and Robert III than any other late medieval kings.'[1] The perennial lack of interest, both academic and popular, in the careers of the founding fathers of Scotland's most durable and famous royal dynasty is at once regrettable and understandable. The contemporary or near-contemporary chroniclers who reported on Robert II and Robert III's reigns certainly did not leave an overall impression of scintillating or forceful personalities with which to excite the interest of later generations. Jean Froissart's picture of the decrepit sixty-nine-year-old Robert II in 1384, bowed down with age, bleary-eyed, wishing for peace with England but openly despised and ignored by his bellicose nobility, was the earliest and one of the most important elements in the development of an enduring tradition which saw the first two Stewart kings as weak, ineffective and inadequate monarchs.[2]

For most subsequent historians the opening of the Stewart age was marked by a sad decline in the stature and competence of Scottish kings. W. C. Dickinson, for example, observed that 'The early Stewarts were strong neither in body nor in character', with 'both unfitted for strong and active rule', and concluded that Robert II's kingship 'was weak and inefficient, and that of his son, . . . was even weaker still'.[3] Gordon Donaldson summed up the two reigns with the memorably acerbic comment that 'after nineteen years of the increasingly senile Robert II, Scotland was to have sixteen years of the infirm Robert III'.[4] The apparent degeneration of the royal house was accentuated by the fame of Robert I, the 'hero-king' of the Wars of Independence, whose reputation cast a long shadow over his successors. Thus, in lamenting the passing of Robert I, R. L. Mackie could comment that 'unfortunately for Scotland, a hundred years had to pass before a worthy successor sat on the throne of Bruce'.[5]

The patent lack of enthusiasm for any detailed consideration of the first two Stewart kings was no doubt largely generated by their own lacklustre reputations, but the indifference of scholars was also grounded in a general opinion that the late fourteenth century was an era with few intrinsic merits as a field of endeavour. Most nineteenth and early twentieth-century writers on Scottish history saw in the accession of the Stewarts the opening of an age characterised by a long and dreary clash between 'a succession of Scottish kings and their great vassals for the ruling power in the direction of the national destinies'.[6] In this view, early Stewart kingship had no great ennobling mission to sustain an historian's interest, for, as P. Hume Brown averred, the two 'great causes of early Scottish kingship' had come to an end with the unification of the kingdom by the Canmore dynasty, and the defence of its independence by the Bruces. The rule of the early Stewarts was thus stigmatised as a period of 'chronic misery and arrested national development'.[7] This generally negative view of Robert II and Robert III, and the age in which they ruled, goes some way to explain the otherwise remarkable fact that the two kings have never been the subject of a scholarly biography.

Although historians were repelled by the aura of casual barbarism and magnate violence which surrounded the late fourteenth century, the period's dramatic episodes and forceful personalities attracted the attention of historical novelists. Sir Walter Scott's *The Fair Maid of Perth* is set in the reign of Robert III and revolves around the fierce clan duel of 1396 on the North Inch in Perth. A far less accomplished literary foray into the same reign is T. D. Lauder's *The Wolf of Badenoch*, a work whose awfulness eventually attains a kind of grandeur. Lauder's insight into the Wolf's unruly domestic arrangements, which today would demand an immediate intervention by the Social Services, is capped by a quite hilarious account of the lord of Badenoch's repentance and moral redemption after the burning of Elgin cathedral.[8]

In the last thirty years, the comparative neglect of the history of Scotland during the second half of the fourteenth century has been ameliorated by the work of a number of historians. Although the reign of David II (1329–71) still requires a full-scale evaluation, R. G. Nicholson, A. B. Webster, and A. A. M. Duncan have produced a series of detailed studies which collectively shed a great deal of light on the rule of that enigmatic king.[9] The period after 1371 has benefited from a similar expansion in scholarly activity. Dr Nicholson's impressive and wide-ranging overview of the politics of the late medieval kingdom, *Scotland: The Later Middle Ages*, provides a brief account of the early Stewart kings which retains the critical tone of earlier analyses. Nicholson dismisses early Stewart kingship as 'futile and aimless', and asserts that, under the new dynasty, 'Scotland was to be racked by a misgovernance which proved . . . that there was no substitute for a masterful king'.[10]

In contrast, the most recent general survey of the late medieval kingdom, Alexander Grant's stimulating *Independence and Nationhood*, offers a much more positive appraisal of the early Stewart monarchs and the kingdom which they ruled. For Dr Grant the distinguishing feature of Robert II's reign was the political peace and stability achieved by a king whose ambitions and methods were in harmony with the political and social structure of a highly decentralised kingdom, although Robert III retains his reputation as 'probably Scotland's least impressive king'.[11] Outwith the general histories, the study of specific aspects of late fourteenth-century Scotland has been advanced by a series of illuminating articles, largely by Dr Grant, on topics such as the development of the Lordship of the Isles, Anglo-Scottish relations in the reign of Robert II, and the career of Alexander Stewart, the Wolf of Badenoch.[12] To these studies we may now add the brief but incisive analysis of the political situation in Scotland at the end of Robert III's reign provided by the opening chapter of Dr Michael Brown's excellent biography of James I.[13] Further clarification of the state of the kingdom in the late fourteenth century should be provided by Alastair Macdonald's current doctoral research on Anglo-Scottish relations in the reigns of Robert II and Robert III, while Karen Hunt's work on the Albany governorships between 1406–1424 will illuminate the period in the immediate aftermath of Robert III's death.

However, despite the quickening pace of research and interpretation, many of the most basic questions as to the ambitions, policies, achievements and personalities of the first two Stewart kings remain unanswered. It is to be hoped that this book will clarify at least some of the areas of uncertainty.

One of the key elements of the present study is a detailed examination of the political relationship between the early Stewart kings and their greatest aristocratic subjects, a relationship which, as the recent work of Drs Grant and Wormald has stressed, lies at the very heart of medieval Scottish government.[14] For most historians, the crucial feature of crown-magnate relations in the reign of Robert II was the emergence of a highly decentralised style of kingship, which involved an extensive delegation of royal authority to major regional aristocrats, particularly the king's Stewart kinsmen. The early chapters of this analysis seek to place the development of this loosely-bound and informal network of royal power in its immediate political context, rather than explaining its appearance entirely in terms of the personal and political mediocrity of the early Stewart kings. There were clearly other factors at work in the establishment of a monarchy which laid so little stress on the promotion and exploitation of the formal rights attached to the royal office.

When Robert the Steward came to the throne in 1371, at the age of fifty-five, he was already the head of a great aristocratic kindred with wide-ranging territorial interests, many of which had been personally secured by Robert during a long and ruthless baronial career. It was natural that the Stewart dynasty's control of the kingdom after 1371 should rest on, and be advanced through, the established local power of the various members of the new royal family. The king's sons and kinsmen were a valuable political resource, protecting the interests of the new dynasty and discharging many of the functions of royal government within their own areas of influence.

In contrast, the actions of noblemen who sought to oppose or restrict the authority of the new dynasty also contributed to a decentralisation of power. In 1371, the Stewart's claim to the throne was challenged in a display of political disaffection at Linlithgow headed by William, 1st earl of Douglas, and supported by men who had been closely linked to the former king, David II. Robert responded to this threat using the techniques of a man long schooled in the practicalities of baronial politics, by cutting deals and establishing marriage alliances which left his principal opponents with their regional or local influence intact.

All these developments took place against a background of long-term political and social disruption which had encouraged a recasting and entrenching of magnate power across much of the kingdom. The civil wars of the early fourteenth century and the ongoing Anglo-Scottish conflict contributed to the rise of new regional lordships, most notably the MacDonald Lordship of the Isles in the west and the Douglas earldom in the south, whose place in the political structure of the kingdom was already firmly established by the time of Robert II's coronation.

When the early Stewart kings are assessed within this environment they emerge as rather more than a hopelessly incompetent double act, staggering from one disastrous public appearance to the next. Robert II, in particular, was clearly a shrewd and capable politician, although a manipulator rather than a shaper of events.

Away from the central concern with royal personalities, aims and ambitions, the study touches on a number of other themes. One recurring motif is the growing political and cultural tension between the Gaelic and English-speaking societies of the kingdom, and the effect which this had on both the operation of royal government and the power of great regional lords such as Alexander Stewart, the Wolf of Badenoch.

Overall, the book aims to provide a coherent political narrative for the late fourteenth century, and a framework within which the reigns of the first two Stewart kings, so long synonymous with inadequacy and failure, can be properly assessed.

NOTES

1. M. Lynch, *Scotland: A New History* (London, 1991), 138.

2. *Sir John Froissart's Chronicles*, trans. T. Johnes (London, 1868), ii, 19–20.

3. W. C. Dickinson, *Scotland from the Earliest Times to 1603*, revised by A. A. M. Duncan (Oxford, 1977), 197, 200.

4. G. Donaldson, *Scottish Kings* (London, 1967), 36.

5. R. L. Mackie, *A Short History of Scotland* (Oxford, 1930), 149. The observation opened a chapter strikingly entitled "Dark and Drublie Days': 1329–1406'.

6. P. Hume Brown, *History of Scotland* (Cambridge, 1911), i, 149.

7. *Ibid.*, 150.

8. Sir W. Scott, *The Fair Maid of Perth* (Edinburgh, 1828); T. D. Lauder, *The Wolf of Badenoch* (Edinburgh, 1827).

9. R. G. Nicholson, 'David II, the Historians and the Chroniclers', *SHR* xlv (1966), 59–78; B. Webster, 'David II and the Government of Fourteenth Century Scotland', *Transactions of the Royal Historical Society*, 5th series, xvi (1966), 115–30; B. Webster, 'Scotland without a King, 1329–1341', in *Medieval Scotland: Crown, Lordship and Community* (Edinburgh, 1993), 223–238; A. A. M. Duncan, 'Honi soit qui mal y pense: David II and Edward III, 1346–52', *SHR* lxvii (1988), 113–141.

10. R. Nicholson, *Scotland: The Later Middle Ages* (Edinburgh, 1974), 184, 203 (in a chapter entitled 'The Accession of the Stewarts, The beginning of the Great Schism and other afflictions').

11. A. Grant, *Independence and Nationhood: Scotland 1306–1469* (London, 1984), 171–99; Chapter 7, 'Kings and Magnates'.

12. A. Grant, 'Earls and Earldoms in late medieval Scotland, c1310–1460', in *Essays presented to Michael Roberts*, eds J. Bossy and P. Jupp (Belfast, 1976), 24–41; A. Grant, 'Scotland's "Celtic Fringe" in the Late Middle Ages: The MacDonald Lords of the Isles and the Kingdom of Scotland', in *The British Isles 1100–1500*, ed. R. R. Davies (Edinburgh, 1988); 'The Otterburn War from the Scottish point of view', in *War and Border Societies in the Middle Ages*, eds A. Tuck and A. Goodman (London, 1992), 30–64; 'The Wolf of Badenoch', in *Moray: Province and People*, ed. W. D. H. Sellar (Scottish Society for Northern Studies, 1993), 143–161.

13. M. Brown, *James I* (Edinburgh, 1994).

14. J. M. Brown, 'The Exercise of Power' in J. M. Brown (ed.), *Scottish Society in the Fifteenth Century* (London, 1977), 33–65; J. M. Wormald, 'Taming the Magnates', in K. J. Stringer (ed.), *Essays on the Nobility of Medieval Scotland* (Edinburgh, 1985), 270–80; A. Grant, *Independence and Nationhood*, 129–99.

Stewart Earldoms, Lordships and Castles in the Lifetime of Robert II

KEY: ROSS (1382) Date of Acquisition : E. Earldom : L. Lordship: ● ROTHESAY castles : BUTE : held before 1371

I

A New Dawn for Yesterday's Man

On 22 February 1371 David II, son of the hero-king Robert I, died unexpectedly at the age of forty-seven and at the height of his political power, in his castle of Edinburgh.[1] During a long and eventful marital career the king had failed to produce any children to sustain the Bruce dynasty after his death. However, the prospect of dynastic and political crisis descending on the realm seemed remote, for the king's nearest male heir, his nephew Robert, hereditary Steward of Scotland and earl of Strathearn, was already an adult and one of the most powerful noblemen in Scotland, with fifteen years' experience of running the kingdom as guardian during David II's enforced absences. Robert's claims to the kingship appeared overpowering, for he was not only nearest in blood to the dead monarch, but was also the heir to the throne under the terms of parliamentary entails which had been drawn up under Robert I's direction in 1318 and 1326.[2]

The impression that the Steward's succession offered an element of political continuity is, however, wholly misleading. For most of his reign David II, not without reason, had regarded the Steward as his principal political opponent within Scotland. The last ten years of David II's rule had seen the Steward and his most significant allies politically marginalised by the rapid rise to territorial and political influence of a number of individuals who found favour at David's court either through their membership of the chivalric crusading cadre which grew up around the king, or their kinship to the king's queen and mistresses. The effect of David's patronage was to produce a royal establishment in which important elements, taking their lead from, and protected by, the king were indifferent or openly hostile to the Steward. The political risks in offending the heir to the throne appeared increasingly slight, for the Steward was already fifty-five years of age in 1371, some eight years older than David II. To many, the Steward must have appeared a spent political force whose chances of ascending the throne were becoming more remote with each passing year. On David II's death in February 1371, therefore, Robert was

1) THE STEWART CLAIM

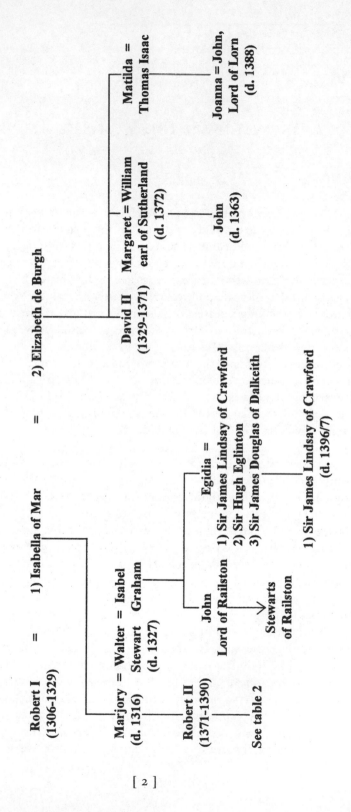

faced with a royal establishment which was not politically sympathetic to, or prepared for, his succession. This fact was to have important consequences not only in terms of the open resistance the Steward would face in enforcing his rights to the crown during 1371, but also in the long-term development of his kingship up to 1390.

When the Steward made the short crossing from his island lordship of Bute to the rocky harbour of Portencross in March 1371, en route to his coronation at Scone, he was bringing to the throne a set of ambitions, alliances and enmities which had been built up over four decades of political activity. Many of Robert II's political prejudices and policies were grounded in his long non-royal career.

In the spring of 1315 Robert I and his brother, Edward, were in the midst of preparations for a great summer campaign in Ireland.[3] Perhaps with an eye on the forthcoming Irish expedition Robert I was contemplating the marriage of his daughter, Marjory, to Walter, Steward of Scotland, a west coast magnate with a large galley force at his disposal and a family history of loyalty to the Bruce dynasty. Walter and his family were to play a prominent part in Edward Bruce's attempt to enforce his claims to the high kingship of Ireland between 1315 and 1318.[4] In 1315 Bruce had no son to succeed him, and any child born to Walter and Marjory would have become the king's heir. The likelihood of a Stewart succession was a far-off improbability, however, for not only did Robert I still hope to produce a son by his second wife, Elizabeth de Burgh, but a parliament at Ayr in April 1315 approved an entailing of the rights to the crown by which the king's brother, Edward, with Marjory's consent, was made heir presumptive in the event of Robert I dying without male heirs.[5]

Within a year of their marriage Walter and Marjory's union was blessed and ended by the birth of a son, named Robert 'eftre hys gud eldfader' in 1316, with Marjory apparently dying shortly after child-birth.[6] The infant Robert, the king's grandson, assumed the position of heir presumptive after the death of his great uncle Edward Bruce in Ireland in 1318.[7] In the years after 1318 Robert I favoured his grandson with grants of the lordship of Cunningham, Kintyre and, following on the suppression of the Soules conspiracy in 1320, the baronies of Methven and Kellie forfeited by Roger Mowbray and William Soules.[8] For six years Robert was the king's heir until the birth of a son, David, to Robert I in 1324. Robert's place in the succession behind his infant uncle was confirmed during a parliament at Cambuskenneth in 1326.[9] In 1327 Robert's father Walter died, and leadership of the Stewart family and care of the Steward passed to Walter's brother, James Stewart of Durisdeer.[10] An orphan at the age of eleven, the young Robert's personal life and political future were further blighted by the death of his grandfather, Robert I, in 1329. The royal dynasty, of which the Steward was now the oldest male member, was brought close to ruin after Robert I's death by the opening of the second phase of the wars of independence and the resurgence of the Balliol claim to the Scottish throne in the person of Edward Balliol, King John's son, backed by the Scottish and English noblemen disinherited by Robert I and by the military might of Edward III. Political and military disasters overwhelmed the supporters of the Bruce dynasty after the death of the king. At Dupplin in 1332, and at Halidon Hill in 1333, the guardians exercising control of the kingdom on behalf of the young David II experienced catastrophic military reverses which handed effective political and territorial control of large areas of southern Scotland to Edward Balliol and the English forces who sustained his claim to the Scottish throne.[11] In 1333 the Steward's own ancestral estates in the Stewartry, Bute and Cowal were granted by the triumphant Edward Balliol to one of his own partisans, David of Strathbogie, the recently restored earl of Atholl who appointed his own officers in Bute and Cowal and personally accepted the submission and fealty of his new tenants in Renfrew.[12] By the summer of 1334 the general situation in Scotland was so desperate that David II was sent for his own safety to France.

It is difficult to disentangle the reality of the Steward's role during David II's first period of exile between 1334 and 1341 from the distortions imposed by the propaganda of later Scottish chroniclers, but it is clear even at this stage that there was some level of political mistrust between the Steward and men associated with his uncle's royal court. There is a marked regional and political clash between the accounts produced by the chroniclers writing closest to the events of the 1330s: an anonymous account incorporated in Andrew of Wyntoun's *Orygenale cronikil* and the Gesta Annalia attached to John of Fordun's *Chronica Gentis Scotorum*.[13] Both accounts saw John Randolph, earl of Moray, a man firmly associated with David II, as an heroic figure in the struggle against Edward Balliol, but they diverge dramatically in their treatment of the Steward. The version preserved in Wyntoun narrates the desperate state into which the kingdom had fallen in 1334, and then launches into an account of the fightback by Bruce partisans in which the Steward was seen as playing the central role. With David of Strathbogie imposing his authority over Cowal, Bute and the Stewartry, the Steward is reputed to have hidden in Rothesay until two faithful retainers arranged a boat to spirit their lord to the mainland at Inverkip, from where a night ride to Overcummnock

> Wyth twa men, that his charterys bare,
> And a chawmbyr boy wythowtyn mare[14]

brought Robert to a small boat which took him to join David II in the
impregnable fortress of Dumbarton held by Sir Malcolm Fleming in
the Bruce interest. The account of the Steward's frantic but heroic flight
from his ancestral estates clearly came from a tradition which placed the
Steward at the centre of Scottish resistance to Balliol after 1333.
Wyntoun's chronicle trumpeted,

> The myscheff here i have yhow tauld:
> Now ware gud to tell, quha sa wauld,
> Qwham in ras fyrst recoveryng
> Off comfowrt, and the begynnyng[15]

before launching into an account of the Steward's recovery of his
lordships of Cowal and Bute. The earliest version of Wyntoun's
chronicle made this point more explicitly with a chapter title 'How
Robert Stewart, at syne wes king, Faucht and first maid releving'.[16]
From his refuge in Dumbarton the Steward sought and received the
assistance of Dougall Campbell of Loch Awe who 'had a great
affectyown' for Robert. In early 1334 the Steward's men swept down
Loch Fyne on Campbell galleys 'till wyn his land, And to mak it his
awyn fre', retaking Dunoon castle in Cowal, a feat which encouraged a
rising of the inhabitants of Bute who killed Strathbogie's sheriff.[17] By
25 May 1334 the Steward was on Bute issuing a charter in favour of
Iwar Campbell, a son of Sir Arthur Campbell of Strachur, of the castle
and bailiary of Rosneath near Dumbarton, no doubt as a reward for the
Strachur Campbells' part in the attack on Dunoon.[18]

The cause of the Bruce dynasty was apparently further bolstered by
the return of John Randolph, the young earl of Moray, from France in
1334. After his return Moray was named alongside the Steward as a
joint guardian of the kingdom for David II, but although Randolph
and the Steward co-operated in campaigns against Balliol interests in
1334, there was clearly considerable political tension between the two
young men. The idea of the joint guardianship probably originated in
David II's court before David's departure to France, and it was an
arrangement which seems to have annoyed the Steward, who was the
king's nephew and probably older than Randolph.[19] Randolph was
clearly the more dynamic of the two guardians, exploiting a falling out
amongst Balliol's allies to force David of Strathbogie, earl of Atholl, to
come to David II's peace in September 1334, and in the following year
appearing at Tarbert, in the Steward's lordship of Kintyre, in an

attempt to win John of the Isles back to David II's allegiance.[20] Chronicle accounts suggested of Randolph that

> . . . men hym callyd wtraly
> The best begynnyng off a man,
> That in Scotland wes lyvand than.[21]

The tensions between the Steward and Randolph became manifest during a parliament held by the two guardians at Dairsie in Fife in April 1335. The council was disrupted by a clash between David of Strathbogie and Randolph. The two men were engaged in a struggle for control of the northern lands and lordships which had belonged to Strathbogie's uncle, John Comyn lord of Badenoch. Strathbogie enjoyed the support of Randolph's fellow guardian, the Steward, whom Fordun accuses of being 'not then ruled by great wisdom'.[22] The dispute escalated into a widespread conflict between adherents of the Steward and Randolph in the north.[23]

In the summer of 1335, while the Steward/Randolph lieutenancy dissolved into political chaos, a huge English force, personally led by Edward III, advanced into Scotland in support of Edward Balliol.[24] In the areas through which the English armies had passed John Randolph led a war of disruption and resistance until his capture near the border in July 1335, the prelude to his imprisonment in England until 1340.[25] The arrival of the English army at Perth brought several men back into Balliol's allegiance, including David of Strathbogie who, on his submission to Edward III and Edward Balliol, was created 'warden of Scotland on behalf of those kings'.[26] Strathbogie's envoys to Edward were empowered to negotiate not only for the earl, but also Robert the Steward, whose lordships had been subject to a series of devastating attacks during 1335, including a direct assault on Bute in August and September 1335 by an English fleet from Ireland. The Steward probably submitted to Edward III at Edinburgh in September 1335, and had certainly demitted the office of lieutenant of the kingdom for David II before 4 December 1335, when Sir Andrew Moray appeared as guardian of the realm having defeated and killed David of Strathbogie, earl of Atholl, Balliol's warden of the north, on 30 November 1335 at the battle of Kilblean.[27] The Steward, despite his position as the king's nephew and heir presumptive, did not re-emerge as guardian of the kingdom until after Sir Andrew's death in 1338.

The pro-Steward account employed in Wyntoun's chronicle suggests that the renewal of the Steward's guardianship brought great benefit to the kingdom:

> That he mantenyt mare and mare,
> As yhe ma here forthirmare[28]

so that by 2 June 1341 the situation in Scotland was considered safe enough for David II to return from France.[29]

It is unlikely that David II and John Randolph shared Wyntoun's positive assessment of the Steward's political contribution to the kingdom during the crisis years of 1334–41. There was, however, little indication of open political hostility between the king and the Steward in the years after 1341. In fact, in February 1342, the king allowed the Steward to obtain title to the lordship of the earldom of Atholl through a curious series of grants and deals with William Douglas over the lordship of Liddesdale.[30] There is little record of the Steward's exercise of lordship in Atholl after 1342, but it seems clear that his new earldom, like other central Highland lordships in the early fourteenth century, was experiencing a measure of social and political reorganisation and realignment. As lord of Atholl Robert established an apparently amicable relationship with the *Clann Donnchaidh*, a kindred descended from the male line of the old celtic earls of Atholl, which had experienced a rapid rise to territorial and political power in highland Perthshire during the turbulent years of the early fourteenth century. The Steward also ratified or initiated the physical expansion of powerful west-coast kindreds into the earldom, with a grant of the thanage of Glen Tilt to Ewen MacRuari, a brother of the great west-coast magnate Ranald MacRuari of Garmoran.[31]

Between 1341 and 1346 any further advance of the Steward's territorial influence in the north of Scotland was made unlikely by David II's association with the warlike and chivalric John Randolph, earl of Moray, Robert's adversary from 1335.[32] The political situation in Scotland was transformed, however, by the battle of Neville's Cross near Durham in October 1346, as David II led the last in a series of punitive raids on northern England designed to force English recognition of his own status and that of his kingdom.[33] The encounter not only resulted in the capture of the Scottish king, but also saw the death or imprisonment of a large number of Scottish noblemen. John Randolph, earl of Moray, and Maurice Moray, earl of Strathearn, were both killed in battle, while John Graham, earl of Menteith, was captured and executed for treasonably breaking the allegiance given to Edward III in 1335. Duncan, earl of Fife, was sentenced to death for the same offence, but was spared because of his blood relationship to the English king.[34] The Steward's behaviour during the battle of Neville's Cross became a matter of chronicle propaganda. Fordun claimed that Robert and Patrick, earl of March, had taken 'flight and got away unhurt', and the allegations against March and the Steward were echoed in English chronicles.[35] Even the earliest version of Wyntoun's chronicle records that 'the Stewart eschapit then, And with him mony of his men, And the Erl of the Marche alsua; Hame to Scotland come thai twa'. However, this passage was removed from later versions, and the general tenor of Wyntoun's account of the campaign was more critical of the king than the Steward.[36]

With David II in captivity in England the magnates and prelates left at liberty in Scotland after Neville's Cross had little option but to choose the Steward, the king's nephew, as guardian of the realm. Fordun was distinctly unimpressed with the Steward's efforts as guardian.[37] The eleven years between 1346 and 1357 during which he ran the kingdom as David II's lieutenant were dominated by two themes: firstly, the increasingly desperate attempts by David II to procure his release from English captivity and, secondly, the political and territorial advance of the Steward and his family in the north of Scotland.

One of the Steward's earliest actions as guardian was to secure a retrospective papal legitimation for the children produced by his relationship with Elizabeth Mure, the daughter of Adam Mure of Rowallan, a landowner in the Steward's lordship of Cunningham. In the late 1330s Robert had co-habited with Elizabeth and produced children by her, in what appears to have been a secular marriage.[38] Many factors would have concentrated the Steward's mind on the issue of the status of his children in 1346. David II was a prisoner of the English whose release could not be guaranteed. It was unlikely that the childless king would be given the opportunity to father a successor during his period of captivity. Moreover, the king had been badly injured at the battle of Neville's Cross, and this fact alone would have focused the Steward's attention on the possibility of his succession to the throne in 1346–7.[39] In this situation the legitimacy of the Steward's offspring became an issue of some importance. The Steward's supplication to the pope certainly indicates that it was more than a personal issue, for it was supported by the kings of France and Scotland, and seven Scottish bishops.[48]

Another consideration was that in 1346 a rival and undoubtedly legitimate line of descent had appeared within the Bruce dynasty. After David II's return from France in 1341 the king had personally arranged for the marriage of his full sister, Margaret, to William, earl of Sutherland, a noble with a good record as a Bruce partisan. William and Margaret's marriage produced a son, John, early in 1346. David II provided a substantial territorial endowment for William and John, who was a full rather than a half nephew to the king.[41] The king's sister seems to have died in childbirth, but before the legitimation of the

Steward's children in 1347, Margaret's son was third in line to the throne behind the Steward, and certainly had a better claim than the Steward's 'illegitimate' offspring. Some fifteenth-century chronicles even suggest that until John Sutherland's death in 1361 at the age of fourteen, he was regarded as David II's nearest male heir and that, if he had lived, he would have succeeded to the crown before the Steward.[42] The 1347 dispensation has all the hallmarks of the Steward protecting the position of his own family in the succession, a preoccupation which may have disturbed the captive David II, especially given the Steward's apparent inactivity over obtaining his king's release.[43]

By 1350 the captive David II was trying to secure his own release by actively supporting proposals that a younger son of the English king, John of Gaunt, earl of Richmond, should be accepted as the heir presumptive to the Scottish throne if David died without producing a male heir. Essentially David II's nephew by marriage, John of Gaunt, would replace the king's nephews by blood, the Steward and John Sutherland, as the king's acknowledged heir.[44] Anglo-Scottish negotiations culminated in a draft agreement in November 1351, by which David could be permanently released in return for an undertaking that, if he died without an heir, his successor as king would be a son of Edward III who was not heir to the English throne. The 1351 agreement also proposed the restoration to the Scots of English-occupied lands and castles, the return of the kingdom to the boundaries of Robert I's time, the waiving of David II's ransom and a truce of 1000 years. As Duncan suggests, this was, in the circumstances, a fair deal, which may have enjoyed some measure of support and approval within Scotland. The proposals also had the backing of the king, and in November 1351 David II was released in order to press his subjects to accept the settlement.[45] The terms were presented to a Scottish parliament in late February/early March 1352 but, despite David's presence, were rejected, forcing the king to return to captivity in England in April 1352. The chief opponent of the proposed terms for David's release was undoubtedly the Steward, whose place in the succession was under direct threat. As Anglo-Scottish negotiations were proceeding during late 1351, the guardian had been in communication with the French king, sending reports on the situation and appealing for help. The nature of the French replies suggests that the Steward was presenting them with a doomsday scenario in which he and his allies faced military defeat and exile from Scotland at the hands of David II and his supporters within the kingdom, possibly backed by English forces.[46] In the early months of 1352 a civil war between the Steward and David II, with political and perhaps military interventions from France and England, could not be ruled out. In the end it was

David II who pulled back from the brink by accepting his parliament's rejection of the Newcastle agreement and returning to captivity.

From 1352 onwards Anglo-Scottish diplomacy revolved around the aim of obtaining David's release in return for the payment of a ransom and the establishment of an Anglo-Scottish truce. A draft treaty for David's release under these terms was put together at Berwick in July 1354. A ransom of 90,000 merks was to be paid in nine annual instalments during a nine-year Anglo-Scottish truce. As surety for payment of the ransom the Scots were to deliver up twenty noble hostages. By October 1354 Edward III was making preparation for David's liberation, and the handing over of the Scottish hostages, but David's hopes for release were dashed by the Steward, who effectively wrecked the treaty by committing the Scots to a French military initiative against England in 1355.[47] Fordun presents the events of 1355 as a colossal political and military mistake, with the Scots 'led away, by lust for gold'. In the end 'they achieved little worthy of remembrance. . . . But from this agreement and greed of gold, there followed . . . the destruction of Lothian by the king of England'.[48]

Wyntoun's chronicle gives a rather more positive assessment of the Scots activities in 1355.[49] Thomas Stewart, earl of Angus and Patrick, earl of March briefly captured Berwick from the English in 1355, but the town was swiftly retaken by Edward III on his return from a campaign in France in late 1355. By 20 January 1356 Edward III was at Roxburgh, where he received the resignation of Edward Balliol's rights to the Scottish kingdom.[50] However, the Scots were brought back to the negotiating table, not by Edward III's destructive foray into Lothian, but by the decisive defeat of the French at the battle of Poitiers on 19 September 1356, which resulted in the capture of King John by the English.[51] With the French effectively out of the conflict, the Scots needed to reopen diplomatic links with the English. In January 1357 negotiations over David II's release recommenced and on 3 October a treaty was concluded by which the king was to be set free in exchange for a ransom of 100,000 merks, payable over ten years and beginning at Midsummer 1358. Until the ransom was paid there was to be a truce during which the territorial *status quo* was to be observed. Twenty noble hostages were to be delivered as surety for payment, while three supplementary hostages were to be chosen from amongst the leading nobles of the kingdom, including the Steward.[52] On 7 October 1357 King David returned to Scotland and in November his council at Scone formally ratified the Berwick ransom treaty and enacted various measures to enable the king to pay his ransom.[53]

ALL THE KING'S MEN? DAVID II, 1357–71

David returned to a realm which had been governed by his nephew for eleven years. If the king harboured thoughts of revenge for the Steward's role at Neville's Cross, or his opposition to plans which could have seen David released in 1352 and 1354, there was to be no immediate manifestation of this ill will. The king was hardly in a position to contemplate attacking the Steward and his allies in 1357–8, for he returned from England to a kingdom in which the former guardian wielded huge territorial and political influence, particularly north of the Forth. The king's most favoured associates in that region, John Randolph, earl of Moray and Maurice Moray, earl of Strathearn, had died at Neville's Cross. David's return, far from initiating a decline in the Steward's power, ushered in a four-year period in which most of the gains made by the Steward during the king's absence received royal approval and the Stewart family expanded their influence into new areas.

The Steward was given an immediate mark of royal favour on David II's return, with his creation as earl of Strathearn between 6 and 13 November 1357.[54] The earldom had been unfilled since the death of Maurice Moray at the battle of Neville's Cross in 1346. Moray had no heirs and he had held Strathearn as a male entail under a reversion to the crown.[55] The king's grant did no more than confirm the Steward's hold on Strathearn. As guardian of the kingdom after 1346 and as possessor of the neighbouring lordships of Methven and Atholl, the Steward had been in an ideal position to establish control in Strathearn after Maurice Moray's death. The only significant opposition to Robert's position in the earldom after 1346 was likely to come from William, earl of Ross. Ross was the brother-in-law of Malise, the former earl of Strathearn, who had been deprived of the earldom by David II in 1343/4 for treasonable dealings with Edward Balliol and Sir John de Warenne.[56] David II's capture and Maurice Moray's death in 1346 seemed to provide an ideal opportunity for Malise, with the backing of Ross, to recover possession of Strathearn. A reconciliation of the conflicting interests of the Steward and Ross in Strathearn may have been finalised by Robert's marriage to William's sister Euphemia, countess of Moray, in 1355.[57] The marriage to Euphemia also gave the Steward an opportunity to exploit his new wife's substantial property rights as the widow of John Randolph, earl of Moray. Grant may well be right in suggesting that it was through Euphemia's terce rights that the Steward gained effective control of the lordship of Badenoch before 1367.[58]

The Steward also concluded a marriage agreement with the other great nobleman left in the north after the disasters of 1346 when, in 1350, his daughter Margaret became the second wife of John, lord of the Isles.[59] John, from the safety of his vast west-coast lordship, had viewed and exploited the upheavals of the Bruce/Balliol civil wars as a largely indifferent observer, at first backing Edward Balliol and then returning to David's allegiance in 1343.[60] Following on the assassination of Ranald MacRuari by William, earl of Ross, in the monastery of Elcho in 1346, effective control of the MacRuari lands of Garmoran also passed to John of the Isles as Ranald's brother-in-law.[61] The Steward/Isles marriage probably involved not only the guardian's recognition of John's lordship over the MacRuari lands, but also the settlement of conflicting territorial interests in Kintyre, which had been granted to John by Edward Balliol in 1336, and which David II had reconfirmed to Robert Steward in a male entail around 1346.[62]

The Steward's policy as guardian in the north after 1346 is instructive, for Robert generally sought to maintain and extend his authority through the establishment of marriage alliances and territorial deals with the most powerful magnates in the region. It was a method which the Steward was to continue to employ as king. His own interests in Highland Perthshire had also expanded during the 1340s through his position as bailie of all the lands in the kingdom of Scotland held by Duncan, earl of Fife, for Fife was the superior of a number of major lordships in western Perthshire including Strath Tay, Strath Braan and Strathord.[63] Although Fife managed to obtain his release from captivity in 1350 he died in 1353, and control of Fife and the Perthshire lordships probably reverted to the Steward as guardian.

By the time of David II's return, then, the Steward was entrenched in Atholl and the neighbouring lordships and earldoms of Strathearn, Badenoch, Methven and the Appin of Dull. The expansion of the Steward's influence into these largely highland earldoms and lordships coincided with and exploited longer-term processes. As Grant has pointed out, the early fourteenth century saw a significant collapse in the position of the governing level of feudal lordship in the Highlands, most notably the eclipse of Comyn power after 1306.[64] Forfeitures, expulsions, prolonged imprisonments, executions, deaths in battle or the simple biological failure to produce male heirs caused severe disruption to effective local lordship over much of the central Highlands. The relative political vacuum produced by this situation tended to be filled by a form of highly militarised lordship exercised by a number of Gaelic male descent kindreds who began to emerge as distinct political and military units in the early fourteenth century. The burgeoning power of these Gaelic lordships was probably connected with a wider political and military reorganisation of Gaelic society across Scotland and Ireland in the fourteenth century, a key feature of which was the maintenance of professional or semi-professional mercenaries in the service of great regional lords and their vassals.[65] In political terms the Steward was ideally placed to take advantage of these wider changes, for he was himself a major west-coast magnate whose lordship embraced highland territories and Gaelic kindreds as well as extensive lowland estates. It seems certain that throughout the 1340s and 1350s the Steward was employing and maintaining mercenary troops, known as caterans (from the Gaelic *ceatharn*, a troop of warriors), in order to impose his lordship in Atholl, Badenoch and elsewhere. By the late 1360s the identification of the earldoms and lordships over which the Steward, his sons and their allies exercised control as centres for cateran forces who raided neighbouring lands and lordships, was forcibly made by a series of general councils and parliaments.[66]

The Steward's political, military and territorial predominance in the north, bolstered by the marriage alliances he had contracted with the earl of Ross and the Lord of the Isles, meant that at first David II had little choice other than to ratify the gains made by the Steward in the region. The king, in fact, showed little inclination to cross swords with his nephew, and in 1358/9 backed away from a potential political clash with Robert over the fate of the premier earldom in the kingdom, Fife, which had lain vacant since the death of Duncan, earl of Fife, in 1353. In March 1358 David II made a grant of the earldom to a minor Fife laird, William Ramsay of Colluthie, who had been one of the king's fellow prisoners in England after 1346, had been employed by the king as an emmisary to Scotland in attempts to secure his release in 1346–8, and who was an associate of one of the king's favourites, Sir Archibald Douglas.[67] The assumption that Ramsay was made earl of Fife as a result of his marriage to Isabella, the daughter and heiress of Duncan, earl of Fife, is flatly refuted by the account of the contemporary chronicler Sir Thomas Gray, who suggests that the king 'created William de Ramsay Earl of Fife, . . . by persuasion of his [Ramsay's] wife'. Gray declares that Duncan had forfeited the earldom to the crown in the reign of Robert I for the murder of an esquire named Michael Beaton and had received it back as a male entail which had reverted to the crown on Duncan's death without male heirs.[68] The king's right to gift Fife to Ramsay was contested by earl Duncan's daughter. 'This daughter was in England, and it was intended that she should be sold to Robert the Steward of Scotland, but she married for love William de Felton, a knight of Northumberland, who was her guardian at the time, and she laid claim to the earldom which had been renounced by that contract.'[69] After the death of Sir William Felton in 1358, Isabella returned to Scotland where her claims to Fife were backed by the Steward. Robert succeeded in validating Isabella's title to Fife in late 1359, and the countess went on to marry the Steward's second son, Walter, between 21 July 1360 and 20 July 1361.[70]

Despite the Steward's triumph in the dispute over Fife in 1359/60, the startling if short-lived promotion of a royal favourite into the kingdom's premier earldom was a taste of things to come. The Steward's victory was, in any case, ephemeral, for late in 1362 Walter Stewart, lord of Fife, died. The timing of Walter's demise was unfortunate, for it occurred while David II was adopting a more aggressive and confrontational approach towards the assertion of royal rights and the promotion of royal favourites within his realm. David's new aggression may have arisen partly from the involvement of 'certain great men of Scotland' in the assassination of his English mistress, Katherine Mortimer, in 1360.[71] In late 1362 David II was certainly not inclined to acquiesce in the Steward's designs on Fife as he had in 1359. After Walter Stewart's death his widow, countess Isabella, was immediately surrounded by men closely associated with the king, including William de Landallis, bishop of St Andrews, Sir Robert Erskine, and Sir Thomas Bisset of Upsetlington, a Berwickshire knight who was one of the select band of royal favourites and officials linked by their attendance on David II during his captivity in England and their involvement in chivalric and crusading enterprises.[72] By 10 January 1363 it had become clear that David II was proposing that Isabella should marry Sir Thomas Bisset. It must have been equally apparent that the king was not about to allow the operation of any entailing of Fife in favour of Walter Stewart's younger brothers. David II is described in various chronicles as having an interest in crusades, and is reputed to have 'showed great and special favour and friendship to his knights and esquires, of whom at that time there were many, who had enlisted and engaged in works of that kind; and he gave and granted to them wide possessions and military honours'.[73] The earliest version of Wyntoun's chronicle concurred with this view and noted that David was

> . . . chevalrouss and worthy;
> Forthy he schupe him halely
> On Goddis fais to travale,
> And for that way he can him taill,
> Had he nocht beyne prevenyt with deid,
> That all his folk maid will of reid,
> And lattit him of that purpose.[74]

Even Sir Robert Erskine, David II's arch-administrator, paid lip service to the crusading ideals which were favoured at his sovereign's court by vowing to bear arms against the Saracen in the Holy Land and to visit St Catherine's in Sinai, although by 1359 he was looking to be released from these obligations on the basis that David II refused to release him from his service.[75]

The grant of Isabella of Fife's marriage to Sir Thomas Bisset was clearly part of the 'special favour' displayed by David II to this crusading knight. It was also guaranteed to arouse the hostility of the Steward and his family, whose careful cultivation of claims to Fife was in danger of complete collapse. The Steward was in St Andrews on 10 January 1363 when Bisset gave over to Isabella the life rent of his barony of Glasclune and other lands 'ante matrimonium' in a charter witnessed by the bishops of St Andrews, Dunkeld and Brechin, Patrick, earl of March and Moray, and the David II loyalists Robert Erskine, David Barclay and William Dischington.[76] Even if the insertion of David II's favourite had been acceptable to the Steward, the terms of the grant of the earldom to Thomas and Isabella on 8 June 1363 seem to have been designed to thwart Stewart ambitions. The descent of the earldom was limited to heirs male produced between the ageing Isabella and Sir Thomas, on the failure of whom the earldom was to revert to David II and his heirs.[77] After being forced or persuaded to acknowledge Isabella's rights in Fife to the exclusion of Sir William Ramsay in 1359, David II used Walter Steward's early death as a means of reasserting his control over the eventual destination of the earldom.

The Steward's disappointment over Fife in early 1363 was symptomatic of a deteriorating political relationship between Robert and his uncle, and it came on top of a number of other threats emanating from the royal court to the territorial and political interests of Robert and his family. One source of friction lay in David II's new mistress, Margaret Logie. In 1357 David II's English queen, Joan, had returned to England, where she stayed until her death in August 1362. During his queen's prolonged absence the king had enjoyed the favours of Katherine Mortimer, until her assassination in 1360. Thereafter he fixed upon Margaret Logie, daughter of Sir Malcolm Drummond and the wife of Sir John Logie of that Ilk, as his new consort. Following on Queen Joan's death, David II made an open acknowledgement of his feelings towards Margaret in a grant of 20 January 1363, and it may have become apparent at that stage that David, now a widower, intended to marry Margaret.[78] It was claimed that the match was made purely for love, but Margaret Logie held several practical attractions for David II, not least the fact that she had already proven her fertility by producing a son for her previous husband.

Besides any potential threat to the Steward's succession posed by David's liaison with Margaret, the Steward had a number of more immediate reasons to resent and fear the growing influence of Margaret and her family at the royal court. In the years around 1360 Margaret's brothers, John and Maurice Drummond, and their ally Walter Moray of Tullibardine, had been involved in a ferocious feud with the Steward's kinsmen and allies, the Menteiths of Rusky and the Campbells of Loch Awe. The dispute was brought to arbitration by the king's justiciars in May 1360, by which stage the Drummonds had caused the deaths of three Menteith brothers.[79] The cause of the dispute is unclear, but it was closely bound up with the marriage of John Drummond to Margaret Graham, countess and heiress of the earldom of Menteith, sometime before April 1360.[80] There is no indication that the Steward took an active part in the dispute, although as one of the four heads of kin of the dead Menteith brothers he was required formally to renounce the pursuit of the feud against John and Maurice Drummond for the slaughter of his kinsmen in the arbitration of May 1360. John Drummond seems to have died shortly after the May 1360 settlement, for by 9 September 1361 the Steward's third son, Robert, had obtained a papal dispensation for his marriage to the countess of Menteith.[81] Margaret Graham's marriage to the Steward's son meant that in the four years following David II's return to Scotland Robert and his family had successfully annexed the earldoms of Strathearn, Fife and Menteith to their already substantial interests in the Stewartry and Atholl, while the death of John Sutherland in England in 1361 left the Steward in an uncontested position as the king's heir apparent.

David II was no doubt perturbed, if not alarmed, by the seemingly irresistible territorial and dynastic rise of the Steward and his family, and in November 1361 the king began a low-key campaign against Stewart interests in Menteith; he confirmed a grant made by Margaret Graham in favour of her previous husband John Drummond and their children of the lands of Aberfoyle in the west of the earldom.[82] David II intervened again in the Menteith inheritance against the interests of the Steward's son in January 1362 in order to support the royal favourite Bartholomew Leon and his wife Philippa Mowbray in their possession of the barony of Barnbougle.[83] David II's proposed marriage to Margaret Logie, the sister of John Drummond, may have raised the spectre of a more aggressive royal intervention against Stewart interests in Menteith, for the queen-to-be was the aunt of the children produced between John Drummond and Margaret Graham, children who could be expected to contest the eventual destination of Menteith with the offspring of Margaret and Robert Stewart. For the Steward, his family already worked out of the Fife succession by David II, the king's proposed Drummond marriage must have seemed like the prelude to the eventual displacement of the Stewart line in Menteith.[84] The advance of Margaret Logie may also have had implications for the Steward in his own earldom of Strathearn. In the 1360s Robert Steward made a series of grants of land and office inside Strathearn in favour of Margaret's brother Maurice Drummond and his ally in the Menteith feud, Walter Moray of Tullibardine. These grants seem to date from late 1362 onwards, and they may have been forced on the Steward after Maurice's sister became the king's mistress.[85] Stewart interests in the earldoms of Fife, Menteith and Strathearn were thus threatened by a small group of individuals closely connected with the royal court.

Exasperation over the fate of the earldom of Fife and the king's proposed marriage to a woman whose family were a potential threat to the Stewarts' hold on Menteith undoubtedly contributed to the involvement of Robert and his sons in a baronial rebellion against David II in early 1363.

Chronicle accounts composed long after David II's reign have seriously misrepresented the aims of the 1363 rebellion by manipulating the chronology of the revolt. Bower's *Scotichronicon*, for example, presented the rebellion of 1363 as a response to proposals that the English king Edward III should be accepted as David II's heir presumptive, and this led later historians to view the Steward as the guardian of some kind of patriotic cause in 1363.[86] The proposals for a change in the succession were not, in fact, put before a Scottish parliament until March 1364, at least nine months after the end of the rebellion. It seems more plausible that the great aristocratic coalition which formed against David II in early 1363 was pursuing a number of separate territorial and political grievances against a king whose behaviour was increasingly aggressive and independent. The earl of Douglas's involvement seems to have been based on his fears that David II's banishment in late 1362 of the childless Thomas, earl of Mar, to whom Douglas was brother-in-law and heir presumptive, was the prelude to the king's seizure of the earldom and Douglas's effective disinheritance.[87]

Although the chronology of the rebellion is obscure, two independent chronicle sources make clear that at some stage the Steward and his sons John, lord of Kyle, and Robert, lord of Menteith, set their seals to a joint resolution with William, earl of Douglas, and Patrick, earl of March, which was presented to the king in the form of a petition calling for the reform of royal government.[88] The *Scalacronica* suggests that the petition complained about the misuse of money levied for the king's ransom, which had been 'squandered by evil counsel, wherefore they demanded reparation and wiser government'.[89] The terms of the Steward's eventual submission to David II in May 1363 probably reflected other elements of the rebels' agenda, for it committed the Steward to defend not only the king but also his officials and 'those faithful to him, whomsoever they be, namely such persons as my lord king shall himself wish to call and style his faithful people'.[90] More strikingly *Scalacronica* suggests that Douglas's part in the rebellion grew naturally from his dispute with the king over David's treatment of the earl of Mar, and that Douglas was already close to rebellion before co-ordinating his actions with the Steward and March.[91] Douglas's position in early 1363 thus seemed to mirror that of the Steward, who had also seen long-cultivated claims to a major earldom wrecked by aggressive royal action.

The Steward hardly played a leading role in the physical defiance of the king. The rebellion was probably underway by late March 1363 and certainly extended into the following month.[92] The Steward was still witnessing royal charters on 9 March 1363 and had apparently rejoined his uncle by 24 April, perhaps in time to attend the king's marriage to Margaret Logie at Inchmurdoch in Fife.[93] There are no indications of the Steward's involvement in direct confrontation with the king's forces. Indeed the *Scalacronica* commented that the Steward came to terms with David 'without the knowledge or consent of his allies'.[94] As early as 14 May 1363 the Steward publicly renewed his fealty to David II and renounced his league with March and Douglas in a ceremony at Inchmurdoch. The ceremony was witnessed by many of the men whom the Steward may have intended to remove from positions of influence around the king.[95] The Steward was certainly back at David's court much earlier than either March or Douglas, the latter the most active and aggressive of the rebels, who did not reappear as a witness to royal charters until July 1363.[96] Douglas may well have fought on alone after the Steward's submission, for the earl captured Sir Robert Ramsay, sheriff of Angus, presumably after Ramsay had appeared as a witness to the Steward's submission at Inchmurdoch on 14 May, in a night attack on Inverkeithing as Ramsay and his men sought to support the king.[97]

One reason for the Steward's early submission may have been that he had a larger prize to lose than either Douglas or March. The Steward's renewal of fealty was made 'sub pena amissionis omnis juris successionis regni Scocie', and it seems likely that David II had specifically threatened the Steward with the loss of his position as heir presumptive during his brief defiance of the crown in 1363.[98] It may be that the Steward had invited this form of royal threat for if, as Fordun suggests, the rebels were prepared to send David into exile if he did not accede to their demands, then they would have required an effective political alternative to the king.[99] In medieval kingdoms aristocratic rebellion usually found its legitimising focus in the person of the adult male within the royal dynasty nearest the king. In 1363 this would have been the Steward, and it seems likely that the 1363 rebellion carried with it a threat to David's untrammelled exercise of power which would have to have been based, in some way, on an increased role for the Steward in royal government.

In many ways the rebellion of 1363 was a political disaster for the Steward. Robert had become involved in a rebellion which had not only failed miserably, but in which his claims in the succession had been used openly to threaten the king's authority within his own realm. Robert had exacerbated the breakdown of his relationship with the king by abandoning his fellow rebels in such a way as to make their support for his political position after 1363 extremely unlikely.

The Steward's political vulnerability was exploited to the full during November 1363 when David II was in England to deal with the issue of the ransom and the securing of a permanent peace between the two kingdoms.[100] David II and Edward III's negotiators produced a draft agreement which was to be taken back to the Scottish parliament for approval. The agreement offered English concessions over all the outstanding issues between the kingdoms in return for the designation of Edward III as David's heir presumptive on the death of the Scottish king without legitimate issue. The English offered to release the Scots from all ransom payments, free all hostages, give back all occupied lands and the burgh of Berwick, buy out the claims of the disinherited, and to return to the Scottish king all the lands held in England by his predecessors. Moreover, the exact relationship between the two kingdoms in any situation where they shared a king was defined in a series of clauses which laid out extensive safeguards and guarantees for the preservation of the institutions, status and customary rights of the nobility and clergy of the kingdom of Scotland within a regnal union.[101]

Doubts about David's sincerity in taking these proposals back to the Scottish parliament for consideration are based on the apparently implacable opposition of the Scottish parliament to any concessions to the English crown over the succession.[102] The certainty of overwhelming parliamentary opposition to a plan offering immediate financial and territorial benefits to the Scottish kingdom, proposals which would also adversely affect only the political interests of the Steward and his family, is perhaps overstated. David II had apparently secured some measure of political support for the proposals by involving William, earl of Douglas, the most powerful magnate south of the Forth, in the negotiations. Douglas received an incentive to work for acceptance of the agreement in Scotland with the promise that he would be restored to the English estates held by his uncle and father, or to lands of equivalent value, on Edward III's designation as heir presumptive.[103] Douglas clearly felt no obligation to defend the interests of the man who had left him to face royal forces alone in April.

On 12 January 1364 the Steward began to make his preparations for the parliament of March, which would discuss the proposed changes in the succession by providing a chaplaincy in Glasgow with an annual rent of forty pounds in fulfilment of the conditions for the legitimation of his marriage with Elizabeth Mure. The Steward's action was some sixteen years late, but given that David II and his negotiators had just returned from England with a proposal which would have bypassed the Stewart succession, he clearly had every incentive in early 1364 to ensure the canonical legitimacy of his three elder sons.[104] Scottish chronicles have given the impression that these proposals were rejected out of hand by the Scottish parliament which met to consider the terms in March 1364. The second version of Wyntoun's chronicle, for example, suggests that David

> . . . movit and said, He wald, that ane
> Off the Kyng Edwardis sonnys ware tane
> To be King in to his sted
> Off Scotland, eftyr that he ware dede.
> Til that said all his liegis, Nay:
> Na thai consent wald be na way,
> That ony Ynglis mannys sone
> In to that honoure suld be done,
> Or succede to bere the Crown
> Off Scotland in successione
> Sine of age and off wertew thare
> The launchful airis apperand ware[105]

The suggestion that David proposed the succession of one of Edward's sons in 1363 and that this was unanimously rejected by the three estates in favour of the Steward's claims gives a rather false picture of unanimity behind the Stewart succession. Certainly, the parliament of March 1364 rejected the proposition that Edward III should be made David's heir presumptive, but that was only part of the story. As Bower and Wyntoun imply, there was a parallel argument, which clearly had some level of support within Scotland, that Edward III's son John of Gaunt should be accepted as David's heir.[106] The accounts of Wyntoun and Bower suggest that David II himself favoured the option of Gaunt's succession, while the enigmatic document entitled *Debate in General Council* seems to indicate that a detailed and coherent case for the acceptance of Gaunt was prepared before the meeting of the three estates.

The arguments put forward in favour of Gaunt provided a systematic rejection of the claims of Edward III and then rounded off with a description of the positive benefits to be expected from Gaunt's succession, expressed in highly patriotic terms. The chief points were that Gaunt's succession would be a thoroughly effective guarantee of the continued existence of an independent Scottish kingdom, because he was not the heir to the English throne; that Gaunt's wife was of Scottish stock, being descended from the Comyn earls of Buchan, so that Gaunt's son and successor as king of Scotland would be half a Scot; and that the Scots had already chosen Gaunt as a possible heir presumptive during the Anglo-Scottish negotiations of the 1350s.[107]

Moreover, the Steward's political reputation in early 1364 hardly guaranteed general support for his claims as heir presumptive. The contemporary chronicler John of Fordun, despite the patriotic tenor of the bulk of his chronicle, clearly sympathised with a viewpoint which saw the Steward as politically incompetent and disruptive. Fordun's account portrayed the Steward as an incapable lieutenant in 1335, associated with the malign and disruptive influence of David of Strathbogie; as a man who had abandoned his king to capture and imprisonment at Neville's Cross; as an ineffective lieutenant after 1346 and then, finally, as a man involved in a treasonable and unjust rebellion against David II in 1363. Fordun's view of the Steward's past behaviour is particularly crucial if we can accept a dating of about 1363 for the compilation of the first version of the chronicler's 'Gesta Annalia'. The presentation of the Steward as a man who had already proved his inability to govern the kingdom was clearly a powerful political statement at a time when the succession was a matter of open debate.[108]

Overall, the evidence of Fordun and the *Debate in General Council* suggests that the Steward's succession did not command universal support within Scotland, nor did it monopolise patriotic rhetoric. The acceptance of John of Gaunt as heir presumptive continued to appear an attractive option to many, perhaps especially to David II himself and those associated with the royal court.

The rejection of the proposals for a change in the succession entailed renewed and prolonged Anglo-Scottish negotiations, in which the English were willing to offer the Scots a truce during which David II's ransom could be paid, while the Scots were prepared to make significant concessions, except over the issues of homage and the succession, in order to obtain a permanent peace. Generally the English conditions for the establishment of a permanent peace remained too exacting for the Scots to accept.[109]

The Steward's position as heir presumptive survived the traumas of 1363–4, but Robert's relationship with the king was not noticeably improved. The five years after 1364 were characterised by David II's aggressive promotion of the interests of the surrogate royal family provided by the kinsmen of his hugely influential new queen, Margaret Drummond. The king showered favours on the kinsfolk of queen Margaret, their political importance displayed in the prestigious marriage alliances they contracted, and in the willingness of major magnates to sanction or contribute to their territorial aggrandisement.[110] The Steward contributed to this process with a series of grants in favour of John Logie, the king's stepson.[111] By March 1366 it was clear that David II was supporting plans for the marriage of Annabella Drummond, the queen's niece, and John Stewart of Kyle, the Steward's son and heir.[112] Grant points out the significance of this match in producing what was, in effect, a Stewart/Drummond line of succession which could be expected to be politically sympathetic to David and Margaret's kinsmen and adherents. The king, having been unable to displace the Steward as heir presumptive in 1363/4, was now forcing the marriage of his step-niece to the man most likely to be the first Stewart king.

The marriage was completed before 31 May 1367, when the Steward granted the earldom of Atholl to John and Annabella, who was styled daughter of the deceased John Drummond.[113] On 22 June 1368 David II made his own contribution to the Stewart/Drummond marriage with a grant of the earldom of Carrick to John and Annabella and their heirs.[114] Carrick was more than just a territorial addition to John's own inheritance in the Stewartry, for the earldom was part of the Bruce dynasty's patrimony. David himself had borne the title earl of Carrick as heir to the throne before 1329.[115] The king's decision to grant Carrick to his nephew's son was near to an explicit acknowledgement of John Stewart's position as the king's heir. After five years of childless association with queen Margaret it seemed that David II had fully accepted the likelihood of a Stewart succession. A letter of c.1368–71 by David to the bishops of Scotland, renouncing any rights claimed by the crown to the moveable goods of bishops after their death, was issued with the consent of Robert the Steward and his children, presumably on the basis that they were the king's heirs.[116] John and Annabella certainly regarded themselves as the heirs to David II and his Drummond queen, for the eldest son and daughter produced by their marriage were given the names David and Margaret.

By 1368 the Steward's son, if not the Steward himself, seems to have had the prize of an uncontested succession within his grasp. It was a victory secured largely on David II's terms; the king's step-niece was to be the first queen of Stewart Scotland, and the Steward's allies had been forced to endure some bitter reverses.

David II, however, had one last joker to play. In 1369 the king's personal and political relationships underwent a radical transformation when he obtained a divorce from queen Margaret Drummond. The separation was finalised, in face of Margaret's outright opposition, on or around 20 March 1369, and by January 1370 Margaret was simply the 'onetime queen'.[117] The Steward's view of Margaret's downfall is uncertain. Later chroniclers claimed that Margaret had encouraged David II to arrest the Steward and his three eldest sons shortly before her divorce. The Steward and his son Alexander were certainly imprisoned in Loch Leven castle in late 1368 and early 1369.[118] David II's divorce is thus usually seen as a triumph for the Steward's political interests, with Bower linking the annulment of the marriage with the release of the Steward and his sons from royal custody. The real political beneficiaries of queen Margaret's downfall, however, were not the Stewarts, but a small faction from within David's own court, clustered around the figure of the arch-administrator and David II loyalist, Sir Robert Erskine.

David II's insistence on forcing through a formal divorce from Margaret in 1369 indicates that his plans extended beyond simply acquiring a new mistress, for the divorce gave the king the opportunity to remarry. David's intended replacement for queen Margaret was Agnes Dunbar, sister of George, earl of March. Royal payments to Agnes commenced in 1369 and these indicate that the king's mistress was in the care of Sir Robert Erskine, probably in the royal castle of Stirling of which Erskine was custodian, while Agnes's brother, John Dunbar, was noted as serving as Erskine's squire in June 1370.[119] Little is known of Agnes's personal history, but George, earl of March, certainly had a sister Agnes married to Robert Maitland. On 23 August 1369 the earl granted the lands of the barony of Tibbers to the heirs of Robert and Agnes, his sister.[120] Unless March was taking the highly unusual step of endowing the heirs of an illegitimate sister with substantial estates we must assume that this Agnes and the king's mistress were one and the same. It may be that George Dunbar's grants to Robert and his heirs were part of the preparation for Maitland's formal separation from Agnes, which would allow the earl's sister to marry the king. Agnes Dunbar, like Margaret Logie, had thus produced children for a previous husband before her association with David II. In terms of producing a son and heir for the king, Agnes Dunbar had all the right credentials, and it would appear that David II, still only forty-seven years of age, had not given up the hope of fathering a Bruce heir for the kingdom.

Agnes Dunbar's brothers, George and John, had a family background typical of the men who were high in David II's favour. Their father, Sir Patrick Dunbar, had been captured with the king at the battle of Neville's Cross in 1346, acted as an envoy for David II in the early years of his imprisonment, had fought at Poitiers in 1356, and had died during a pilgrimage to the Holy Land in the following year.[121] The Dunbar brothers thus boasted a family history of chivalric martial achievement and crusading sentiment which found favour at David II's court. David II almost certainly intended to make Agnes Dunbar his new queen, for on 21 January 1371, a month before his death, the king granted Agnes a huge annual rent of 1000 merks from the customs of Aberdeen and Haddington.[122] The grant reflected the domination of royal patronage by the Erskine/Dunbar faction during the last two years of David's reign. In April 1370 Robert Erskine, Agnes's guardian, had received a lifetime grant of the keepership of Stirling castle. The king also arranged a lucrative marriage for Erskine's son, Thomas, and gave the burgh of Dunbar the status of a free burgh at the request of Agnes's brother, George, earl of March.[123]

As far as the Steward was concerned, however, the most significant and offensive beneficiary of Agnes Dunbar's relationship with David II was her brother John. By 11 July 1370 John Dunbar had received a papal dispensation allowing him to marry Marjory Stewart, the Steward's daughter. The Steward was bitterly opposed to the marriage of his daughter to a man who had not even attained knightly status in June 1370. A sixteenth-century chronicler suggested that Marjory was married 'but ony avise of hir fader', and that the Steward, once king, would accuse Dunbar of the 'tresonabill seducing of his dochter to mariage withoute his avise'.[124] David II forced the Steward to acquiesce in Marjory's marriage to the brother of the king's mistress by threatening Robert with the loss of his earldom of Strathearn. Between September 1369 and May 1370, royal charters did not style the Steward as earl of Strathearn, although the Steward continued to use the title in his own charters.[125]

Besides having to accept his daughter's marriage to John Dunbar, the Steward was also forced into resignations of Strathearn lands in favour of another of David's rising young favourites, Sir James Douglas of Dalkeith.[126] In his dealings with the Steward's brother-in-law, William, earl of Ross, David II had already displayed a capacity for the ruthless application of pressure on major noblemen in order to obtain desirable marriages for his favourites. In 1369 and 1370 it was the Steward's turn to feel the full blast of the king's intimidatory tactics.

Moreover, David II's plan for the elevation of John Dunbar went far beyond the procurement of a prestigious marriage to the Steward's daughter. Like William Ramsay of Colluthie and Sir Thomas Bisset of Upsetlington before him, Dunbar was about to be catapulted into the top rank of the Scottish nobility as lord of Fife. At some point in the autumn of 1370, David II forced Isabella, countess of Fife, to resign her earldom to the king, who promptly regranted Fife to his mistress's brother.[127] The acquisition of Fife, under what may have been heritable title, by the young John Dunbar signalled the end of the Steward's hopes of securing the earldom for one of his sons under the terms of the entail drawn up by countess Isabella and Walter Stewart in the early 1360s.

On 21 February 1371 the immediate future looked as bright for Robert Erskine and the Dunbar brothers, now respectively earl of March and lord of Fife, as it looked bleak for the battle-weary Steward and his allies. Agnes Dunbar was on the verge of becoming David II's queen; the possibility of her producing a son for the king was remote, but it was a possibility. In the meantime Erskine and the Dunbars could content themselves with the patronage dispensed by a royal brother-in-law who was still only forty-seven years of age, and who could be expected to dominate the kingdom for some time to come. Erskine and the Dunbar brothers had played the game shrewdly; their rise to political influence and territorial aggrandisement may have offended the Steward, but the protection of their royal patron meant they had little to fear from that quarter. On the following day, 22 February 1371, David II died in his castle of Edinburgh: the roof had fallen in on the king's men.

The evening of 22 February was unlikely to have been one of restful repose for the political associates and favourites of the dead monarch. The thoughts of many were no doubt racing west with the messengers bearing news of the king's death along the long road to Rothesay. Sir Robert Erskine, George Dunbar, earl of March, John Dunbar, lord of Fife, Walter Leslie, lord of Philorth and his Lindsay half brothers, James Douglas of Dalkeith and a host of lesser men had built their territorial and political fortunes on David II's favour and, in many instances, his willingness and ability to intimidate and coerce the Steward and his brother-in-law William, earl of Ross. They had made a horrible and perhaps fatal political miscalculation. An unanticipated hour of reckoning was now upon the king's men for, sooner rather than later, the Steward would be on the march, coming in to claim his royal inheritance.

NOTES

1. R. Nicholson, *Scotland: The Later Middle Ages* (Edinburgh, 1974), 184.
2. *The [A]cts of the [P]arliaments of [S]cotland*, edd. T. Thomson and C. Innes (Edinburgh, 1814–75), i, 465–6; *Johannis de Fordun, Chronica Gentis Scotorum*, ed. W. F. Skene (Edinburgh, 1871–2), i, 351.
3. G. W. S. Barrow, *Robert Bruce and the Community of the Realm of Scotland*, 3rd edition (Edinburgh, 1988), 314–7.
4. *Barbour's Bruce*, edd. M. P. McDiarmid and J. A. C. Stevenson (The [S]cottish [T]ext [S]ociety, 1985), ii, 80, 89, 94, 103, 186–187 (but see note vol. i, 102–3), 190; *Rot.Scot*, i, 31–2.
5. *APS*, i, 464–5. The entail guaranteed Edward's place in the succession before his departure to Ireland in the following month; A. A. M. Duncan, 'The Scots Invasion of Ireland, 1315', in R. R. Davies, ed., *The British Isles 1100–1500* (Edinburgh, 1988), 100–117.
6. Barbour, *Bruce*, iii, 76; Walter received Bathgate, various lands around Linlithgow, Bondington, an annual rent from the Carse of Stirling, Ednam in Roxburghshire and perhaps Kilbride from his royal father-in-law. *[R]egistrum [M]agni [S]igilii Regum Scotorum*, edd. J. M. Thomson and others (Edinburgh, 1882–1914), i, App. 2, nos. 219, 220.
7. *APS*, i, 465–6; Barbour, *Bruce*, iii, 189–90.
8. *RMS*, i, no. 54; App. 2, nos. 221, 222, 661.
9. *Chron.Fordun*, i, 351.
10. Barbour, *Bruce*, iii, 216–7; W. Fraser, *The Lennox* (Edinburgh, 1874), ii, 23.
11. R. Nicholson, *Edward III and The Scots* (Oxford, 1965), Chapters v–xiv, esp. 85–90, 134–8.
12. By 30 August 1333 Strathbogie was styled Steward of Scotland. R. Nicholson, *Edward III*, 148 note 6; Androw of Wyntoun, *The Orygynale Cronykil of Scotland*, ed. D. Laing (Edinburgh, 1872–9), ii, 407–8.
13. The anonymous account and the final version of Fordun's annals were probably produced within a few years of each other in the late 1380s and early 1390s. The anonymous account used by Wyntoun appears to have been written up shortly after the death of Robert II. Although mostly concerned with events in Lothian and the borders, the anonymous account preserved a positive view of the Steward's political record before 1371 and incorporated details perhaps derived from Stewart family traditions. John of Fordun wrote and reworked his chronicle account in a period stretching from the 1360s to around 1389. Fordun's annals display a consistent personal hostility towards the Steward and are usually assumed to have been complete by 1363, although this point is still debatable: *Chron.Fordun*, i, 317. Fordun was writing from a northern perspective, regularly describing Scotland

north of the Forth as lying on this (*citra*) side of the river: *Chron.Fordun*, i, 310. Scotland south of the Forth was noted as lying beyond (*ultra*) the river: *Ibid.*, i, 333. Similarly, Fordun spoke of the northern parts (*partes boreales*) lying beyond the mountains, to which people crossed from 'this' side of the hills: *Ibid.*, i, 335, 360. Fordun's geographical viewpoint was thus north of the Forth but on *this* side of the hills, either south of the Mounth in Angus and Fife or east of the Grampians in Aberdeenshire.

14. *Chron.Wyntoun* (Laing), ii, 407–8.
15. *Chron.Wyntoun* (Laing), ii, 413–4.
16. *The Original Chronicle of Andrew of Wyntoun* (STS, 1903–14), vi, 40.
17. *Chron.Wyntoun* (Laing), ii, 414–5.
18. *Highland Papers*, ed. J. R. N. Macphail ([S]cottish [H]istory [S]ociety, 1914–34), iv, p. 11; the Campbells of Loch Awe may also have received reward for the attack on Cowal: *Origines Parochiales Scotiae* (Bannatyne Club, 1851–5), ii, Part 1, p. 59.
19. *Chron.Wyntoun* (Laing), ii, 415–7; A. Grant, *Independence and Nationhood: Scotland 1306–1469* (Edinburgh, 1984), 20, 174–5; [R]egesta [R]egum [S]cotorum, 1153–1424, vi, 60.
20. Nicholson, *Later Middle Ages*, 130; *Chron.Fordun*, i, 357; *Chron.Wyntoun* (Laing), ii, 417.
21. *Chron.Wyntoun* (Laing), ii, 419.
22. *Chron.Fordun*, i, 358–9; *Chron Wyntoun* (Laing), ii, 413, 421. Fordun suggests that Strathbogie's 'tyrannous' behaviour in the north forced Randolph from the region. Strathbogie did make good his claims to Lochindorb, which was held by his widow after his death in November 1335, and also probably occupied Badenoch. The Wyntoun version does not suggest a Steward/Strathbogie connection.
23. *The [E]xchequer [R]olls of [S]cotland*, edd. J. Stuart and others (Edinburgh, 1878–1908), i, 435. A customs account rendered in 1337 recorded that the customs north of the Forth could not be collected because of the 'disagreements between the lord Steward and the earl of Moray'.
24. Nicholson, *Edward III*, 203–36.
25. *Chron.Wyntoun* (Laing), ii, 420–1, 462; Nicholson, *Later Middle Ages*, 139.
26. *Chron.Fordun*, i, 359.
27. Nicholson, *Edward III*, 215–6, 218–221, 227, 230–5; *Scalacronica* (Maxwell), pp. 99, 100–1; *Rot.Scot*, i, 382. 10 November 1335, English safe conduct for Nigel Carruthers, Steward's chancellor. *RRS*, vi, no. 14.
28. *Chron. Wyntoun* (Laing), iii, 440. The patriotic deeds Wyntoun's chronicle then goes on to recount were thus attributable to the overall political leadership provided by the Steward. The Steward's

most notable personal involvement in action against *pro* Balliol or English forces was the organisation of the sieges of Perth and Stirling: *Chron.Fordun*, i, 363–4; *Chron.Wyntoun* (Laing), ii, 456–7.

29. *Chron.Wyntoun* (Laing), ii, 466.

30. On 18 July 1341 David II granted the earldom of Atholl to William Douglas: *RRS*, vi, 78. On 14 February 1342 the Steward brought a claim against Douglas over the lordship of Liddesdale, which the Steward claimed by reason of David II's gift to him, and which Douglas occupied as ward of the son and heir of Archibald Douglas. The court found in the Steward's favour and within two days of the judgement Douglas and the Steward had swapped Atholl and Liddesdale: *RRS*, vi, 89–90; *RMS*, i, app. 2, no. 1124; no. 410, 437–8.

31. *Highland Papers*, i, 18–20. The seventeenth-century Clanranald history preserves a tale in which Robert II was apprehended and then entertained by *Clann Donnchaidh* while he undertook a journey 'accompanied only by one gentleman, (as often his manner was)'. On the following day the clan provided the king with an escort to Perth and received reward in a grant of land. The garbled tale probably reflects a genuine *Clann Donnchaidh* tradition of hospitality given to Robert II on very intimate terms. The head of *Clan Donnachaidh* was chief forester of Strath Braan in 1346, a location which was one of Robert II's favourite hunting spots; for the grant to Ewen, Duke of Atholl's Muniments, Blair Castle, Blair Atholl, Box 9/ Parcel XIV/ Glen Tilt; speculation that Ewen was a son of John MacDonald is probably mistaken: *Acts of the Lords of the Isles, 1336–1943*, eds. J. and R. W. Munro (SHS, 1986), 298. The Steward's charter was witnessed by Richard Pilmor, bishop of Dunkeld, who died in 1346/7. At that stage Ewen, who was described in the charter as the brother of Ranald of the Isles, would surely have been identified as the son of John, rather than the brother of John's, at best, teenage son Ranald. A relationship to Ranald MacRuari of Garmoran, whose family did use the style 'de Insulis', would, on the other hand, have been a matter of note before 1346: *RRS*, vi, 114–15. Given the MacRuaris' formidable reputation as Galloglass mercenaries in Ireland, Ewen's appearance in Glen Tilt may have been connected to the Steward's attempt to impose political control in Atholl after 1342: G. A. Hayes-McCoy, *Scots Mercenary Forces in Ireland (1565–1603)* (Dublin, 1937), 23, 34–5; for the expansion of Clan Donald's cultural influence into Atholl, Bannerman, 'The Lordship of the Isles', in *Scottish Society in the Fifteenth Century*, ed. J. M. Brown (London, 1977), 212.

32. *Chron.Wyntoun* (Laing), ii, 467.

33. Nicholson, *Later Middle Ages*, 146–7.

34. *Ibid.*, 147.

35. *Chron.Fordun*, i, 367; *Chron.Lanercost*, 350.

36. *Chron. Wyntoun*, vi, 186; the chronicle noted David II's impetuosity in undertaking the campaign and in scorning the advice of William of Douglas, 'That off weris mast wys than was', to turn the expedition home after the successful storming of the tower of Liddell. Wyntoun explains defeat in terms of tactical mistakes made by Randolph and the king, with David II's division assembling 'In till a full anoyus place' in which 'nane, but hurt, mycht lyfft his hand'. The Steward's division, in contrast, 'had . . . rowme to stand in fycht': *Chron. Wyntoun* (Laing), ii, 470–3, 475–6.

37. 'But how he governed in the office of warden — how he governed the kingdom intrusted unto him, his deeds show forth unto all times': *Fordun*, i, 368; ii, 358–9.

38. G. W. S. Barrow, 'The lost Gaidhealtachd of Medieval Scotland', in *Gaelic and Scotland*, ed. W. Gillies (Edinburgh, 1989), 73.

39. Nicholson, *Middle Ages*, 147.

40. *[C]alender of Entries in the [P]apal Registers relating to Great Britain and Ireland: [P]etitions to the Pope*, ed. W. H. Bliss (London, 1896) i, p. 124; *Vetera Monumenta Hibernorum et Scotorum Historiam Illustrantia*, ed. A. Theiner (Rome, 1864), 289.

41. *Chron.Wyntoun* (Laing), ii, 320. Sutherland besieged the castle of Cupar in Fife and raided England in 1340 with the earl of March: *Chron.Lanercost*, 385; *Scalacronica*, 112; *Chron.Froissart* (Johnes), i, 77, 97–8; W. Fraser, *The Sutherland Book* (Edinburgh, 1892), iii, no. 13; *RMS*, App. 1, nos. 120, 121, 122; SRO Yule Collection GD 90/26.

42. *Chron.Bower* (Watt), vi, 377; *Chron.Pluscarden*, i, 240. The idea that David regarded John Sutherland as his heir by blood before the Steward was first suggested by Bower and was further elaborated by Boece who suggests that David actually forced through a formal recognition of his nephew Alexander (*recte* John) Sutherland as his heir on his return to Scotland in 1357: *The Chronicles of Scotland compiled by Hector Boece*, translated into Scots by John Bellenden 1531 (STS, 1938–41), ii, 333.

43. A. A. M. Duncan, 'Honi soit qui mal y pense: David II and Edward III, 1346–52', in *SHR*, lxvii, October 1988, 115.

44. Duncan, 'David II and Edward III', 121–5.

45. Duncan, 'David II and Edward III', 121–6, 132; *Rot.Scot*, i, 741.

46. Duncan, 'David II and Edward III', 126–131; *Oevres de Froissart publiées avec les variants des divers manuscrits*, ed. Baron Kervyn de Lettenhove, xviii (Brussels, 1867–77), 336–7; Edward III made some preparations for a military intervention in the event of a forcible rejection of the proposals. On 1 February 1352 the English king gave leave to all Scots that were at his peace to join William Douglas of Liddesdale in putting down any Scots who rebelled against David II in his pursuit of agreement to the Newcastle terms.

47. Nicholson, *Later Middle Ages*, 160; *Rot.Scot*, i, 768–71. In March 1355 King John of France despatched the Sire de Gerncières and fifty men at arms to Scotland to lead the Scottish war effort and to distribute a substantial war subsidy amongst the prelates and barons of Scotland to encourage them to wage war upon the king of England.

48. *Chron.Fordun*, i, 371; ii, 360–1; *Scalacronica* (Maxwell), 118.

49. *Chron.Wyntoun* (Laing), ii, 482–4.

50. Nicholson, *Middle Ages*, 161; *Rot.Scot*, i, 787–8.

51. *CDS*, iii, no. 1616; *Rot.Scot*, i, 795–6.

52. *RRS*, vi, 168–9; *CDS*, iii, no. 1629; Nicholson, *Middle Ages*, 163; *Rot.Scot*, i, 811–4; *RRS*, vi, 173–83.

53. Nicholson, *Middle Ages*, 163–7.

54. *APS*, i, 518–9; *HMC Report*, xv, App. 8, 6; the Steward also received a pension of 40 pounds c.1358: *RMS*, App. 2, 1266.55; *RRS*, vi, 118.

56. Malise, earl of Strathearn, had been tried and cleared on the treason charge in 1338–41 by Robert the Steward as the king's lieutenant. Despite this, on 31 October 1343 David II granted Strathearn to the Bruce loyalist Maurice Moray: *RRS*, vi, 118. Malise had four daughters and co-heiresses, and on 28 May 1344 he nominated his daughter Isabella as his heir in Caithness and gave over her marriage to his brother-in-law William, earl of Ross: *RMS*, i, App. 1, no. 150. A little over a week later, on 7 June 1344, Ross defended Malise's claims to Strathearn before parliament, although as the king had already granted the earldom to Maurice Moray the previous October, this was clearly a lost cause.

57. *CPP*, i, 287. The supplication certainly suggested that the match was intended to bring to an end discord between the Steward and Euphemia's brother, William, earl of Ross. It seems significant that it was the eldest son of this Stewart/Ross marriage, David, who was groomed to inherit Strathearn, and that grants made by the Steward from Strathearn required the confirmation of Euphemia.

58. A. Grant, 'The Wolf of Badenoch', in *Moray: Province and People*, ed. W. D. H. Sellar (The Scottish Society for Northern Studies, 1992), p. 143.

59. *CPL*, iii, 381.

60. *Acts of the Lords of the Isles: 1336–1493* (SHS, 1986), nos. 1–3; *RRS*, vi, 113–4. In September 1336 the lord of the Isles had offered his support to Edward Balliol in return for a substantial grant of lands which included Kintyre and the ward of Lochaber. In June 1343, after a marked decline in Balliol's fortunes and David II's return from France, John and his brother-in-law, Ranald MacRuari, returned to David's allegiance 'for the common profit and tranquillity of the realm' in a settlement concluded in Ayr. David II confirmed John in the possession of his island lordships and also the lands of Morvern and Lochaber

'free from all action and dispute', and Duror and Glencoe on the southern shores of Loch Linnhe. The reference to disputes over Lochaber probably related to the claims of the king's man John Randolph, earl of Moray, whose father had received Lochaber from Robert I as part of the huge Moray regality in 1312. The 1343 agreement essentially recognised the reality of the lordship's power in the area.

61. *Chron.Wyntoun* (Laing), ii, 472.

62. *RMS*, i, App. 2, no. 1066.

63. Robert appears as Duncan's bailie in documents issued in March 1346 at Kilwinning. The dating seems strange, for Fife was not physically or mentally incapacitated in March 1346. Later in the year he accompanied David II on the expedition which resulted in the earl's capture at Neville's Cross. March 1347, after Fife was in English captivity, might seem a more likely date, but there is no indication that Fife was allowed a temporary release from custody at that stage: SRO Murthly Castle Muniments GD 121/Box 4/Bundle 10/ no. 3; Fraser, *Red Book of Grandtully*, i, 2–3, nos. 2–3; in Strath Braan and Strath Tay the most important local figure was Duncan Andrewson, chief of the *Clann Donnchaidh*, who acted as the head forester of Braan and who held the lands of Discher and Toyer in Strath Tay of the earl of Fife. *RMS*, i, App. 2., no. 1396. By 1360 the Steward was also intromitting with the lands of the Abthania of Dull in Perthshire. *ER*, ii, 48, 73, 111.

64. For the political importance of the Comyns in the north, see Alan Young, 'The Earls and Earldom of Buchan in the Thirteenth Century', in A. Grant and K. Stringer, eds., *Medieval Scotland: Crown, Lordship and Community* (Edinburgh, 1993), 174–202; Grant, *Independence*, 204–6.

65. K. Simms, *From Kings to Warlords: The Changing Political Structure of Gaelic Ireland in the Later Middle Ages* (Woodbridge, 1987), 18–9; R. Frame, *Colonial Ireland, 1169–1369* (Dublin, 1981), 111–113, where the general arguments with regard to the effect of climatic factors and plague on the populations of urban and lowland, cereal-growing, areas are laid out. Evidence for a similar depopulation in Scotland arising from war, famine and, after 1349, the Black Death, tends to be fragmentary and anecdotal. *Charters, Bulls and other Documents relating to the Abbey of Inchaffray* (SHS, 1908), no. 130, where in 1344 the rents from the lands of Dunning in Strathearn were said to be reduced by 'the misfortunes of war and the fewness of the inhabitants'; *CPL*, iv, 56.

66. The parliament of July 1366 complained about the activities of the rebels of Atholl, Argyll, Badenoch, Lochaber and Ross. Atholl and Badenoch were under the control of the Steward, Lochaber was held by the Steward's son-in-law John of the Isles and Ross by his brother-in-law William, earl of Ross. In June 1368 the Steward and his sons

John, lord of Kyle, and Robert, lord of Menteith, were forced to swear oaths with regard to the behaviour of the inhabitants of their lordships, and to promise that they would not allow malefactors to cross their territories or be reset within them. The key lordship in this complaint was probably Badenoch, for by late June 1368 it was the Steward and his son Alexander who were warded in Loch Leven castle. Alexander remained in ward until the parliament of March 1369, in which assembly the Steward and his sons were once again urged to enforce justice against malefactors in their earldoms of Strathearn, Atholl and Menteith and other Highland possessions, to prevent their reset there, and to enforce the payment of taxes: *APS*, i, 497–8, 503, 528–9.

67. A. A. M. Duncan, 'David II and Edward III', 115–16; *CDS*, iii, nos. 1519, 1549; *Rot.Scot*, i, 707–8, 709, 714, 794; *RMS*, i, App. 1, no. 127, App. 2, nos. 1228, 1249; *RRS*, vi, 213; *Chron. Wyntoun* (Laing), ii, 496 for the Douglas/Ramsay connection.

68. *Scalacronica* (Maxwell), 125–6; the brief notes on the grants to William Ramsay do not indicate that they were made to him and his wife: *RMS*, i, App. 2, nos. 1228, 1249.

69. *Scalacronica*, 125–6. There is strong circumstantial evidence to support the substance of Gray's tale that Isabella of Fife was in England and married to Sir William Felton at the time of Ramsay's acquisition of the earldom. When Sir William Felton died in September 1358 his widow was named Isabella. Moreover, Felton had a son with the highly suggestive name Duncan, and Duncan's mother was stated in a papal petition of 1351 to be of kindred to the English king Edward III. Isabella of Fife was the great grand-daughter of Edward I. Duncan Felton's appearance in 1351 suggests that his parents married in the 1330s. This is possible, for Duncan, earl of Fife, fluctuated in allegiance between Edward Balliol and David II for most of the 1330s, while William de Felton was heavily engaged in Scottish affairs as keeper of Roxburgh castle: *A History of Northumberland* (Newcastle-upon-Tyne, 1904), 116; *CPP*, i, 210; J. Raine, ed., *Wills and inventories illustrative of the History, Manners, Language statistics etc., of the Northern Counties of England from the 11th century onwards*, part 1 (Surtees Society, 1835), 29; *Lanercost*, 283; *ER*, i, 437; *Edward III Calendar of Close Rolls 1354–1360*, 563.

70. Isabella had returned to Scotland by 20 November 1359 when she was issuing charters as Isabella de Fyffe, widow (of Felton rather than Ramsay), and daughter of the deceased Duncan, earl of Fife: SRO Calendar of Craigmillar Writs GD 122/141. The charter was issued from the Steward's castle of Methven and Robert's seal was used to attest the grant. William Ramsay was still styled earl of Fife on 8 April 1359 (*RRS*, vi, 243–4), but by 21 July 1360 Isabella was described as a

widow and as daughter and *heiress* of Duncan, earl of Fife (*RRS*, vi, 269) when resigning the barony of Kinnoul in favour of David II's 'confederato' Robert Erskine. By 21 July 1361 Isabella had married Walter Stewart who was styled lord of Fife when witnessing a charter issued by his father at Cluny on that date: *Registrum Monasterii de Passelet* (Maitland Club, 1832), 67–8. At some stage during their brief marriage Isabella and Walter Stewart drew up an entail specifying a descent of the earldom to Walter or Walter's younger brothers in the event of the failure of the marriage to produce male heirs. The entail anticipated Walter outliving his new bride, who was probably in her late thirties by 1360, and reflected the likelihood that the union would not be blessed with children: Fraser, *Menteith*, ii, 251–4. Isabella could not have been born before 1315 (Barrow, *Bruce*, 278), but may have been born in the early 1320s.

71. *Scalacronica* (Maxwell), pp. 162–3.

72. NLS Ch.no.47; *RRS*, vi, 374–5. In 1356 Bisset's valet, Thomas de l'Despense, attended David II in London while later in the same year, and again in 1359, Bisset was associated with David II's favourites, the crusading brothers Norman and Walter Leslie and Sir Walter Moigne, in the preparation for expeditions to Prussia and the Holy Land to crusade against the Lithuanians and Saracens: *Rot.Scot*, i, 757–8, 763, 764, 797, 799, 837; *CPP*, i, 345.

73. A. MacQuarrie, *Scotland and the Crusades 1095–1560* (Edinburgh, 1985), 81. Cf. W. Goodall, *Joannis de Fordun Scotichronicon cum supplementis ac Continuatione Walteri Boweri Insulae Sancti Columbae Abbatis* (Edinburgh, 1759), ii, 380. Wyntoun's chronicle seems to suggest that as early as the 1340s David saw himself as the political, military and social focus for a group of young knights whom he had created: *Wyntoun* (Laing), ii, 467–8.

74. *Wyntoun*, vi, 244.

75. *CPP*, i, 346.

76. *RMS*, i, no. 221; *RMS*, i, no. 825.

77. *RMS*, i, no. 158.

78. *RMS*, i, no. 124.

79. W. Fraser, *The Red Book of Menteith* (Edinburgh, 1880), i, 239–46.

80. Theiner, *Monumenta*, 315. The marriage may have initiated the feud by giving Drummond rights to property held by the Menteiths and the Campbells, although Drummond's application for a papal dispensation claimed that the match was intended to bring the feud to an end. At least part of Drummond's marriage settlement, the lands of Rosneath granted to him by his bride's mother Mary, countess of Menteith, were given over to Alexander Menteith as the result of the arbitration of 1360: *RMS*, i, no. 505. The identification of the John Drummond married to the countess of Menteith with the John

Drummond involved in the Menteith feud is not certain, but probable.

81. Theiner, *Monumenta*, 347.

82. *RRS*, vi, 296; Fraser, *Menteith*, ii, 246–7. The evidence of the papal dispensation of April 1360 suggests that the countess of Menteith's liaison with John Drummond had produced children.

83. *RRS*, vi, 299. Bartholomew Leon had recovered Barnbougle in 1346 as the result of a crown-sponsored deal between Leon and John Graham, earl of Menteith, and his wife Mary, who gave over the barony in payment of a sum of 2000 merks owed to the crown for their marriage and relief. David II's 1362 grant included the provision that if the heirs of John Graham and his wife Mary, clearly a reference to their daughter Margaret and her new husband Robert Stewart, attempted to reclaim the barony they would first have to repay the sum of 2000 merks which Leon had paid to the crown in 1346, and gave Bartholomew the automatic right to distrain the goods of the earldom of Menteith for that sum: *RRS*, vi, 136, 299. For Leon's various diplomatic services to David II see A. A. M. Duncan, 'David II and Edward III'; Fraser, *Menteith*, ii, 232; *ER*, ii, 200.

84. Robert Stewart, lord of Menteith, was clearly prepared to make a fight of the Menteith succession. His first child by Margaret Graham was born in mid to late 1362 and named Murdoch, probably after Margaret's grand uncle, the last of the old line of the Stewart/Menteith earls of Menteith who had died at the battle of Dupplin in 1332. At Murdoch's baptism Robert was already engineering powerful local support for his son, with Duncan, the future earl of Lennox, bordering Menteith's western flank, acting as the infant's godfather. The exact status of Margaret's children by John Drummond is unclear; despite the papal dispensation of 1360 the Stewarts may have regarded them as illegitimate.

85. SRO Drummond Castle Writs GD 160/1/3/2. Robert Steward, earl of Strathearn to Maurice Drummond lands of Dromane and Tullicharin in Strathearn: GD 160/1/3/1. Robert Steward of Scotland and earl of Strathearn to Maurice Drummond lands and the office of coroner of the earldom of Strathearn: GD 160/1/2. Robert Steward, earl of Strathearn to 'speciali consanguineo' Maurice Drummond, son of Malcolm Drummond, office of Forester of Strathearn: cf. *RRS*, vi, no. 281, 313–4. Before 3 December 1362, Robert Steward of Scotland, earl of Strathearn, confirmed the lands of Tullibardine and others to Walter Murray: *RMS*, i, no. 125.

86. R. Nicholson, 'David II, the historians and the chroniclers', *SHR*, xlv (1966), 65–6.

87. A. A. M. Duncan, The 'Laws of Malcolm MacKenneth', in A. Grant and K. Stringer, eds., *Medieval Scotland: Crown Lordship and Community* (Edinburgh, 1993), 264–5. Duncan also raises the possibility that

Douglas, Steward and March were alarmed by the fact that David's repeated failure to pay the English ransom meant that they were potentially liable to be sent as hostages to England. Cf. *RRS*, vi, p. 187. Arrangements were in hand in early 1363 for an embassy to London, and it is not impossible that the rebels were given some notification of the solution which David II and his councillors were about to propose for the problem of his ransom: *Rot.Scot*, i, 872. The petition could have been timed to give the nobles some say over the way David was to conduct his planned negotiations with Edward III.

88. *Chron.Fordun*, i, 381–2, ii, 369–70; *Scalacronica* (Maxwell), 173–4.
89. *Scalacronica* (Maxwell), 173.
90. *Chron.Bower* (Goodall), ii, 369–70.
91. *Scalacronica* (Maxwell), 173.
92. B. Webster, 'David II and the Government of Fourteenth Century Scotland', in *Transactions of the Royal Historical Society*, 5th series, xvi (1966), 118–9.
93. *RRS*, vi, 319–20, 321–2. The Steward probably recognised Sir Thomas Bisset's claims to Fife as part of his reconciliation with the king, for Bisset was a fellow witness to David II's charter of 24 April. David and Margaret's marriage was said to have been completed at Inchmurdoch, a manor house of the bishop of St Andrews, in April 1363: *Chron.Wyntoun* (Laing), ii, 506; *Chron.Fordun*, i, 382.
94. *Scalacronica* (Maxwell), 174.
95. *Chron.Bower* (Goodall), ii, 369–70. The witnesses included the bishops of St Andrews and Brechin, the abbot of Dunfermline, Walter Wardlaw, archdeacon of Lothian, Gilbert Armstrong, Sir Robert Erskine, chamberlain, Sir Archibald Douglas, Sir Robert Ramsay and the half brothers Norman Leslie and Alexander Lindsay.
96. *RRS*, vi, no. 298.
97. *Scalacronica* (Maxwell), 174. For Ramsay as sheriff of Angus in 1363, *ER*, i, 114, 117, 140.
98. *Chron. Bower*, ii, 369–70.
99. *Chron.Fordun*, i, 381, ii, 369.
100. Nicholson, *Later Middle Ages*, 170–1; Duncan, 'David II and Edward III'.
101. *APS*, i, 494.102. R. Nicholson, 'David II, the historians and the chroniclers', 67–8.
103. *CDS*, iv, no. 93. Payment by Edward III on 8 December 1363 to Douglas as one of the lords with David II.
104. J. Riddell, *Stewartiana* (Edinburgh, 1843), App. ii, 135–7.
105. *Chron.Wyntoun* (Laing), ii, 506. The earliest version does not mention this episode at all and closes with a highly sympathetic and positive gloss of the closing years of David's reign: *Chron. Wyntoun*, vi, 242–6. The details of the 1363 parliament were added to Wyntoun's account in the period after 1390.

106. *Chron.Bower* (Goodall), ii, 366; *APS*, i, 493; *SHS Miscellany*, ix, 1–56; Duncan, 'David II and Edward III', 135–6.

107. *SHS Miscellany*, ix, 'Debate in General Council', 36–56, esp. 49–50. Gaunt was married to Blanche, daughter of Henry of Grosmont, duke of Lancaster by his wife Isabella, daughter and heiress of Henry Beaumont, earl of Buchan. Beaumont's wife had been Alicia Comyn, the daughter of Alexander Comyn and the niece of John Comyn, earl of Buchan.

108. Unfortunately Fordun's personal and political connections are obscure. He may have been a chantry priest attached to the cathedral of Aberdeen: *Chron.Fordun*, i, xiv. An Aberdeenshire base is possible given the regional bias displayed in the Annals, that part of Fordun's work most likely to reflect contemporary local sources and the personal experiences of the chronicler and his associates. The Annals were written for an audience dwelling north of the Forth and south or east of the Mounth and Grampians, that is, in Fife, Angus, the Mearns and Aberdeenshire. See note 13 *supra*. It was this region which provided David II with some of his most committed retainers, notably the Leslie brothers, Norman and Walter, their half brother Alexander Lindsay of Glen Esk and Sir Robert Ramsay, sheriff of Angus. It was also men from these areas who viewed the activities of the Steward and his sons in Perthshire and the central highlands with the gravest suspicion. Fordun may have had a direct link to David II's court through Walter Wardlaw, who was archdeacon of Lothian and David II's secretary in 1363, and who witnessed the Steward's submission to the king in May of that year. There was certainly a personal link between the two men by c.1384–87, if not well before, when Wardlaw supplied the chronicler with a genealogy of David I. Dating Fordun's correspondence with Wardlaw depends on whether the phrase 'dudum' is taken to mean that Wardlaw sent him the genealogy 'lately' or 'long ago': *Chron. Fordun*, ii, 244. 109; *CDS*, iv, no. 108; *Rot. Scot.*, i, 894–5; *RRS*, vi, 375–7; *APS*, i, 496–7, 503.

110. In 1363 Maurice Drummond, Margaret's nephew, married Marion Erskine, daughter of Sir Robert Erskine, receiving lands in Perthshire from Sir Thomas Bisset: W. Drummond, Viscount Strathallan, *The Genealogie of the Noble and Ancient House of Drummond* (Edinburgh, 1831), 40. The marriage of Malcolm Drummond to Isabella Douglas, daughter of the earl of Douglas, was another element in the creation of what Grant has called the 'Drummond affinity'.

111. On 12 May 1365 Logie received the lands of Foulis, Gask and others in Strathearn. At a parliament at Scone in July 1366 the Steward as earl of Strathearn gave over the lands of Logie to John Logie to be held in a free barony and regality directly of the crown. On the same day the assembled peers gave their consent to a grant by the king to

John of the royal lands in Annandale: *RRS*, vi, 385–6; Fraser, *Grandtully*, 131–2*.

112. SRO Register House Transcripts RH2/6/4, 81.

113. *RRS*, vi, 404.

114. *RRS*, vi, 428.

115. *ER*, i, 184.

116. *RMS*, i, no. 372.

117. *ER*, ii, 344–6.

118. *Chron.Bower* (Goodall), ii, 380; *The Book of Pluscarden*, ed. F. J. H. Skene (Edinburgh, 1880), 234; *ER*, ii, 309, 347. The imprisonment of Robert and Alexander seems to have been related to repeated parliamentary complaints about disorder in their Highland lordships. The Steward and his family did not receive any territorial benefits from the eclipse of the Drummonds with the exception of a minor grant in favour of David Stewart in October 1370: *RMS*, i, no. 360.

119. *ER*, ii, 328, 345, 357; *CDS*, iii, no. 173.

120. *APS*, vii, 159; cf. *RRS*, vi, 473, where other charters in favour of John Maitland were given royal confirmation in September 1369.

121. *Rot.Scot*, i, 707–9; *Chron.Fordun*, i, 377 note 3.

122. *RRS*, vi, 498.

123. *RMS*, i, nos. 305, 318, 340.

124. A. Stewart, *Genealogical History of the Stewarts* (London, 1798), 439; Hector Boece, *The Chronicles of Scotland*, translated into Scots by John Bellenden 1531 (STS, Third Series, no. 15, 1941), ii, 337. The accusation of seduction was echoed in the papal dispensation.

125. *RRS*, vi, 472–4. Perhaps as early as July, *RRS*, vi, no. 447; *RRS*, vi, 491–2; SRO Inventory of Fraser Charters GD 86/7: Robert Steward, earl of Strathearn and baron of Renfrew, to Alan of Lauder, bailiary of lands in Berwickshire 19 October 1369. David II may also have threatened the Steward's title to the barony of Methven: *RMS*, i, no. 351.

126. SRO Morton Muniments GD 150/21; *Mort.Reg.*, ii, 60: Grant by Robert, as earl of Strathearn, of Kellor in Strathearn, to Sir James Douglas of Dalkeith. The witnesses included Sir Robert Erskine, his son Thomas and a number of men associated with George and John Dunbar, John Heryce, David de Anand, and Patrick de Hepburn. The charter is undated but was confirmed by the Steward's wife, Euphemia, as countess of Moray and Strathearn, on 28 February 1370: GD 150/22; *Mort.Reg.*, ii, 86; GD 150/105: Lands in Bathgate granted to William Douglas, Douglas of Dalkeith's brother, shortly before 2 January 1370.

127. Fraser, *Menteith*, ii, 254–6; *RMS*, i, App.2, no. 1624; SRO RH6/176. The last is a badly damaged obligation issued sometime in 1370 by

which Dunbar, styled 'Dominus de Ffyffe', agreed to pay a lifetime annuity of £145 to Isabella, as had been guaranteed at the time of the countess's resignation. The view that John Dunbar married Isabella is almost certainly mistaken. Isabella was not styled as Dunbar's spouse in the agreement between them and John was, or was soon to be, married to the Steward's daughter. Isabella was simply coerced into resigning her rights in Fife and other lands to John Dunbar: cf. *RMS*, i, no. 350. In September 1370 lands which had been given to the countess in life rent by her third husband, Thomas Bisset, who had died in 1366, were regranted to associates of the Dunbars. Isabella was also forced into grants to James Douglas of Dalkeith in late 1369: *Mort.Reg.*, ii, 80; GD 150/20. The witnesses included Sir Alexander Lindsay and Sir William Dischington.

2

The Foundation of a Dynasty: Politics, Power and Propaganda

At the time of David II's death in February 1371 the king's court was dominated by men whose political and personal relationships with the Steward were decidedly equivocal. The morning of 23 February 1371 would not bring much cheer to the dead king's most favoured and trusted allies, Sir Robert Erskine, his son Thomas, and the brothers of David II's mistress and bride-to-be, George Dunbar, earl of March, and John, lord of Fife. The succession of the Steward clearly threatened the patronage which David had lavished on this tight-knit social/political grouping and raised the prospect of political marginalisation and some measure of revenge for the treatment meted out to the Steward in 1369–71. The concern would prove to be well founded, for within two years of Robert II becoming king the Erskines and John Dunbar would lose possession of most of the titles and offices granted to them by David II.

Within the wider circle of men who had prospered in the service of David II the prospect of the Steward as king was one to inspire fear and apprehension. The immediate reaction of some of the less powerful members of David II's entourage to the death of their patron was to seek safety in England, with Edward III issuing year-long safe conducts on 17 March 1371 to members of David's household. The group included Simon Reid, David's well-favoured constable of Edinburgh castle, Murdach of Glassary, the Steward of David II's household, the diplomat Bartholomew de Leon and Sir William Ramsay of Colluthie.[1]

While many may have feared the accession of the Steward, there seemed to be no practical way in which opposition could be manifested, for since the death of John Sutherland in 1361 the Steward was clearly David II's nearest male heir, and he was also the heir to the throne under the terms of the entails which had been drawn up under Robert I's direction in 1318 and 1326.[2] Yet despite the Steward's apparently overwhelming dynastic claims it soon became clear that Robert was not to enjoy an easy and automatic succession. While David II appears to have been buried almost immediately after his death in Holyrood abbey, the Steward's coronation at Scone did not take place until 26 March 1371, over a month after his uncle's demise. There was no symbolic continuity between the laying to rest of the old king and the coronation of his successor.[3] The long delay between David's death and Robert's coronation is explained by the emergence of a major, although rather obscure, challenge to the Steward's succession in the form of a gathering of forces at Linlithgow by William, earl of Douglas, and his supporters.[4] The earliest account of this episode suggests only that Douglas appeared at Linlithgow in order to oppose the Steward's claim to the throne, with no explanation of the earl's aims or justifications.[5] Bower, writing in the 1440s, elaborates on this sparse story line with the claim that Douglas's display of defiance came after a meeting of the three estates at Linlithgow had discussed 'the choice of their future king' and had found in favour of the Steward because of his hereditary right and the entails drawn up in 1315 and 1318. Bower also suggests that Douglas was personally claiming the throne for himself on the basis of Balliol and Comyn rights to the crown, an idea further developed by the mid-fifteenth century Pluscarden chronicle, which boldly states that Douglas claimed a right in the succession derived from Edward Balliol, the son of king John Balliol.[6]

There are a number of problems with Bower's account. Firstly, there is no indication in contemporary record, or in Wyntoun's version of the events of 1371, that there was ever a meeting of the three estates at Linlithgow. The picture of general political consensus amongst the three estates in favour of the claims of Robert the Steward would, however, fit well with Bower's consistent emphasis on the widespread support enjoyed by the Stewart claim to the throne before 1371.[7] If there was an assembly of some kind at Linlithgow in late February or early March it would hardly have been welcomed by the Steward who, as David II's heir by blood and entail, would surely have seen no political advantage in the holding of a 'council' to discuss the merits of alternative claims to the throne. The choice of Linlithgow, rather than Perth or Scone where Robert would eventually be crowned, reinforces the point that any gathering in West Lothian could not have been intended simply to approve the Steward's succession and allow his immediate coronation. The political impetus for Bower's 'meeting of the three estates' must have come from those seeking or supporting an alternative to the Steward's succession, and it seems likely that the Linlithgow 'council' was in fact little more than an armed gathering of those men desperate and determined enough to oppose the Steward, led by William, earl of Douglas, in the immediate aftermath of David II's death.[8]

2) SONS AND DAUGHTERS : THE FAMILY OF ROBERT II

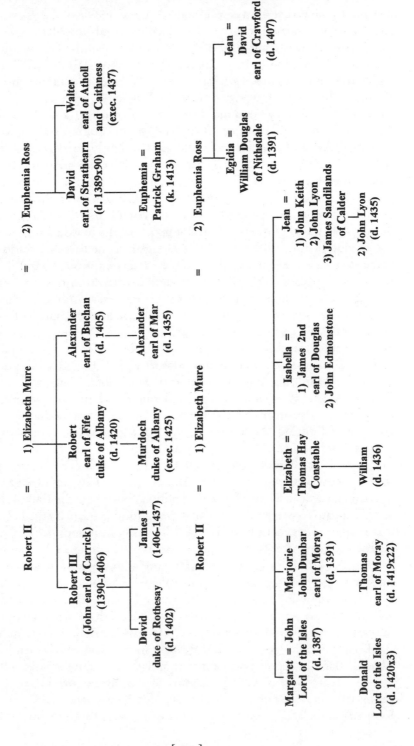

For any chance of success Douglas's opposition to the Steward's succession would have to have been based on a viable political/dynastic alternative. Bower's suggestion that Douglas put himself forward as a candidate for the kingship as the representative of Balliol and Comyn rights has sent a number of historians on a largely fruitless quest to establish the earl's Comyn and Balliol descent. In fact, the only discernible, and very tenuous, link between the earl and the Balliol family was through Douglas's brother-in-law Thomas, earl of Mar.[9]

The weakness of any personal claim advanced by the earl of Douglas to the Scottish crown in 1371 was manifest, for while the Steward's role as heir by blood and entail to the last of the Bruce kings was unquestionable, there was absolutely no indication that Douglas was the rightful heir to any claims to royal status vested in the Balliol and Comyn families. Bower's portrayal of near-universal support for the Steward's rights and the obviously flimsy nature of any Douglas claim to royal status has resulted in the entire episode being viewed as an opportunistic and almost frivolous exercise, in which Douglas sought to extract various concessions from the Steward before agreeing to support Robert's claim to the throne. A politically isolated, unsupported and unsustainable display of force against the heir presumptive and future king would, however, have been an act of supreme political folly and would surely not have merited the substantial concessions made by the Steward to Douglas and his supporters in order to bring their defiance to an end. The evidence suggests, in fact, that Douglas's demonstration enjoyed significant support from men determined to protect the territorial and jurisdictional influence they had acquired during David's reign, and that the Steward, at least, saw a very real political threat in their actions.

In 1371 the raising of a rebellion in the name of Balliol and Comyn by the most powerful magnate south of the Forth may have appeared a very grave threat indeed to the Steward's position. Since 1332 the Balliol claim to the Scottish crown had been maintained almost entirely by the political and military interventions of Edward III, at first in support of Edward Balliol and later, after Edward Balliol had expressly resigned his claims to the Scottish kingdom in favour of Edward III in 1356, in pursuit of the English king's own rights as Balliol's assignee.[10] Douglas's stance in 1371 was therefore bound to excite the interest of Edward III, and it raised the spectre of a new political intervention by the English crown in a disputed Scottish succession, either in support of Douglas as a Balliol claimant or in vindication of Edward's own rights, for if anyone had a well-established claim as Balliol's representative it was, in fact, the English king.

The resurrection of Comyn claims to the throne would also have generated interest south of the border, for Henry, the young son of John of Gaunt and grandson of Edward III was, through his mother

Blanche, a lineal descendant of the Comyn earls of Buchan. The Comyn descent of Gaunt's son had been one of the reasons put forward in the run-up to the parliament of March 1364 for the adoption of John of Gaunt as heir presumptive to the Scottish throne.[11] It seems possible that in raising Balliol and Comyn claims in February 1371 Douglas was not, in fact, claiming the throne for himself, but threatening the Steward with a revival of the only political alternative to the Stewart succession which had been under serious consideration in the previous decade, that is, the acceptance of Edward III or John of Gaunt as David II's heir. The terms of a treaty concluded between Robert II and Charles V of France later in 1371 certainly betray Robert's anxiety about potential English interventions in future Scottish succession disputes, an anxiety which may have been based on the king's experiences in February and March 1371.[12] As it was, there was to be no effective assertion of the interests of the English dynasty in the Scottish succession. Although Edward III was clearly in personal contact with disaffected members of David II's household before 17 March 1371, including Simon Reid, the constable of Edinburgh castle, the ageing king was not the man to embark on a new Scottish adventure. Perhaps the most significant point was that in February 1371 the man who had been promoted as a possible successor to David II on at least two occasions, John of Gaunt, was serving as a lieutenant of the English crown in Aquitaine and was clearly in no position to intervene personally in Scotland. In the autumn of 1371 Gaunt would marry Constance, the daughter and heir of Pedro king of Castile, a match which increasingly pulled Gaunt into Iberian affairs and the pursuit of the Castilian crown.[13]

Whatever the basis of the earl of Douglas's display of opposition to the Steward's succession, the earl's plans were thwarted by the men who had dominated David II's court in 1369–71: Sir Robert Erskine, George Dunbar, earl of March, and John Dunbar, lord of Fife. Wyntoun informs us that Erskine who was 'worthy, wiss, and lele', knew the 'Stewartis rycht' and brought a great force to Douglas's gathering at Linlithgow, where he was joined by the Dunbar brothers who 'Come with the Stewartis rycht to be'. The end result was that Douglas 'Throu thare powere sa stonayit was' that he entered into negotiations for a settlement with the Steward.[14] Given the events of 1369–71, Erskine and the Dunbar brothers, the three noblemen named as upholding the Steward's claim at Linlithgow, can hardly be regarded as long-standing political allies of the Steward. Nor were they guaranteed to view any potential intervention by Edward III or John of Gaunt in the Scottish succession with a patriotic horror, for only eight months before David's death, Robert and Thomas Erskine and

John Dunbar had been in London receiving a loan of £666 13s 4d from the English exchequer.[15] In the context of attempting to secure control of the kingdom after David's death, the support or opposition of Erskine, March and John Dunbar was crucial to both the Steward and his opponents. In the chronicle accounts Erskine is described as custodian of the three major royal castles of Edinburgh, Dumbarton and Stirling. Sir Robert was certainly the keeper of Stirling, while his son Thomas is recorded as custodian of Edinburgh castle for the first time in the year 1371–2, a position which he may have gained through one of David II's last acts of patronage.[16] Although Erskine had briefly held Dumbarton in the late 1360s, in 1371 the royal stronghold on the Clyde was in the care of Sir John Danielston, a man who had been a fairly regular witness to the Steward's charters before 1371, and who can probably be regarded as a Stewart loyalist.[17]

The Erskines' hold on the vital royal castles of Stirling and Edinburgh in February 1371 made them significant figures in the dispute over the succession, and Douglas's attempt to pre-empt the Steward's claim to the throne effectively foundered when Erskine, March and John Dunbar, perhaps unexpectedly, came out in favour of the Steward's rights at Linlithgow. It seems likely that until that point Douglas had actually regarded the Erskines and Dunbars as potential allies, men who had every reason to fear that the Steward's succession would bring about a rapid decline in their territorial and political fortunes.[18]

There is no indication of any significant military confrontation at Linlithgow, and the chronicle accounts suggest that Douglas abandoned his opposition and entered into negotiations with the Steward once Erskine and the Dunbars had made their support for the Steward's rights plain. With the castles of Stirling and Edinburgh held in the Steward's interest, the lord of Fife unwilling to acknowledge the virtue of any alternative claim, and with no prospect of an immediate English intervention, Douglas's political options were severely limited. The Steward, however, was more than prepared to make concessions in order to neutralise Douglas opposition to his succession. Douglas's own formidable territorial power and the fact that his resurrection of the Balliol/Comyn cause potentially, and probably deliberately, threatened a renewed English interest in the Scottish kingdom, meant that there was considerable pressure on the Steward to achieve a swift political settlement. The Steward was clearly eager to avoid any long and damaging confrontation with the earl of Douglas which could have delayed his coronation and encouraged the intervention of external powers into the succession dispute, a concern specifically mentioned in the Franco-Scottish treaty concluded in July 1371 by Scottish ambassadors who had been commissioned for the task in the first parliament of Robert II's reign.[19] The Steward's concessions included a marriage for the earl's son and heir into the new royal house:

> Swa tretyt thai, that his son suld wed
> This Kingis dochtyr off lawchful bed,
> Ande he suld tyl his lord ay do
> Honoure, that till hym efferyte to:
> And the King to this mariage
> Gawe silver and land in heritage.[20]

Sir James Douglas was probably knighted by Robert II at his coronation in March 1371, and a dispensation was obtained for his marriage to Robert II's daughter, Isabel, on 24 September of the same year. As part of the marriage settlement James Douglas received a 100-merk pension from the royal customs. Sir James's father, William, also prospered in the year after Robert II's coronation. By 23 January 1372, the earl had become the royal justiciar south of Forth, an office with an attractive annual salary of 200 pounds, apparently replacing Sir Robert Erskine who had served as David II's justiciar of Lothian.[21] Besides these gains, Sir James Douglas's marriage to Isabel Stewart eventually produced a huge payment of £500 from the crown to the earl in 1373 and a further annuity in the same year of £100 to James Douglas from the lands of Ednam, an annuity which had to be topped up from the royal revenues because half the lands of Ednam were in the hands of the English.[22] Altogether, the pre-coronation settlement of March 1371 saw the earl of Douglas obtain the principal royal judicial office south of the Forth, a royal marriage for his son, a lump sum of £500, and a combined annual income from royal offices and pensions for father and son of close on £370. The earl of Douglas and his son emerged from 1371 with their jurisdictional, social and financial position very much enhanced, and their political primacy in the south of Scotland unchallenged.

The marriage alliance and territorial deal with Douglas appears to have been one of a number concluded by the Steward in early 1371 as he sought to obtain the loyalty and support of magnates driven into real or potential opposition by the fear that their political and territorial interests would be swiftly undermined by the new king. There are no means of identifying the men who supported Douglas at Linlithgow, but the group probably included the powerful northern affinity, based around the formidable Sir Walter Leslie and his half-brother Sir Alexander Lindsay of Glen Esk, which had risen to great influence in the service of David II.[23] The close personal and political relationship between David II and Sir Walter Leslie rested squarely on the latter's crusading exploits during the 1350s and 1360s. Walter Leslie and his elder brother Norman, who was one of David II's most trusted diplomats, planned crusades against the heathens of Lithuania in 1356 and the Saracens in 1359. In 1365, probably at the personal instigation of David II, the two brothers were involved in the storming of Alexandria by Peter I of Cyprus, during which action Norman appears to have been killed.[24] Walter Leslie's achievements as a crusader were well known; in the fourteenth-century Armorial of Gelres, Leslie's coat-of-arms displayed a crest bearing a turbaned Saracen's head, but these were simply one part of an extensive career as a continental mercenary which formed the basis for a now lost chivalric/crusading epic, 'the tail of syr valtir the bald leslye'.[25]

On Walter Leslie's return to Scotland in 1366, the crusading knight became the recipient of considerable royal patronage; most importantly, before 13 September 1366 he was married to Euphemia, the daughter and heiress by line of the earl of Ross, a match imposed on the aged earl by David II.[26] In the late 1360s Walter Leslie was the beneficiary of several grants extorted from Ross and his brother Hugh by Leslie's royal patron.[27] The most important of these transactions was Ross's forced resignation of his earldom of Ross and the lordship of Skye to the crown in October 1370. David II regranted the earldom and lordship to Ross under an entail which ensured the succession of the earl's daughter Euphemia and her spouse Walter Leslie.[28] The resignation and regrant were required by the crown because since the 1350s the earldom had been in a male entail which would have seen the title of earl pass, on earl William's death, to the earl's nearest male heir, his nephew, William Ross of Balnagowan.[29]

Leslie's position in the Ross inheritance had thus been engineered entirely by David II's intimidation of the Steward's brother-in-law. It seemed inevitable that David II's premature death and the accession of Robert II would see Leslie's territorial interests swept away as the new king and Ross gained their revenge for the humiliations of 1369–71. Leslie, in particular, must have feared that his claims to the earldom of Ross and his occupation of the royal lands granted to him by David II would not survive the Steward's uncontested succession. William, earl of Ross, certainly anticipated a changed attitude towards Leslie's claims in the north on the part of the new king. In June 1371 Ross complained to Robert II's royal council that he had been forced to accept his daughter's marriage to Walter Leslie and to surrender elements of the Ross inheritance in Buchan in Leslie's favour, through David II's intimidation and coercion. Ross further asserted that none of the grants he had made in favour of his daughter and Walter Leslie had been made freely, an allegation which cast doubt on the legality of the earl's resignation of the earldom of Ross and the lordship of Skye to David II in October 1370, and the subsequent royal regrant of the earldom and lordship to the earl with the entail which ensured the succession of his daughter Euphemia and Walter Leslie.[30] Since the earldom of Ross had been in a male entail in the 1350s there was a distinct possibility that Robert II could simply revoke the 1370 entail and allow the earldom to descend to the earl's nephew, William Ross of Balnagowan, rather than Walter Leslie and his spouse. Besides the threat to his position in Ross, Walter Leslie must also have feared for his claims to the thanages of Kincardine, Aberluthnott, Fettercairn, and Aberchirder, which had been granted to him by David II.[31]

It seems likely that 'the bald syr valtir' was one of the men prepared to support the earl of Douglas's stand against the Steward's succession in 1371, largely to protect, or obtain guarantees for, his suddenly threatened territorial position in the north. Leslie's opposition to a Stewart succession would have represented a serious political problem for the Steward, because Sir Walter was part of a powerful and closely knit kin group which included his half brothers Alexander Lindsay of Glen Esk and Sir William Lindsay of the Byres, and his nephew, Sir James Lindsay of Crawford. Both before and after 1371 Leslie and his Lindsay kinsmen maintained a high level of contact and co-operation which made them a formidable aristocratic coalition.[32] Sir Alexander Lindsay of Glen Esk had also been a close associate of David II, witnessing the Steward's submission to David in 1363, and appearing as a fairly regular witness to David's great seal charters in 1369–71, usually alongside Sir Walter.[33]

David II's death left both Sir Walter Leslie and Sir Alexander Lindsay in a very vulnerable position, but their probable role in opposing a Stewart succession in February/March 1371 seems to have forced the Steward into a political and territorial settlement with the Lindsay/Leslie affinity which allowed them to survive the change of regime in 1371 with their influence not only preserved but enhanced. The Steward's agreement with the Lindsay/Leslie affinity mirrored his settlement with the earl of Douglas and was secured in exactly the same way, that is through marriage alliances with the new royal family and the dispensation of considerable royal patronage. A marriage alliance appears to have been contracted around 1371 between Robert II's immediate family and the Lindsays of Glen Esk, with Alexander Lindsay marrying, as his second wife, Robert II's niece Marjory.[34] The marriage links between the crown and the Lindsays of Glen Esk were further strengthened in early 1375, with Alexander Lindsay's son and heir, David, obtaining a dispensation for his marriage to Robert II's daughter Elizabeth on 22 February.[35] The marriage saw the payment of a substantial dowry of £233 8s 6d to Sir Alexander, indicative of Robert II's continuing financial patronage of the Lindsays.[36]

Alexander Lindsay, James Lindsay and Walter Leslie all attended Robert II's coronation in 1371, and Alexander Lindsay was immediately established as a regular great seal charter witness for the new king, as he had been for David II.[37] None of the patronage directed to Walter Leslie by David II was rescinded. Leslie became lord of Ross after the death of William, earl of Ross, in 1372, and the reversionary rights to a number of royal thanages which David II had granted to Leslie in the 1360s were honoured and upheld by the new king. Sir Walter redistributed most of these estates to his Lindsay kinsmen.[38] Most importantly of all, by 1373, and probably from 1371, Alexander and James Lindsay were acting as the royal justiciars north of the Forth, and from 1374 until his death in 1382 the office was exercised by Alexander Lindsay alone.[39] It seems likely that the justiciarship north of Forth was one of the key concessions offered by Robert II to the Lindsay/Leslie affinity for their support or acquiescence during the succession dispute of 1371. For a decade after 1371 Sir Walter and his kinsmen would act as a powerful political, territorial and jurisdictional counterweight to the growing influence of the king's son Alexander, lord of Badenoch, in the north of the kingdom.

Neither of the justiciars appointed north and south of the Forth in 1371 were men who had displayed previous political loyalty to the new king and his family, indeed quite the reverse, and they cannot be regarded as Robert II's own preferred choice for upholding the new dynasty's policies and ambitions in the localities. The Douglas and Lindsay justiciarships were part of the price of the political settlement reached between Robert II and the powerful factions which had been openly opposed to his succession in 1371. During the last ten years of his reign David II had drawn his justiciars from within the crown administration or his own household. In 1371 David II men such as Sir Robert Erskine, Sir Hugh Eglintoun and Sir William Dischington of Ardross were swept aside to be replaced not by Stewart adherents, but by major regional magnates, Douglas in the south, Lindsay in the north, whose political support and loyalty had to be secured for the new royal dynasty.[40]

Robert the Steward bargained his way to the throne in February/ March 1371 by recognising, guaranteeing and winning over to his cause entrenched political power groups in the localities. After a decade of arbitrary, abrasive and assertive kingship, of increasingly onerous financial demands, of confrontation, imprisonment and coercion, of the promotion of junior members of David II's chivalric crusading cadre at the expense of the great magnates, a very different type of monarch was about to ascend the throne. As king, Robert II was to follow the political path he had laid down, as Steward, before 1371. The promotion of Stewart family interests was paramount, but the methods used to achieve this after 1371 were understandably cautious and conservative. In the years after 1371 Robert showed a distinct disinclination to interfere in the affairs, or thwart the territorial ambitions, of the great regional magnates, except where the interests of his own family demanded an intervention. The king's low-key and non-confrontational approach was an understandable reaction to the problems of 1371, for it was in the newly established royal dynasty's best interests to see that a period of relative political calm followed Robert II's coronation. The new king's privy council immediately reflected a mix of magnate interests. Besides his two sons Carrick and Menteith, the king's early charters were witnessed by the earl of Douglas and his brother-in-law Thomas, earl of Mar, Sir Robert Erskine and Sir Alexander Lindsay. Although Mar soon disappeared as a witness to great seal charters Douglas remained, and Alexander Lindsay was joined by his nephew, who was also the king's nephew, Sir James Lindsay. The important point was that all the major magnate groups which had been involved in the political disturbances of 1371/2 continued to command a place and to be represented in the king's council, and to have a say in the distribution of royal patronage.

The elevation of Robert the Steward to the kingship seems to have proceeded smoothly once an accommodation had been reached with the earl of Douglas and those who had supported him in February/March 1371, and the earl and his son were both present on 27 March 1371 when Robert II was crowned at Scone.[41] The coronation parliament was marked by further royal concessions, this time to Sir Archibald Douglas, lord of Galloway, and Sir James Douglas of Dalkeith, both David II loyalists who may well have been involved in their kinsman's display of force at Linlithgow.[42] Not surprisingly perhaps, given the political problems of the preceding month, Robert II immediately nominated his eldest son John, earl of Carrick, as his successor and caused the assembled prelates and magnates to acknowledge both Carrick's right to the kingship after his own death, and to promise to uphold and defend that right. Notarial instruments were drawn up recording the public assent of the three estates to the succession arrangements, to which the seals of the noblemen and clerics present were appended 'for a perpetual and future memorial' and 'lest anyone on this matter might pretend ignorance in future'. Robert II found a prestigious precedent to justify his entailing of the crown, for he claimed to be acting 'after the manner and example of the said good king . . ., Robert his grandfather'. The fifty-five-year-old Robert II was obviously concerned to obtain as many guarantees as possible for the uncontested succession of his son to the throne after his own death (which, given his age, cannot have been thought too distant) from the prelates and magnates of the realm. The search for dynastic security would remain the dominant political theme in the early years of Robert's reign.

Some highly significant figures were absent from Robert II's coronation ceremony. The senior Scottish earl, Fife, traditionally played a key role in the ritual of coronation, and the founder of a new dynasty would clearly be anxious to stress and ensure the legitimacy and authority of the ceremony which formally invested him with his power as king.[43] In 1371, however, the lord of Fife was John Dunbar, whose political relationship with the new king was, despite Dunbar's apparent support for Robert II against Douglas in the month before the coronation, decidedly frosty. Robert II certainly gave little indication that he was overcome with gratitude towards the earl of March and his brother for their role in February–March 1371, and the chronicle accounts may well overplay the importance of the Dunbar brothers in the successful pursuit of the Steward's claim in 1371.[44] The chronicles certainly misrepresent the nature of the political relationship between Robert II and the Dunbars, for by 30 March 1371 it was clear that the new king and his sons did not recognise the legality of Dunbar's claim to be lord of Fife. This no doubt explains why John Dunbar and his brother George did not witness any of the great public declarations drawn up on or around 27 March, although March's seal was appended to the instrument confirming Carrick's position as Robert II's heir. It seems most likely that it was Isabella, countess of Fife, who performed the traditional functions of the earl of Fife at Robert's coronation.

Isabella was certainly in nearby Perth on 30 March, where she concluded a remarkable indenture with the new king's second son, Robert, earl of Menteith.[45] In the indenture Isabella formally recognised Menteith as heir to the earldom of Fife under the terms of two entails. The first dated from August 1315 and was part of a political reconciliation between Duncan, earl of Fife, Isabella's father, and Robert I.[46] The 1315 agreement stipulated that the earldom of Fife was to descend, on the failure of earl Duncan's legitimate heirs, to Robert I and any of the king's lawful heirs to whom he wished to give the earldom. There were various clauses designed to ensure that the earldom could not, in future, be held directly by the king and that it would remain distinct from the royal patrimony. The chief concern here was that the earls of Fife played a pivotal role in the inauguration of the Scottish monarch; future kings could hardly be expected to perform these services themselves at their own coronation. If Robert I died without a lawful heir to whom the earldom could be assigned, then it was to revert to the earl of Fife's heir of line, Allan, son and heir of Allan, earl of Menteith. In 1371 Isabella recognised Robert Stewart, the husband of Alan of Menteith's grand-niece and heiress and the new earl of Menteith, as her heir in the earldom of Fife. Robert would also have had a strong claim under the terms of a descent to the heirs of Robert I. This would have brought the earldom to Robert II and, since the terms of the entail precluded the king from holding the earldom, it was most likely that Robert II would settle Fife on his second son, rather than the heir to the throne.

The second entail, by which Robert, earl of Menteith, claimed Fife, had been drawn up sometime in 1360–2 by Isabella and her then husband Walter Stewart, Robert's elder brother. Robert's indenture with the countess of Fife directly threatened the position of John Dunbar, lord of Fife. Robert and Isabella agreed that Robert should recover possession of the earldom which the countess had been forced to resign, a clear reference to David II's grant to John Dunbar in 1369/70, whereupon Isabella would resign the earldom to the crown to be regranted to Robert of Menteith. From March 1371, then, Robert, earl of Menteith, was committed to removing John Dunbar from the earldom of Fife.

The dispute between the new royal family and the Dunbars over the earldom of Fife was to last for almost a year after Robert II's coronation, and between March 1371 and March 1372 the king's second son was styled simply earl of Menteith. In early 1372, however, a major territorial deal between Robert II and the Dunbar brothers allowed the king's son Robert to acquire the earldom of Fife. The arrangement centred on Robert II acknowledging the claims of George and John Dunbar to elements of the inheritance of the Randolph earls of Moray, lords of Annandale and Man. John and George Dunbar were the sons of Isabella Randolph, a daughter of Thomas Randolph, 1st earl of Moray, and a sister of John Randolph, third and last of the Randolph earls of Moray who had died without heirs at the battle of Neville's Cross in 1346. In strictly legal terms the Dunbars' claims to be the descendants and heirs of the Randolph earls of Moray were not particularly strong, because the 1312 grant to Thomas Randolph, the first earl, had explicitly made the earldom a male entail with a reversion to the crown on the failure of male heirs. In 1368 David II had recovered control of the earldom of Moray under the terms of the 1312 entail, and until 1372 the earldom remained part of the royal financial and territorial system.[47] In a parliament at Scone on 9

March 1372, however, John Dunbar and his spouse, the king's daughter Marjory, were granted the earldom of Moray in free regality, excepting the lordships of Lochaber, Badenoch and the castle of Urquhart, which had already been granted out to the lord of the Isles and the king's sons Alexander and David.[48] The grant of Moray was clearly intended to be a permanent alienation to the Dunbar interest since, on the failure of heirs between John and Marjory, the earldom was to descend to John's brother George, earl of March, and his heirs. March was probably given possession of other elements of the Randolph inheritance, the 'royal' lordship of Annandale and claims to the Isle of Man, as part of the settlement over Fife; George was certainly styling himself lord of Annandale and Man in 1372.[49] At around the same time as the grant of Moray to John Dunbar, Robert Stewart began to style himself earl of Fife and Menteith.[50]

Robert II had thus, at last, secured the ancient earldom of Fife in the hands of the Stewarts and had thereby indirectly increased the stranglehold exerted by the new dynasty on the kingship itself, since the earl played such a crucial role in the inauguration ceremony of a new king. Robert had paid for John Dunbar's resignation of his claims to Fife with a grant of Moray to John, and the lordships of Annandale and Man to his brother George. There may also have been an element of political coercion involved, if there is any substance in the later tale that Robert II brought charges against John Dunbar in a parliament at Perth for the 'treasonable' seducing of his daughter in 1370.[51]

Robert II's grant of Moray to John Dunbar may have caused some resentment on the part of the king's third son Alexander, lord of Badenoch, who probably hoped to be elevated to the top rank of the peerage as the new earl of Moray. Alexander had certainly uplifted some of the revenues due to the crown from the earldom of Moray in the year 1371–2, and on 10 November 1371 he had witnessed a royal charter dealing with the settlement of a dispute between Richard Comyn and Thomas Grant over possession of the office of forester of the park and forest of Darnaway.[52] Alexander Stewart became the recipient of an unrelenting stream of crown patronage in the years after 1371, but the loss of Moray in order to secure Fife for his elder brother must have been a blow to Alexander, who did not attain comital rank until 1382.

The Dunbars' chief ally in 1369–71, Sir Robert Erskine, was also gently eased from many of the positions of power and influence he had enjoyed under David II, as Robert II and his sons came increasingly to dominate the royal establishment. On 7 February 1373, Robert II granted Robert, earl of Fife and Menteith, and his male heirs, the heritable custodianship of Stirling castle with an associated pension of

200 merks.[53] The keepership of the royal castle was thus to be permanently annexed to a junior branch of the Stewart royal family. Fife was directly replacing Sir Robert Erskine as custodian of Stirling, and the transfer of the fortress was accompanied by an agreement, made on the same day, between the earl and Sir Robert. The agreement took the form of a bond of friendship between the two men in which Fife undertook to be a good and faithful lord and kind friend to Sir Robert, his sons, his brother and his men and to protect him in his lands, rents, possessions and other goods.[54] The agreement was clearly designed to counteract the growth of any political resentment harboured by Sir Robert Erskine and his son Sir Thomas against the king and his sons in the wake of the Erskines' relentless loss of crown office after 1371. Sir Robert had already been replaced as justiciar of Lothian by the earl of Douglas, while his son had been displaced as custodian of Edinburgh castle by John, earl of Carrick, in early 1372, and as Sheriff of Edinburgh by Carrick's adherent Sir Malcolm Fleming before February 1374. In early 1373, besides the loss of Stirling castle, the barony of Ednam which the Steward had granted to Sir Robert Erskine in 1357 was transferred to the custody of James Douglas, the earl's son.[55]

The Erskines had raised themselves to an unusual level of political influence within David II's royal administration through loyal service to the crown, but unlike the earl of Douglas they did not enjoy a significant regional military and political status from which to defy, threaten and bargain with the new king. After 1371 the Erskines' only option was to continue in royal service despite the manifest loss of power and influence which they experienced, and Sir Robert doggedly remained as a witness to Robert II's great seal charters. Erskine resentment at the loss of the justiciarship of Lothian and the barony of Ednam to the Douglases, and the keepership of Edinburgh and Stirling castles and the sheriffship of Edinburgh to the king's sons, was also bought off with a handsome financial settlement in February 1373. Sir Robert Erskine received a gift of 500 merks from Robert II, to be paid over five years, which was clearly intended as a compensation for the loss of the office of keeper of Stirling castle, with its annual pension of 200 merks, which David II had gifted in liferent to Erskine. Erskine was also given an annuity of £100 from the fermes of Aberdeen to compensate for the loss of Ednam, an issue which was raised by Erskine during the parliament of April 1373. Sir Thomas Erskine, meanwhile, was given 400 merks for the ward of Margaret, the heiress of Sir David Barclay of Brechin.[56] Erskine had married Margaret's mother Janet Keith shortly before 16 April 1370, probably a match arranged for Thomas by David II at the height of Erskine/Dunbar influence over the king. Despite the significant sum of 400 merks given over to Erskine, the purchase of the ward of Margaret Barclay by the crown was little more than the removal from Erskine control of the last significant piece of territorial or jurisdictional patronage granted to them by David II. Eventually the marriage of Margaret Barclay and the considerable Brechin inheritance which went with her would be settled on the king's youngest son, Walter.[57]

In Robert II's dealings with the Dunbar/Erskine faction after 1371 we see the hallmarks of the politics of the opening years of the new king's reign. The king exhibited a fierce determination to support the territorial ambitions of his sons and to place the Stewart dynasty in an unassailable political position within the kingdom. Robert seems to have regarded these two processes as essentially interlinked. The most notable aspect of the 1370s has, for some historians, been the tremendous territorial and jurisdictional aggrandisement of the new king's extensive family network. Robert II's settlement of earldoms, lordships, offices and pensions on his sons and sons-in-law may have looked unusual in the wake of two Bruce kings who had few close relatives survive to adulthood, but it was hardly untypical of the way in which major mediaeval magnates with sufficient resources provided for and employed an extended family. The 'Stewartisation' of the higher nobility in the 1370s has generally been regarded as a dangerous political development, especially when combined with Robert II's 'futile and aimless' kingship, with the king portrayed as allowing his sons, relations and the other great magnates to acquire too much independent territorial and political power.[58] The view that Robert II's large family was a politically destabilising element in Scottish politics first took hold in Walter Bower's *Scotichronicon*, written in the 1440s. After describing the events of 1371 Bower gives a brief and positive portrayal of Robert II, but then launches into a lament about the king's children: 'some were peace-loving and benign, some were arrogant and malign'.[59] The crucial point about Bower's description is that the Abbot of Inchcolm was writing his history in the aftermath of the assassination of James I in 1437. Walter Stewart, earl of Atholl, by that stage the last surviving son of Robert II, had been involved in the assassination plot and had been executed for his crime.[60] Bower's bitter condemnation of some of Robert II's offspring thus arises from the political conditions of the 1440s rather than the 1370s.

Much of the negative imagery surrounding Robert II's political control over his kingdom in fact stemmed from the activities of his sons, especially Alexander and Walter, after the king's death. In the years after 1371 Robert II clearly regarded the territorial and political advance of his sons as the most effective way to pursue his primary aim of securing the hold of the new Stewart dynasty on the kingdom. The aggrandisement of the king's sons was a key part of the process of consolidating Stewart rule and was largely supervised and controlled by Robert II himself. Given the insecurity of the new dynasty and the problems of 1371, the king's policy of promoting his own family was subject to certain political limits. The king's pursuit of the earldom of Fife and the royal offices occupied by Sir Robert Erskine, for example, was marked by his willingness to offer John Dunbar and the Erskines considerable territorial and financial compensation. Moreover, it was not necessarily the case that the king's relatives became powerful regional magnates on the basis of their royal connection; very often the reverse was true, as Robert II sought to marry his daughters into influential, and in the immediate aftermath of 1371, potentially hostile noble affinities.

After Robert II's accession to the throne his two eldest sons, John, earl of Carrick, and Robert, earl of Fife and Menteith, became regular witnesses to the king's great seal charters and spearheaded the Stewart takeover of the crown administration. By the time of Robert II's coronation, Carrick had already received the lands and title of the Steward of Scotland resigned by the king.[61] With a parliamentary confirmation of his position as heir apparent John, earl of Carrick and Atholl and Steward of Scotland, was speedily established as the foremost magnate in the kingdom after his father. In the following year, 1372, Robert II made Carrick keeper of the vital royal fortress of Edinburgh with a huge annual pension of 500 merks from the customs of the burgh, more than doubling the 200-merk annuity which had been paid to previous custodians, along with control of the associated office of sheriff of Edinburgh.[62] In the years after 1371 Carrick established himself as the principal representative of the royal dynasty south of the Forth and the leading figure in Anglo-Scottish diplomacy. Carrick would seek marriages for his sons and daughters amongst the nobility of Lothian and the borders, while his council and political affinity came to be dominated by men from the same region, notably the earl of Douglas and Sir James Lindsay of Crawford. Carrick's political influence south of the Forth would soon outweigh his father's, a process accelerated by the fact that Robert II's kingship was essentially based in and around Perth rather than Edinburgh.[63]

Robert II's second son, Robert, earl of Fife and Menteith, also prospered during and after 1371. Robert's provisional status in the earldom of Menteith had been brought to an end by the time of his father's coronation, with Robert styled earl rather than lord of Menteith.[64] Robert Stewart's use of the comital title suggests that the children born to John Drummond and the countess of Menteith had either died, or that their claims to Menteith had insufficient political backing to withstand the ambitions of the earl and his royal father. By July 1372 Robert had concluded an amicable settlement with another of David II's favourites who had disrupted his control of the Menteith inheritance during the 1360s, Bartholomew Leon.[65]

Aside from the securing of his title to Menteith, the 1370s proved to be a decade of spectacular territorial and political gains for the king's second son. The acquisition of Fife in March 1372 gave Robert the status of the second most important magnate in the kingdom after his brother John, earl of Carrick, the king's heir. In early 1373 Fife received another substantial boost to his position in the kingdom with the grant of the constabulary of Stirling castle in heritage, giving the earl and his successors a permanent interest in one of the royal establishment's three major fortresses.[66]

In the same year Robert II's determination to secure the hold of the Stewart dynasty on the crown brought further rewards to Fife, but may also have resulted in a measure of political tension between the king and Fife on the one hand, and John, earl of Carrick, the heir to the throne, on the other. On 4 April 1373 Robert II attained the highest possible degree of dynastic security for the Stewart family when a parliament at Scone approved the creation of a male entail to govern the descent of the kingship.[67] By the terms of the entail it was agreed that the right to govern the kingdom would, on Robert II's death, pass to his eldest son John, earl of Carrick (as had been laid out in the legislation of 1371). If John produced no male heirs before his death, then the succession was to pass to the king's second son Robert, earl of Fife and Menteith, and his heirs male; if Fife died without male heirs, then the king's third son Alexander, lord of Badenoch, and his male heirs would succeed to the throne and so on, with the entail naming the five sons of Robert II by his first and second wives in order of seniority. Robert II's concern to establish the Scottish crown as a male entail may well have been spurred, in part, by the failure of John, earl of Carrick's five-year-old marriage to Annabella Drummond to produce a male heir by 1373. Carrick and Annabella had produced two daughters, Margaret and Elizabeth, before April 1378, and both were probably born before the entail of 1373.[68] Margaret was certainly old enough to marry Archibald Douglas, the son of Archibald the Grim, before 1390. By 1373 Fife's marriage had produced one son, Murdoch, who was probably ten or eleven years old when the entail was proposed. Alexander Stewart, lord of Badenoch, was unmarried, although he may already have produced the eldest of his eventually numerous illegitimate sons and daughters. David, earl of Strathearn, and Walter Stewart were not yet of age. The entailing of the crown in 1373 seems to have provoked political opposition. Boece's *Lives of the Bishops of Aberdeen*, a not entirely reliable early sixteenth-century chronicle, suggests that Adam Tynyngham, dean of Aberdeen, after working as an ambassador for Robert II, which he did in 1371–3, 'fell under the suspicion of the king for . . . he was accused of sympathising with the views of certain leading men in the country on the question of the succession to the throne. This matter came up in connection with the passing of a law on the succession which these nobles disapproved of'.[69] If Boece's tale is in any way accurate, it seems most likely that he was referring to baronial disapproval of the entailing of the crown in 1373. The most obvious source of opposition to the proposed entail was the earl of Carrick, his wife Annabella, and her Drummond kinsmen. Carrick was being asked to abandon his daughter's rights in the succession in favour of his brother's children. While Carrick and Annabella might still produce a male heir, in 1373 the entail must have seemed to be a grievous blow against the Stewart/Drummond dynasty which David II had envisaged in 1367–8.[70] Aside from Robert II himself, obviously anxious that his dynasty should not, like the Bruces, last for only two generations, the chief political begetter and beneficiary of the entail was obviously Carrick's younger brother Robert, earl of Fife and Menteith.

Fife, as the events of the previous two years had shown, was high in the king's favour. Between 1373 and the belated birth of Carrick's first son, David, after eleven years of marriage, in October 1378, Fife's son Murdoch Stewart was Robert II's only legitimate male grandchild. The position of Carrick's daughters was obviously a matter of some concern for the earl after the entail of 1373. On 1 June 1374 John resigned his earldom of Carrick to the king and received it back in conjunctfeftment with Annabella his wife with a descent, after their deaths, to any heirs produced between them. Carrick clearly wanted his father's confirmation of the descent outlined in David II's original grant of the earldom. If Carrick and Annabella had failed to produce a male heir, then the earldom would have passed to Carrick's daughters, and would not have gone with the kingship and the rest of his estates to the children of one of Carrick's brothers.[71] Some of the later political animosity and rivalry between Fife and Carrick may well have had its origin in this dispute over the entailing of the crown in 1373.

The men supporting Carrick's opposition to the entailing of the crown probably included the earl of Douglas and his son James, who would certainly be closely associated with the political interests of the heir to the throne later in the reign. The earl of Douglas's family had also been politically tied to the fortunes of the Stewart/Drummond royal line by David II, who seems to have arranged the marriage of the earl's daughter, Isabella, to Malcolm Drummond, the brother of Carrick's wife Annabella, and uncle of the two young girls whose potential claims to the crown were bypassed by the entail of 1373.[72] In addition, James Douglas may have objected to the fact that the entail gave any heirs produced in his marriage to Carrick's full sister Isabel an inferior claim to the crown to that of the heirs of Carrick's half brothers. It seems significant that Adam Tynynghame, the cleric who was said to be allied to the noblemen opposing the regulation of the succession, had acted as a clerk for David II and queen Margaret Drummond in 1364, had been employed in that king's service and associated with his favourites in 1366 and 1369, and had also acted as the earl of Douglas's secretary in 1360 and was still associated with the earl in 1378.[73] Douglas opposition to the entailing of the crown may explain the renewed financial concessions made by Robert II to the earl and his son in early 1373. The royal largesse included the payment of £500 to the earl for the marriage of James Douglas and the king's daughter Isabel, the granting of the lands of Ednam to the younger Douglas, and a grant of a port at North Berwick to earl William. All three grants were probably made during, or shortly before, the meeting of the parliament which ratified the entailing of the crown.[74] It seems likely that the financial settlement of early 1373 was designed to guarantee the Douglases' political acquiescence in an act which overturned the rights of Carrick's daughters to a place in the Scottish succession and which, temporarily as it turned out, meant the eclipse of the Stewart/Drummond royal line which they represented.

Robert I's entailing of the crown in 1315 and 1318 gave Robert II a precedent for regulating the succession which he used explicitly and implicitly in the provisions of 1371 and 1373.[75] In 1371, in confirming John, earl of Carrick, as his heir, Robert II claimed to be following the example of his illustrious grandfather Robert I in nominating his successor before his death. The political disasters and discords which had beset the Scottish kingdom in the early fourteenth century were invoked to justify the entailing of the crown in 1373. In the entail Robert II claimed that he desired to avoid the 'uncertainty of succession' and 'the misfortunes and calamities which in most places and kingdoms happen, and in times bygone have happened, from the succession of female heirs'.[76] The presentation of male succession as a guarantee of the political stability and security of the kingdom happily coincided with Robert II's own political interests in securing the new Stewart dynasty. In John Barbour's *Brus*, completed within two years of the entailing of the crown in 1373, the Great Cause between Bruce and Balliol in 1292 was presented as a clash between a male (Bruce) and female (Balliol) claim. Barbour's account was thus 'politically correct', in terms of Robert II's promotion of the benefits of a defined male succession, in suggesting that the consideration given to

Balliol's 'female' claim had brought about the disastrous intervention of Edward I into Scottish politics in the 1290s.[77]

By the end of 1373 Robert II had gone a considerable way towards achieving his primary political objective, which was the establishment of the dynastic/political primacy of the Stewarts as kings of Scotland. In April 1373 Robert II had been able to introduce succession laws which gave the various branches of his own family an effective monopoly of claims to regal status within Scotland. The king's two eldest sons, John and Robert, controlled the vital royal castles of Edinburgh and Stirling, while Robert had also been established as earl of Fife, the magnate who played a critical symbolic role in the creation of a new king. The Stewart family thus increasingly dominated all the formal mechanisms of royal power, a development which went hand in hand with a renewed burst of propaganda encouraging the nobility of Scotland to render their service and loyalty to the new royal dynasty.

The propaganda produced by the new dynasty understandably laid great stress on Robert II's descent from Robert I, the hero king of the Wars of Independence, but there may also have been an attempt to rework the early history of the Stewart family in order to reflect and justify their new royal status. The poet John Barbour certainly composed a now lost Stewart genealogy, 'The Stewartis Orygenale', which apparently traced the Stewarts' line of descent from Dardanus, lord of Frigia.[78] Such an origin legend, giving the Stewarts a descent from Brutus, king of Britain, may have had a long history in the baronial house of Stewart before 1371. A prestigious Brittonic origin would have had useful political applications for a Breton noble family establishing itself in the British Isles in the eleventh and twelfth centuries, and the Stewarts, occupying lands in the north of the old Brittonic kingdom of Strathclyde, would have found agreeable a history which gave them an ancient claim to social and political pre-eminence in the region.[79] The value of Brittonic descent outside the local context of the Stewart lordships around the Firth of Clyde was likely to be limited. This was especially true in terms of the Scottish kingship, for from the early fourteenth century onwards, perhaps in response to the use of the Brut legend by English chroniclers and historians to justify the contemporary political claims of the English crown to overlordship over the entire British Isles, the Scottish chronicle tradition had tended to stress the independent origin of the Scottish royal dynasty and kingdom, and the essential irrelevance of the Brut legend.[80]

The most powerful and attractive focus for aristocratic loyalty remained the figure of Robert I and his leadership of the Scottish nation in arms. There was little to be gained in attempting to refocus the loyalties of the Scottish aristocracy on the baronial house of Steward when Robert II could portray himself as the inheritor and upholder of the Bruce legacy. The 'Armorial de Gelres', compiled by a father and son who were successively Gelres herault d'armes to the Dukes of Gueldres from 1334 to 1411, contains three folios of Scottish arms from the late fourteenth century. The bulk of the arms can be shown to date from a period after 1378 and in many cases after 1384. The royal arms are included and show a crowned helm displaying a caperline with a Bruce saltire. The compilers seem to have anachronistically recorded the Scottish royal arms pre-1371 in a collection otherwise clearly reflecting the arms of the Scottish nobility in the late 1370s and 1380s, but the mistake, if such it was, happily reflected Robert II's desire to represent the continuity of the Bruce/Stewart dynasty in his own kingship.[81] Between 1375 and 1378, some five to seven years after Robert II's succession, John Barbour, the author also of the Stewart genealogy and a man who had entered royal service on Robert II's accession in 1371, produced the most potent literary reworking of the Bruce legend in his vernacular chivalric epic *The Bruce*.[82] Although some reservations have been expressed about the level of Robert II's direct support for the production of *The Bruce*, there is little doubt that the king would have found Barbour's portrayal of aristocratic unity in the service of Robert I as he fought to preserve his dynasty and the Scottish kingdom a very gratifying picture.[83] It is also evident that Barbour himself intended his work to influence the behaviour of his own contemporaries. After narrating the circumstances of the deaths of Bruce, Sir James Douglas, and Thomas Randolph, earl of Moray, seen by Barbour as the principal leaders of the Scottish nation, the poet brings his great work to an end with the declaration that

> Thir lordis deyt apon this wis
> He that hey lord off all thing is
> Up till his mekill blis thaim bring
> And graunt his grace that thar ofspring
> Leid weill [the land], and ententyve
> Be to folow in all thar lyve
> Thar nobill eldrys gret bounte.[84]

Barbour had already expressed similar hopes for Bruce's heirs:

> thai that cummyn ar
> Off his ofspring manteyme the land
> And hald the folk weill to warrand
> And manteyme rycht and leawte
> Als wele as in hys tyme did he.[85]

It is uncertain whether Barbour intended the term 'offspring' to refer generically to the Scottish royal family and nobility as a whole, or if he was directing his comments to the actual heirs of Bruce, Douglas and Randolph. In 1375–8 these men were Robert II, William, earl of Douglas, George Dunbar, earl of March, and John Dunbar, earl of Moray. Given the political tensions between these men in 1371–2, Barbour's evocation of an age of mutual co-operation and loyal service in the defence of the crown and kingdom, and his prayer that these qualities should be displayed in his own day, can be seen as a powerful political statement.

It seems certain that men did regard the role of their families in the wars of the early fourteenth century as a matter of political pride and prestige, worthy of consideration by the crown and the subject of special pleading before the royal courts. When, in November 1371, Thomas Grant was restored by arbitration to lands in Moray which had been held by his father John, Robert II's confirmatory charter narrated that the grant had been made because of the service done by John Grant to Thomas Randolph, earl of Moray, Thomas and John his sons and in the defence of the kingdom in the time of Robert I and David II, the king's grandfather and uncle.[86]

The early years of Robert II's rule were thus a qualified political success. The wily old campaigner had overcome initial opposition through a series of territorial and political deals with aristocratic rivals who were seeking to defend their territorial and regional power against a new king whom they regarded as politically hostile. The king's own policy for establishing his dynasty rested firmly on entrenching his sons as powerful regional magnates, often wielding extensive royal rights. From the start of Robert II's reign, then, partly as a result of policy and partly as a result of political circumstance, there developed a remarkably decentralised and regionalised form of kingship, largely held together by kinship ties and marriage alliances. The king's council which emerged from the political discords of 1371 was certainly not dominated by royal favourites but was composed of representatives of major regional magnates and their affinities. The king's justiciars north and south of the Forth were, in fact, men who had been opposed to his succession in 1371, their creation as royal officers probably intended to limit rather than augment the crown's ability to intervene in their localities. While Robert II's non-interventionist approach undoubtedly reduced political tensions, it also meant that the king's personal control over what had previously been regarded as key areas of the kingdom was rather uncertain. In particular, the king's influence in the south-east of Scotland was curtailed by the regional importance of the earl of Douglas and, as the 1370s progressed, the king's son and heir, Carrick.

In the north-east, the earldoms of Angus, Mar and Moray were dominated by men whose political acceptance of Robert II's kingship had only been secured in the territorial deals and marriage alliances of 1371–2.

Despite these qualifications the years after 1371 saw some real political achievements. The future of the new dynasty became more assured in physical terms with the Stewart takeover of Edinburgh and Stirling castles, and in legal terms with the entailing of the crown in 1371 and 1373. These developments were coupled with the general territorial advance of Robert II's sons in the localities and what appears to have been a considerable propaganda campaign on behalf of the new dynasty. The disputed entail of 1373 also, however, gave the first indication of political tensions within the new royal family. These tensions were to become more pronounced as the divergent territorial and political ambitions of the king's sons, to some extent derived from the nature of Steward expansion before 1371, became apparent during the 1370s. It was ironic that the first manifestation of the coming storm would occur north of the Forth, in the heartland of the territorial empire which Robert the Steward had created for his family before 1371.

NOTES

1. *Rot.Scot.*, i, 943.
2. *APS*, i, 465–6; *Chron.Fordun*, i, 351.
3. *Chron.Fordun*, i, 382; *Chron.Wyntoun* (Laing), ii, 507.
4. *Chron.Bower* (Goodall), ii, 382; *Chron. Wyntoun* (Laing), iii, 8. Our knowledge of the Douglas rebellion rests entirely on these two chronicle accounts, and both are clearly derived from a common source.
5. *Chron.Wyntoun*, vi, 264–5: Douglas 'schup hym for to mak hym bare'. Cf. Wyntoun's description of the ceremonial stripping of the kingship from John Balliol in·1296, when Edward I 'made hym off the kynryk bare': *Chron.Wyntoun* (Laing), ii, 337.
6. *Chron.Bower* (Goodall), ii, 382; *Chron.Pluscarden*, i, 310.
7. R. Nicholson, 'David II, the historians and the chroniclers', *SHR*, xlv (1966), 75–77.
8. The point is supported by the fact that the Steward and his adherents have no recorded part in confronting Douglas at Linlithgow, which they would surely have done had they been present at a council in the town when the earl unveiled his alternative claim to the throne. The only reference to the Steward's whereabouts between David II's death and his coronation as Robert II at Scone on 27 March 1371 apparently places Robert at Ardneil on the Ayrshire coast on 18 March 1371 in

the company of his eldest son, John, earl of Carrick: SRO Ailsa Muniments GD 25/1/10. Ardneil is on the Farland Head, facing the Isle of Little Cumbrae, and the nearby castle of Portencross, with its well-developed harbour, seems to have been used by the Steward as the chief transit point between his mainland Ayrshire and Renfrewshire estates and his island possessions of Bute, Arran, the Cumbraes and Cowal. If the Steward and his eldest son had attended a council in Linlithgow which had upheld Robert's claim to the throne, their appearance in Ardneil as late as 18 March, suggesting that the Steward had only just arrived on the mainland, seems rather strange.

9. Most of these speculative links have subsequently been disproved. A very conjectural argument can be made that Douglas was putting himself forward on the basis of his position as heir presumptive to his brother-in-law, Thomas, earl of Mar. Thomas, earl of Mar, had a brother called Thomas Balliol who in 1368 resigned various lands in the barony of Cavers, which had been given to him by his brother Mar, in favour of the earl of Douglas, the lord of Cavers: *Melrose Liber*, ii, 435–37; *RRS*, vi, 354; *Rot.Scot.*, i, 880. It is unlikely that Thomas Balliol was Mar's brother-in-law, for there is no record of Mar having any sister apart from Margaret, the wife of Douglas. If Balliol had been married to an unknown sister of Mar he would also have been Douglas's brother-in-law, but this relationship is not mentioned in the above charter. It seems, then, that Balliol was a uterine brother of Mar from an unrecorded marriage of Mar's mother into a Balliol family, perhaps, given Thomas' landholdings in 1368, descended from Alexander Balliol of Cavers, the brother of king John Balliol: cf. P. F. Tytler, *History of Scotland* (Edinburgh, 1841), ii, 333–4. If, as the 1368 agreement seems to indicate, Thomas Balliol had no heirs, then the Douglas claim would rest on his position as heir presumptive to Mar, who was himself heir presumptive to Thomas Balliol. If that was the case, then the rebellion of 1371 would have been in support of Mar's rights. It is interesting to note the prominence given to Mar in the 1371 settlement, Thomas being the first earl to seal the acknowledgement of Carrick's position as heir apparent, and his position on Robert II's council for the next few months: SRO GD 25/10; *RMS*, i, no. 558; SRO Eglinton Muniments GD 3/1/275; SRO RH1/1/2/1.

10. *Chron.Fordun*, i, 373; *Rot.Scot.*, i, 787–8; *CDS*, iii, nos. 1591–2, 1596, 1603. As late as 1366 the claims of Edward III's family to Balliol's Scottish lands were still a matter of discussion in Anglo-Scottish diplomacy: *APS*, i, 497.

11. *SHS Misc.*, ix, 49. Henry's Scottish descent was also noted in the earl of March's appeal to Henry, then king Henry IV, in February 1400.

12. SRO State Papers, Treaties with France, SP7/2; *ER*, iii, xcvii–civ.

13. A. Goodman, *John of Gaunt* (Harlow, 1992), 47–8.

14. *Chron.Wyntoun*, vi, 264.
15. *CDS*, iv, no. 173. The sum was repaid on 7 November.
16. *ER*, ii, 221, 260, 289, 307, 344, 357, 364, 393. There are no Edinburgh custumars accounts for the year 1370–1.
17. E.g. SRO Inventory of Fraser Charters GD 86/7; SRO GD 150/15; Fraser, *Melville*, iii, 12–13; *ER*, ii, 344, 357.
18. Erskine and Dunbar support for Douglas's stance would have made the Steward's position very tricky indeed. With the castles of Stirling, Edinburgh and Dunbar held against him, and the lord of Fife unwilling to crown him, the Steward would have faced a long struggle to vindicate his rights with the persistent threat of an English intervention in the background. By the sixteenth century some chroniclers suggested that Douglas believed that March and Erskine 'fauoritt his accioun': Bellenden, *Chronicles*, ii, 336.
19. SRO SP7/2; *ER*, iii, cii. The treaty specified that if the king of Scotland died without an heir (although Robert II was hardly likely to die heirless) and a dispute arose over the succession, then France was not to intervene in support of any individual until the dispute had been discussed by the prelates and magnates of the Scottish kingdom according to the rules and statutes of the kingdom. The French were then bound to recognise the contender approved of by the largest and wisest group of Scottish nobles and clerics and to offer him support if his rivals engaged in warfare against him with the assistance of the king of England. While the clause reflected the general sensitivity of the Scots towards the issue of foreign, especially English, involvement in succession disputes, it was also, clearly, a response to the particular fears and anxieties of Robert II in 1371. The French commitment to support the choice of the bulk of the Scottish magnates as king according to the rules and statutes of the kingdom in the event of any dispute after Robert II's death strengthened the hand of John, earl of Carrick, whose right to succeed to the crown after Robert II had already been specifically acknowledged by the three estates in March 1371.
20. *Chron.Wyntoun* (Laing), iii, 8.
21. *ER*, ii, 363, 393; J. Raine, *History and Antiquities of North Durham* (London, 1852), Appendix, 34, 62; *ER*, ii, 394; Douglas's adherent, Alan Lauder, became clerk of justiciary before 14 January 1374: NRAS Lauderdale Muniments, Bundle 44/36.
22. *ER*, ii, 433.
23. For David II grants in favour of Alexander Lindsay: *RRS*, vi, 330; *RMS*, i, nos. 173, 226, 315, 337.
24. *Rot.Scot.*, i, 979; *CPP*, 345–6; A. MacQuarrie, *Scotland and the Crusades* (Edinburgh, 1985), 80–2; In October 1363, shortly before Walter left on his expedition to the Mediterranean, he received a royal pension of forty pounds for his lifetime: *RMS*, i, no. 171.

25. Col. K. H. Leslie of Balquhain, *Historical Records of the Family of Leslie* (Edinburgh, 1869), 65–6; Bishop John Leslie, *Rebus Gestis Scotorum* (Rome, 1578), 201; R. J. Lyall, 'The lost literature of Medieval Scotland', in *Bryght Lanternis: Essays on the Language and Literature of Medieval and Renaissance Scotland*, edd. J. D. McClure and M. R. G. Spiller (Aberdeen, 1989), 41.

26. *RMS*, i, no. 258, where Euphemia is not described as her father's heir; SRO J and F Anderson Collection, Balnagowan Titles GD 297/193; *A.B.Ill*, ii, 387. The papal dispensation for the marriage was not issued until 24 November 1366: *CPL*, iv, 59.

27. For the king's intimidation of Ross and his brother and Leslie's political influence with the king, see SRO GD 297/193; cf. *RMS*, i, nos. 300–1; SRO GD 297/161, 198.

28. *RMS*, i, no. 354.

29. SRO GD 297/163. In April 1350 William had named his brother Hugh as his heir, subject to royal approval. This must have been granted for in September 1351 Hugh appears as the brother and heir of the earl of Ross: *Rot.Scot.*, i, 744. Ross made a number of grants of lands within the earldom in favour of Hugh, perhaps in anticipation of the latter's succession to the earldom: SRO GD 297/173, 176. William, earl of Ross, appears to have had a son, also William, *after* the entailing in 1350/1, for in October 1354 the English noted that of the potential Scottish hostages to secure the release of David II the son and heir of the earl of Ross was not of age to travel: *Rot.Scot.*, i, 768. After the premature death of the earl's son William, it seems likely that the earl reverted to his original plan that the earldom should descend to his brother and his heirs. William Ross, the earl's nephew, appears as the deceased Hugh's son and heir on 14 February 1370: SRO GD 297/178, 179. The Rosses of Balnagowan remained an important and powerful family within the earldom.

30. SRO GD 297/193; *A.B.Ill*, ii, 387. The fact that Ross's complaint was preserved in this collection of titles relating to the inheritance of his nephew William Ross of Balnagowan is highly significant.

31. *RMS*, i, nos. 311, 354, 338–9.

32. NRAS 885, Earl of Strathmore Muniments, Glamis Charters, Box 2: Sir James Lindsay, lord of Crawford, and Sir Alexander Lindsay of Glen Esk acting as procurators for Walter Leslie; *RMS*, i, No. 247: A charter by Margaret the widow of Sir Norman Leslie, witnessed by Margaret, countess of Angus, and Sir Walter and Sir Alexander Lindsay; Col. K. H. Leslie of Balquhain, *Historical Records of the Family of Leslie* (Edinburgh, 1869), Vol. 1, 25; *A.B.Ill*, ii, 389; *Ibid.*, iv, 83, Alexander and William Lindsay, 'our brothers', witnessing a Walter Leslie charter of August 1381.

33. *Chron.Bower* (Goodall), ii, 367–70; *RRS*, vi, 431, 444, 446, 450, 452, 456, 461–2, 475, 483, 485, 496–7, 500. Alexander was also involved in

at least some of Sir Walter's foreign adventures: *Rot.Scot.*, i, 919.

34. Marjory was the daughter of Robert II's half-brother, John Stewart of Railston. John Stewart had been a regular witness to Robert's charters before 1371, and on Robert's coronation he became Steward of the king's household: *ER*, ii, 365, 395, 436, 461, 501, 551.

35. SRO Register House Transcripts RH2/6/4, 103.

36. *ER*, ii, 458; In 1373 Sir James Lindsay was given a pension of £100 to be taken from the wards, reliefs and marriages falling to the crown from north of the Forth: *ER*, ii, 407. In the same year Lindsay's fee as sheriff of Lanark was augmented 'de gracia regis': *Ibid.*, 418. From 18 February 1374 Lindsay also served as an auditor of accounts: *Ibid.*, 428. Some of these grants may have been intended to compensate James Lindsay for the crown's failure to warrant a grant of the lordship of Wigtown to James, made on 20 April 1372, following on the resignation of Thomas Fleming, grandson and heir of Sir Malcolm Fleming, former earl of Wigtown: *RMS*, i, no. 527. In fact Fleming had already sold all his rights in the earldom of Wigtown to Archibald Douglas, lord of Galloway east of the Cree on 8 February 1372: *RMS*, i, no. 507. The conflicting claims to Galloway west of the Cree were decided before a general council on 7 October 1372 which ended with Robert II confirming Archibald's charter. James Lindsay never used the title lord of Wigtown, while Archibald increasingly used the title lord of Galloway to embrace the entire lordship, both west and east of the Cree.

37. Eg. *RMS*, i, no. 558, 30 March 1371: Alexander Lindsay as a royal charter witness. Alexander would continue as a regular witness until his death in 1382. Alexander was swiftly joined on Robert II's council by his nephew Sir James Lindsay of Crawford.

38. In 1373 the New Forest in Galloway was resigned by Walter Leslie in favour of his nephew Sir James Lindsay, and in 1375 Leslie resigned the lands of Aberchirder in favour of his brother Sir William Lindsay: *RMS*, i, nos. 446, 621.

39. *ER*, ii, 435, 458, 620.

40. *RRS*, vi, 257, 485.

41. *APS*, i, 545–7.

42. Archibald and James Douglas were two of the royal ambassadors to France: *APS*, i, 559–60. Both received charters in the March parliament: *RMS*, i, no. 401; *Mort. Reg.*, ii, 94–5. The charter to Archibald Douglas narrated that, because of Archibald's service to David II and the work he was about to do in France, he was to have all rights and claims pertaining to the crown if his wife, Joanna Moray, died without heirs. The grant confirmed Archibald's hold on the estates of his wife, including the extensive lordships of her former husband Sir Thomas Moray of Bothwell. Archibald Douglas was already styling himself

lord of Bothwell in 1369. Some elements of the Bothwell inheritance had been disputed between Douglas and the king's son Robert in 1369, and the March grant was clearly intended to win Archibald over by securing him in the patronage granted to him by David II: *Laing Charters*, no. 379; *CPL*, iv, 76. The grant in favour of Douglas of Dalkeith seems to have enabled him to recover estates whose possession had been contested during the 1360s: *Mort.Reg.*, ii, 111–13. In January 1372 James Douglas of Dalkeith was confirmed in the lands in Strathearn which the Steward had been forced to resign to him in 1369, by Robert II's son David, the new earl of Strathearn: SRO GD 150/26.

43. *Chron. Bower* (Watt), viii, 220–1, for the earl of Fife's role in the coronation of James I.

44. Wyntoun freely admits that his description of the reign of Robert II is derived from an anonymous chronicle. Bower's treatment of the reign is so similar in terms of material and detail that the abbot of Inchcolm must have been using the same or a very similar source. The anonymous chronicle seems to be the product of someone resident in, or with local knowledge of, East Lothian. MacDiarmid speculates that the author may be the 'Heriot' mentioned in Dunbar's 'Lament for the Makars'. The chronicler's concern with giving the earl of March and his brother a heroic and decisive role in the events of 1371 may reflect this local bias: *Barbour's Bruce* (STS, 1985), i, 4.

45. NLS Charter no. 698; W. Fraser, *The Red Book of Menteith* (Edinburgh, 1880), ii, 251–4. The indenture also raised the possibility that Robert could recover possession of other lands, besides the earldom itself, which David II had forced Isabella to resign.

46. *RRS*, v, 354–60. For A. A. M. Duncan's detailed discussion of the background to this agreement see *RRS*, v, 356–60.

47. *RRS*, v, 633–5. Despite the entailing Patrick, earl of March, the husband of Isabella's sister Agnes, had taken the title earl of Moray after the death of his brother-in-law John Randolph at Neville's Cross and had continued to extract rents from the earldom until his death in 1368: *APS*, i, 528–29. David II had recovered control of the earldom after Patrick's death in 1368, presumably under the terms of the 1312 entail.

48. *RMS*, i, no. 405.

49. *Mort. Reg.*, ii, 101–2; *RMS*, i, nos. 521, 553; SRO GD 1/202/1; *RMS*, i, no. 473. George Dunbar received a resignation from one of his new tenants in Annandale at Duddingston in Lothian on 15 April 1372, shortly after the parliamentary settlement: *The Miscellany of the Scottish History Society* (SHS, 1893–), v, no. 17; *HMC Report* xv, viii, no. 74.

50. Edinburgh University Library, John Maitland Thomson Collection, no. 71: 10 March 1372 in St Andrews, Robert Stewart still styled earl

of Menteith; Fraser, *Cromartie*, ii, no. 524, 8 April 1372: Robert now earl of Fife and Menteith; *APS*, xii, 17–8.

51. Bellenden, *Chronicles*, 337.
52. *ER*, ii, 363; *Mort.Reg.*, 473–5. The settlement of this dispute over important lands and offices in the then royal earldom of Moray was also witnessed by George, earl of March. This may indicate that the Dunbars were recognised as having interests in the earldom well before the settlement of March 1372.
53. *RMS*, i, no. 554.
54. SRO Mar and Kellie GD 124/7/1. The bond was concluded at Perth in the presence of king Robert and John, earl of Carrick, who both sealed the document. The provision concerning Erskine's brother may well have been designed to stop the earl of Fife pursuing the Erskines for the barony of Kinnoul which had been resigned in their favour by Isabella, countess of Fife, in 1360: *RRS*, vi, 269.
55. *ER* ii, 364, 393, 462, 434, 460, 501. Douglas received a £100 pension from the royal exchequer because half the barony was in English hands.
56. SRO GD 124/1/416; *ER*, ii, 415, 433, 460, 472, 494, 515, 517, 543, 555, 577.
57. *RMS*, i, no. 652.
58. R. Nicholson, *Later Middle Ages*, 186–7, 203.
59. *Chron.Bower* (Goodall), ii, 383.
60. M. H. Brown, ' 'That Old Serpent and Ancient of Evil Days': Walter, Earl of Atholl and the Death of James I', *SHR*, lxxi (1992), 23–45. The observations on Robert II's sons were not paralleled in Wyntoun's chronicle, which used the same source as Bower for the events of 1371–90. The negative view of the king's family was thus probably Bower's own interpolation.
61. John may have been given the Stewartry as early as 18 March 1371: SRO GD 25/1/10; *APS*, i, 545; *RMS*, i, no. 558.
62. *ER*, ii, 92, 364, 393, 435, 458.
63. See Table 1: Robert II's Itinerary.
64. *APS*, i, 545; *RMS*, i, no. 558.
65. Leon was one of David II's favourites included on Edward III's safe conduct of 17 March 1371. Leon either remained in Scotland or had returned by July 1372, when it was arranged that Janet, Robert's daughter, should marry Bartholomew's son David: SRO Register House Charters RH6/157. The marriage arrangements ensured that Bartholomew and his spouse Philippa would bear the cost of maintaining the couple. It was further agreed that the earl would assist Bartholomew in the recovery of all the old Mowbray lands to which his wife had a right, an obligation which Robert reiterated in November 1375, although apparently with no tangible result: SRO RH6/163.

66. *RMS*, i, no. 554.
67. *APS*, i, 549.
68. *Mort. Reg.*, ii, 136–7.
69. *Hectoris Boetii Murthlacensium et Aberdonensium Episcoporum Vitae* (New Spalding Club, 1894), 25. For Tyninghame's role as a crown diplomat, *APS*, i, 559; *ER*, ii, 435.
70. Chapter 1; A. Grant, *Independence*, 177–8.
71. *RMS*, i, nos. 462, 488. Carrick, of course, had been David II's own personal territorial investment in the Stewart/Drummond line, and it was logical that this should be the property to descend to the heirs of David's niece, Annabella.
72. A. Grant, *Independence*, 177–8. Malcolm Drummond was a man who provided an important personal and political link between the Carrick and Douglas affinities: *Melrose Liber*, ii, 465–6.
73. *CPP*, i, 350, 480, 538; *Rot.Scot.*, i, 901, 932.
74. *ER*, ii, 433; W. Robertson, ed., *An Index, drawn up about the year 1629, of many Records of Charters* (Edinburgh, 1798), 111, no. 63. Sir Robert Erskine certainly brought his request for compensation for the grant of Ednam to Douglas before the parliament on 3 April, the day before the entailing of the crown received parliamentary approval: SRO GD 124/1/416. The dispensation for the marriage of James Douglas and Isabel Stewart had been granted in September 1371 but it is unclear whether the ceremony took place before early 1373. The grant of a port at North Berwick to earl William had clearly been made shortly before April 1373.
75. *APS*, i, 424, 464–5, 465–6, 545–7.
76. *Ibid.*, i, 549.
77. *Barbour's Bruce* (STS, 1985), ii, 3.
78. *Chron. Wyntoun* (Laing) ii, 152, 200, 314; *Chron. Wyntoun*, v, 256.
79. A. Gransden, *Historical Writing in England c. 550 to c. 1307* (London, 1974), 204–6. The Stewarts were certainly in close social and political contact with a number of important families around the Firth of Clyde who boasted a real or mythical Brittonic descent. See W. D. H. Sellar, 'The Earliest Campbells — Norman, Briton or Gael?' in *Scottish Studies*, xvii (1973), 109–122, where a Brittonic descent is suggested for the Clan Campbell and a number of other families, Galbraiths, MacNaughtons and Drummonds, whose ancestors seem to have shared an origin in the old British kingdom of Strathclyde north of the firth of Clyde which became part of the medieval earldom of Lennox. The most recent editor of Barbour's *Bruce* suggests that the genealogy simply gave the Stewarts a generic claim to an illustrious Brittonic descent through their Breton origins and brief stay in Wales before their arrival in Scotland: *Barbour's Bruce* (STS, 1985), i, 17–22. R. J. Lyall, however, sees no particular reason why the genealogy

might not, in fact, have traced a direct line from Dardanus to Robert
II: Lyall 'Lost Literature', 39.

80. See R. A. Mason, 'Scotching the Brut: Politics, History and National
Myth in 16th Century Britain', in R. A. Mason (ed.), *Scotland and
England 1286–1815* (Edinburgh, 1987), 60–84.
81. *Proceedings of the Society of Antiquaries of Scotland*, xxv (1890–1), 9.
82. *Barbour's Bruce* (STS, 1985), i, 7–10.
83. *Ibid.*, i, 7.
84. *Ibid.*, iii, 263.
85. *Ibid.*, iii, 76–7.
86. *Moray Reg.*, 473–5.

3

Unleashing the Hounds:
The Stewart Settlement in the North

T he period after Robert II's accession saw what appeared to be a rapid expansion of the political and territorial influence of the new royal family north of the Forth. In fact, the acquisition of the earldoms of Atholl, Strathearn, and Menteith and the lordships of Methven and Badenoch before 1371 had already transformed the Stewarts from a family whose territorial and political ambitions had been confined largely to the Firth of Clyde into the most powerful magnate grouping in Perthshire and the central Highlands. Robert II's acquisition of the crown gave his sons the opportunity to consolidate and enhance an already formidable territorial position. While Robert II's eldest son and heir John, earl of Carrick, inherited the family's secure south-western patrimony and was established as the sole representative of the royal line south of the Forth, the king's younger sons operated in a rather more competitive political environment north of the 'Scottish sea'.

Since the death of his son Walter in 1362 the main beneficiary and spearhead of Robert II's expansionist policies and political interests in Fife, Menteith and the south-western Highlands had been his second surviving son Robert, by 1372 established as earl of Fife and Menteith. Apart from his successful campaign to acquire Fife in 1371–2, the younger Robert's territorial and political ambitions were largely focused on consolidating his hold on the area around his earldom of Menteith. Inside the earldom, Robert began the construction of a hugely impressive new castle at Doune. Robert also made a number of significant territorial gains in the areas of Perthshire bordering Menteith during the 1370s, notably the barony of Glen Dochart, lying on Menteith's northern flank, in 1375–6, and the profitable lordship of Strath Gartney, adjoining Menteith's western border, probably shortly after 1371, and certainly before 1385.[1] The lands of Strath Gartney had a troubled history which would eventually involve Fife in a prolonged dispute with a rival claimant, Sir John Logie, the son of David II's queen, Margaret Drummond.[2]

Fife's dominant position within and around Menteith was augmented by Robert II's permanent alienation of the constableship of Stirling castle to his son in 1373. The grant tied the royal castle, and possibly also the sheriffship of Stirling, into the burgeoning regional power of Robert and his family as earls of Menteith, and complemented Fife's new fortress at nearby Doune.[3] The 1373 grant in favour of Fife typified a process seen throughout Robert II's reign, whereby royal financial, jurisdictional and territorial resources in the localities tended to be absorbed within the regional lordships exercised by the king's sons, allies and, in the case of the justiciarships, his one-time political enemies.

Fife's position in Menteith was also important in the overall governance of the kingdom, for it allowed the earl to dominate the politics of, and to project his interests westwards into, the great lordships of Lennox and Argyll. Thus by the mid-1370s Fife had been established in a formidable position as a powerful territorial magnate with wide-ranging interests across central Scotland, running from Fife in the east to the borders of the Lennox, who nevertheless remained an important figure at his father's court and in the royal administration. The political and territorial conflicts which would develop between Fife and his elder and younger brothers, Carrick and Alexander, lord of Badenoch, were as yet a distant murmur. As he surveyed his kingdom in 1380, Robert II must have regarded the power wielded by his second son as another indication and guarantee of the triumph of the royal Stewarts.

The most fascinating and maligned figure in the Stewart settlement of the north was Fife's younger brother, the king's third son, Alexander Stewart, whose activities would eventually earn him the nickname, from lowland chroniclers at least, of the 'Wolf of Badenoch'.[4] Alexander's territorial interests, as his by-name suggests, were initially based around the lordship of Badenoch. Alexander inherited control of the lordship from his father, who seems to have established a temporary claim to Badenoch through the terce rights of his second wife, Euphemia Ross, the widow of John Randolph, earl of Moray, who had died at Neville's Cross in 1346. Badenoch itself was one of the Highland lordships subsumed in the huge Moray regality created by Robert I for Randolph's father, Thomas, in 1312.[5] Badenoch was noted as being in the hands of Robert the Steward in 1368, and by August 1370 it was clear that the Steward's young son, Alexander, was actually exercising local lordship within Badenoch on his father's behalf. On 14 August 1370 Alexander issued letters of protection for the lands and men of Alexander, bishop of Moray, in Strathspey and Badenoch. The letters were issued from Ruthven, the chief stronghold of Badenoch, and were sealed by Alexander's father, Robert the Steward.[6] Even at this early stage there is some evidence that Alexander's style of lordship was arousing political resentment. In a parliament of June 1368 David II ordered that Robert the Steward and his two eldest sons should publicly pledge themselves to control the activities of the inhabitants of their lordships and to prevent 'malefactors' from moving through or being harboured within those lordships.[7] One of the key areas of complaint seems to have been Badenoch, for in late 1368 it was the Steward and his third son Alexander who were warded in the royal castle of Loch Leven, presumably for their failure to comply with the instructions of the June parliament. Alexander remained in Loch Leven for at least three months until the parliament of March 1369, during which the Steward and his sons were again ordered to take action against 'malefactors' within their earldoms and Highland lordships.[8]

Alexander's political and territorial position in the north was secured by the death of David II and the accession of Robert II to the throne. On 30 March 1371, in Robert's first parliament, Alexander received secure title to Badenoch with a formal grant of the lordship which included custody of Lochindorb castle.[9] Lochindorb was a vital addition to Alexander's lordship in Badenoch, and its tranfer to the king's son represented a significant blow to the settlement of the north which David II had attempted to construct in the last few years of his reign. After the death of John Randolph, earl of Moray, in 1346, control of the earldom of Moray had been assumed by Randolph's brother-in-law, Patrick, earl of March. David II disputed March's title to Moray in 1367–8, and reclaimed control of the earldom and Lochindorb for the crown.[10] Once established in control of Moray, David II began to make grants of earldom lands to trusted royal servants such as Simon Reid, the constable of Edinburgh castle, who received the lands and forest of Lochindorb in November 1367, and Richard Comyn, who became Forester of Darnaway.[11] Richard Comyn was a political associate of David II's crusading favourite Sir Walter Leslie.[12] If David II had lived beyond 1371, then Leslie would have become Lord of Ross in February 1372, while the chief fortresses of the neighbouring 'royal' earldom of Moray would have been in the control of Reid and Leslie's ally Richard Comyn. On the Steward's accession in 1371 Reid apparently fled the kingdom, and his Moray lands, including Lochindorb, were assigned over to Alexander Stewart, while Richard Comyn lost his claim to Darnaway in November 1371.[13]

Besides the confirmation of his hold on Badenoch, Alexander may well have hoped, as Grant suggests, that his father would create him earl of Moray in 1371–2.[14] The huge 1312 Randolph regality, which had embraced Badenoch, Lochaber, Mamore, Glenelg, Glengarry and

Locharkaig, if it had ever functioned as an effective unit, had ceased to be a political or territorial reality long before 1371. From the start of his reign Robert II began the process of ratifying the break-up of the wider earldom into its component lordships, matching feudal title to the actual exercise of lordship across much of the central and western highlands. The comital title and the lands of the earldom on the Moray coastal plain and around Inverness, however, were still at the crown's disposal. Robert II retained direct control of this portion of Moray for a full year before it was granted away in March 1372, with the title earl of Moray, to John Dunbar. For the year before the grant to Dunbar, Alexander had uplifted the fermes and rents of the earldom, and it must have appeared to the young lord of Badenoch that his own local ambitions and interests were being sacrificed in order to acquire Fife for his elder brother Robert.[15]

Robert II also evidently intended that Alexander should share the patronage available to the royal house in the north of Scotland with his younger half-brother David, still a minor in 1371, but already created earl of Strathearn. Some versions of the grant of Badenoch to Alexander contained an entail specifying that if Alexander died without heirs, then the lordship was to revert to David.[16] When David received a grant of the strategically vital castle and barony of Urquhart on the western shore of Loch Ness, in June 1371, there was a similar entailing arrangement in Alexander's favour.[17]

Despite the political and territorial limits set on Alexander's aggrandisement in the north by the king's need to give patronage to his other sons, the years after 1371 saw a spectacular advance in Alexander's power and influence in the central Highlands. His meteoric rise to regional dominance in the north was to some extent founded on the near-complete collapse of alternative local lordship in the area in the period from 1370 to 1372. On 7 October 1372, Alexander Stewart received a commission of lieutenancy covering all of Scotland north of the bounds of the earldom of Moray to the Pentland Firth and all of the sheriffdom of Inverness outside the regality of Moray.[18] The lieutenancy reflected a very real crisis in the exercise of local lordship within the huge area covered by the grant, which embraced the earldoms of Ross, Sutherland and Caithness and the Gaelic lordships lying to the west of the earldoms.

William, earl of Sutherland, had died sometime between 27 February 1370 and 19 June 1371, leaving a son and heir, Robert, who may still have been a minor in 1371.[19] It seems likely that by October 1372 Alexander Stewart was already running Sutherland as ward to William's young heir, Robert, who would eventually marry Alexander's daughter Margaret.[20] Alexander was certainly in the chief Sutherland stronghold of Dunrobin in the year 1373/4.[21] North of Sutherland, the earldom of Caithness had long ceased to be an effective territorial unit, but the title of earl and possession of the vestigial estates attached to the earldom had been a matter of dispute between the various heirs of Malise, earl of Strathearn, Caithness and Orkney, since the 1340s.[22] Alexander Stewart's lieutenancy saw the effective end of the dispute over Caithness, with one of the principal claimants, Alexander de Ard, making a series of resignations to the crown in favour of the new lieutenant and his brother David, who was created earl palatine of Caithness before 28 December 1377.[23] Robert II seems to have concluded a deal with Alexander de Ard by which the latter resigned all his rights within mainland Scotland to the royal house, perhaps in return for the Scottish crown's support in his attempt to become earl of Orkney.[24]

Alexander, lord of Badenoch, may have felt aggrieved that his younger brother had received a second earldom, this time with palatinate powers which would clearly have long-term implications for Badenoch's lieutenancy in Caithness. David's promotion in both Strathearn and Caithness may well have been due to the influence of his mother, Queen Euphemia, the sister of William, earl of Ross.[25]

The general problem of political control in the northern earldoms of Sutherland and Caithness was made more acute by the death, in February 1372, of William, earl of Ross, the brother-in-law of Robert II, at his residence of Delny.[26] In Ross, the husband of the late earl's daughter and heiress, the redoubtable Sir Walter Leslie, was likely to resent the creation of a lieutenancy for Alexander Stewart which would undermine Leslie's authority within Ross. Walter Leslie may, however, have been out of the kingdom when his father-in-law died, having obtained an English safe conduct on 12 February 1372.[27] In any case, Robert II's grant to Alexander probably reflected the long-established political animosity between the king and Walter Leslie. The earl of Ross's death in February 1372 had cut short the campaign which the aged earl had been waging against the claims of his daughter and Walter Leslie to various parts of the Ross inheritance, but the establishment of a royal lieutenancy which included the earldom suggests that there was to be little help from the crown for Leslie's attempts to consolidate his hold over Ross. For a time after earl William's death in 1372, parts of the earldom were held by the crown, and Alexander Stewart gained yet more influence inside Ross when he was assigned the task of upholding the terce rights of earl William's widow, Mary of the Isles.[28] Walter Leslie and Alexander Stewart may have tried to patch up their political differences by planning a pilgrimage together in August 1374, although there is no indication that this ever took place. Nevertheless, from early

1375 Leslie appears as lord of Ross in English safe conducts and had established his rights in at least some elements of the Ross inheritance by 4 June 1375, although it seems probable that his political influence within the earldom was severely limited, his local position not helped by his repeated absences from Scotland during the 1370s.[29]

Thus by 1373 Alexander, lord of Badenoch, was established as a figure of great territorial and jurisdictional power in the central and northern Highlands. Complementing his own lordship of Badenoch was the vital barony and castle of Urquhart on the western shore of Loch Ness, which he was leasing from his young brother David, earl of Strathearn, and the wide-ranging powers of a royal lieutenancy over an immense area of northern Scotland.[30] Besides his advances in the central Highlands and far north, Alexander Stewart was also used to reconfirm Stewart control over northern Perthshire. By 1372, Alexander was the royal justiciar in the Appin of Dull, and in the following year he was noted as withholding the rents due to the crown from the Appin of Dull and Glen Lyon, and refusing to allow taxation to be levied in the area.[31] Alexander's control of the Appin of Dull and northern Perthshire swept away the influence of David II's representative in the area, John of Lorn.[32] For most of the 1370s, then, Alexander Stewart, the man warded by David II in 1368-9 for his failure to control his adherents in Badenoch, was operating as the chief political representative of the crown and enforcer of royal justice over an area of Scotland stretching from northern Perthshire to the Pentland Firth. Alexander's own territorial acquisitions were scattered over the same wide area, ranging from Caithness to Rannoch and Strath Tummel. Holding a lordship of this size and diversity together was a task requiring almost manic energy, and it is hardly surprising that Alexander was not often to be found at his father's royal court.

Despite the impressive build-up in his power and influence, Alexander may have felt some dissatisfaction with the lordships and offices granted to him after 1371. Confirmation in Badenoch, which he already held, and temporary control over a number of northern earldoms and lordships hardly matched the prestigious and lucrative titles which had been bestowed not only on Alexander's two elder brothers, but also his younger half-brother David, earl of Strathearn and Caithness. A major opportunity for territorial advance was, however, to present itself to Alexander in 1382.

In 1382 the political and territorial balance in the north of the kingdom was shattered by the deaths, in quick succession, of the half-brothers who headed the Lindsay/Leslie affinity. Sometime between December 1381 and March 1382, Alexander Lindsay of Glen Esk, royal councillor and justiciar north of the Forth, died at Candia on the Isle of Crete as he made his way to the Holy Land.[33] Lindsay's death on a far-off Mediterranean island reflected the social and political cohesion of the entire extended Lindsay/Leslie family and their adherents around the crusading ideal. Alexander's brother Norman Leslie had died beneath the walls of Alexandria in 1365, his full brother William Lindsay of the Byres had knighted the son of St Bridget of Sweden at the Holy Sepulchre, while another brother, Sir Walter Leslie, lord of Ross, was the most famous crusading Scot of the fourteenth century.[34] The political effect within Scotland of Lindsay's demise on Crete was made far worse by Walter's death, at Perth, on 30 February 1382.[35]

The first man to move into the political vacuum created by the removal of Alexander Lindsay and Walter Leslie was the king's son and lieutenant Alexander Stewart. Charters issued by Walter Leslie's widow, Euphemia Ross, on 9 and 14 March 1382 at Dingwall were witnessed by Alexander Bur, the bishop of Moray, who was involved in a long-standing dispute with the lord of Badenoch, Alexander, bishop of Ross, and local clerics and laymen who had been associated with the deceased lord of Ross, notably Sir Walter Stewart of Railston, Sir Robert Innes and Sir Richard Comyn.[36] By 30 April 1382, Alexander Stewart, lord of Badenoch, was in Dingwall, where he witnessed a grant made by Euphemia, countess of Ross, in her widowhood, to Hugh Munro. Walter Leslie's adherents, his brother-in-law Sir Walter Stewart of Railston, Sir Richard Comyn and Sir Robert Innes, did not witness this charter, their place being taken by men associated with the lord of Badenoch.[37] Alexander Stewart's appearance in Euphemia Ross's company in April 1382 was the prelude to his marriage to the widowed countess later that same year.

Growing concern over the future of the Ross inheritance and the behaviour of Alexander Stewart may have been one of the principal reasons for the calling of a general council which met in Edinburgh in June 1382.[38] Any opposition in the council to the marriage of the king's son to Euphemia Ross appears to have been swept aside. The marriage certainly had the full support of Robert II, who came to Inverness on 22 July 1382 to supervise personally the transfer of Euphemia's estates to the control of his son. On 22 July Euphemia, lady of Ross, resigned the barony of Kingedward into the king's hands. This comprised the northern half of the old earldom of Buchan which had been dismembered by Robert I in the wake of the death without male heirs of John Comyn, earl of Buchan, in 1308.[39] Within two days of the grant of Kingedward, Alexander had been advanced to the dignity of earl of Buchan, and it was under that designation that he received further royal confirmations of the lands resigned by Euphemia on 24–25 July.[40] The terms of descent stipulated in the royal charters are crucial in explaining the political reaction to Alexander Stewart's acquisition of Ross. The end result of Euphemia's resignations was that the lordships of Skye and Lewis, the thanages of Dingwall, Glendowachy and Deskford and all Euphemia's lands in Caithness, Sutherland, Atholl, Galloway and elsewhere were to be held jointly with Alexander and were to descend to any heirs produced between them; if the marriage remained childless the lands were to go to Euphemia's heirs. The earldom of Ross itself was only given to Alexander Stewart in liferent, with no mention of a descent to heirs produced between the newly married couple.[41] In 1382 Euphemia Ross was probably in her mid to late thirties, the dispensation for her father's marriage to Mary of the Isles having been granted on 25 May 1342, and it was unlikely, although not impossible, that she would produce an heir for her new husband.[42] If the marriage of Alexander and Euphemia had produced any children, Alexander Leslie, Euphemia's son by her marriage to Walter Leslie, would have inherited only the earldom of Ross, stripped of the western lordships of Lewis and Skye and the core eastern thanage and castle of Dingwall. Even if Alexander and Euphemia produced no heirs, the terms of the various grants ensured that the lord of Badenoch would enjoy lifetime possession of the earldom of Ross and its associated lands and lordships. Alexander Stewart had probably been born around 1343 and would have been in his late thirties in 1382. The young Alexander Leslie thus faced exclusion from all or part of his inheritance until the death of his new stepfather, an event which was certainly not likely in the foreseeable future.

For Robert II, Alexander Stewart's intrusion into the earldom must have seemed a sensible move, allowing the royal lieutenant, a man already active in Ross and the most powerful magnate in the region, to protect Ross and its associated lordships from the political and territorial pressures which had affected the earldom even at the height of the power of earl William.[43] From the viewpoint of Alexander Leslie's kinsmen and allies, however, the king's actions potentially threatened Alexander's claims to significant elements of the Ross inheritance and at the least meant that Leslie's ability to exercise full authority within Ross would be delayed for the lifetime of his powerful stepfather.

The mood of the Leslie/Lindsay affinity and their allies was not likely to be improved by the king's treatment of the office of justiciar north of the Forth in 1382. The office had been held by Alexander Lindsay, lord of Glen Esk, probably from 1371, and certainly from 1373 onwards.[44] Sir James Lindsay of Crawford, Alexander Lindsay's nephew, had acted as justiciar north of the Forth in conjunction with his uncle during 1373, and in 1382 he may have hoped that the justiciarship would be returned to himself or given to his cousin, Glen Esk's son and heir, Sir David Lindsay.[45] The office of justiciar north of the Forth seems, in fact, to have remained unfilled for some time after Sir Alexander's death, before eventually being granted, before February 1387, to Alexander Stewart, by that stage earl of Buchan, lord of Ross and Badenoch, royal lieutenant in the north, and unquestionably the most powerful figure in northern Scotland.[46]

SEEDS OF DISCORD

The huge territorial gains made by Alexander Stewart in the Ross inheritance in 1382, apparently with the support and approval of Robert II and at the expense of the Leslie heir, amounted to the first significant change in the overall political settlement of 1371. The promotion of Alexander Stewart to the lordship of Ross and the loss of the northern justiciarship provoked a furious response from the effective leader of the Lindsay/Leslie affinity, Sir James Lindsay, lord of Crawford. On 4 November 1382, Sir James assassinated the royal chamberlain and Robert II's son-in-law and favourite, Sir John Lyon, thane of Glamis.[47] Later accounts elaborated on the circumstances of John Lyon's death, but perhaps the most interesting version is that found in the sixteenth-century *Extracta*, a work compiled from a number of earlier chronicles, but with additional and apparently original material largely concerned with the affairs of Angus. The *Extracta* explains Lyon's assassination in terms of the chamberlain's ingratitude towards Lindsay, who was said to have secured Lyon a place in Robert II's royal administration and to have protected him against the king's anger after Lyon's seduction of Robert's daughter Johanna.[48] The gist of the story, that Lyon was a former political associate of Sir James Lindsay who had failed to use his influence in Lindsay's interest, may have a basis in fact. Lyon had been connected with the Leslie/Lindsay affinity late in the reign of David II, whom he served as clerk of the privy seal, and played a part in the royal assault on the territorial interests of William, earl of Ross, and other northern landowners in 1368–9, alongside Sir Walter Leslie.[49] From 1371 onwards, however, Lyon developed a lucrative career as Robert II's personal favourite and chamberlain, making spectacular territorial gains through royal favour and his ability, as chamberlain, to exploit the crown's feudal rights.[50]

The death of the king's favourite in 1382 thus seems to have resulted from Lindsay's frustration over the direction of royal policy and patronage in the north. Sir James Lindsay harboured a number of political grievances against the royal government. Alexander Stewart's

3) BROTHERS-IN-ARMS : THE LINDSAY-LESLIE AFFINITY

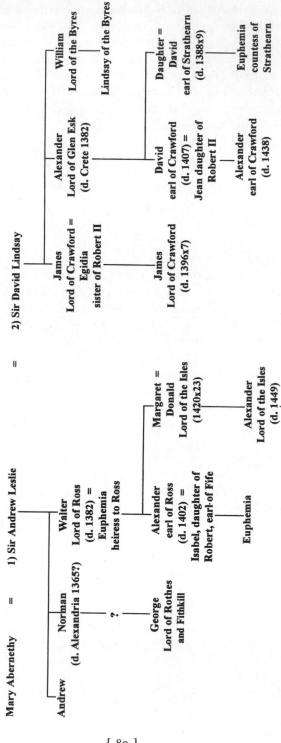

creation as earl of Buchan in July 1382 clearly invalidated Sir James's own shadowy claim to the lordship of Buchan. Sir James would eventually enter litigation with Alexander Stewart over the Buchan lordship, and he habitually styled himself lord of Crawford and Buchan until his death in 1395.[51] In addition, Alexander Stewart's gains in 1382 clearly affected the position of Sir James's two young cousins, Alexander Leslie and David Lindsay. Alexander Stewart's marriage to Euphemia Ross threatened Alexander Leslie with partial disinheritance, while the justiciarship north of the Forth, an office held by the Lindsays since 1371, was denied to both Sir James and his cousin David Lindsay in 1382. Sir James Lindsay clearly suspected Lyon, Robert II's confidant, of playing a critical role in the losses he and his family had sustained in 1382. Lyon, as chamberlain, did in fact supervise, and benefit from, the implementation of royal rights in the Ross inheritance after Walter Leslie's death.[52]

The assassination of Lyon seems to have been the first serious manifestation of the growing political rivalry between the affinity of the king's son and heir-apparent John, earl of Carrick, and Robert II's own favourites. Sir James Lindsay was certainly one of Carrick's closest political associates, and only five days before he killed the chamberlain he had witnessed a charter issued by Carrick during a general council at Scone on 30 October 1382.[53] The other witnesses to the charter included Carrick's brothers Fife and Strathearn, William, earl of Douglas, and Sir Walter Stewart of Railston. Most of these men had developed strong connections with the Lindsay/Leslie affinity and would have been perturbed by the direction of Robert II's policies in the north during 1382.[54]

After Lyon's death James Lindsay, unsurprisingly, disappeared as a witness to Robert II's charters, and in January 1383 he procured a year-long safe conduct for himself and a hundred others in order to visit the shrine of St Thomas Becket in Canterbury and other English pilgrimage centres, probably as part of a ritual atonement for his crime.[55] Despite incurring the king's wrath, Sir James Lindsay had a number of powerful patrons to protect him. Lindsay was sufficiently close to Carrick, the heir apparent, for the latter (after he had become king as Robert III in 1390) to make Sir James custodian of his first-born son David.[56]

Lindsay also had a close political relationship with William, 1st earl of Douglas, and his son and heir James.[57] Douglas and Lindsay interests north and south of the Forth had become increasingly entwined during the 1370s following on the succession of William, earl of Douglas, to the earldom of Mar in late July 1377 after the death of his brother-in-law Thomas, earl of Mar.[58]

After establishing himself in Mar, Douglas quickly persuaded Thomas's widow, Margaret Stewart, to assign over her terce rights in the earldom and to vacate the chief castle, Kildrummy, in return for a 200-merk annuity and the right to occupy Douglas's East Lothian fortress of Tantallon. Once in Tantallon, Margaret also became William's mistress and produced a bastard son George. Douglas may have hoped to arrange the succession of George to the estates of his maternal grandfather, Thomas Stewart, earl of Angus.[59]

Douglas's relationship with Margaret Stewart and his growing influence in Angus intensified the political and social links between the earl and the Lindsays of Glen Esk and Walter Leslie, lord of Ross. Alexander Lindsay of Glen Esk was a cousin and a former adherent of Thomas, earl of Angus, the father of Douglas's new mistress. Throughout the 1360s and 1370s Alexander Lindsay had been the beneficiary of a series of grants made by his aunt, Margaret Abernethy, countess of Angus, the grandmother of Douglas's mistress.[60] Douglas's liaison with Margaret Stewart, his control of the lands to which she was heiress, and the earl's probable long-term interest in securing the Angus inheritance for his bastard son inevitably resulted in a close political relationship between Douglas and Alexander Lindsay, as the two men set about dividing the Angus estates between themselves. The social links between the two affinities were also undoubtedly strengthened by the joint participation of Angus, Lothian and Berwickshire knights in crusading and chivalric enterprises during the 1370s.

By 1382 the combined political and territorial power of the Douglas/ Lindsay affinity was immense, holding the justiciarships north and south of the Forth, the earldoms of Douglas, Mar, and Ross and effective control of Angus. Robert II's policy in the north during 1382 thus managed to offend the most powerful aristocratic coalition in the kingdom, a situation made even more dangerous by the fact that all these men were politically aligned with the king's heir apparent, Carrick. By 1382 it was clear that Carrick's court was to some extent forming a shadow administration within the kingdom, preparing for John's accession to the throne, and exerting an ever-increasing influence on royal policy and government. Carrick was already politically dominant in the south of the kingdom, and by the early 1380s some men were seeking confirmations from the heir apparent of royal decrees and charters.[61] The traditional view of Carrick as an unambitious and 'indolent' man incapable of, and uninterested in, the exercise of royal office is entirely groundless. All the indications are that Carrick, already forty-five years of age in 1382, was a man expecting, eager and prepared for power.[62] Robert II's continued hold on royal patronage and the key functions of government seems to have been a source of increasing frustration for the king's ambitious and vigorous son, and his allies. The Carrick lieutenancy of 1384–8 would be firmly based on the Carrick-Douglas-Lindsay triumvirate, whose political and territorial interests in the north had been damaged by Robert II's policies in 1382.

Thus, although royal grants of lieutenancy and justiciary and the liferent of the Ross inheritance helped to make Alexander Stewart the most powerful figure in the north by the early 1380s, his promotion had serious political repercussions for Robert II. The fact that Alexander's exercise of lordship in the north became a matter of political complaint was no doubt partly inspired by the short-term politics of faction, but there may also have been long-term factors.

To some extent, Alexander's territorial power and personal lordship in areas such as Ross, Urquhart and Sutherland, although impressive, was inherently unstable because it was largely based on his ability to control these areas during the minorities of the rightful heirs. Sooner or later Alexander's right to exercise untrammelled lordship in these earldoms and baronies was bound to be challenged.

It may also be that the methods of lordship which gave Alexander the necessary local power to function as a royal lieutenant in the central and northern Highlands created local resentment. The parliaments, general councils and chronicles of late fourteenth and early fifteenth-century Scotland were awash with complaints about the activities of caterans, a name derived from the Gaelic *ceatharn*, denoting a troop of warriors.[63] From the lowland viewpoint the issue was seen largely in legal terms; caterans occupied and exploited lands to which they had no legal title and raided the estates of neighbouring landowners. The stress in contemporary record on the illegality of the activities of the cateran led to a view, much elaborated by later chroniclers and historians, which defined and translated the very name cateran in terms of his criminal activity; cateran meant 'broken man', 'Highland robber' or 'Highland marauder'.[64] This view of the cateran as an ungovernable Highland bandit operating outside any recognisable form of authority hardly fits with the available contemporary evidence. Lowland chronicle accounts tend to mention caterans in a specifically military context, in which they are invariably seen as being in the service of great Highland lords or kindreds.[65] The impression is that in many circumstances the term was used in a technical, military sense, and referred to native mercenary troops maintained by, and in the service of, the great magnates of the central Highlands. Certainly it seems significant that in medieval Ireland the same Gaelic expression developed into the Anglo-Irish term *kerne*, denoting 'professional native soldiers', employed in the service of both Gaelic and Anglo-Irish lords.[66]

A number of aristocratic agreements made late in the fourteenth century also tend to support the idea that at the heart of lowland parliamentary and chronicle complaints lay a class of professional or semi-professional Gaelic mercenaries. In 1389, for example, in an arbitration of a dispute between John Dunbar, the earl of Moray, and the bishop of Moray, the earl cleared himself on oath of having introduced caterans into his lordship to the detriment of the bishop. Since the caterans had failed to indemnify the earl as he had commanded, presumably for the losses sustained by the bishop's tenants, Moray was ordered to appoint officers to execute justice on the evil doers (*malefactoribus*), a term often used as a synonym for cateran.[67] The 1389 agreement implied that caterans were a distinct class of men who were considered to be in the service of a secular lord but who were not always responsive to his commands, and whose presence presented problems for their neighbours. An agreement of 1394 between John's successor as earl of Moray, Thomas Dunbar, and Alexander of the Isles of Lochaber reinforced these points. By the concord, Alexander of the Isles promised to protect the lands of the earldom and bishopric of Moray for the next seven years in return for an annual fee of 80 merks. It was stipulated that Alexander should not permit 'his men, nor other caterans he is able to, of whatever rank they shall be, to beg (*mendicare*) through the lands of Moray nor to consume (*comedere*) or ruin them'.[68] The key feature of the agreement was that caterans were characterised as men who moved from one area to another consuming the produce of the land. The process being described here, and complained about in very similar language in the general council of 1385, was clearly that of the maintenance of large-scale cateran forces through the systematic billeting of troops by a great lord on the lordships and populations subject to his authority. It was a system already well established in Ireland, where the quartering of a lord's troops on his tenants was given the name *buannacht*.[69]

By the late fourteenth century, the exercise of lordship over much of the central Highlands was largely dependent on the construction of a military following large enough to intimidate rival lords and to dominate smaller clans and cateran groups who had an alarming capacity for freelance political and military action. In one Highland chronicle, John of the Isles was noted as maintaining 'a strong party of standing forces, under the command of Hector More Macillechoan, for defending Lochaber and the frontiers of the country from robbery and incursions of the rest of the Scots'.[70]

It was in this highly militarised society that Alexander Stewart, lord of Badenoch, sought to exercise his power as royal lieutenant. From the crown's viewpoint the delegation of wide-ranging powers over justice, overriding or ignoring the rights of the titular lords of the territorial lordships in the north, was the only sensible response to a 'law and order' problem which did not respect the neat boundaries of feudal lordship and which required the concentration of military resources in the hands of a trusted royal agent. The effectiveness of Alexander's lieutenancy would rest on his ability to raise substantial cateran forces from within his own lordships to follow the royal banner into the west, especially as he had no major lowland earldom or lordship which could have provided him with a significant force of armoured knights or feudal levies.

The upkeep of professional cateran forces placed a heavy strain on resources, and entailed the imposition of a wide range of unpopular exactions, similar to the *buannacht* of the lordships of Ireland, on the tenants of the various territories under Alexander's control. Resistance on the part of the tenantry would be overcome by physical violence and intimidation. It seems likely that the lord of Badenoch's well-documented disagreements with the bishops of Moray and Aberdeen actually centred on the demands imposed on church lands by Alexander's adherents within Badenoch and his other central Highland lordships[71]. The twists and turns of the long running dispute between the lord of Badenoch and the bishop of Moray, in fact, bear an uncanny resemblance to a similar struggle in fourteenth-century Ireland between the archbishops of Armagh and the O'Neills. In both cases the beleaguered clerics tried to defend church lands and tenants against the impositions of the soldiery and adherents of an overbearing regional lord through the use of the ecclesiastical censure of excommunication, desperate appeals to the 'legitimate secular authority' for assistance, and/or the recruitment of a secular lord powerful enough to protect church lands from the exactions of his rival.[72] The position of the bishops of Moray and Aberdeen was made particularly galling by the fact that Alexander Stewart, as lord of Badenoch and the royal lieutenant, *was* the legitimate secular authority at the local level, a situation which forced both bishops into direct appeals to the court of Alexander's father, Robert II. An echo of these disputes is, perhaps, to be found in the charges levelled against Alexander in Boece's sixteenth-century history of the bishops of Aberdeen. The outraged chronicler claimed that Alexander was a man 'whose wickedness had earned him universal hatred'. In particular, Alexander was 'joined by certain vile creatures, and . . . drove off all the bishop's cattle, and carried away his property, killing at the same time in the most high-handed way the peasants. . . . He divided as he pleased the lands stolen from the church, and gave them to be cultivated by certain wicked men who had no regard for God or man'.[73] The aggrieved tone of the chronicle account mirrored the substance of the complaints made by the bishop of Aberdeen to the king and his council in 1382 against one Farquhar Mackintosh, probably one of Badenoch's adherents. The bishop lamented that he and the tenants of the church's lands of Birse had suffered great losses, and that because of the continuous threats of Farquhar and his adherents, the inhabitants of the land were not able, nor did they dare, to remain in their homes or cultivate the land.[74] The imposition or independent arrival of cateran troops on certain estates made them essentially worthless to the titled landowners, and this fact may well lie behind many of the 'voluntary' resignations of land made in Alexander's favour by the bishop of Moray and a number of secular landowners.[75]

To some extent, the lord of Badenoch was caught in a cleft stick. In order to impose his authority effectively in the north he had to compete with, and outstrip in terms of military power, the clans and lords of the central Highlands. The recruitment of a substantial mercenary force in the service of the royal lieutenant seemed an obvious solution to the problem; it was certainly a strategy adopted by those upholding the political interests of the English crown in Ireland.[76] However, the process of raising and sustaining cateran forces from within his own centre of power in Badenoch and Strathspey involved Alexander in damaging political clashes with prelates and magnates who held title to lands in these areas.

Robert II's political standing seems to have suffered as a result of his support for Alexander's activities in the north. Boece claimed that Alexander justified all his wickedness in terms of 'avenging his father's wrongs' and prosecuting royal rights, that Robert II failed to act on repeated complaints from the bishop of Aberdeen, and that Alexander was long protected by his royal connection because 'no one cared to punish his insolence lest in so doing he might seem to offend the king'.[77] The history probably reflects, although in a highly garbled form, contemporary complaints about Alexander's use of the office of royal lieutenant. Lowland Scots clearly had a general distaste for the type of lordship being exercised by the lord of Badenoch. Besides the repeated parliamentary complaints against caterans and malefactors, the well-known, and much-quoted, comparison of the habits and lifestyles of the English and Gaelic-speaking Scots by the fourteenth-century Angus/Aberdeenshire-based chronicler John of Fordun stressed the need for effective royal action in order to make the Highland Scot answer to justice. Despite their savagery, the Highland Scots were 'faithful and obedient to their king and country, and easily made to submit to law, *if* controlled'.[78] Fordun clearly saw any problems in the implementation of justice in the north largely in terms of the failure of royal government, and his comment seems implicitly to criticise the chief representative of royal power in the region, Alexander Stewart, whom

The Wolf's Lair: 1382 - 1388

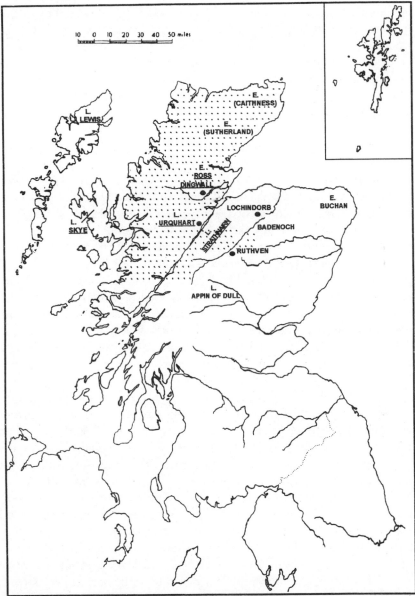

KEY: ꞌ ꞌ ꞌ ꞌ   **Approximate area of Wolf's Lieutenancy:** **LEWIS** - Earldoms and Lordships help in liferent or leased:
         (CAITHNESS) - Earldoms incorporated within the Lieutenancy:
      ●   **LOCHINDORB** - Major Fortresses held by the Wolf.

Fordun probably regarded as part of the problem, rather than the solution.

The growing tension between the lord of Badenoch and his near neighbours may, then, have been as much cultural as political. For much of the second half of the fourteenth century the earldoms of Ross, Mar and Moray were held by newcomers, men with few established connections with Gaelic society, whose kinship links and political interests were centred in Angus or south of the Forth. Walter Leslie, lord of Ross, John Dunbar, earl of Moray, and William, earl of Douglas and Mar, were often absent from their northern earldoms, and their careers give little indication of the development of effective local leadership or the establishment of good working relationships with the Gaelic kindreds within their own or neighbouring lordships. Unable successfully to exploit or contain the power of Gaelic kindreds, Leslie, Dunbar and Douglas undoubtedly added their voices to the general condemnation of the processes of lordship which underpinned the power of their chief rivals in the region. Alexander Stewart, in contrast, seems to have become almost wholly absorbed into the social and political world of Gaelic Scotland.[79] The lord of Badenoch's by-name of the 'Wolf of Badenoch' was a lowland appellation, presenting Alexander, like the cateran forces which sustained his lordship, as a type of elemental and dangerous natural phenomenon, deserving persecution and extermination. Within Gaelic Scotland Alexander had a different persona; when the lord of Badenoch came branking through the bounds of his lieutenancy, it was as *Alasdair Mòr Mac an Rìgh*, 'great Alexander, the king's son'.[80]

While Robert II clearly regarded and promoted Alexander, lord of Badenoch, as the chief agent of royal authority in the central Highlands and the far north, the king's two sons by his second wife Euphemia Ross were also destined to become great landholders north of the Forth. By the time of the first parliament of the king's reign the eldest son of this second marriage, David, was already using the title earl of Strathearn which had been resigned by his father. In June 1371 David's position received a further boost with a grant of the strategically vital barony and castle of Urquhart on the western shore of Loch Ness, entailed to David's heirs, whom failing the king's third son Alexander Stewart. David was still a minor in 1371 and Urquhart was leased to David's brother Alexander, the heir by entail in the barony, who seems to have occupied the castle and barony for the remainder of the 1370s.[81] On the same day David received a renewed grant of the earldom of Strathearn, this time with the extensive judicial rights of regality jurisdiction.[82]

The grant of the highly profitable earldom of Strathearn to David had probably been a feature of Robert II's plans for his vast conquest lands before his accession to the throne. For some time before 1371 David's mother, Euphemia Ross, had confirmed charters issued by the Steward dealing with lands in Strathearn.[83] David's creation as earl of Caithness before 28 December 1377 probably also reflected the political influence of his mother, queen Euphemia.[84] During the 1370s David, earl of Strathearn, became closely tied in social and political terms to Alexander Lindsay of Glen Esk. David married one of Alexander Lindsay's daughters in the late 1370s or early 1380s, while David's cousin and retainer, Sir Walter Stewart of Railston, was Alexander Lindsay's brother-in-law.[85] David's Lindsay links and his own dispute with the lord of Badenoch over the latter's occupation of the barony and castle of Urquhart placed the young earl of Strathearn amongst those expressing dissatisfaction with the conduct of the royal lieutenant. The youngest of Robert II's legitimate sons, Walter, was also given a considerable territorial stake north of the Forth, with his marriage to the heiress to the lordship of Brechin. Walter would eventually become earl of Atholl and Caithness and one of the most powerful and ruthless of the great Stewart magnates, but the full flowering of his territorial and political power would not occur until the reign of James I.[86]

Besides the king's sons, the most significant figure in the settlement of Scotland north of the Forth after 1371 was Robert II's son-in-law, John of the Isles.[87] John controlled a huge west-coast lordship, which had expanded greatly during the early fourteenth century. The Lord of the Isles had displayed a commendable opportunism in his dealings with Bruce and Balliol kings and the English crown throughout the 1330s, 1340s and 1350s. A deal with Edward Balliol in 1336 saw John obtain a grant of Islay, Kintyre, Knapdale, Mull, Skye, Lewis, Ardnamurchan and other lands, with the ward of Lochaber, in return for John's assistance against Edward's enemies and rebels.[88] By June 1343 John had been forced to abandon Balliol, and he and his brother-in-law, Ranald MacRuari, made their peace with David II for the 'common profit and tranquillity of the realm' at Ayr. David confirmed John in his possession of Islay, Lewis, and the other islands, as well as the lands of Morvern, Lochaber, and Duror and Glencoe on the southern shores of Loch Linnhe, but John's claims to Skye, held by William, earl of Ross, and Kintyre and Knapdale, held by the Steward and his kinsman Sir John Menteith, were not allowed. On the same day Ranald MacRuari also came into David II's peace and received confirmation of his claims to Uist, Barra, Eigg, Rhum, Moidart, Morar, Arisaig and Knoydart.[89] However, in 1346 the lord of the Isles' territorial position received a further boost, when he seized effective control of the inheritance of his brother-in-law Ranald MacRuari, after the latter's assassination by adherents of William, earl of Ross.[90] In 1368 lands noted as being under the control of John of the Isles included Lewis, Lochaber, Garmoran (from MacRuari), and lands in Kintyre and Argyll.[91]

David II seems to have regarded John's claims to all these territories as dubious, and the last few years of his reign were marked by a more or less continuous dispute between himself and the lord of the Isles, who refused to submit to the financial and territorial demands arising from David II's ransom payments and the royal revocation of 1367. Eventually, in November 1369, David forced John's submission at Inverness.[92] The king's expedition against John of the Isles was clearly part of the wider attack being made by David II against the great northern magnates who were regarded as fomenters of Highland disorder and abusers of royal authority, and who were generally politically aligned with the Steward and his sons. Significantly, the first-named of the three hostages delivered up by John to the king as guarantees for his future behaviour was Donald, his son by the Steward's daughter. The Steward also stood as a guarantor for John's general compliance with the terms of his submission and, in particular, as a surety that John would deliver the hostages as he had promised. The Steward was required to place his own seal alongside John's on the submission.

The accession of Robert II thus saw the crown pass to a man with extensive political and social links to the lordship of the Isles, and held out the prospect of a more amicable relationship between the crown and the lordship than had been the case for some time. In a parliament at Scone on 9 March 1372, Robert II formally confirmed, for the first time, John's title to the Garmoran lands which had belonged to Ranald MacRuari.[93] In January of the following year Robert II confirmed John's grant of the Garmoran lands to Ranald, the eldest son of the Lord of the Isles' first marriage to Amy MacRuari.[94] The settlement of his mother's estates on Ranald seems to have been the prelude to the transfer of the lordship lands proper, and the leadership of Clan Donald, to Donald, the first son of John's marriage to the king's daughter. A series of charters issued in June 1376 suggests that Donald's claim to be the next lord of the Isles was already established. By these charters, Robert II granted to John, and his daughter Margaret, the isle of Colonsay and the lands of Lochaber, which had been resigned by John, to be held by John and Margaret and the heirs produced between them. The deal gave John's son Donald secure title to Lochaber and the lands in Kintyre and Knapdale, which had been long disputed between John and the Stewarts, and linked the ruling dynasty within the Lordship of the Isles to the royal house. For Robert II the arrangement ensured, at the least, that the king's own grandsons would control the mainland territories into which the lordship had expanded during the early fourteenth century, particularly the areas of the lordship adjoining Stewart interests in the Firth of Clyde and the central Highlands. In the long term there was the distinct prospect that the next lord of the Isles, with the lordship's mainland acquisitions having been given royal sanction, would simply become part of the great Stewart family network that increasingly dominated the north.[95] According to later Highland chronicles, the transfer of the lordship to John's sons by his second wife, Margaret Stewart, generated significant political divisions within the lordship itself.[96] Whatever the internal repercussions of the creation of Donald as lord of the Isles, the new lordship line established in the 1370s clearly saw their royal descent as a feature which gave them political prestige both within the lordship and in their dealings with other magnates. Donald himself took the royal tressure to surround his own coat of arms.[97] The practice of allowing magnates who had married into the royal dynasty, and their descendants of royal blood, the use of the royal tressure in their arms seems to have originated in the reign of Robert I, probably in the hope of creating and rewarding a wider magnate group who would identify themselves, by marriage, with the preservation and promotion of the Bruce dynasty. Robert II had no lack of male kinsmen, but did have a similar need to establish a new dynasty, and he continued the practice of allowing his sons-in-law to bear the royal tressure.[98]

Overall, Robert II's dealings with his son-in-law John, lord of the Isles, illustrate a clear willingness to ratify the lordship's territorial advances and an eagerness to incorporate the new heir to the lordship, the king's own grandson, into the wider Stewart settlement of the north. Although political and cultural conflict between the crown and the lordship of the Isles became an established feature of the fifteenth-century Scottish kingdom, Robert II came to the throne with a personal background of political and social co-operation with the great lords of the west, and some sympathy with their culture and the methods of lordship they employed. It is hardly surprising, then, that the first Stewart king's political attitudes in dealing with the lordship stressed inclusion rather than exclusion. On the seal employed by Donald, lord of the Isles, Robert II's grandson, in the early fifteenth century the MacDonald galley sailed on a sea bounded by the royal tressure of the Stewart kings.

The final, and most ignored, figure in the establishment of royal control of the north was the king himself, for Robert II's itinerary as king reveals a marked change from that of David II, whose most frequent place of residence was Edinburgh.[99] Robert II, particularly in

Locations of Royal Acts: Robert II

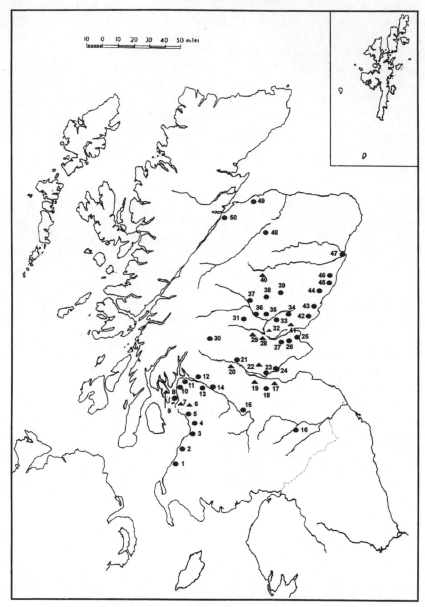

KEY: ● 1–10 Acts issued ▲ Over 10 Acts issued

KEY

STEWARTRY

(1)	Ardstinchar	1
(2)	Kirkoswald	1
(3)	Ayr	6
(4)	Dundonald	4
(5)	Irvine	3
(6)	Kilwinning	10
(7)	Ardneil	12
(8)	Cumbrae	2
(9)	Rothesay–Bute	10
(10)	Inverkip	2
(11)	Dunrod	1
(12)	Dumbarton	4
(13)	Renfrew	3
(14)	Glasgow	3
	TOTAL	62

BORDERS

(15)	Lanark	1
(16)	Selkirk/Edybredschelis	2
	TOTAL	3

LOTHIAN

(17)	Edinburgh	75
(18)	Calder	1
(19)	Linlithgow	14
	TOTAL	90

(20)	Stirling	22
(21)	Cambuskenneth	2
(22)	Dunfermline	11
(23)	Inverkeithing	3
(24)	Kinghorn	1
(25)	St. Andrews	6
(26)	Cupar	11
(27)	Lindores	1

PERTHSHIRE AND
CENTRAL HIGHLANDS

(28)	Perth	80
(29)	Methven	26
(30)	Glen Finglas	4
(31)	Loch Freuchie (Strath Braan)	1
(32)	Scone	22
(33)	Coupar-Angus	2
(34)	Glamis	1
(35)	Clunie	4
(36)	Dunkeld	2
(37)	Logierait	1
(38)	Glenshee	2
(39)	Glen Prosen	1
(40)	Kindrochit	10
	TOTAL	156

(41)	Dundee	11
(42)	Arbroath	2
(43)	Montrose	2
(44)	Kincardine	2
(45)	Inverbervie	1
(46)	Kinneff	1
(47)	Aberdeen	3
(48)	Badenoch	1
(49)	Darnaway	1
(50)	Inverness	5

the first ten years of his reign, issued most of his charters in and around Perthshire, either in Perth itself, Scone, or his own residence at Methven. The king's itinerary also displayed a continued heavy use of the old Stewartry lands in Renfrew, Bute and Ayrshire, with the king's numerous appearances at Ardneil reflecting the fact that nearby Portencross was Robert's preferred transit point for his island lordships in the Firth of Clyde.[100]

Some distinct and regular patterns may be discerned in Robert's annual circuit around his kingdom. In May, for example, the king was usually to be found in Bute, perhaps timing his arrival there to coincide with the feast days of the island's two most important saints, Brendan and Brioc. In August, Robert headed for the hunting grounds around Kindrochit (Braemar), while the king's frequent visits to the monastery of Kilwinning were typically confined to the late autumn.

Some more general points may be made about Robert II's itinerary. Firstly, it can be guessed that Robert's kingship made relatively light demands on his subjects in terms of physical provision for the royal household, since for much of the time the king and his entourage were actually resident in the king's own lordships or those of his sons. The issue of purveyance, the king's right to requisition transport and goods for the support of the royal household from the surrounding area, could arouse considerable political resentment.[101] It was not likely to be an issue in the reign of Robert II.

Secondly, the massive territorial resources which the Steward and his family brought to the crown in 1371 to some extent counteracted the long-term decline in the crown's landed base which had been a marked feature of fourteenth-century kingshp. Grant's analysis of the history of royal thanages establishes the significant effect the permanent alienation of crown estates had, not only on the finances of kingship, but also on the crown's political control in the north of the kingdom. Robert II's own territorial resources, the expanding income from the great customs, and the king's desire to consolidate the political position of his dynasty pushed Robert to deliver the final blow to the older system of crown lands by continuing the process of granting out royal thanages and other lands in heritage as patronage to major noblemen in the localities.[102]

Thirdly, Robert's itinerary and personal connections reveal a king whose political and social life was a remarkable contrast to that of his uncle and predecessor, David II. David's kingship had been overwhelmingly based in Lothian, his court heavily influenced by chivalric and crusading ideals, and his political and personal favourites largely drawn from the chivalry of Angus, Fife and Lothian. Robert II's chief passion, in contrast, was the hunt, with the king issuing a number of charters from obscure as well as well-known hunting seats in Highland Perthshire and other areas.[103] Robert's expeditions to Kindrochit (Braemar), Glen Finglas, Strath Braan, Glen Almond, Glen Shee, Glen Prosen, Badenoch and the hunting areas within his own ancestral estates such as Bute and the Cumbraes undoubtedly brought the king into regular contact with his sons and other great magnates, but it also confirmed the king's long-standing connections with Gaelic aristocratic society, a society in which the celebration of prowess in the hunt regularly found an expression in the praise poems composed by Gaelic bards for their noble patrons.[104] Robert's regular visits to Strath Braan undoubtedly lie behind the curious account of the king's 'arrest' by the Clann Donnchaidh, whose head was chief forester of Strath Braan, while Robert wandered through the country with only two gentlemen for company.[105]

The king's links with Perthshire were furthered by his long-standing liaison with Mariota de Cardeny, the daughter of the lord of Cardeny and Foss. Mariota may well have been the widow of Alexander MacNaughton, head of the MacNaughtons of Argyll, and the mother of Donald MacNaughton whose clerical career was supported by the king and who went on to become bishop of Dunkeld, the diocese in which the Stewart king exerted greatest influence.[106]

By 1382, Robert II and his family had achieved a remarkable domination of Scotland north of the Forth. The extent and speed of this Stewart advance after 1371 has, however, been exaggerated. Much of the settlement after Robert's coronation simply involved a confirmation in, or redistribution of, lands and lordships which Robert and his family had acquired before 1371. Moreover, the political circumstances of the king's accession, Robert II's own personal preference, and the long-term collapse of the royal territorial establishment in the north-east, produced a major re-orientation of the political and geographical centre of Scottish kingship. After 1371, the influence of the crown as a major regional magnate, perhaps unsurprisingly, remained in Perthshire and the Stewartry, the areas which Robert II had dominated before he became king. This fact may go some way to explain Jean Froissart's hostile characterisation of Robert II, undoubtedly derived from the south-east of Scotland, as a man with little interest in, or influence over, Anglo-Scottish warfare and diplomacy, who abandoned the affairs of state at critical junctures to reside in the Highlands ('la sauvage Escose'). When Robert II died in 1390, Andrew of Wyntoun, a chronicler generally sympathetic to the king, recorded that the monarch met his end at Dundonald in the Stewartry, 'in his cuntre', a rather strange description for a king of Scots.[107] The extension of Robert II's authority and influence outside this core area was largely achieved through the expansion of the territorial and jurisdictional powers of the king's sons, notably Carrick south of the Forth and Badenoch in the north, and the conclusion of a series of territorial deals and marriage settlements with powerful magnate groups in the localities. The king's political influence in the north-east and in Scotland south of the Forth remained restricted.

At first this loose family network, and a style of kingship which tended to deal with and through established magnatial power rather than stressing formal royal rights and authority, produced a measure of political stability. The king's generous patronage to both his sons and other noblemen was noted on his death:

> Till lordis rowmly he landis gave:
> His swnnys he maid rych and mychty.[108]

By 1382 Robert's sons controlled the earldoms of Strathearn, Atholl, Menteith, and Ross, and the lordships of Badenoch, Urquhart, Glen Dochart, Strath Gartney and the Appin of Dull. Alexander Stewart was lieutenant over most of northern Scotland. In Argyll, the chiefly line within Clan Campbell, the king's long-time political associates, were granted powers of lieutenancy within mid-Argyll.[109] Robert's sons-in-law included the earl of Moray, the heir to the earldom of Mar and the heir to the lordship of Glen Esk. Robert's grandson was to be the next lord of the Isles. Robert II's family network seemed to dominate all of Scotland from the Forth to the Pentland Firth, from the North Sea to the Atlantic.

By 1382, however, it was clear that this appearance of political unity was deceptive. John Lyon's assassination in November of that year illustrated growing tension between the king and his heir apparent, John, earl of Carrick. Carrick, ambitious and impatient for power, became the political focus for resentment against his brother and royal lieutenant in the north, Alexander Stewart, earl of Buchan, lord of Badenoch and Ross. Alexander's seizure of the Ross inheritance in 1382 and the king's apparent reluctance or inability to bring Alexander's adherents to justice swung the Lindsay/Leslie affinity behind Carrick as an alternative source of power and influence within the royal administration. Carrick's hour was fast approaching, but the heir apparent's rise to power, whilst reflecting and affecting the political situation in the north, was also dependent on the course of Anglo-Scottish diplomacy, and the affairs of the great magnates south of the Forth.

NOTES

1. *RMS*, i, nos. 458, 562; SRO Breadlabane Collection GD 112/1/4.
2. In 1320 Strath Gartney had been forfeited by Sir John Logie of that ilk for his part in the de Soules conspiracy against Robert I. Sir John's son, also John, recovered the estate in 1339 as the result of negotiations between the Steward, who was conducting a siege of Perth, and the garrison of disinherited Scottish noblemen, including Logie, who were holding the town in the name of Edward Balliol. In September 1343 Logie received title to Strath Gartney in accordance with the terms made at Perth, despite the fact that the lands were in the hands of Sir John Menteith. By 5 April 1359 John Logie had died and David II restored Strath Gartney to John Menteith, the son of the Sir John Menteith to whom Robert I had granted the forfeited Logie estates. When Sir John Menteith, lord of Arran and Knapdale, died without male heirs shortly after 17 May 1360, possession of Strath Gartney passed to Sir John's sister Christian and her husband, Sir Robert Erskine. In 1363, the widow of Sir John Logie, Margaret Drummond, was married to David II. Margaret's son from her marriage to Sir John Logie, also John, enjoyed his royal stepfather's patronage and support in the recovery of his paternal estates. In August 1364 Sir Robert Erskine and his wife received a grant of Alloa from David II in exchange for their resignation of Strath Gartney to the crown. Although it is not specified, it seems certain that David was recovering Strath Gartney for his stepson. John Logie was certainly restored to the lands of Logie, which had also been forfeited by his grandfather, before 1366: Fraser, *Menteith*, ii, 239; *RRS*, vi, 357, 385; SRO GD 124/1/514, 518. John Logie's position in Perthshire had collapsed after his mother's divorce from David II in 1369–70. Margaret and her son fled to the court of pope Gregory XI and in 1373 Gregory wrote to Robert II recommending to him John Logie 'who in the time of king David received many injuries, touching which justice should be done'. Despite the papal pleas it seems certain that Strath Gartney was simply occupied by Fife after 1371: *CPL*, iv, 99, 129; *Chron.Bower* (Goodall), ii, 379–80.
3. *RMS*, i, no. 554.
4. *Chron. Bower* (Goodall), ii, 416.
5. *RRS*, v, 633–5; A. Grant, 'The Wolf of Badenoch', in *Moray: Province and People*, ed. W. D. H. Sellar (The Scottish Society for Northern Studies, 1993), 143–163, at 143.
6. *APS*, i, 528–9; *Moray Reg.*, 171.
7. *APS*, i, 503, 528–9.
8. *ER*, ii, 309, 347; *APS*, i, 506–7.
9. *Moray Reg.*, 472–3; *RMS*, i, nos. 382, 530, 558; SRO RH1/1/2/1. See

A. Grant, 'The Wolf', 146, for a discussion of the strange variations in the terms under which Badenoch was granted out to Alexander in March 1371, and the suggestion that this was linked to the continuing jurisdictional dispute between Alexander and the bishop of Moray with regard to church lands and tenants in Badenoch.

10. *ER*, ii, 343, 352, 363.

11. *RMS*, i, no. 279; App. 2, no. 1577; *Ibid.*, no. 353; *RRS*, vi, 418, no. 387; *RMS*, i, no. 285; *Moray Reg.*, 473–5. The grants may have been intended to surround the Steward's son in Badenoch with a number of men wholly loyal to David II. The grants were almost immediately followed by the parliamentary complaints of 1368–9 against the Steward and his sons' inability or unwillingness to move against 'malefactors' in their own lordships.

12. Like Walter Leslie and a number of other David II favourites, Richard Comyn was originally a member of the affinity of Thomas Stewart, earl of Angus: *Rot.Scot.*, i, 821, 828, 901. 919.

13. Reid was named on the English safe conducts obtained by David II adherents in March 1371. He disappears entirely from Scottish records after 1371: *RMS*, i, nos. 285, 353; *ER*, ii 348, for Comyn's links to David II; *Moray Reg.*, 473–5, for Comyn's loss of the lands granted to him by David II.

14. A. Grant, 'The Wolf', 144.

15. *ER*, ii, 186, 197, 360, 363.

16. *RMS*, i, nos. 382, 530 contain the reversion in favour of David. *Ibid.*, no. 558 does not. *Moray Reg.*, 472–3 does not have the reversion and the text gives a different version of the rights attached to the lordship, claiming that Alexander was to hold Badenoch as it had been held by Thomas Randolph. The other versions have Alexander holding the lordship as it had been held by John Comyn, the last lord of Badenoch to hold the lordship before its absorption into Moray in 1312. All the charters carry the same date, but the existence of three different versions suggests a protracted dispute over the terms under which Badenoch was granted to Alexander.

17. *RMS*, i, nos. 389, 537.

18. *RMS*, i, no. 556.

19. Sutherland was presumably still alive in February 1370 when David II granted Walter Leslie a reversionary right to the thanages of Kincardine, Aberluthnott and Fettercairn which were said to be then held by Sutherland in liferent: *RMS*, i, no. 338. Sutherland had been given a grant of Urquhart by David II in February 1359, and had thus probably died before the June 1371 grants of Urquhart in favour of David, earl of Strathearn: *RRS*, vi, 239; *RMS*, i, nos. 389, 537. Robert's mother and father were married between October 1346 and November 1347.

20. *Chron. Wyntoun* (Laing), iii, 112.

21. *ER*, ii, 414.

22. B. E. Crawford, 'The Earls of Orkney-Caithness and their relations with Norway and Scotland: 1158–1470' (unpublished Ph.D. thesis, St Andrews 1971), 30–38, 130–133, 170–77.

23. *RMS*, i, no. 666. David was earl palatine of Strathearn and Caithness by 28 December 1377.

24. Alexander de Ard's most significant resignations in favour of the king's sons began around 21 March 1375 (*RMS*, i, nos. 614, 165), some three months before he was given a one-year governorship of Orkney by Haakon, king of Norway: *Records of the Earldom of Orkney* (SHS, 1914), 18–20. Ard's claims in Orkney may have been supported by the Scottish crown in negotiations which were underway in 1373: *ER*, ii, 390. Alexander de Ard's resignations to the crown continued in 1377 and 1378: SRO Lord Forbes Collection GD 52/1034; RH6/167; *RMS*, i, nos. 600, 601. But thereafter Alexander disappears from record, and it is conceivable that he died in 1378/9, for by August 1379 Henry Sinclair, lord of Roslin, a rival claimant to Orkney, had been made earl of Orkney by king Haakon.

25. Ross had supported Malise, earl of Strathearn's claims to Strathearn, and his daughter Isabella's rights to Caithness throughout the 1350s and 1360s, and had clearly dominated Caithness for much of the period. Advancing Ross's nephew, the queen's son David, as the Stewart candidate in the earldoms of Strathearn and Caithness, was probably part of a long-term political compromise of the conflicting claims: B. E. Crawford, 'The Earls of Orkney-Caithness', op. cit., 30–38, 130–133, 170–77.

26. *The Calendar of Fearn: text and additions, 1471–1667*, ed. R. J. Adam (STS, 1991), 85.

27. *Rot. Scot.*, i, 955.

28. *ER*, ii, 430; iii, 14, 44, 45.

29. *Rot.Scot.*, i, 965, 968, 969, 982; *Ibid.*, ii, 14, 17; *Frasers of Philorth*, ii, 211; SRO GD 297/ no. 229, 26 November 1380; SRO GD 274/no. 93: Walter Leslie, lord of Ross, granting six davochs to William Ross, for his homage and service, in the bailiary of Ferdonald and Delgeny.

30. See A. Grant, 'The Wolf', 143–145, for a more detailed examination of the build-up of the Wolf's power in the 1370s.

31. *ER*, ii, 425; SRO RH1/2/134.

32. *ER*, ii, 352; *RMS*, i, no. 237: David II charter to John of Lorn of the lands of Glen Lyon dated 12 March 1369. Alexander's role in Perthshire also brought his expanding territorial lordship into contact with that of his elder brother Robert, earl of Fife and Menteith, who had obtained possession of the barony of Glen Dochart, lying to the south and west of Loch Tay, in 1375–6. Fife's gains here were made as

the result of a resignation by Alexander Menzies of Fortingall and Redhall. The destination of the Menzies inheritance may have been a matter of some dispute between the Stewart brothers. In 1379 Alexander Stewart received royal confirmation of a grant of various lands in Rannoch, Strath Tummel, and Loch Tay resigned by a Janet Menzies: *RMS*, i, no. 676. This may be the same Janet Menzies who was described as a widow and as the daughter and heir of the deceased Alexander Menzies, when she issued a charter on 5 June 1381 from Fife's castle of Doune in Menteith. The competing claims of Fife and Alexander Stewart in northern Perthshire would eventually prove to be highly significant, but for most of the 1370s there was little sign of open tension between the two men.

33. *Rot.Scot.*, ii, 40; *ER*, ii, 102, 105; *Chron.Bower* (Goodall), ii, 395; Lindsay seems to have been accompanied by his kinsman Sir John Abernethy, a crusading knight frequently found in the company of Lindsay's brother Walter Leslie, and by three knights from south of the Forth, Patrick Hepburn, John Towers, and John Edmonstone. Abernethy, Towers and Edmonstone had all been associated with each other in crusades against the Lithuanians and, probably in the 1370s, were witnesses to a charter involving fellow Scots at Königsberg: SRO Inventory of Whitehill Papers GD 143/Box 1/2; *Rot.Scot.*, ii, 48–9, 27 February 1383. Hepburn, Towers and Edmonstone were also associated with William and James, 1st and 2nd earls of Douglas: *Melrose Liber*, ii, 78–80.

34. *Chron. Bower* (Goodall), ii, 386.

35. *Cal.Fearn*, 86.

36. *A.B.Ill*, ii, 389; SRO Cromartie Muniments GD 305/ Section 1/ Bundle 112/1; Comyn, in particular, was a long-standing adherent of Sir Walter. NRAS 1492, Perth Museum and Art Gallery, Bundle 641, Titles of Fordel, no. 1; NRAS 885, Earl of Strathmore Muniments, Glamis Charters, Box 2. Charter 1367x1372 by Walter Leslie, lord of Philorth, witnessed by Sir Alexander Lindsay, Sir Robert Ramsay, James Lindsay, and Richard Comyn; NRAS 885 Earl of Strathmore Muniments, Glamis Charters, Box 3, nos. 54, 56. 26 December 1375 Walter Leslie, lord of Ross, charter, witnessed by Alexander Lindsay of Glen Esk and William Lindsay, described as Walter's brothers, and Richard Comyn; *A.B.Ill*, iv, 84. A Walter Leslie charter from August 1381 was witnessed by his brothers, Alexander and William Lindsay, Sir Walter Stewart, Sir Robert Innes and Sir Richard Comyn, at Elgin: SRO Munro of Foulis Writs GD 93/ 12; SRO GD 297/ 229. A 1380 charter at Tain in Ross by Walter Leslie, lord of Ross, to Hugh Ross of Kinfauns, was witnessed by, amongst others, Alexander, bishop of Ross, Sir John Sutherland, Sir Robert Innes and Sir Richard Comyn.

37. SRO GD 93/ 11. The charter is curiously misdated 30 April 1379, but the fact that Euphemia makes the grant in her widowhood means that date is impossible. Alexander is styled lord of Badenoch rather than earl of Buchan or lord of Ross as he would become in July 1382. The charter must have been issued between March and July 1382.

38. *Abdn.Reg.*, 136–38. The council certainly dealt with complaints from northern prelates, for on 7 and 8 June the bishop of Aberdeen brought a case before the king against Farquhar Mackintosh for his illegal occupation of the bishop's lands of Birse. Mackintosh was probably an adherent of the lord of Badenoch, and the king sent letters to Alexander commanding him to take action over the issue.

39. The nieces and heiresses of the last Comyn earl were married to Henry Beaumont and Sir John Ross, the brother of Hugh, earl of Ross. Beaumont and his wife forfeited their portion of the earldom to the crown because of their adherence to Edward II, but the portion given over to John Ross and Margaret Comyn was allowed to descend to John's nephew, William, earl of Ross, on John's death without male heirs: Barrow, *Bruce*, 271–4.

40. *RMS*, i, nos. 736, 741, 742. Curiously, Alexander Stewart retained the Buchan title even after he had lost possession of the barony of Kingedward, with which the title was associated, after his divorce from Euphemia in the 1390s.

41. *RMS*, i, no. 736.

42. *CPL*, iii, 85.

43. Earl William seems to have been engaged in a long, bitter, and ultimately unsuccessful battle to retain control of lands and lordships on the western seaboard. Edward Balliol's 1336 grant to John of the Isles gave John a claim to Ross's lordships of Skye and Lewis. David II's 1343 rapprochement with John of the Isles and Ranald MacRuari was preceded by an agreement between Ross and the two islesmen. In 1342 Ross married John's sister Mary and in the same year granted Kintail to Ranald MacRuari: *RRS*, vi, 505; *CPL*, iii, 85. The grant of Kintail was presumably made under duress; four years later the earl would be responsible for MacRuari's assassination. In 1369 Robert Munro, one of earl William's retainers, was killed in 'defence' of the earl in unknown circumstances: SRO GD 93/6.

44. *ER*, iii, 30, 73, 81, 652.

45. Sir David Lindsay would certainly express an interest in the justiciarship after Alexander Stewart's demission of the office in 1388.

46. *Moray Reg.*, 196–7; see Grant, 'The Wolf', 148–50.

47. *ER*, iii, 657; *Chron.Bower* (Goodall), ii, 395: Lindsay styled lord of Buchan and Crawford.

48. *Extracta e Variis Cronicis Scocie* (Bannatyne Club, 1842), 194; C. McGladdery, *James II* (Edinburgh, 1990), 126–8.

49. NRAS 1492, Perth Museum and Art Gallery, Bundle 641, Titles of
    Fordel, no. 1; NRAS 885, Earl of Strathmore Muniments, Glamis
    Charters, Box 2: Charter 1367x1372 by Walter Leslie, lord of Philorth,
    granting Lyon lands in Monorgan, witnessed by Sir Alexander
    Lindsay, Sir Robert Ramsay, James Lindsay, and Richard Comyn;
    NRAS 885 Earl of Strathmore Muniments, Glamis charters, Box 3,
    nos. 54, 56. On 26 December 1375 Walter Leslie, lord of Ross, gave
    the same lands to Lyon in a new charter, witnessed by Alexander
    Lindsay of Glen Esk and William Lindsay, described as Walter's
    brothers, and Richard Comyn: Glamis Charters Box 1, nos. 2, 4;
    ER, ii, 339, 358; *CDS*, iv, no. 173; SRO Lord Forbes Collection GD
    52/1562; SRO Henderson of Fordell GD 172/121, Elgin 28 November
    1369: John Hay of Tollybothil, at that stage in trouble with the king,
    to John Lyon 'pro fideli consilio sui michi impenso et impendendo',
    witnessed by James Douglas, Walter Leslie and William Dischington,
    all David II men. There is also little doubt that there was some
    irregularity in Lyon's marriage to Robert II's daughter Johanna
    which required the king to issue remissions to the couple in 1378.
50. See NRAS, Earl of Strathmore Writs, Glamis charters; *RMS*, i, nos.
    411, 549, 575, 641, 642, 679, 693, 699, 734, 738, 744, 781, 787.
51. *APS*, i, 550–3; *Chron.Bower* (Goodall), ii, 395. The claim was probably
    derived from James Lindsay's great-uncle William Lindsay, lord of
    Symington, who had been married to Margaret Comyn, countess of
    Buchan, after the death of her first husband, John Ross: *A.B.Ill*, iv, 4.
52. *RMS*, i, nos. 734, 738: Grants on 30 August 1382. Both grants involved
    Lyon receiving lands which had been retained by the crown because
    they had been alienated without the king's licence. One was of the
    thanage of Glendowachy, which had been given to Alexander Stewart
    and the countess of Ross in the previous month.
53. SRO Calendar of the Swinton Charters GD 12/6.
54. The young earl of Strathearn, for example, was Alexander Lindsay of
    Glen Esk's son-in-law. Walter Stewart of Railston was one of
    Strathearn's retainers, (SRO RH1/2/148), but he was also Alexander
    Lindsay of Glen Esk's brother-in-law and a charter witness for Walter
    Leslie and his widowed countess. Euphemia Ross had given Walter
    Stewart a grant of the superiority of western Kinfauns shortly after
    Walter Leslie's death in 1382 but before her marriage to Alexander
    Stewart: *RMS*, i, no. 743.
55. SRO GD 25/1/18; *Rot.Scot.*, ii, 46. James Lindsay did apparently
    witness a royal charter on 21 November 1382, concerning the terce
    rights of his mother Egidia, although the need for the confirmation
    may suggest that the king was about to make some move against James
    Lindsay's estates: NLS Crawford and Balcarres Inventory, Section B,
    no. 7.

56. See below, Chapter 6.

57. Lindsay and the earl's son had planned to travel to England together in late 1381/2, and Sir James was a frequent witness to the earl's charters. Lindsay would eventually prove himself to be one of the loyalest members of the 2nd earl of Douglas's affinity: *Rot.Scot.*, ii, 40; SRO GD 12/1, James Lindsay and his uncles Alexander Lindsay of Glen Esk and Sir William Lindsay of the Byres in the earl's company in 1379; Fraser, *Douglas*, iii, 397, 398.

58. Thomas, earl of Mar's widow, Margaret Stewart, was given possession of her terce lands on 14 July 1377: Fraser, *Douglas*, iii, 24. On 30 June 1377 Douglas was still simply earl of Douglas, but in July and August 1377 Robert II made a trip to Mar during which Douglas received the earldom on some date around 26 July 1377: RH6/167, 168, 169; Fraser, *Douglas*, iii, 651–2. On 26 July 1377 Douglas issued a charter as earl of Mar from his castle of Kildrummy.

59. On 2 January 1379 Margaret Stewart, countess of Mar, granted her brother John Sinclair of Herdmanston all her lands in the town of Kimmerghame, resigned by Margaret's younger sister Elizabeth in her virginity. The witnesses included Douglas and the Lindsay brothers Alexander Lindsay, lord of Glen Esk, and William Lindsay of the Byres: *A.B.Ill*, iv, 724; Fraser, *Douglas*, iii, 27–8. In February 1379, Robert II granted licence to Elizabeth Stewart, to give to Margaret all lands and rents within the kingdom falling to Elizabeth by hereditary right. Since both sisters were named as heirs to their father Thomas, earl of Angus, the aim of the licence was clearly to allow a consolidation of the Angus inheritance in the hands of Douglas's mistress, and the process was complete by 9 April 1379: Fraser, *Douglas*, iii, 29–30; RH6/173.

60. On 12 March 1380 Alexander Lindsay 'at the instance of a noble and mychty Lorde, sir William, erle of Douglas and of Marr' renounced his claims against Margaret, countess of Mar, and Elizabeth her sister for the forty merks' worth of land which their father Thomas, earl of Angus, had promised to him 'efter that i had tane the ordre of Knycht': Fraser, *Douglas*, iii, 28–9; cf. SRO GD 121/3/21. A charter of Margaret, countess of Mar, witnessed by the earl of Douglas, James his son, Walter Leslie, lord of Ross, and Alexander Lindsay of Glen Esk, described as Margaret's relatives; *RMS*, i, nos. 389, 523.

61. *Abdn.Reg.*, 137–8. In June 1382, for example, Carrick was clearly enjoying a leading role alongside the king during the royal council which heard complaints from the bishop of Aberdeen against Farquhar MacKintosh. On 7 June Robert II commanded Alexander, lord of Badenoch, to take action over the issue. On the following day Carrick issued his own letters to the same effect, the terms of which suggested he was in some senses exercising royal authority alongside his father.

Carrick's letters were given to the bishop of Aberdeen,who may have specifically requested them from Carrick as an alternative source of power and authority within the royal administration: NLS Crawford and Balcarres Inventory. Section B, no. 6. Transactions in a parliament of 19 October 1378 were said to have taken place in the presence of the king and the earl of Carrick, these being the only two men named: E. C. Lodge and R. Somerville, edd., *John of Gaunt's Register* (Camden 3rd series, 1937), no. 1097. In June 1381 Carrick was styling himself lieutenant of the Scottish king 'versus marchias Anglie'. Carrick's position as heir apparent obviously gave him political influence and from 1382 onwards men, particularly Carrick's supporters in the south, sought confirmations of royal patronage from the heir to the throne: SRO GD 12/6.

62. Carrick's seals give an interesting indication of the earl's perception of his place within the kingdom. The seal used in c.1380 basically mirrors the royal seal in showing an armed knight, sword drawn, with a shield and surcoat bearing the Scottish royal arms, although distinguished with a label of three points. The implication was that Carrick played a special 'semi-regal' role in the military defence of the kingdom, and this would obviously fit in with his position as royal lieutenant on the marches. Carrick's privy seal seems to have made a clear reference to his impending accession to the throne: *Descriptive Catalogue of Impressions from Ancient Scottish Seals* (Bannatyne Club, 1850), 129, no. 783.

63. *APS*, i, 553; *Chron. Wyntoun* (Laing), iii, 55; *Chron. Bower* (Watt), viii, 6–8, 265–7, 363.

64. R. Nicholson, *Later Middle Ages*, 205–6; *The Concise Scots Dictionary*, ed. M. Robinson (Aberdeen, 1987), under 'Cateran'.

65. *Chron. Wyntoun* (Laing), iii, 55; *Chron. Bower* (Watt), viii, 6–8, 265–7, 363. It should be noted, however, that in Ireland the activities of unemployed bodies of mercenary troops did shade into outright banditry. The existence of such groups simply reinforced the need for lords to maintain sufficient forces to protect their own lands and men: K. Simms, *Kings to Warlords*, 120, 149.

66. K. Simms, *Kings to Warlords*, 18, 20, 93–95, 120, 125–8, 135, 143; J. Lydon, 'The Scottish Soldier in Medieval Ireland: The Bruce Invasion and the Galloglass', in *The Scottish Soldier Abroad 1247–1967*, ed. G. G. Simpson (Edinburgh, 1992), 1–15, at 7.

67. *Moray Reg.*, 197–201; *Ibid.*, 201–2: An indenture of 1390 by which Thomas Dunbar agreed to defend the lands of the bishopric of Moray against 'omnes malefactores viros Kethranicos et alios'.

68. *Ibid.*, 354–5.

69. K. Simms, *Kings to Warlords*, 17–19, 93–5, 116–128, 131, 134–5, 138–9, 149; J. Lydon, 'The Scottish Soldier', 9. The term appears in one early

fifteenth-century Scottish Gaelic praise poem composed for Malcolm MacGregor: 'From Hallowe'en to Beltane the warrior bands had right of quarters (*buannacht*) in every house', *Scottish Verse from the Book of the Dean of Lismore* (Scottish Gaelic Texts Society, 1937), 29, 262–3, although this section of the poem, dealing with ancient Irish heroes, may make deliberate use of distinctively Irish terminology; *APS*, i, 553. The terminology of the complaints against caterans in the 1385 general council reinforces the point that they were not permanently resident in any one area, but moved from one location to another, 'consuming' victuals often seized through physical violence.

70. *Highland Papers*, i, 25.
71. A. Grant, 'The Wolf', 145–9, for a detailed analysis of the clash between Alexander and the bishop over regalian jurisdiction within Badenoch and Strathspey.
72. K. Simms, 'The archbishops of Armagh and the O'Neills 1347–71', *Irish Historical Studies*, xix (1974–5), 38–55; J. Lydon, 'The Scottish Soldier', 9.
73. Boece, *Vitae*, 25–8.
74. *Abdn.Reg.*, 136–8.
75. E.g. *Moray Reg.*, 189–91 (no. 162), 196–7 (no. 168). The type of pressure underlying the resignations by the bishop of Moray is revealed in the bishop's lease of Rothiemurchus to Alexander and two heirs of his body legitimately procreated on 20 April 1383. In return for the grant Alexander agreed to 'protect' the church's lands, particularly the three towns of Finlargys, from 'malefactors'. It is interesting to note that in the late fourteenth century recipients of crown pensions in lieu of land grants began to specify that any land eventually granted to them should be in the 'partes inferiores' of certain sheriffdoms, suggesting that possession of Highland estates was regarded as a dubious pleasure: SRO GD 124/1/416.
76. R. Frame, *Colonial Ireland*, 124.
77. Boece, *Vitae*, 25–8.
78. *Chron. Fordun*, i, 42, ii, 38.
79. Alexander apparently contracted a Gaelic secular marriage with one *Mairead inghean Eachainn*: G. W. S. Barrow, 'The lost Gaidhealtachd of Medieval Scotland', in W. Gillies ed., *Gaelic and Scotland, Alba Agus a'Ghaidhlig* (Edinburgh, 1989).
80. *Chron. Pluscarden*, i, 329.
81. *RMS*, i, no. 537.
82. *RMS*, i, nos. 404, 526, 538.
83. Fraser, *Maxwells of Pollock*, 130; SRO GD 150/22; Fraser, *Grandtully*, 128–28*. Euphemia's special interest in Strathearn probably derived from the circumstances in which the Steward had acquired control of the earldom in the 1340s.

84. In March 1375 Alexander de Ard, the son of the eldest daughter of Malise, earl of Strathearn, Caithness and Orkney resigned all his claims and rights to the earldom of Strathearn and the castle of Bradewelle in Caithness, in favour of David: *RMS*, i, nos. 614, 615, 666. David was thus placed into two elements of earl Malise's inheritance, earl Malise being his mother's brother-in-law. The other components of the early settlement made on David, Urquhart and a reversionary interest in Badenoch, may have been derived from his mother's terce rights as widow of John Randolph, earl of Moray.

85. SRO RH2/6/4, 103.

86. *RMS*, i, nos. 652, 689.

87. *CPL*, iii, 381. John's marriage to Margaret Stewart took place c.1350.

88. *Acts of the Lords of the Isles* (SHS, 1986), 1–2.

89. *RRS*, vi, 113–5.

90. *Chron. Wyntoun* (Laing), ii, 472.

91. *APS*, i, 528.

92. *APS*, i, 503, 506; *Acts of the Lords of the Isles* (SHS, 1986), 8–9, no. 6.

93. *RMS*, i, nos. 412, 551.

94. *Ibid.*, i, no. 520.

95. *Ibid.*, i, nos. 567–9.

96. *Highland Papers*, i, 25–7; *Reliquiae Scoticae*, ii, 161.

97. *Acts of the Lords of the Isles*, 318.

98. The families bearing the royal tressure as part of Robert I's surrogate royal dynasty had marriage links through the king's daughters and sisters, and included the Randolph earls of Moray, the Setons, and the earls of Ross: *Ancient Scottish Seals* (Bannatyne Club, 1850), 114–15, nos. 688, 690 (Randolph), 116, nos. 698, 699 (Ross), 122, nos. 737, 738 (Seton).

99. *RRS*, vi, map at end.

100. Table 1. Place-Dates Robert II.

101. C. A. Madden, 'The royal demesne in northern Scotland during the later middle ages', *Northern Scotland*, iii (1977–8), 1–24, esp. 3–4.

102. A. Grant, 'Thanes and Thanages, from the Eleventh to the Fourteenth Centuries', in *Medieval Scotland, Crown, Lordship and Community*, edd. A. Grant and K. J. Stringer (Edinburgh, 1993), 39–79, esp. 65–71; Madden, 'The royal demesne', 8–10.

103. See Place-Dates; J. M. Gilbert, *Hunting and Hunting Reserves in Medieval Scotland* (Edinburgh, 1979), 36, 61, 66, 80, 95; *Chron. Pluscarden*, i, 311.

104. Interestingly, a Gaelic ballad concerning the death of a Fian warrior, Diarmaid Ua Duibhne, was composed in the area around Glen Shee around 1400, apparently by an Allan MacRuari. He may have been a descendant of the Ewan MacRuari brought into neighbouring Glen Tilt by Robert II in the 1340s: D. E. Meek, 'The Gaelic Ballads of

Medieval Scotland', *TGSI*, lv (1986–7), 47–72, at 52–6; *Scottish Verse*, op. cit., 27–9; J. M. Gilbert, *Hunting Reserves*, 60, 72–6.

105. *Highland Papers*, ii, 18–20.

106. *RMS*, i, no. 552, 27 March 1372, Robert's relationship with Mariota is first acknowledged, although it seems likely to have been underway well beforehand. The sons of this liaison were old enough to receive grants of land from the king in 1383: *RMS*, i, nos. 729, 730, 731; *Highland Papers*, i, 111–12. In 1439 Duncan Robertson of Atholl styled Donald MacNaughton his cousin: SRO GD1/947/1. Donald seems to have been a member of Robert II's royal household: *ER*, ii, 557. Mariota's brother, Thomas, also received royal support in his ecclesiastical career: *CPL*, iv, 226.

107. *Froissart*, xiii, 201; *Chron. Wyntoun* (Laing), iii, 44.

108. *Ibid.*, 45.

109. *RMS*, ii, no. 2028.

4

Anglo-Scottish Relations, 1371–84

T he conduct of Anglo-Scottish relations and warfare during the 1370s and 1380s lies at the very heart of the historical perception of Robert II as a weak and ineffective king. An account by the French chronicler, Jean Froissart, of the combined Franco-Scottish campaign against England during 1385 contains a damning description of Robert II's personal appearance and political marginalisation which has become the single most important basis for historical condemnation of the king's handling of Anglo-Scottish affairs in particular, and his governance of Scotland in general. Froissart's account presents a picture of a king wanting peace, but unable to control the ambitions and activities of a number of powerful border magnates who spearheaded warfare against England for their own personal political objectives.[1] Froissart's view is at odds with at least one strand of Scottish chronicle and poetic tradition, which for much of the fifteenth and sixteenth centuries actually presented Robert II as a Scottish patriotic hero, a defender of the integrity of the Scottish kingdom, and as the direct heir to Robert I's political legacy of successful defiance of the English crown.[2] Moreover, Froissart's reliability as a chronicler of the 1385 campaign, and as a useful source for Robert II's government of the kingdom, has been seriously questioned in a recent article which sets out a convincing argument for strong royal direction of the border warfare of the late 1370s and early 1380s.[3]

In 1371, when Robert II became king of Scots, the great Anglo-Scottish conflict which had dominated the political life of the Scottish crown and nobility since the late thirteenth century was in temporary abeyance, contained but not resolved. Robert inherited a kingdom which was still partially occupied by English forces or Scots who acknowledged the superiority of the English king. In the south of Scotland the major castles of Berwick, Roxburgh, Jedburgh and Lochmaben were controlled by English garrisons, forming the military and administrative backbone of an English 'pale' which embraced Berwickshire south of the Lammermuir hills, Teviotdale, lower Tweeddale, and half of Annandale. The zone of English political and territorial control had been established largely during Edward III's invasions of Scotland in David II's reign. A fourteen-year truce concluded between David II and Edward III in 1369, which came into force on 2 February 1370, was made on the basis of continued English occupation of this extensive tract of land in the south of Scotland.[4] The truce of 1369 also committed the Scots to pay 4,000 merks a year to the English king as part of David II's ransom agreement.

While Edward III remained alive the Scots largely adhered to these terms. In truth, however, the fourteen-year truce was precisely what it appeared to be, a temporary arrangement to suspend warfare between two kingdoms which remained basically hostile to one another, and which failed to address in any permanent way the unresolved territorial and political problems which sustained the conflict, most notably the occupation of large areas of Berwickshire, Teviotdale, Annandale and Roxburghshire by English assignees.

Robert II's own personal relationship with the English king was unlikely to replicate the apparently amicable dealings, the 'rycht gret specialte', between David II and his brother-in-law Edward III. The new king had none of David II's personal experience of the English court, and he did not share David II and Edward III's fascination with the chivalric/crusading ethic.[5] Moreover, Edward III's negotiations with David II in the 1350s and 1360s had established the English king as a prime mover in the various schemes to thwart a Stewart succession. The Douglas demonstration against Robert II's accession in February/March 1371 had probably threatened the new Stewart king with the possibility of an intervention by the English royal house in the disputed succession.[6] In 1371, then, Edward III must have seemed to represent a considerable political threat to the new Stewart dynasty. The Anglo-Scottish 'cold war' of the 1360s was about to become distinctly chillier.

The first parliament of Robert's reign unsurprisingly saw an embassy despatched to Charles V of France, headed by Archibald Douglas, lord of Galloway (who had fought for the French at Poitiers in 1356, and been on embassy to France in 1369 for David II), and Sir James Douglas of Dalkeith, which secured a renewal of the Franco-Scottish alliance.[7] The treaty which they negotiated provided for French assistance and advice to the Scots against the king of England whenever it was required, in peace or war. The Scots agreed to assist the French in the event of an Anglo-French war after the expiry of the present truce, or whenever the truce had been annulled in some other way by default of the English. The Scots also obtained an assurance that the French would not conclude a truce or peace with the English without the consent of the Scots and unless the Scottish kingdom was included in its provisions. It seems that Robert II's desire to conclude a deal with the

French was largely concerned with obtaining a powerful ally to bolster the kingdom and the new dynasty against English intervention. The essentially defensive aim of Robert's diplomacy is illustrated by the fact that Robert and his council rejected an alternative offer by Charles V to pay off the remainder of David II's ransom and to send a French expeditionary force to Scotland.[8] Given the events of 1371, and Robert II's uncertain political and personal relationships with the chief border magnates, the earls of Douglas and March and the lord of Galloway, it was hardly likely that the new king would seek to embark on any course of action which could provoke a political/military response from the English crown.

The same caution is seen in Robert II's decision to continue the payment of the 4,000-merk annuity owed to the English crown for the ransom of David II.[9] Nevertheless, a dispute over the form of address employed by the English chancery in the receipts given to Robert II for the ransom payments reveals the very real change in the personal relationship between the Scottish and English monarchs after 1371. The Scottish representatives who appeared in Berwick in June 1372 to hand over the ransom payment refused to accept the English receipt because it styled Robert II simply as Edward III's cousin, rather than as king of Scots. The Scots were prepared to counter the English argument that David II had accepted earlier receipts using exactly the same style, with the highly significant assertion that these writs had only been accepted because of David's personal fondness for Edward III, and that 'out of love for the king' David had not contested the issue, in prejudice of his own rights. Robert II's representatives further claimed that the form of the earlier writs had pleased no-one in Scotland except David II himself.[10] This, surely, was an early expression of the official Stewart view of David II's kingship and his political policies and diplomacy during the 1360s, perhaps even a reflection of the political propaganda employed by the Steward in the succession dispute of 1363/4, presenting David as an Anglophile whose personal relationship with the English king had led him to neglect his own rights and status as 'king of Scots'. It was an image of David which would be further developed by the fourteenth- and fifteenth-century chroniclers of Stewart Scotland.[11]

The dispute over the style employed in the English receipts fizzled out in December 1372 with Edward III's refusal to change the wording of the documents, but the episode demonstrated that Robert's maintenance of the truce and ransom payments actually cloaked a new and more hostile personal relationship between the Scottish and English kings.[12]

The political desire within Scotland for the recovery of the English-occupied zone was undoubtedly at its strongest amongst those land-owners directly dispossessed by the English, but the recovery of what was certainly regarded as part of Scotland was a cause which the king was expected to lead and co-ordinate. There is, indeed, every indication that Robert II was prepared to exploit English political confusion after the death of Edward III in 1377, and there was never any sign that the new king, never mind the border magnates, ever accepted the permanent loss of territory in Berwickshire, Roxburghshire and the western march.[13] Robert II's personal political history and the devel-opment of a kingship firmly based in Perthshire, however, hardly suited the king to the task of personally leading the chivalry of Lothian, Berwickshire and the western March in the recovery of their lost estates. From very early in Robert's reign it became clear that the new dynasty's representatives in the conduct of Anglo-Scottish warfare and diplomacy would be the king's two eldest sons, Carrick and Fife. The long-term danger for Robert II in this situation was that Carrick's effective control over the implementation of foreign policy would lead to an increasing desire on his part to control the formulation of policy.

In the mid-1370s, as Edward III declined into his dotage, the Scots opened a piecemeal campaign against the English enclaves in the south, which seems to have enjoyed the implicit support of Robert II. As early as 1375 it became clear that George Dunbar, earl of March, was increasing the pressure on the English-occupied zone in both Berwick-shire and the lordship of Annandale, which George claimed as the heir to the Randolph earls of Moray.[14] With the death of Edward III in 1377, and the accession of the ten-year-old Richard II, the Scots embarked on an intensified campaign against the English political and territorial presence in Scotland. The new English king was concerned about the state of the Scottish border from the very start of his reign. In July 1377 Richard ordered Thomas, bishop of Durham, to go with his household to his lands nearest the Scottish border in order to defend the March.[15] Richard was right to be concerned, for although Robert II was not about to lead or sanction a full-scale Scottish assault on the north of England, he and his magnates were clearly intent on making life as uncomfortable as possible for those upholding English interests. Probably in August 1377, George, earl of March, launched a dawn attack on Englishmen gathered in Roxburgh for the fair, in revenge for the death of one of his own men in the previous year. Wyntoun and Bower suggest that March gave the entire town to the flames and that many of the earl's enemies died in the lofts of the burgh's dwelling houses, where they had made a desperate stand against March's men.[16] Although the devastating nature of Dunbar's assault is probably exaggerated by the Scottish chroniclers, the earl's destructive and apparently indiscriminate attack on a nominally Scottish burgh suggests that the Scots living within the English 'pale' and cooperating with, and perhaps earning a good living from, the English garrisons in Berwick and Roxburgh were not likely to view March and his fellow border warlords as liberating saviours.

Although March's actions in 1377 appear like a unilateral declaration of war, they fitted in with an increasingly belligerent royal attitude towards Scottish interests on the border. From 1377 onwards, Robert II simply abandoned payment of David II's ransom, while, on 25 July 1378, the king transferred control of the priory of Coldingham in Berwickshire, formerly a dependent cell of the English priory of Durham, from its English superior to Dunfermline abbey.[17] The dispute between Dunfermline and Durham over Coldingham had probably begun some time before 1378, and the first Scottish prior of Coldingham, Adam of Crail, a Dunfermline monk, had been imprisoned by the bishop of Durham as early as 12 September 1376.[18] The case between Durham and Dunfermline continued at Holyrood on 28 April 1379, where the bishop of St Andrews opened proceedings against Robert Claxton, the English prior of Coldingham appointed by the Durham prior, in order to remove him from that office.[19]

By this stage the abbot of Dunfermline would have been able to present Claxton as a schismatic adherent of the Roman pope Urban VI. The Great Schism of 1378 had seen the Scots and English adhere to rival popes. On 9 August 1378 the cardinals who had elected pope Urban VI in April declared their first election null and void, and on 20 September they elected cardinal Robert of Geneva as pope Clement VII. The English king made clear his support for Urban VI in October/ November 1378, while Charles V of France declared his allegiance to Clement on 16 November.[20] The schism undoubtedly made the Avignon pope, Clement VII, eager to reward those secular princes who acknowledged and supported his claim, more receptive to the request of Robert II for letters allowing the bishops of St Andrews and Glasgow to summon Robert Claxton to answer criminal charges before them. Clement issued letters to that effect on 20 March 1379.[21]

Claxton was clearly deprived of Coldingham by the Holyrood court of April 1379, for in the following month, on 19 May 1379, the abbot of Dunfermline issued a charter, as superior of the barony of Colding-ham, to Sir John Swinton of the lands of Little Swinton.[22] Swinton was a remarkable figure who had developed a considerable military reputation, and a lucrative career, as an indentured retainer in the service of Edward III's son, John of Gaunt.[23] In late 1377 or early 1378 Swinton returned to Scotland with a retinue of sixty men from service to the English crown in France, and an early biographer may be correct in suggesting that it was the opportunity to reclaim the ancestral Swinton estates in Berwickshire presented by the Scottish advance in 1376–7, particularly the seizure of control of Coldingham priory, which drew Swinton home. Swinton swiftly established a good relationship with the key figure in the Scottish border campaigns, William, earl of Douglas and Mar. Sometime before 19 May 1379 Douglas witnessed, and probably arranged, an exchange between Sir Henry Swinton and Sir John of the lands of Little Swinton for those of Mykery in Douglas's barony of Strathord in Perthshire.[24] The exchange reflected the earl of Douglas's extensive political connections with the Lindsay kindred, with Sir James Lindsay, lord of Crawford, and his two uncles Sir Alexander Lindsay of Glen Esk and Sir William Lindsay of the Byres, all witnessing the transaction alongside the earl. The insertion of Sir John Swinton, a man with a proven record of military expertise and valour and a considerable following, into lands in the heart of the English-occupied zone in Berwickshire was obviously part of the process of the reclamation of political and tenurial control of this region by the Scots, although Swinton's record of service to John of Gaunt, the chief representative of the English king in Anglo-Scottish diplomacy, may have made his territorial gains less provocative than might otherwise have been the case.

The promotion of Sir John Swinton was probably symptomatic of wider tenurial changes within the occupied zone, as Scottish land-owners with long-redundant claims to lands in Roxburghshire and elsewhere sold or otherwise surrendered their rights to men who were directly engaged in the reclamation of these estates from English control.[25] Implicit royal support for the men involved in the recovery of border estates from the English was reflected in Robert II's confirmation, on 20 May 1380, of a charter by John, abbot of Dunfermline, granting Sir John Swinton, lord of Little Swinton (the manor of which had been held by an English assignee, Sir Edward Letham, during the 1360s), all the lands of Meikle Swinton which belonged to the newly Scotticised priory of Coldingham.[26] The abbot's confirmed charter had been witnessed by all the leading figures in the Scottish assault on the occupied zone, the earls of Carrick, Fife, Douglas, March and Moray, James Douglas, lord of Liddesdale, and Archibald Douglas, lord of Galloway. Royal financial support for Swinton's role is indicated by the pension of £20 granted by Robert II to Sir John on 4 June 1381.[27] Curiously, on 30 October 1382, Sir John received a confirmation of the 1380 grant by the abbot of Dunfermline of the lands of Meikle Swinton from John, earl of Carrick.[28] Carrick was not the feudal superior of these lands and the charter had already received the confirmation of Robert II. The value of a confirmation from Carrick lay, not only in the long-term guarantees offered by obtaining the support of the heir to the throne, but also in the earl's growing influence in royal government, especially in the conduct of Anglo-Scottish diplomacy. John, earl of Carrick, had been the chief Scottish representative in Anglo-Scottish negotiations throughout the 1370s and 1380s, and his grant assured Swinton that his claims to the lands of Meikle and Little Swinton would not be sacrificed or ignored in any future negotiations.

The Carrick charter also clearly identifies the heir to the throne with the most belligerent members of the border aristocracy. Sir John Swinton, whose estates had been wrested from English control in the 1370s, was described as Carrick's bachelor, while the charter was also witnessed by the major figure in the recovery of Scottish lands from English control, and Swinton's patron, Wiliam, 1st earl of Douglas. As earl of Carrick, Steward of Scotland, and custodian of the castle of Edinburgh, the heir to the throne was the only royal Stewart with an extensive territorial interest south of the Forth. It was natural that Carrick should serve as the chief representative of the king in Anglo-Scottish diplomacy during the 1370s and 1380s, and that this should lead to a close relationship between the earl and the border magnates.[29] Along with his brother Fife, Carrick fulfilled the task of representing royal interests at March Days, at which infractions of the truce were dealt with, and other Anglo-Scottish negotiations throughout the 1370s.[30] Carrick's developing status as a regional overlord south of the Forth, and his role as a leader and co-ordinator of the southern nobility in the defence of the kingdom, was confirmed by his appointment as the king's 'lieutenant for the Marches' on some date before 21 June 1381.[31]

It was presumably his role as royal lieutenant and defender of the Marches which justified Carrick's use of a seal which in style and imagery mirrored those employed by the king. Carrick's seal depicted the earl as a knight charging at full speed, sword drawn, with shield, surcoat and the trappings of his horse all blazoned with the royal arms, but bearing a label of three points, to distinguish him from the king. The seal suggests that from an early point in his career Carrick regarded himself as the man effectively exercising the duty of the king to defend the kingdom and to lead his subjects in war.[32] Carrick's expanding political and social links with the nobility of southern Scotland were strengthened by the marriages of his daughters Margaret and Elizabeth to the first-born sons and heirs of Archibald Douglas, lord of Galloway, and Sir James Douglas of Dalkeith.[33]

Carrick's growing regional dominance south of the Forth increasingly tied the southern magnates who had been largely hostile to Robert II's accession in 1371 to the royal Stewart line, but the process also carried an element of danger for the king. In 1382 Carrick was probably around forty-five years of age, and his apprenticeship in government had carried him into middle age. The general council of June 1382 carries hints that Carrick, already the leading figure in the defence of the kingdom, was also beginning to exercise, alongside his father, a role in the execution and enforcement of royal justice in areas of the kingdom outside the earl's own power base in the south.[34] Carrick's confirmation of royal charters issued by his father in October 1382 shows that the earl was acutely aware of his destiny. Powerful but not paramount, Carrick's position in the succession and in the governance of the kingdom made him a natural focus for any dissatisfaction with the policies and patronage of Robert II.

The chronicle and documentary evidence suggests, then, that from 1377 onwards the conflict on the borders became dominated by a cycle of cross-border raiding, although March Days continued to be held and obligations to maintain the truce exchanged.[35] Overall, there seems little doubt that the years 1377–1380 saw the steady recovery by the Scots of English-occupied lands in Berwickshire, Roxburghshire, Teviotdale and elsewhere, and that Robert II and, in particular, the earl of Carrick were perfectly willing to sanction and encourage these gains.

A series of charters issued by the king in May 1380 illustrates the point. Between 13 and 15 May Robert II was in Edinburgh, and confirmed resignations and grants concerning the lands of Chamberlain Newton and Denum in Roxburghshire, and granted a 200-merk pension to Sir James Douglas, lord of Liddesdale (earl William's son), from the great customs of the burgh of Haddington, for his service and retinue to the king and John, earl of Carrick.[36] The significance of all the May 1380 grants in Edinburgh is made clear by a document sent by the English court to John of Gaunt and other English commissioners who were to hold a March Day with the Scots on 1 October 1380.[37] The memorandum specified lands which the English crown and its assignees claimed had been wrongfully occupied by the Scots since the great truce of 1369. The list included the desmesne of Denum, lands in Chamberlain Newton, and all of Liddesdale. The pension to Sir James Douglas is one of the earliest examples of an annuity given out by the crown in return for the 'special retinue' service of the recipient. The exact significance of this form of crown-noble contract has been widely discussed.[38] One view sees these retaining pensions as a 'sinister' development, arising from the political weakness of royal government under Robert II and Robert III, which allowed the great magnates of the realm increasingly to monopolise royal financial resources. In fact, the retaining pensions granted out in the reign of Robert II seem to have differed in purpose and intent from those found in the reign of Robert III. Before 1390 all the recipients of 'special retinue' pensions were men playing a prominent and active role in border warfare, and in the context of 1380 it is hard not to view the pension given to the earl of Douglas's son as something of a war subsidy. Moreover, the terms of special retinue service required the recipient to be ready to assist the granter in peace and war outside the normal restrictions of feudal service. Since James Douglas, like most of those given crown special retinue pensions before 1390, was also bound to the earl of Carrick, the royal lieutenant on the Marches, it is tempting to speculate that the 200-merk pension was at least partly designed to ensure and reward the appearance of Douglas's own following in Carrick's entourage, either during diplomatic meetings or military expeditions. This was no doubt regarded as desirable at a time when John of Gaunt, Carrick's opposite number south of the border, appears to have attended Anglo-Scottish March days with, on occasion, a retinue of 2,000 men.[39]

The contemporary anonymous chronicler, from whom both Wyntoun and Bower derive their accounts of the border wars of the 1370s and 1380s, records the relentless pattern of raid and counter-raid, but conveys an impression of Scottish ascendancy: the triumph of Sir John Gordon, one of the leaders of the earl of March's assault on Roxburgh, over Sir John Lilburn at Carham; the beating off of a raid by the earl of Northumberland in Duns and Sir John Gordon's capture of Sir Thomas Musgrave, the warden of Berwick Castle, at the same time; the triumphs of the laird of Johnstone on the western March (significantly not reported in any detail); and the raid by the earl of Douglas on Penrith in 1380, and the defeat of a retaliatory English raid on the Solway.[40] The success of the Scots in this period is to some extent reflected in English official records. Richard II, for example, was evidently unhappy with the defence of the borders against Scottish incursions, and in March 1380 appointed the earl of Northumberland and the baron of Greystoke to ensure that all landowners holding 100 merks of land in Northumberland and the liberty of Durham resided constantly in the Marches, and that all castles and strongholds within three or four leagues of the border were to be fortified and supplied with men and stores to resist the Scots.[41] The Scots had certainly caused severe damage to the barony of Liddell in Cumberland before August 1380, perhaps as part of the earl of Douglas's raid on Penrith.[42]

Despite the many infractions, the Great Truce of 1369 staggered on as the official basis of Anglo-Scottish relations, with occasional attempts to revive its effectiveness. On 1 November 1380 at Berwick, the lieutenant of the English king on the Marches, John of Gaunt, concluded an indenture with the commissioners of the Scottish king, the earls of Douglas and March, and Archibald Douglas, lord of Galloway, which confirmed a truce (within the wider but greatly infringed fourteen-year truce of 1369) which was to last until 9 June 1381, and appointed a March Day at Ayton on 12 June 1381 between Gaunt and Carrick.[43] On 18 June Carrick and Gaunt met at Ebchester near Ayton, to seal the indentures for a further truce, to extend for two years to June 1383.[44] The March Day was interrupted by news of the peasants' revolt in southern England, which briefly forced John of Gaunt to take refuge in Scotland. Gaunt's short exile in Scotland in June/July 1381 confirmed the control of Carrick and his allies over Scottish diplomacy. On 21 June Carrick, as lieutenant of the Marches, issued a safe conduct to Gaunt allowing him to come to Edinburgh. By 25 June Gaunt had arrived in Edinburgh and lodged in Holyrood abbey. Robert II rather belatedly issued his own safe conduct for Gaunt from Scone on 28 June. On 10 July Gaunt gave gifts to the Scottish noblemen who had arranged his flight and offered him hospitality. These men were Carrick, James, the Master of Douglas, and the lord Lindsay.[45] The entire episode confirmed Carrick's predominant role in Anglo-Scottish diplomacy, and his close relationship with James Douglas, the earl's son, and Sir James Lindsay.

In January 1382 Robert II made a rare, indeed almost unique, appearance in the Scottish counties south of Edinburgh. Starting out from Edinburgh on 1 January, the king journeyed to Edybredschelis, near Selkirk, by 13 January, granting charters in favour of the Lindsay lords of Crawford and the Byres, adherents and allies of the earls of Carrick and Douglas.[46] The king's presence in the area not only reflected the recently secured truce, and may have been intended to bolster it, but there was surely also a symbolic aspect to the king's court appearing at Edybredschelis, from where the earl of Douglas seems to have co-ordinated his assault on the occupied zone to the south. By February 1382 Robert II had returned to Perthshire, although the ratification or encouragement of Scottish gains in the border area continued in the grant made by the king, on 23 March 1382 (from Ardneil), by which he gave over 100 shillings of the castlewards of Roxburgh (still held by the English) to Laurence of Govan, an adherent of the earl of Douglas, from the lands of Whitechester, Edrystone, Wilton, Chamberlain Newton and Minto.[47]

On 12 July 1383 Carrick and Gaunt held a further meeting on the border which arranged for compensation to the English for damage done to Wark castle and for infringements of the truce by the earl of

March.[48] There was, however, no indication of any arrangement to extend the Great Truce of 1369, which was due to expire in eight months' time. Robert II and his advisers were evidently not relying on a renewal of the truce, and on 20 August 1383, in the month following the Anglo-Scottish meeting on the March, the Scots concluded an agreement with Charles VI's government, by which the French agreed to support Robert's kingdom with troops and money should war break out between England and Scotland the next year.[49] The conclusion of a military alliance with the French may have been a reaction to a change in English foreign policy which laid less emphasis on continental war, and concentrated instead on the expansion of the English king's power within the British Isles.[50] In many ways, however, it seems to have been the Scots who were keenest to intensify the conflict on the border. Despite their ascendancy in the border wars of 1377–1380, and the reclamation of some areas from English control, the Scots had received no indication that the English were willing to renounce their claims to these territories. Indeed, the English negotiators at the Anglo–Scottish meetings in June/July 1383 were under specific instructions not to give up control of any lands held or claimed by the English crown and its agents in Scotland. Moreover, areas such as Teviotdale and fortresses such as Roxburgh and Lochmaben remained firmly in English control and could not be reclaimed without significant military action.

The preservation or prolongation of the truce thus held little attraction for the Scots who felt, probably justifiably, that they had held the military initiative for the previous seven years and yet were not being offered any concessions by Richard II's government. In January 1384, shortly before the expiry of the truce, Richard II attempted to increase the pressure on the Scots with a commission to the earl of Northumberland and lord Neville to obtain compensation for breaches of the truce by the Scots and to request the balance of David II's ransom. If the Scots did not comply, then the English lords were to demand the rendering of homage and fealty by Robert II to Richard II and, if this too were refused, they were to recruit an army and invade Scotland in order to punish the king and his men.[51] In reality, it was the Scots who were prepared for war on the Marches in February 1384.

Shortly before the expiry of the Great Truce, on 26 January 1384, the French and English concluded a truce at Leulighen to last until 1 October that same year, in which the Scots could join if they wished.[52] Apparently unaware that the French had established a truce with the English, the Scots mounted a full-scale assault on the occupied zone in early February 1384 during which the earl of March and Archibald Douglas recaptured Lochmaben castle and the earl of Douglas brought Teviotdale under Scottish control. The successful assaults on Annandale and Teviotdale predictably provoked an English counter-attack. In April 1384 John of Gaunt led a retaliatory English raid as far as Edinburgh.[53] The burgesses of Edinburgh saved their town from the flames by offering a ransom, but the English advance through East Lothian seems to have involved a particularly destructive attack on Haddington. The chronicler Froissart evidently has the same occasion in mind when he suggests that, soon after Easter 1384 (10 April), the earls of Northumberland and Nottingham launched a raid against Scotland, in which they 'burnt all the lands of the earl of Douglas and the lord Lindsay'.[54]

The tale of the 1384 raid, as told by Froissart, is significant because it presents the earl of Douglas and his ally Sir James Lindsay as the Scottish nobles with the greatest motivation to prolong the conflict in the summer of 1384, although the raid through Lothian could hardly have affected Lindsay's estates which lay mainly in the western March. The earl of Douglas at the time of Gaunt's raid was probably James, 2nd earl of Douglas, whose father was noted as having died shortly after leading the assault on Teviotdale, and who was certainly dead before 25 April 1384.[55] The new Douglas earl and James Lindsay were both, as we have seen, political associates of the king's eldest son Carrick. Moreover, an English seaborne expeditionary force, which was part of Gaunt's campaign in 1384, was worsted at South Queensferry by a Scottish company made up of the retinues of Sir Thomas and Sir Nicholas Erskine, Alexander Lindsay (probably the son of Sir William of the Byres) and Sir William Cunningham of Kilmaurs. Thomas Erskine and William Cunningham were Carrick retainers, and were probably in Lothian in the earl's service.[56] The Edinburgh-based Carrick had long regarded himself as a defender of the Scottish Marches for the royal dynasty, and had built a powerful regional lordship as one of the principal political and military leaders of the southern nobility. It was hardly surprising that in early 1384 he seems to have shared the desire of the adherents of the earl of Douglas to respond to the English raid into Lothian with military action. The determination of the heir to the throne and the young and aggressive earl of Douglas to retaliate for Gaunt's invasion seems to have contributed to a growing political crisis within Scotland which increasingly brought Robert II's authority within his own realm into question.

Froissart's chronicle suggests that Robert II initially shared Carrick's enthusiasm for a forceful reply to the English attack. He goes on to narrate, however, that French ambassadors arrived in Edinburgh during the deliberations of the king's council with notification of the truce established between England and France.[57]

Robert II, according to Froissart, felt that having received formal

notification of the Anglo-French truce and been offered the chance to
have Scotland included, it would be inappropriate to launch an attack
on England. More pertinently, it must have been clear to the king and
his advisers that the French were not about to fulfill their promise of
August 1383 to reinforce the Scots with troops, arms and money by
May 1384. Any further Scottish attacks in the summer of 1384 would
have threatened the inclusion of the Scots in the truce running to
October 1385 and in the Anglo-French peace negotiations which were
due to resume in Boulogne in June/July, and would have left Robert's
kingdom alone to face the inevitable English retaliation.

Froissart also suggests, however, that many of the Scots nobility,
notably James, 2nd earl of Douglas, John Dunbar, the earl of Moray, Sir
William Seton, the Lindsays and the Ramsays were not much inclined
to accept entry to the Anglo-French truce without avenging themselves
on the English for the raid of April 1384. Froissart's account has these
men holding a secret meeting in St Giles' Kirk, in the company of
freebooting French knights from Flanders, during which they decided
to attack northern England in defiance of Robert II's wishes.[58]
Froissart's interpretation should be treated with extreme caution
because his account reflects political propaganda produced within
Scotland during the late 1380s.[59] Yet there seems little doubt that
the summer of 1384 did see a considerable divergence between the
'official' diplomatic stance of the king and the 'unofficial' activities of
Scottish forces operating against England. Robert II's apparently self-
professed inability to control the actions of some of his magnates may
have been little more than a diplomatic device designed to allow
Scottish military action in the summer of 1384 without derailing the
wider truce negotiations, but the fact that within five months the king
would be replaced by his son Carrick in the task of upholding justice
within Scotland hardly suggests that Robert had impressed his subjects,
and consolidated his authority, with a display of shrewd diplomacy
during 1384.

The king was in Rothesay on 1 June 1384, where his confirmation to
Walter of Faslane, lord of Lennox, of the right to hold the weapon-
showings of the earldom, probably indicates that there had been a plan
for a general call-up of the Scottish host in the early summer of 1384.[60]
The Scottish response to the offer of inclusion in the truce and further
Anglo-French negotiations must have been decided, not in Edinburgh
as Froissart suggests, but while Robert II was on Bute, for by the
following day the king had sailed to Dumbarton, and had evidently
already decided to send cardinal Walter Wardlaw, bishop of Glasgow,
to the Anglo-French negotiations at Boulogne.[61] Richard II and his
council had obviously heard encouraging noises from the Scottish

government by 12 June, when English commissioners were appointed to negotiate a truce with the Scots. Carrick, who had been with the king at Dumbarton on 2 June, seems to have come out of the west with rather different objectives in mind, for the English chroniclers make clear that the Scots launched a number of raids into northern England in the early summer of 1384.[62] Carrick's personal involvement in organising these raids is made clear in a charter issued on 16 June 1384 by Sir Thomas Erskine of Dun, in favour of his cousin Sir William, at Elilaw in Northumberland.[63] Sir Thomas Erskine was an adherent of the earl of Carrick, and was one of the men who had fought against Gaunt's forces at South Queensferry two months previously.[64]

The witnesses to Erskine's charter were a mix of diehard Douglas and Carrick supporters, including Sir William Seton, Sir Robert Colville, Sir John Towers, Adam Forrester and John Shaw. Froissart names a William 'asneton', probably William Seton, as one of the men who had refused to accept the proposed truce of June 1384 and was eager for revenge for the English raid which had caused great damage to Haddington and East Lothian.[65] Sir Robert Colville was likely to approach Anglo-Scottish conflict with the zeal of the converted, having only recently been won over from allegiance to the English king. Colville immediately became a regular witness to charters issued by James, 2nd earl of Douglas, while his son Thomas married the daughter of Sir James Lindsay.[66] Sir John Towers was a well-known Douglas adherent with estates in the ravaged constabulary of Haddington.[67] Adam Forrester was a man of business around the court of the king and the earl of Carrick, and also the custumar of Edinburgh. He also seems to have been the sheriff of Lothian, an office in Carrick's gift, in July 1382. John Shaw was the laird of Hailey in Ayrshire and, like Adam Forrester, a regular witness to Carrick charters.[68]

If Robert II had been truly unaware of the young earl of Douglas's aggressive intent in early June, it is clear that Carrick, the heir to the throne and the member of the royal house most intimately involved in the conduct of Anglo-Scottish diplomacy and warfare, knew and approved of the plans, and had allowed members of his own retinue to take part in the raids on northern England. Froissart's story about Robert II's despatch of a Scottish herald to explain away the raid to Richard II may be reflected in the payments made to Lyon Herald for his expenses in travelling to England in 1384/5 and the English safe conduct obtained by the herald on 15 June, while Sir Thomas Erskine and his associates were ravaging the earl of Northumberland's estates around Elilaw.[69] Robert II was either engaging in diplomacy of the most duplicitous nature, or he was being openly defied not only by Douglas, but by his own son Carrick. While, as Grant suggests, there is no indication that Robert II's overall attitude towards the recovery of lands in the occupied zone differed markedly from that of Carrick and Douglas (the whole process had, after all, been explicitly supported by the king throughout the 1370s and early 1380s), the apparent dispute over the specific Scottish response to the events of 1384 demonstrated clearly that the heir to the throne had powerful political support in the south of the kingdom which cared little for Robert II's authority in the conduct of diplomacy and the defence of the Scottish Marches.[70]

Carrick was already the most influential royal Stewart south of the Forth. The earl's behaviour in the summer of 1384 indicates that he was, in fact, established as the political patron of the most bellicose Scottish noblemen involved in border warfare, with the unqualified backing of the earl of Douglas and the Lindsay affinity, and that he was increasingly prepared to take independent political action in contravention of the king's wishes. There is no dispute over the political attitude of James, 2nd earl of Douglas. Even chronicle accounts which were, generally, politically hostile to the earl admitted that he displayed a commendably consistent, if rather elemental, approach to Anglo-Scottish relations. According to Bower, Douglas was 'a relentless knight who was always hostile to the English'.[71] As Grant has noted, the political and military leadership of the kingdom was swinging towards a younger and more aggressive generation of Scottish noblemen.[72]

Despite the Douglas/Carrick raid on Northumberland in June 1384, the English do not seem to have abandoned hopes of a meaningful truce with the Scots, and by 26 July the terms of Scotland's entry to the truce until 1 October 1384 had been agreed.[73] It is doubtful if Douglas and Carrick wholly observed the terms of the truce, for there were persistent complaints about attacks on the English king's faithful subjects, and by 18 September 1384 Richard II was mobilising forces to go against the Scots who had invaded England.[74]

In the same month Robert II held a council in Glasgow which confirmed the growing domination of royal patronage by the young men personally involved in border warfare. During the council, on 21 September 1384, Sir William Douglas, the illegitimate son of Archibald Douglas, lord of Galloway, who was developing a formidable reputation for his military exploits in the Anglo-Scottish conflicts, received a £40 pension from royal customs revenues south of the Forth. On the same day Robert II promised to confirm to William £100 worth of land in Roxburghshire, which had been, or was to be, granted to him by his father.[75] The pension can be regarded as another war subsidy, while the king's obligation over the Roxburgh lands committed the crown to the defence of the gains made by Archibald the Grim and his family in the shattered English 'pale' after 1384. It seems likely that Carrick's was the guiding hand behind the patronage directed to William Douglas, the brother-in-law of Carrick's daughter Margaret.

The September council had probably been called to discuss Scottish diplomatic and military policy in the coming months. The truce which the Scots had joined in July 1384 was due to expire on 1 October, and the Glasgow council may have made preliminary preparations for any intensification of the military conflict on the border after that date. The English were also apparently making ready for the end of the truce, with Richard II calling out a number of noble retinues for an expedition against the Scots on 18 September.[76] As it was, any immediate escalation of hostilities was prevented by the conclusion of the Anglo-French peace conference in late September, and the establishment of a general truce which was to remain in place until May 1385.[77] On 10 October 1384 the Scottish envoys, cardinal Wardlaw and the bishop of Dunkeld, received English safe conducts for their return from France.[78] It is clear that the two men brought back more than simply notification of the general truce, for they were later named as having concluded the treaties and agreements which brought a French expeditionary force to Scotland in 1385.[79] It seems certain that one of the reasons for the calling of a general council in November 1384 was to secure the approval of the major magnates of the realm for Scottish involvement in a combined invasion of northern England with the French at the expiry of the truce in the following May, proposals which Wardlaw and Dunkeld had brought back from France in mid to late October.

By their very nature, deliberations of this sort were unlikely to find their way into official record. While there is no suggestion that Robert II was in any way reluctant to commit the Scots to an invasion — he himself had agreed to Franco-Scottish military co-operation as early as August 1383 under terms almost identical to those under which the campaign of 1385 was conducted — there seems little doubt that during the summer of 1384 political control of the Scottish war campaign had slipped from Robert II's hands. The king's personal political authority and control over the aristocracy of southern Scotland had been tenuous from the start of his reign. The earl of Carrick's emergence as an Edinburgh-based representative of royal power with extensive social and political links south of the Forth had succeeded in bringing the region into the wider Stewart settlement of Scotland. The price for Robert II was that by 1384 the heir to the throne had an established regional power base and committed aristocratic supporters who were prepared to see their patron oust his father from power. Even if Froissart's account is distorted by Douglas/Carrick propaganda, the portrayal of Robert II as a futile figure attempting to pacify the English king surely served a political purpose in November 1384 when the Scots were committing themselves to full-scale warfare. Moreover, Froissart's account identifies the magnates who had prolonged and intensified the conflict in 1384, and by implication those with the greatest qualification to lead the Scottish kingdom in arms, as the earl of Douglas and Sir James Lindsay, both of them political allies of the earl of Carrick. Froissart even implies that the freebooting French knights of 1384 took back the idea of a French army invading England through Scotland after it had been suggested to them by the earl of Douglas. Froissart's chronicle thus places Douglas and his allies at the very heart of the Scottish war effort in 1384–5 and reduces Robert II to a peripheral and powerless figure.[80]

The presentation of Robert II as a man who had failed to take the lead in the warfare of 1384 was simply one element of the propaganda deployed by Carrick and his allies in late 1384 to justify the political sidelining of the king. Robert II's presumed failings as a war leader reinforced rather more serious complaints about the king's exercise of justice and distribution of patronage in the north of the kingdom, and in particular the abuses of his royal lieutenant in the north, Alexander, earl of Buchan, lord of Badenoch and Ross. It was a curious and largely accidental feature of aristocratic landholding in the north of Scotland that many of those who were most alarmed by the behaviour of Alexander Stewart were also major figures in the south of Scotland, closely connected with Carrick, and heavily involved in the earl's border campaigns. James, earl of Douglas and Mar, John Dunbar, earl of Moray, and Sir James Lindsay all had extensive northern connections, and Lindsay and Dunbar, in particular, harboured specific grievances against Buchan's lordship in the north. Political discontent with the king's policies both north and south of the Forth was thus dovetailed in Carrick's affinity. The king's supposed unwillingness or physical inability to lead the kingdom in war constituted a powerful additional argument for political change in October/November 1384 when the Scots were discussing the proposed Franco-Scottish military alliance.

At the Holyrood general council of November 1384 the growing political discontent caught up with the king. Enforcement of royal justice was removed from the hands of Robert II and given over to Carrick, who became guardian of the kingdom.[81]

The aged king's demission of power may not have been entirely voluntary. A strange tale in the anonymous fifteenth-century abridgement of Bower's *Scotichronicon*, the Book of Pluscarden, suggests that the death of Sir David Fleming of Cumbernauld in 1406, during a battle with adherents of Sir James Douglas of Balvenie, was excused by the argument that Fleming had 'been one of the chief actors in the seizure of King Robert II'.[82] David Fleming was the son of Sir Malcolm Fleming, who had been the custodian of Edinburgh castle and sheriff of Edinburgh for the earl of Carrick in the 1370s, and was once again acting as sheriff of Edinburgh in 1388.[83]. If there had been a palace coup in November 1384, ratified by a general council held in the heartland of Carrick's political power, then David Fleming, as a Carrick adherent of long standing, would be a good candidate for involvement in an arrest of the king.

In November 1384 the founding father of the Stewart dynasty was pushed aside by his vigorous and ambitious heir, whose guardianship seemed to promise war in the south and a curtailing of the power of his brother, Buchan, in the north. Carrick's political future was bright: guardian of the realm and king-to-be. Robert II, on the other hand, seemed consigned to a slow decline into comfortable political obscurity. The great Stewart family settlement of the 1370s had experienced its first irrevocable breach. But, as Carrick would discover, the old king, the great political survivor, had not quite finished yet.

NOTES

1. *Sir John Froissart's Chronicles*, trans. T. Johnes (London, 1868), ii, 19–20.

2. This positive assessment of Robert II's record in Anglo-Scottish warfare and diplomacy first appears shortly after his death in the 'anonymous' chronicle utilised by Wyntoun and Bower: *Chron. Wyntoun* (Laing), iii, 45. The most bizarre product of this tradition was 'The Ring of the Roy Robert', a fifteenth- or sixteenth-century poem which mistakenly makes Robert II contemporaneous with Henry IV of England. The author of 'The Ring' places into the mouth of Robert II a vigorous defence of the ancient independence of the Scottish royal lineage and kingdom from English overlordship, starting from 'scota of egipt' and progressing through the heroes of the Wars of Independence, Wallace, Bruce, Douglas and Randolph. The important point was that Robert II was clearly regarded as a figure who upheld this tradition and ideology, and the poem finishes with Robert sending an offer to Henry IV for the issue of homage to be settled by a combat between a limited number of Scots and English, or by a personal combat between the two kings: *Maitland Folio MS* (STS, 1917–27), ii, 127–33. I should like to thank Dr Carol Edington for this reference.

3. A. Grant, 'The Otterburn War from the Scottish point of view', in *War and Border Societies in the Middle Ages*, edd. A. Goodman and A. Tuck (London, 1992), 30–65.

4. *Rot.Scot.*, i, 934, 938–9; *CDS*, iv, no. 154; R. Nicholson, *Later Middle Ages*, 126–35, 146–8; J. A. Tuck, 'Richard II and the Border Magnates', *Northern History*, vol. 3 (1968), 36; B. Webster, 'The English Occupations of Dumfriesshire in the Fourteenth century', in *Transactions of the Dumfriesshire and Galloway Natural History and Antiquarian Society*, 3rd series, xxxv (1956–7), 75.

5. *Chron. Wyntoun* (Laing), ii, 502.

6. A. A. M. Duncan, 'Honi soit qui mal y pense', *SHR*, lxvii (October 1988), 113–141; E. W. M. Balfour-Melville, 'Edward III and David II', *Historical Association Pamphlet*, 1954.

7. *ER*, ii, 356, 363; *Chron. Wyntoun* (Laing), ii, 496; *Foedera*, iii, 925–6; text of treaty in *ER*, iii, xcviii–civ.

8. J. Campbell, 'England, Scotland and the Hundred Years War in the fourteenth century', in *Europe in the Late Middle Ages*, edd. J. R. Hale, J. R. L. Highfield and B. Smalley (London, 1965), 203.

9. *ER*, iii, liv–lxi.

10. SRO PA 5/4, ff. 34–5; W. Robertson, *The Parliamentary Records of Scotland* (London, 1804), i, 126–7.

11. R. Nicholson, 'David II', 75–8.

12. *Rot.Scot.*, i, 951–2, 953; *Foedera*, vii, 967–8.

13. See A. Grant, 'The Otterburn War', esp. 40–1, for a powerful argument which emphasises Robert II's general support for the territorial goals of the border magnates.

14. *CDS*, iv, nos. 223, 231; J. A. Tuck, 'Richard II', 37.

15. *CDS*, iv, no. 241.

16. *Chron. Fordun*, i, 283; *Chron. Bower* (Goodall), ii, 384; *Chron. Wyntoun* (Laing), iii, 9–10.

17. *CDS*, iv, nos. 242, 265; *Chron. Bower* (Goodall), ii, 161–3; A. L. Brown, 'The Priory of Coldingham in the late Fourteenth Century', *Innes Review*, xxiii (1972), 91–93.

18. *CDS*, iv, no. 235; cf. Brown, 'The Priory of Coldingham', 92.

19. Brown, 'The Priory of Coldingham', 92.

20. W. Ullmann, *The Origins of the Great Schism* (London, 1948), 54–5, 91, 104.

21. Brown, 'The Priory of Coldingham', 92.

22. SRO GD 12/3.

23. A. Goodman, *John of Gaunt: The Exercise of Princely Power in Fourteenth-Century Europe* (1992), 58, 216–7; G. S. C. Swinton, 'John of Swinton: A Border Fighter of the Middle Ages', in *SHR*, xvi (July, 1919), 261–279.

24. SRO GD 12/1–3.

25. *Mort.Reg.*, i, pp. xxxv–vii, nos. 4–7: Alan Stewart, lord of Ochiltree, selling all his lands of Langnewton in Roxburghshire to Sir Henry Douglas, around 20 June 1377.

26. *CDS*, iv, no. 140; SRO GD 12/5; *RMS*, i, no. 647.

27. *RMS*, i, no. 700.

28. SRO GD 12/6.

29. *Rot.Scot.*, ii, 3; *CDS*, iv, no. 242.

30. *Chron. Wyntoun*, iii, 9; *ER*, ii, 433, 554, 602, 621-2.

31. E. C. Lodge and R. Somerville, eds, *John of Gaunt's Register, 1379-1383* (Camden 3rd series, 1937), no. 564.

32. *Ancient Scottish Seals* (Bannatyne Club, 1850), 129 (no. 783).

33. *Mort. Reg.*, ii, 136-7, 148-50. Douglas of Dalkeith was to receive 500 merks for his son's marriage and was to be given all his lands held directly of the king in free regality.

34. *Abdn. Reg.*, 137-8.

35. *Chron. Wyntoun* (Laing), iii, 9-14.

36. *RMS*, i, nos. 636, 646.

37. *CDS*, iv, nos. 294, 295.

38. R. Nicholson, *Later Middle Ages*, 211-12; J. Wormald, *Lords and Men in Scotland: Bonds of Manrent, 1442-1603* (Edinburgh, 1985), 42-6; A. Grant, 'The Higher Nobility in Scotland and their Estates, c. 1371-1424' (Oxford D.Phil., 1975), 321-6. Grant's analysis is the most convincing.

39. R. L. Storey, 'The Wardens of the Marches of England towards Scotland, 1377-1489', in *EHR*, lxxii (October 1957), 595; J. Campbell, 'England, Scotland and the Hundred Years War', 207.

40. *Chron. Wyntoun* (Laing), iii, 10-15.

41. *CDS*, iv, no. 292.

42. *CDS*, iv, no. 292.

43. Goodman, *John of Gaunt*, 76; *CDS*, iv, no. 297; *Foedera*, iv, 101.

44. Goodman, *John of Gaunt*, 80-1; *Rot.Scot.*, ii, 38-9.

45. *J.G.R. 1379-83*, nos. 564, 643, 1097, 1186-7.

46. *RMS*, i, nos. 696, 697. The progress of the king seems to have taken him through East Lothian, for on 6 January, at Seton, Sir William Seton issued a charter which was witnessed by the earl of Moray, and two regular members of the king's privy council, James Lindsay, lord of Crawford, and Sir John Lyon, chamberlain of Scotland. G. Seton, *The Family of Seton* (Edinburgh, 1896), ii, 844-5.

47. *RMS*, i, nos. 365, 692.

48. *CDS*, iv, no. 318.

49. *Foedera*, vii, 406-7; *APS*, xii, 19, no. 36. The commitment amounted to 1,000 men-at-arms, 1,000 suits of armour, and 40,000 gold francs before May 1384.

50. A. Grant, 'The Otterburn War', 41.

51. *Rot.Scot.*, ii, 51, 59.

52. J. Campbell, 'England, Scotland, and the Hundred Years War', 208-9.

53. *Chron. Wyntoun* (Laing), iii, 18-22; *Chron. Bower* (Goodall), ii, 398; *ER*, iii, 117, 120; Goodman, *John of Gaunt*, 99.

54. *Froissart* (Johnes), ii, 18.
55. *Chron. Wyntoun* (Laing), iii, 21; SRO Crown Office Writs AD. 1/23; A. Grant, 'The Otterburn War', 41–2.
56. *Chron. Wyntoun* (Laing), iii, 21; *Chron. Bower* (Goodall), ii, 398–400. Sir Nicholas Erskine seems to have been the recipient of a pension from the French king: R. Fawtier, ed., *Comptes de Trésor* (Paris, 1930), no. 1469.
57. *Froissart* (Johnes), ii, 19.
58. *Froissart* (Johnes), ii, 19–20.
59. See below, Chapter 5. See also A. Grant, 'The Otterburn War', 35–6, for a discussion which raises considerable doubts over the general reliability of Froissart as an accurate chronicler of political events and attitudes.
60. Fraser, *Lennox*, ii, 39–51.
61. *Registrum Monasterii de Passelet* (Maitland Club, 1832), 330–31. The French envoys had thus arrived in Scotland before 1 June 1384. A formal commission to Wardlaw and John, Bishop of Dunkeld, the chancellor, as the king's representatives to the Boulogne peace conference was issued from Edinburgh on 6 June 1384: *Foedera*, viii, 441.
62. Thomas Walsingham, *Historia Anglicana*, ed. H. T. Riley (Rolls Series, 1863–4), ii, 112, 115.
63. SRO GD 124/7/2. I should like to thank Victor Watts, Honorary Director of the English Place-Name Society, for his help in identifying Elilaw from the charter's 'Ealowley in Anglia'. Sir Thomas was granting his cousin a £20 annuity for 'suo bono et fideli servicio mihi impensis et pro toto tempe vite mee impedendo', probably a reward for William's role in Thomas's company during the Northumberland raid.
64. Erskine had an 80-merk annuity from the customs of Linlithgow for his 'retinencia' and service to the king and the earl of Carrick: *ER*, iii, 49, and *passim*. Erskine's heavy involvement in Carrick's military adventures reinforces the view that the retaining pensions granted out in the 1380s were designed to create a body of southern noblemen whose obligation to appear in Carrick's retinue for diplomatic or military purposes extended beyond the customary limits of feudal service: *Chron. Wyntoun* (Laing), iii, 21. Thomas Erskine would be severely wounded in the company of the 2nd earl of Douglas at Otterburn in 1388: *Ibid.*, iii, 38.
65. *ER*, iii, 117, 120, 129, 160, 200; *Froissart* (Johnes), ii, 20.
66. *Rot.Scot.*, ii, 60; Fraser, *Haddington*, ii, 225; J. Young, ed., *The Family of Lauder* (Glasgow, 1884), Appendix lix: 2nd earl charter at Tantallon in favour of Alan of Lauder; SRO RH6/191: 2nd earl charter as lord of the constabulary of Lauder to Alexander of Newton, witnessed by Sir William Lindsay, Sir Robert Colville, Sir William Gledstanes,

Sir Richard Rutherford, Alan Lauder, Adam Forrester, Thomas Turnbull.

67. W. Robertson, *Index of Missing Charters*, 121, no. 82. Towers would die alongside the 2nd earl at the battle of Otterburn in 1388: *Chron. Wyntoun* (Laing), iii, 38.

68. *Abdn.Reg.*, 141; SRO Inventory of Craigans Writs, GD 148/4.

69. *ER*, iii, 120; *Rot.Scot.*, ii, 63.

70. A. Grant, 'The Otterburn War', 40–2.

71. *Chron. Bower* (Goodall), ii, 400.

72. A. Grant, 'The Otterburn War', 43.

73. *Rot.Scot.*, ii, 62–4.

74. *Rot.Scot.*, ii, 66–8; *CDS*, v, no. 857; A. Grant, 'The Otterburn War', 43.

75. *RMS*, i, nos. 752, 770; *Chron. Wyntoun* (Laing), iii, 30–4. Another beneficiary of crown support for the Scottish acquisition of land in Roxburghshire which had been previously held by English assignees was William Stewart of Jedworth, who was given the lands of Synlaws in the barony of Oxenham, which had reverted to the crown because of the forfeiture of Thomas Rydale (who had died as a subject of the English king), on 2 July 1384: *RMS*, i, no. 772; *CDS*, iv, nos. 272, 282.

76. *CDS*, v, no. 857.

77. J. Campbell, 'England, Scotland and the Hundred Years War', 209; E. Marténe and U. Durand, *Voyage littéraire de deux religieux bénédictins* (Paris, 1724), 332–40.

78. *Rot. Scot.*, ii, 68.

79. *Foedera*, vii, 473.

80. *Froissart* (Johnes), ii, 20–22.

81. *APS*, i, 500.

82. *Chron. Pluscarden*, ii, 262.

83. *Mort. Reg.*, ii, 165–6; *ER*, iii, 66.

5

Broken Promise:
The Carrick Guardianship 1384–88

The statutes of the November 1384 general council which saw the earl of Carrick become guardian of the kingdom reflected the widespread concern over Robert II's exercise of justice in the previous few years. The first act of the council recorded the king's desire to administer the laws of his kingdom justly and 'with the advice of his council', while Robert also agreed to reform any of his actions which had been negligent or against the law. It was further stipulated that complaints against the king himself could be brought before the royal council, and that Robert would submit himself to the council's judgement over these claims. The key political change in November 1384, however, was embodied in the act which stipulated that because the king could not personally supervise the execution of justice, his first-born son and heir, the earl of Carrick, was to administer the common law everywhere throughout the kingdom.[1] It was significant that the three estates were sworn to support the new guardian in the exercise of his office even if Carrick incurred the king's displeasure through his actions.

The articles suggest far more than a simple transfer of responsibility for the arduous task of enforcing the common law from an aged king to his younger and more active son. There had clearly been direct and sustained complaints about the king's exercise of justice before November 1384, and it was implied that in some cases the king had acted illegally and ignored justified complaints about his own behaviour. The enforcement of the common law was not a politically neutral, purely judicial, task. Although members of the general council talked only of the administration of justice, this, of course, affected many aspects of crown administration and patronage. Access to a 'just' hearing over disputed lands and offices, royal action or inaction over complaints of intimidation or illegal occupation of land, were all aspects of political favour, reflecting the balance of power in and around the royal court. In 1384 the bulk of the complaints against Robert II probably focused on the king's refusal or inability to take decisive action against the royal lieutenant in the north, Alexander Stewart, earl of Buchan.

The general council of November 1384, and the promotion of Carrick to the guardianship of the kingdom, thus produced a clear change in the direction of royal policy and patronage both north and south of the Forth. By late November 1384 Carrick/Douglas loyalists were manifestly dominating crown patronage. On 20 November it became apparent that Joanna Stewart, the king's daughter and the widow of Sir John Lyon, was to marry James Sandilands of Calder, a cousin and adherent of the 1st earl of Douglas.[2] The marriage gave Sandilands control of some of the baronies and lordships acquired by John Lyon during the 1370s, including Glamis, Belhelvie and Kinghorn.[3]

James Lindsay of Crawford and his kinsmen, especially his young cousin David Lindsay of Glen Esk, also prospered in late 1384. At some stage in 1384/5 Robert II confirmed mutual charters of entail between Sir James and Sir David Lindsay. Sir James had produced no male heirs and the charters ensured that the bulk of his estates would pass over to the control of his cousin David, or David's brothers. In what was an increasingly common formula, the charters narrated that the entailed lands were to descend, in the last resort, to the nearest male heir of the name of Lindsay and bearing the Lindsay arms.[4] The royal confirmation of the entail may have been encouraged by the fact that David Lindsay had a royal bride, Elizabeth Stewart, Robert II's daughter.[5]

The charter which entailed David Lindsay's estates reconfirmed his title to the lands and lordship of Strath Nairn on the eastern shore of Loch Ness. However, it seems unlikely that Lindsay's feudal rights in Strath Nairn had translated into real political control in this central Highland lordship by 1384. In the financial year 1381–2, David Lindsay had received £105 from the custumars of Dundee for the fermes of the lands of Strath Nairn, which had been leased to Alexander Stewart, the king's son, by the king's command.[6] The payment from the royal customs suggests that Robert II was directly supporting Alexander Stewart's control over a number of strategic central Highland lordships in which the royal lieutenant had no hereditary title or right. Alexander Stewart's occupation of Strath Nairn and Urquhart reflected, and at the same time strengthened, his political and military power as royal lieutenant in the north. It seems probable that Robert II had initially justified these arrangements on the basis that Alexander Stewart was the only man capable of exercising any form of effective personal control in these lordships, especially given the tender years of the heirs to Strath Nairn and Urquhart, and that these possessions were essential for the continuing effectiveness of Alexander in his wider role as royal policeman in the north.

Alexander Stewart had probably continued to occupy Strath Nairn in the period 1382–4, but after Carrick's appointment as guardian in November 1384, David Lindsay immediately acted to assert his rights in Strath Nairn. In a charter which probably dated from January 1385, the king granted his permission to Lindsay to come to an agreement with John Dunbar, earl of Moray, who also claimed an interest in Strath Nairn, over possession of the lordship.[7] The grant foreshadowed the resurgence of Lindsay influence in the north, and the attack about to be launched against the position of the earl of Buchan in 1385. On 6 January 1385 Robert II also allowed that the £100 pension due to the earl of Moray from the burgh of Aberdeen should in future be taken from the more obviously convenient burghs of Elgin and Forres.[8] The arrangement was said to have been made at the request of Moray and with the consent of the king's son Carrick, and it may well have been intended to encourage Moray to abandon his claims to Strath Nairn.

By early 1385, then, the Lindsay affinity, with the backing of the new guardian Carrick and an understanding with the earl of Moray, was ready to reassert its territorial and political influence in the north. The collapse of the family's regional power in 1382 was obviously regarded as a temporary and reversible state of affairs by Sir James Lindsay and David Lindsay of Glen Esk, and their powerful allies, the earls of Carrick and Douglas.

A general council of April 1385 saw a full-scale, co-ordinated attack on the earl of Buchan's territorial position and his record as a royal lieutenant, in which the Lindsays and the earl of Moray played a prominent part. The proceedings of the council noted that there were many complaints from prelates, noblemen and others arising from the failure of justice in the Highland and northern parts of the kingdom, especially concerning the activities of caterans who were seen to 'wander about, gather and shelter' in the region, and whose killing, plundering and burning made both clergy and laity destitute.[9] Carrick was reminded that he had promised to uphold the law in the council of November 1384 which had appointed him guardian, and was urged to attend personally to the dispensation of justice in the area, and to call a meeting of northern noblemen and prelates to give him counsel with regard to the identity of the caterans and those who harboured them. The statutes amounted to a clear condemnation of, and a statement of no confidence in, the royal lieutenant in the north, Alexander, earl of Buchan, who was undoubtedly regarded by the bishops of Moray and Aberdeen as the chief supporter and employer of the caterans who had long troubled their lands and tenants in Badenoch and Strathspey.[10]

In the same council a number of specific complaints were brought against Buchan which had clearly been suppressed during Robert II's personal rule (reflecting the thrust of the legislation of November 1384 about the king's council now being open to dispense justice to all). Sir James Lindsay reopened legal proceedings over his claim to the lordship of Buchan, while David, earl of Strathearn, attempted to recover control of his castle and barony of Urquhart from his elder brother, with the young earl delivering in a complaint against Alexander for withholding the fermes of the barony and illegally occupying the lands and castle.[11] Strathearn was Sir David Lindsay's brother-in-law and had other links with the Lindsay affinity; his recovery of Urquhart on the western shore of Loch Ness would have complemented Sir David's recovery of Strath Nairn on the east of the Loch to disrupt Buchan's control of the Great Glen.[12] This development would also have pleased John, earl of Moray, who in the same council complained about the death of some of his adherents, with Buchan being urged to bring those responsible to justice (implying that the culprits were Alexander's own men). The territorial advances of Strathearn and David Lindsay in 1385 were clearly part of a wider political agenda, given formal expression in the April general council, which aimed to restrict Buchan's misuse of royal office, to contest his unjust occupation of lands and lordships in the central Highlands, and to challenge his imposition of cateran forces on the lands and lordships, ecclesiastical and temporal, under his sway. The council represented a concerted attempt by the prelates and magnates inconvenienced by Buchan's power in the north, many of whom had probably, like the bishop of Aberdeen, 'lost all hope of redress' from Robert II, to present their complaints against Alexander and his adherents to a new guardian expected to be sympathetic to their claims.

Carrick had clearly swept into power in November 1384 on a 'law and order' ticket, but his guardianship was to prove a major disappointment to Buchan's beleaguered adversaries in the central Highlands. The council of 1385, for all its direct and implied criticism of Buchan, did not deliver an official condemnation and the earl crucially retained his office of royal lieutenant in the north. Sir James Lindsay's claim to the lordship of Buchan did not apparently meet with any great success after April 1385. The dispute between Buchan and Strathearn over Urquhart was probably ended by Strathearn's premature death on a date between April 1385 and March 1390, an event which seems to have ensured that the vital Great Glen castle remained in Buchan's hands.[13]

It seems, indeed, that towards the end of the Carrick guardianship Alexander Stewart's territorial and political control of the Great Glen was strengthening rather than weakening. On 1 October 1386 Buchan received a royal confirmation of his custody of the barony and castle of

Bona at the northern end of Loch Ness following on the resignation of the earl of Moray.[14] It seems that this was part of a wholesale abandonment by Moray and his adherents of territorial claims around Loch Ness in the late autumn of 1386. On 28 September at Inverness, Sir Robert Chisholm resigned his claims to wester Abriachan, lying uncomfortably between Buchan's newly acquired lordship of Bona and his more established power base in Urquhart, along with other lands within the barony of Urquhart, into the hands of the feudal superior Alexander, bishop of Moray. In the following February the bishop of Moray granted Abriachan and the other lands to Alexander Stewart.[15] Chisholm was an adherent of the earl of Moray's, and had acted as justiciar within the regality of Moray for the earl.[16] The resignations of Chisholm and the earl of Moray indicate that, by late 1386, Buchan had triumphed in the struggle for control of the Great Glen. Some of Buchan's associates also began to receive royal favour in late 1386, with Farquhar the Leech, probably a member of the Beaton medical kindred who had become established as royal physicians in the reign of Robert I, the beneficiary of a substantial grant of lands in Strathnaver on 31 December 1386.[17] Above all, it became clear that by February 1387 Alexander Stewart had been granted the office of justiciar north of the Forth to complement his established powers as a royal lieutenant in central and northern Scotland. The bishop of Moray's feu-ferme charter to Alexander grandly styled him earl of Buchan, lord of Ross and Badenoch, lieutenant of the king and justiciar north of Forth.[18]

Carrick's guardianship ultimately seems to have resulted in profound disillusionment for his northern allies of 1384/5. Far from witnessing the curbing of Alexander Stewart's power in the region, the years after 1385 saw Buchan's territorial and jurisdictional influence increase, particularly in the Great Glen, where the earl of Moray and his adherents seem to have given up any attempt to exercise personal lordship. Even if Buchan and his cateran forces had not contributed directly to the decision of the earl of Moray and his justiciar to pull out of the Great Glen, it seems evident that the process reflected the general political and military pressure being placed on the titular landowners in the area. With the lord of the Isles requiring a standing army to maintain and defend his lands and lordship in Lochaber and, no doubt, to raid neighbouring lordships, it was hardly surprising that men who sought to exploit isolated and vulnerable Highland estates through conventional forms of feudal lordship were unable to protect their lands and tenants adequately. In this situation Carrick seems to have reached the conclusion that Buchan's control of the central Highlands was a necessary evil, ensuring at least some level of political stability.

Carrick's options in the north may well have been limited by the death of the royal dynasty's only obvious political alternative to Buchan as an agent of royal authority in the region, David, earl of Strathearn and Caithness. While Strathearn's death was undoubtedly an important factor in the failure of the Carrick guardianship to secure any reduction in Buchan's power, the earl and bishop of Moray, the bishop of Aberdeen and David Lindsay of Glen Esk were probably more inclined to blame the personal political failings of the guardian. There were indications of exasperation as early as the April 1385 general council, which sought to cajole Carrick into a decisive personal intervention in the north.[19] The decision to grant Alexander Stewart the office of justiciar north of the Forth before February 1387, potentially extending Buchan's influence into the earldoms of Lennox, Menteith, Fife, Angus, Mar and the great sweep of sheriffdoms north of the Forth from Dumbarton to Nairn, would have been greeted with varying degrees of horror by the men who had supported Carrick's ousting of Robert II in November 1384. Carrick, whose political heartland lay south of the Forth and who was heavily involved in Anglo-Scottish diplomacy and warfare after 1384, seems to have had neither the resources nor the inclination to make repeated military/judicial tours into the north. When the heir to the throne's guardianship ran into serious political trouble in late 1388, it may not have required too much persuasion for Carrick's northern associates to accept the transfer of power to a man who could and would organise a concerted political and territorial assault on Buchan's Highland lordship.

Besides the various complaints laid against Buchan, the April 1385 general council gave other members of the royal family an indication that their days of political favour were numbered, and that the earl of Carrick's allies were now in the ascendant. In the month after the council Robert, earl of Fife and Menteith, lost possession of Logie and Strath Gartney as the result of an arbitration of his dispute over these lands with John Logie, the son and heir of Sir John Logie. Logie was the son of David II's queen, Margaret Drummond, and a cousin to Carrick's wife Annabella. The restoration of Logie's fortunes undoubtedly rested on Carrick's acquisition of the guardianship in 1384.[20] Despite the 1385 arbitration, it is clear that the earl of Fife was not inclined to accept Logie's occupation of Strath Gartney and Logie, and the earl does not seem to have surrendered these lands to Carrick's favourite until 1387.

Fife, from his position as chamberlain, was, in fact, the only effective political check within the royal administration on Carrick's ambitions and authority after 1384. On 13 March 1385 it became clear that Carrick had received a huge payment of £700 in gold and silver from

Thomas Forrester, a custumar of Edinburgh, without mandate of the king or the chamberlain.[21] The same account revealed that Carrick had arbitrarily taken his £100 pension due from Aberdeen from the customs of Edinburgh. The custumars were ordered not to allow this unless they received a new mandate from the king or the chamberlain, while Thomas Forrester was held personally responsible for the sum of £700.[22] It may well be significant that this exchequer session was held in Stirling, the burgh with which Fife had the strongest connections, rather than Perth. It appears that in 1384/5 Robert II and, more especially, his second son Fife, were waging a defensive battle to keep Carrick's exploitation of 'royal' resources under control.

The most important aspect of the April 1385 council was the clear anticipation of renewed Anglo-Scottish hostilities in the following month. The Anglo-French truce which the Scots had joined in June/July 1384 was due to expire on 1 May, and it had been clear for some time that the French had no intention of prolonging the cessation of hostilities. Instead they were entertaining plans for a dual invasion of England, with one army landing in Scotland and sweeping into northern England in a combined operation with the Scots, while a second larger force gathering at Sluys in the Low Countries would launch a direct invasion of southern England. Planning for the invasion had begun late the previous year and presumably required some notification from the Scots of their willingness to co-operate in the (for them) high-risk strategy of a full-scale attack on northern England.[23] By April 1385 the Scots were preparing for war and the statutes of the general council asked noblemen to make sure that their adherents were ready to defend the kingdom.[24]

In late May and early June 1385 the French expeditionary force under the command of Jean de Vienne, the French admiral, arrived in Leith and Dunbar, where according to Froissart it was met by the earls of Douglas and Moray.[25] Froissart's account suggests that Robert II was not there to greet the French in person on their arrival, but was in the Highlands. The description of a king resident in the Highlands and essentially uninvolved in the events of 1385 reveals a great deal about the political bias of Froissart's sources, but does not give a particularly accurate account of Robert II's movements during 1385. The king had indeed been on Bute on 8 May 1385, in the company of the bishop of Dunkeld, the royal chancellor, Celestine Campbell, John Kennedy, Sir Andrew Mercer, and Duncan Lamont.[26] However, by 22 May, obviously anticipating the arrival of the French force, the king had left his island lordship and had crossed to the mainland at Ardneil, where he was joined by the earls of Carrick, Fife and Douglas.[27] Two days later the king was staying with his new son-in-law and prominent

Douglas adherent, Sir James Sandilands of Calder, at Sandilands' castle of Calder. While there, the king freed Sandilands and his heirs from the obligation to provide castleguard service to the crown for their lands of Calder.[28]

The king's arrival in Edinburgh does not seem to have left a great impression on the French knights and adherents of the 2nd earl of Douglas who provided Froissart with an account of the expedition. The king was described as having 'red bleared eyes, of the colour of sandalwood, which clearly showed that he was no valiant man, but one who would rather remain at home than march to the field.'[29] Robert II was sixty-nine years of age in June 1385 and on that account alone could hardly have been expected to take a leading personal role in the military campaigns about to be unleashed. Moreover, it was clear that he had not been actively involved in the campaigns undertaken by the border aristocracy in the 1370s and 1380s. For at least a decade before 1385 the physical leadership of war in the south had lain in the hands of the king's son, the earl of Carrick, and his allies. Froissart's description of the ageing king in 1385, probably reflecting the way in which Robert was regarded, or at least portrayed, by the southern noblemen who had helped Carrick move against his father in late 1384, was to prove highly influential in the later development of the king's historical image, largely because of the popularity and wide dissemination of Froissart's chronicles. By the seventeenth century Froissart's account of Robert II's physical appearance had resulted in Scottish chroniclers and historians adopting and developing the entirely spurious 'traditional' nickname Robert 'Blare-eye' for the king, while folk tales appeared to explain the damage to Robert II's eyes in terms of an accident during his birth by caesarian section.[30]

Regardless of the state of his eyesight, the king issued instructions for the assembling of the Scottish host, a task which seems to have occupied much of the following month, until on 1 July 1385 the council drew up regulations for the conduct of a Franco-Scottish force which would begin a foray into England.[31] The delay until 1 July 1385 ensured that the Scots had not breached the terms of a truce which had been concluded on 15 March 1385 between the earl of Northumberland and Archibald Douglas of Galloway, and which also embraced the lands of the lord Neville and the earl of Douglas.[32] The delay seems to have given rise to tension between the French troops and the residents of the areas in which they were quartered. Froissart narrates that the earls of Douglas and Moray were the only regular and friendly visitors to the commanders of the French force, and suggests that the Scots were less keen than the French to open up the war against England because they wished to extort more money from their allies.[33] Any reluctance on the part of the Scots seems to have been connected with a wish not to break the short truce arranged by Archibald, lord of Galloway, and perhaps a desire for evidence of the promised invasion of England by a French army from the Low Countries.

The logistics of the great assault on southern England were, in fact, rapidly coming apart at the seams, and the Scots were in danger of provoking a full-scale confrontation in which they might have to face the entire might of the English kingdom aided only by de Vienne's expeditionary force. However, by July any counsels of caution had been rejected and the Franco-Scottish force advanced into England through the eastern and middle March and attacked the castles of Wark, Ford and Cornhill.[34] The allies then briefly examined the possibility of besieging Carlisle, before turning their attention to a siege of Roxburgh, which must have been a prime target for the 2nd earl of Douglas. The activities of the allied army were brought to an abrupt halt by the news that a huge English force, personally led by Richard II and his uncle John of Gaunt, was hastening northwards. The English king had been aware of the French force in Scotland as early as 4 June 1385, when the preparations for an expedition to crush the Franco-Scottish threat in the north began.[35] Despite Froissart's protestations that de Vienne and his French knights were keen to engage the English and only retreated into Scotland at the insistence of their allies, there seems little doubt that it was the failure of the planned French invasion of southern England which had left the Franco-Scottish force in the north dangerously isolated and hopelessly outgunned, and Scotland itself vulnerable to massive retaliation. The Scots and the French admiral decided to avoid a direct confrontation and instead launched a retaliatory raid through the west March against Cumberland.[36] Froissart managed another gibe at the Scottish king by reporting that Robert II was not in sufficiently good health to accompany the expedition and retired to the Highlands, where he remained during the war, 'and left his subjects to act as well as they could'.[37]

The English army's uncontested advance into Scotland in August 1385 was immensely destructive, with the monasteries of Dryburgh, Melrose and Newbattle, the town of Edinburgh, and the kirk of St Giles all being given to the flames. Richard II was in Newbattle wood by 11 August 1385, from where he took action against those in Teviotdale who had returned to the allegiance of the Scots.[38] The English campaign in Lothian was a short one, but further Franco-Scottish co-operation in 1385 seems to have been made impossible by the breakdown of the relationship between Jean de Vienne's army and their hosts. Froissart claims that the French admiral was keen to winter in Scotland to campaign afresh the following year, but that the mood of the Scots became so hostile that he soon thought better of it. Froissart concentrates on the issue of provisioning and reparation for damage caused by the French as the chief cause of the break between the French and Scots, and suggests that de Vienne was only allowed to depart after the French king had placed sufficient funds in Bruges to cover the sums for which de Vienne had been forced to stand surety.[39] The Scottish chronicles do not suggest a serious breach over these issues, and instead put forward the idea that there was a disagreement over who should retain possession of Roxburgh castle should it be recaptured by the French.[40]

Richard II's campaign through Lothian seems to have had a sobering effect on the Scots, who in September accepted entry to a truce with the English which was to last from 24 October 1385 to 1 July 1386.[41] Despite the possibility of a great French armada attacking England during the summer of 1386 the Scots adhered to the terms of the truce with England and in June agreed to its extension to May 1387. Further negotiations in 1387 eventually extended the truce to 19 June 1388.[42]

There is no direct chronicle record of the earl of Carrick's role in the campaigns of 1385 but, although not specifically named, he was probably one of Robert II's 'nine sons who loved arms', as described by Froissart, who accompanied de Vienne's expedition.[43] There is every reason to suppose that the guardian was at the heart of the Franco-Scottish campaign in 1385. The heir to the throne received 5,500 livres tournais from the subsidy of 40,000 livres tournais allocated by the French crown to the Scottish nobles involved in the expedition (a grant surpassed only by the sum given to the earl of Douglas), while two of the three Scottish knights who supervised the distribution of the French subsidy, Sir Thomas Erskine and Sir William Cunningham, were members of Carrick's household.[44]

The remainder of the Carrick guardianship was dominated by the cold war with the English and, in domestic terms, with the guardian's increasing control and supervision of royal patronage as the moment of his accession to the kingship drew closer. These themes combined in Robert II's grant of 17 September 1385 by which he gave over the ten pound land of Nether Glen App, which had been given by the ancestors of John Kennedy to the canons of Bangor in Ireland but had been forfeited to the crown because of the canons' adherence to the king of England, to the chaplains of St Mary's in Maybole.[45] In the following February Carrick 'confirmed' the royal charter from his castle at Dundonald.[46] The issuing of charters by the guardian confirming grants made by Robert II was an increasingly common occurrence after 1384, and illustrates that, although Carrick was nominally only in charge of the dispensation of justice, his position as heir apparent gave him immediate power and influence. Carrick was, in reality, reviewing royal patronage, if not from an official position, then from the fact that people were anticipating his accession to the throne and wished to have their grants confirmed by the man whom they expected would shortly become their king. Royal grants made by Robert II were likely to be of a limited duration if they did not also have the approval of Carrick. Other grants reflected the severing of cross-kingdom links and the creation of a tenantry of undisputed loyalty to the Scottish crown in the areas over which the border magnates now asserted political control, while royal patronage generally came to concentrate on Carrick adherents and men who had been involved in the warfare of 1385.[47] In April 1385, for example, Sir Robert Colville, the Douglas adherent who had taken part in the raids of 1384 alongside members of Carrick's household, and whose son was married to a daughter of James Lindsay of Crawford, opened proceedings for the reclamation of his Scottish lands, which had been forfeited because of Colville's spell as a liege man of the English king.[48] Moreover, despite the relatively low-key nature of Anglo-Scottish relations in 1386, the men who had been most heavily involved in the warfare of the previous year continued to receive the support of the royal establishment. On 29 November 1386 the king granted a heritable pension of 20 merks to Robert Stewart of Innermeath, for his retinue service, from the great customs of Inverkeithing.[49] The pension for retinue service, in common with other similar grants in Robert II's reign, seems to have been connected with Robert Stewart's service to the crown in the Anglo-Scottish war of 1385; he was certainly later to be found on military expeditions in association with William Douglas, the son of Archibald of Galloway. On 2 February 1387 Carrick 'confirmed' the king's charter to Stewart of Innermeath.[50]

Carrick's influence in government is also revealed in letters patent of 15 January 1387, issued by the earl from Edinburgh, undertaking to cause, within a year, Robert II to infeft Sir Henry Douglas and Marjory his wife in a 20-merk pension or its equivalent in land.[51] Sir Henry Douglas, the brother of Sir James Douglas of Dalkeith, had been heavily engaged in the Carrick/Douglas campaign of 1384 and in the Franco-Scottish expedition of 1385.[52] A little over two months before the January 1387 grant, Carrick had given Sir Henry a 50-merk allowance from his own 500-merk pension from the customs of Edinburgh for Sir Henry's faithful service and retinue to David, Carrick's son and heir.[53]

Carrick was thus initiating, reviewing and confirming crown patronage. The obligation of retinue service by Sir Henry Douglas to David, Carrick's nine-year-old son, indicates that the heir to the throne was already looking to fashion an affinity, drawn largely from the nobility of southern Scotland, which would remain politically loyal to his family for some time to come. Certainly Carrick's growing political and dynastic security in the period after 1384 is undoubted. In the 1370s and early 1380s it had been customary for grants involving the permanent alienation of crown lands to be confirmed by Carrick, Fife, Badenoch, and, on occasion, David, the young earl of Strathearn, no doubt on the basis that any of these men, or their offspring, could eventually succeed to the kingship under the terms of the entail of 1373.[54] By 1384, with the birth of two sons to the heir to the throne, the dubiety over the succession had disappeared and alienations of crown land or customs revenue were made solely with the consent of Carrick.

As Carrick's power and influence increased, that of his brother Fife inevitably waned. By 1387, there were more immediate tensions between the two brothers. On 5 August 1387 Robert II issued a charter under his secret seal in the castle of Bute, in which he confirmed the rights of Duncan, earl of Lennox, to hold the weapon-showings in the earldom of Lennox.[55] The grant, which was not issued under the great seal, suggests tension between Duncan, earl of Lennox, who had strong links to the earl of Fife, and Sir Robert Danielston, sheriff of Dumbarton, a member of Carrick's household. At the same time the dispute between Carrick's retainer, John Logie, and Fife was also in full swing.[56]

The royal favour displayed to prominent war leaders south of the Forth during Carrick's guardianship manifested itself again at Scone on 26 December 1387, when the king granted to William Douglas, the illegitimate son of the lord of Galloway, and his wife, the king's daughter Egidia, a £300 pension from the customs of Edinburgh, Linlithgow, Dundee and Aberdeen until they or their heirs were infeft in £300 worth of land. The huge royal investment in the issue of the marriage was clearly a significant financial and political promotion for a man who, despite his growing reputation as a military leader, was, after all, merely an illegitimate son of the lord of Galloway.[57] Early in the following year further concessions were made to the interests of southern landowners. On 2 February 1388 Robert II granted the burgesses of Haddington the rents, profits of justice, and the little customs of the burgh for a consolidated annual ferm of £15, and on the same day remitted payment of this rent for four years, because of the burgh's penury, obviously as a result of the English raids of 1384/5.[58] On the same day the burgesses of Rutherglen, a burgh associated with the earls of Douglas, received similar rights in their own burgh in return for a ferm of £13.[59]

The burst of royal patronage in favour of southern noblemen and burghs in the winter of 1387/8 may have reflected a growing determination on the part of the Scots to renew the Anglo-Scottish war on the expiry of the temporary truce on 19 June 1388. Significantly, English envoys who had been appointed on 26 March 1388 to renew the Anglo-Scottish truce returned home by 19 April with no agreement, and by 29 April 1388 Robert II was holding what amounted to a council of war in Edinburgh.[60] Shortly before the council, on 16 April, John, earl of Carrick, issued his own confirmation of Robert II's February grant in favour of the burgh of Haddington. Carrick's charter confirmed the guardian's close association with the nobility of Lothian and Berwick, who were gathering in Edinburgh to discuss and arrange the raising of war on the border; the grant was witnessed by the earls of March and Orkney, Douglas of Dalkeith, Sir Thomas Erskine, Sir Walter Haliburton, Sir William Seton, Sir Patrick Hepburn, Sir Alexander Haliburton, John Sinclair, John Maitland and Alexander Cockburn.[61] All of these men were to play a prominent part in the renewed border warfare of 1388.[62] The council in late April/early May 1388 seems to have made arrangements for the preliminary Scottish raids on the north of England once the Anglo-Scottish truce expired in the month following.[63] The Edinburgh council clearly makes nonsense of Froissart's claim that the Scottish war effort during 1388 was arranged by a meeting of noblemen at Aberdeen who simply ignored Robert II. Carrick may have been the political driving force behind the push for renewed war in 1388, but the policy was clearly thrashed out and sanctioned by a well-attended general council presided over by Robert II.[64]

THE OTTERBURN CAMPAIGN AND ITS AFTERMATH

Over the winter of 1387/8 the Scots had been confronted by a series of factors which may have inclined them towards war. One positive incentive was the obvious opportunity for intervention in a kingdom weakened by a series of political coups and counter-rebellions during the summer and winter of 1387, and whose border defences had been seriously disrupted by local political rivalries. Another consideration may have been the obvious intention of the new English regime to open a war against the French in the summer of 1388. The prospect of full-scale Anglo-French conflict would undoubtedly have restricted the ability of the English to counter any Scottish attack in the north.[65]

What, then, were the war aims of the Scots in 1388? One interpretation is that the Otterburn campaign was nothing less than a full-

Left: 'Syr valtir the bald leslye': The coat-of-arms of David II's crusader knight displays a Saracen's head. King David's crusading favourites, including Sir Walter and his Lindsay half-brothers, prospered at the expense of the Steward and his allies. (Armorial de Gelres)

Below: Doune Castle. The construction of this impressive and sophisticated stronghold by Robert 1st duke of Albany and his son, Murdoch, reflects the power, status and ambition of the Albany Stewarts. (Crown Copyright: Royal Commission on the Ancient and Historical Monuments of Scotland)

Pyrrhic Victory: Henry Percy's captured pennon is displayed outside the 2nd earl of Douglas's pavilion at Newcastle. Within days Douglas would be killed at Otterburn, plunging the earl of Carrick's guardianship into crisis. (Photo courtesy of Biblioteka Narodowa, Warsaw)

Guardian of the Great Glen: Urquhart Castle on Loch Ness. Possession of the castle was a crucial feature of the Wolf of Badenoch's Highland lordship. (Crown Copyright: Historic Scotland)

Home in the West: Rothesay Castle on Bute. A traditional Stewart stronghold which continued to be used as a residence by both Robert II and Robert III. (Crown Copyright: Historic Scotland)

Lord of Argyll: The tombs of Sir Duncan Campbell of Loch Awe and his second wife in Kilmun kirk. Duncan was Albany's son-in-law and a major ally of the royal duke in the south-western Highlands. (Crown Copyright: Royal Commission on the Ancient and Historical Monuments of Scotland)

Princes' Bane: The episcopal castle at St. Andrews. In 1401 the duke of Rothesay was arrested on his way to accept the castle's surrender, and was lodged briefly in the bishop's keep before being taken to his final, fatal imprisonment in Falkland. In 1406 Prince James set off from St. Andrews on his disastrous expedition to East Lothian. (Crown Copyright: Royal Commission on the Ancient and Historical Monuments of Scotland)

The Wolf at rest: The tomb of Alexander Stewart, earl of Buchan and lord of Badenoch, in Dunkeld Cathedral. (Author's photograph)

Castle on the Clyde: The mighty castle of Dumbarton. The base for the 1398 expedition against Donald of the Isles. Robert III's attempts to remove Walter Danielstone as keeper of the fortress contributed to the political crisis of that year. (Reproduced by permission of the Trustees of the National Library of Scotland)

Dynasty's End? The Bass Rock, with Tantallon Castle in the background. Prince James and the earl of Orkney waited over a month on this bleak and barren island for a ship to take the heir to the throne to 'safety'. (Reproduced by permission of the Trustees of the National Library of Scotland)

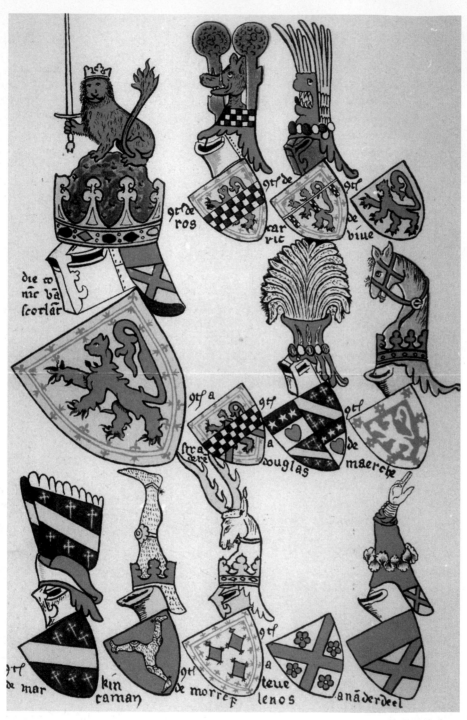

Family firm: The insignia of the Stewart earls of Ross, Carrick, Fife and Strathearn surround the Royal Arms. (Armorial de Gelres)

scale attempt, involving a three-pronged assault on the English east and west Marches and the Anglo-Irish lordship in Ireland, to force a weak and dispirited English regime to accede to Scottish conditions for a perpetual peace, including, no doubt, the permanent abandonment of English claims to the lands and castles recaptured by the Scots in 1377–85.[66] A variation on this theme suggests that the original aim of the invasion of 1388 may have been to isolate, besiege, and occupy Carlisle and other areas in Cumberland in an effort to obtain a territorial bargaining counter which could be exchanged for Scottish castles or territory held by the English.[67] Carlisle's defences were certainly regarded as inadequate by its own inhabitants, a fact which would have been known to the Scots who had accompanied the Franco-Scottish expeditionary force of 1385, when the possibility of besieging the town had certainly been considered. The Scottish army, led by Fife and Archibald the Grim, which invaded the west March in the summer of 1388, did, apparently, pitch camp outside Carlisle on 3 August and defeated a local force of Cumberland levies. In this interpretation, the grand strategic aim was thwarted by the maverick behaviour of the eastern force led by James, 2nd earl of Douglas, which failed to close in on Carlisle as had been agreed.[68] As we shall see, however, the supposedly 'maverick' behaviour of the earl of Douglas in 1388 seems to have been largely a product of political propaganda rather than military fact. Moreover, there is little reason to suppose that the Scots felt that they could mount a successful, prolonged siege of Carlisle in 1388 when they had failed even to attempt a similar operation with expert French assistance in 1385 for fear of severe loss of life.

Although both the eastern and western forces launched brazen attacks on major English towns, Carlisle and Newcastle, these may have been intended to display the Scots' military and political mastery of the north of England rather than to have been genuine attempts to seize the burghs and their castles. If the intention in 1388 was to capture and occupy a major English town, then this would have marked a radical and ambitious departure from established Scottish military practice. It seems more likely that the agreed strategy was to ravage northern England with a series of punitive raids throughout the summer and autumn of 1388. Scottish sources certainly describe the force which invaded the English west March as mounting a pillaging 'rade', and it was left to Froissart, with his extensive experience of the aims and methods of continental warfare, to suggest that the Scots were interested in the physical capture of Newcastle.[69] The first attacks on northern England commenced around 29 June, with the Scots crossing the frontier on both the eastern and western Marches, and returning in mid-July.[70] In late July 1388 two further substantial

Scottish armies headed out across the border. The contrasting fate of these two forces was to have a profound effect on the political situation within Scotland.

The Scottish army which set off through the eastern March shortly after 27 July 1388 was commanded by the earl of Douglas and raided as far as the walls of Newcastle, where it skirmished with the English garrison under the command of Sir Henry Percy, 'Hotspur', the son and heir of the earl of Northumberland. As Douglas's force withdrew towards Scotland, it was overtaken by Hotspur and a large northern English army at Otterburn in Redesdale on, or around, 5 August 1388. The ensuing battle ended in triumph for the Scots with the capture of Hotspur, his brother Ralph Percy, and a number of other Northumbrian noblemen. But the victory came at a price, for, at some stage during the battle, the 'relentless knight', James, 2nd earl of Douglas, was killed. Douglas's death became, under the pen of Froissart, a triumph of individual courage and chivalric sentiment. The dying earl, fatally wounded after turning the tide of battle single-handed, asked his faithful retainers to raise the Douglas banner and keep the news of his death from friend and foe so that their enemies should not gain encouragement. In Froissart's tableau the unvanquished banner of the dead earl, the three stars of Douglas and Bruce's bloody heart, floated over the scene of his last, posthumous, victory.[71]

One of the most interesting features of the chronicle presentation of the Scottish campaigns during the summer of 1388 is the wide divergence in the accounts given by Froissart on the one hand, and those of the Scottish chroniclers writing nearest the event, Andrew Wyntoun and Walter Bower, on the other. Froissart has very little to say about the exploits of the Scottish force on the western March, and concentrates instead on the eastern expedition under the command of the earls of Douglas, March, and Moray. In Froissart's account the division of the Scottish army is explained as a deliberate policy decision by the entire leadership before the two factions entered England. Froissart, significantly, at least partly derived his account from a meeting at Avignon in 1389 with a knight and two squires who had been in the earl of Douglas's service in 1388.[72] The Scottish chroniclers Wyntoun and Bower, on the other hand, clearly share a source that was hostile to any interpretation of the 1388 campaign as a triumph of arms for James, 2nd earl of Douglas, and his adherents.

Wyntoun's chronicle was completed in 1413–1420 during the earl of Fife's governorship of Scotland (as Duke of Albany), and the chronicler's patrons are known to have included Sir John Wemyss of Reres, a prominent adherent of Fife. Wyntoun himself, however, does not claim credit for the pro-Fife description of the military campaigns of the 1380s included in his chronicle. The account of the 1388 campaign, with the rest of the narrative for the reigns of David II and Robert II incorporated in Wyntoun's chronicle, is assigned, by Wyntoun himself, to the pen of a chronicler whom Wyntoun declines to name.[73] The political sympathies of this anonymous chronicler happily coincided with those of Wyntoun. In contrast to Froissart, the earl of Fife is given the leading role in the Scots' campaigns of 1385; and in the description of a retaliatory raid on the area around Cockermouth, allegedly led by Fife in late 1385, the anonymous chronicler manages to associate Fife's military exploits with those of the paragon of Scottish martial achievement, Robert I.[74] In Wyntoun's account, the 1388 campaign is also inspired and led by the earl of Fife, and his narrative concentrates on the exploits of Archibald the Grim's illegitimate son William Douglas.[75] Moreover, Wyntoun introduces his description of the earl of Douglas's Otterburn campaign with the charge that

> The Erle Jamys off Dowglas,
> That had made cunnand for till pas
> Wyth the Erle off Fyff in cumpany,
> Faylyd tharoff allwterly.[76]

The implication of Wyntoun's narrative is that Douglas had acted in an impulsive and reckless manner, ignoring previously arranged plans, a charge flatly refuted in Froissart's account. Bower's account of the domestic politics of Robert II's reign, including the Otterburn campaign, is derived either from the same anonymous chronicler as used by Wyntoun, or from a very similar source. Bower thus mirrors Wyntoun in suggesting that Douglas had promised to join the army of the earl of Fife in the west March, but 'he went back on this, by whose advice i do not know'.[77] The presentation of the second earl as a rather reckless commander permeates the remainder of Wyntoun's narrative of the Otterburn campaign. After gathering close to 7,000 men the earl, we are told,

> Than thoucht, that he mycht tak on hand
> Wyth that menyhe, that he had thare,
> In Ingland, but mare helpe, to fare.[78]

Despite admitting that the earl was 'off corage gret', the anonymous chronicler was, in fact, drawing a fairly clear comparison between Douglas's rashness and Fife's prudent leadership of the western force. At the joining of the battle Douglas was

> . . . sa besy
> For till ordane his cumpany,
> And on his fayis for to pas,
> That rekles he off his armying was.[79]

   The anonymous account laid great stress on the fact that Douglas's
force was wholly unprepared for Percy's attack, with the earl and his
men in their 'syd gownys' and enjoying a meal when they received the
news that Hotspur was almost upon them.[80] Froissart's account of the
opening of the battle, although in agreement with the anonymous
chronicler that many of the Scots were at supper and most were
unarmed, refutes the picture of Douglas's tactical incompetence by
reporting that the Scottish commanders had expected an attack and had
pre-set plans to deal with any assault '. . . during the preceding day, they
had well examined the country around, and said among themselves,
"should the English come to beat up our quarters, we will do so and
so," and thus settled their plans beforehand, which was the saving of
them'.[81] The essentially critical nature of the anonymous account of
Douglas's Otterburn campaign is confirmed by the inclusion of an
obvious fiction. The anonymous chronicler suggests that Sir Henry
Percy initially explored the possibility of engaging Fife's western force,
which the chronicle suggests Douglas should have joined, but declined
to do so because it was 'swa stowt'.[82] A close encounter between Percy
and Fife's army was physically impossible given the routes taken by the
Scottish forces in 1388, but the tale reinforces the anonymous chronicle's basic message, that the battle of Otterburn was an avoidable
conflict, which arose chiefly from the earl of Douglas's initial miscalculation in conducting an independent campaign in the east March.
The Scottish victory and the earl's death are reported with none of
Froissart's heroic details, and Wyntoun follows his brief description of
Douglas's death with another gibe at the earl's imprudence:

> This suld ken chefftanys in to were,
> For till have gud men ay thaim by
> In fycht for to kepe thare body:
> For alswelle ellis may be slane
> A mychty man, as may a swayne:
> Swa fell on hym in to that stede.
> Perchawns he had noucht there bene dede,
> And he had sete on hym yhemselle.[83]

Wyntoun's final description of the 1388 campaign is surely meant to
provide a stark contrast between the reckless earl of Douglas's fate, and

the success of Fife's expedition which, we are told, the king's son
brought home 'Wythowtyn tynsell off his men',[84] echoing the earlier
description of the Fife-led 1385 expedition which

> . . . passyd Sullway but tynsell,
> For thai war wysly led and welle.[85]

   The overall message of the anonymous account was that Douglas
lacked prudence, which was regarded in the theoretical texts of
mediaeval warfare as an essential quality for a war captain, particularly, and significantly in terms of the political context in which the
anonymous chronicle was composed, for a royal lieutenant and
Constable.[86] Froissart's account, derived from supporters of the 2nd
earl of Douglas and with an elaborate explanation and justification of
the decision to divide the Scottish host into two elements in 1388, seems
to represent a direct response to the charges levelled against Douglas by
the anonymous chronicler used by Wyntoun. Standing the anonymous
account on its head, Froissart concludes his description of the Scottish
victory with the observation that if Archibald Douglas and the earl of
Fife's force had been present at Otterburn, then none of the English
would have escaped death or capture, and that the Scots could have
captured the bishop of Durham and the town of Newcastle.[87] For
Froissart it was the victory of the Scots at Otterburn, and the huge
profit they made from the ransoming of their captives, which most
clearly echoed the triumphs of Robert I.[88]
   Froissart's account of the battle was written up between 1389 and
1393, while the anonymous chronicle was almost certainly a product of
the same period, early in Robert III's reign, and undoubtedly before the
death of that king. At the end of his account the anonymous author
describes Robert III's coronation (August 1390), and then expresses the
hope that

> God off swete will gyve hym gras
> To govern and wphald his land
> In na ware state, na he it fand;
> Bot leve it bettyr at his dycese.[89]

It would thus seem that the two accounts were part of a propaganda
battle being waged in Scotland, in the aftermath of the earl of
Douglas's death, between adherents and supporters of the dead
earl, and supporters of the earl of Fife and Archibald the Grim.
The propaganda battle reflected the very real struggle for control over
both the Douglas inheritance and the guardianship of the kingdom,

which broke out in Scotland in late 1388 in the wake of the earl of Douglas's death.

One of the major political issues in the aftermath of Otterburn was that the kingdom required an active and capable war leader to defend it against the massive English counter-attack expected in 1389. The anonymous chronicle provides the proof that Fife possessed all the qualities of bravery, experience and prudence required to lead the Scottish nation in arms in 1388–9. Indeed, in direct contrast to Froissart, the anonymous account suggests that it was Fife, and not Douglas, who had spearheaded the Scottish war effort in 1384 and 1385. The anonymous chronicler and Froissart also clash sharply in their presentation of the king, Robert II. While Froissart, relying on pro-Douglas/Carrick accounts, presents the king as a pathetic and politically powerless figure, the anonymous chronicle includes a tale from 1389 which specifically shows the loyalty and deference of Archibald the Grim and Fife to the aged Robert II. When English envoys to Scotland in 1389 become alarmed at the king's warm greeting for French envoys arriving at the royal court at the same time, they approach Archibald the Grim and ask him to support the truce they desire. According to the account preserved in Wyntoun, Archibald replies that

> . . . Till oure Kyng off the land
> And till the Wardane, as yhe may se,
> That fallis, and litill, or noucht, till me.[90]

When the envoys approach the guardian Fife

> . . . he answeryd thame agane,
> That all wes in the Kyngis wille,
> Till warray, or till hald hym still.[91]

The contrast between the picture of Fife and Archibald Douglas's treatment of, and reverence towards, the king in the anonymous chronicle, and the disparaging descriptions of the bypassing of the futile Robert II by the earl of Douglas in Froissart's chronicle could hardly be starker. The two chronicles reflect highly partisan accounts of the politics of the late 1380s. The anonymous chronicle concentrates on the abilities, achievements and the mutual co-operation of the earl of Fife and Archibald Douglas and his family, and stresses their support for Robert II. Froissart concentrates on the career of the earl of Douglas and his adherents, and stresses the essential ineffectiveness of the king.

The anonymous chronicle thus reflects the political propaganda of the Fife/Archibald Douglas faction which sought to oust Carrick and the remnants of the earl of Douglas's affinity from political power in the aftermath of Otterburn. Significantly, after Froissart has described the earl of Douglas's funeral, he asserts that he does not know who had succeeded to the estate of Douglas but, he adds, 'you must know, that the sir Archibald Douglas whom I have mentioned as a gallant knight, and one much feared by the English, was a bastard'.[92] The comment leaves no doubt as to the Scottish source for Froissart's account of the Otterburn campaign; the men whom the chronicler met in Avignon in 1389 were clearly members, as Froissart says, of the 2nd earl of Douglas's affinity, many of whom were, by 1389, engaged in a struggle with Archibald, lord of Galloway, for control of the Douglas inheritance.

In July 1388 the earl of Carrick's political future had looked assured. Carrick's role as heir apparent (with a statutory right to succeed to the throne) to an elderly and infirm king gave the guardian immense prestige and power; he was clearly not a man to defy. This powerful position was underpinned by Carrick's regional dominance in the south of Scotland, particularly his close relationship to the young earl of Douglas and his formidable political establishment. By 1388 Carrick's marriage had produced two sons, David and Robert, to succeed their father. Carrick was already providing the elder of these sons with feed retainers. In 1388 Carrick, like those men who brought royal charters to his court for confirmation, knew that he was a man whose hour of destiny was fast approaching, and that his succession to the throne was likely to be one of the smoothest and least fraught in the history of the mediaeval Scottish monarchy. The signet seal employed by Carrick as Robert II's lieutenant symbolised the earl's ambition and status, displaying a lion passant, with a crown held tantalisingly above its head by two disembodied hands.[93] Yet by the end of August 1388, Carrick's exercise of power within Scotland was clearly in serious trouble, with his own affinity disintegrating around him in the welter of territorial disputes arising from the earl of Douglas's death.

The death of Carrick's most powerful political associate was compounded by the capture of another of his principal supporters, Sir James Lindsay of Crawford, shortly after the battle of Otterburn by the bishop of Durham.[94] This reverse left the way open for Fife to play for the political support of the remainder of the Lindsay/Leslie affinity, principally Sir James's young cousins, Sir David Lindsay of Glen Esk and Alexander Leslie, heir to the earldom of Ross, who were less committed politically to Carrick and whose principal interests lay in the north of the kingdom. Thus, although Carrick's guardianship was to struggle on for another four months after Otterburn, his political control of the kingdom died alongside the earl of Douglas in Redesdale.

[149]

The deliberations of a general council held in Linlithgow on 18 August 1388, shortly after Otterburn, reflected the immediate debates over the destination of the Douglas inheritance, concern with the defence of the kingdom, and the political ascendancy of the earl of Fife. Robert II, after deliberation of the issue by the council, sent command to the free tenants of the barony of North Berwick and the keeper and constable of Tantallon castle, saying that the barony and castle had been held by the deceased James, earl of Douglas, from the earl of Fife, who was the feudal superior, and that, until Douglas's true heirs recovered possession of the barony and castle by due process of the law, the tenants and constable, in the interests of the defence of the kingdom, were to obey Fife as the legitimate overlord and give him possession of the castle.[95] Fife's attempt to gain possession of Tantallon was being resisted by the formidable Margaret Stewart, dowager countess of Mar, daughter and heiress of Thomas Stewart, earl of Angus, and mistress of William, 1st earl of Douglas. Margaret had resided in Tantallon with George, her illegitimate son by William, earl of Douglas, since c.1379, and in late 1388 she was simply sitting tight behind the castle's impregnable walls surrounded by her own kinsmen, the Sinclairs of Herdmanston, who, according to Froissart, had been the men to carry the dying earl of Douglas's banner to victory at Otterburn, and other notable Douglas adherents such as Alan Lauder, the Constable of Tantallon, Sir William Borthwick, William Lindsay of the Byres and Richard Hangangside.[96]

On 20 September Robert II was dealing with other elements of the Douglas inheritance, issuing a precept to his sheriff and baillies in Selkirk to ensure that his daughter Isabella, the widow of James, 2nd earl of Douglas, received a reasonable terce from the lordship of Selkirk.[97] At some stage before 1390, Isabella was remarried to one of the knights who had fought for her dead husband at Otterburn, Sir John Edmondston. It seems likely that, around the same time, Sir Malcolm Drummond, the husband of the 2nd earl's sister and heiress Isabella, was given a precept of sasine, the first step in obtaining full, legal possession of property, for the lordship of Selkirk. Drummond, who was Carrick's brother-in-law, had a powerful claim to the entire Douglas inheritance through his marriage to Isabella, but in 1388–9 he faced a challenge from Archibald Douglas, lord of Galloway, who claimed many of the most significant elements of the Douglas inheritance, including Selkirk, under the terms of a charter of entail from 1342. Carrick's close relationship to Malcolm Drummond ensured that the lord of Galloway would have to look elsewhere within the royal administration for support for his territorial claims. The fact that Drummond received royal letters of sasine in the forest of Selkirk at some stage before April 1389 indicates that, at first, Sir Malcolm's claims, undoubtedly supported by Carrick, were in the ascendant. Sometime shortly after the 2nd earl's death Malcolm Drummond was styling himself lord of Strathord, a Perthshire lordship which had been held by the 2nd earl, and sheriff of Edinburgh (an office in the gift of the earl of Carrick). Under these designations Drummond witnessed various transactions in Edinburgh involving Alan Lauder, the Douglas constable of Tantallon who was defying Fife, in the company of a number of other Douglas adherents.[98]

Despite Drummond's initial success, however, Carrick and his remaining allies from the Douglas/Lindsay affinity were increasingly forced on to the defensive in late 1388 by Fife, the lord of Galloway, and a resurgent Robert II. On 18 October 1388 Robert II issued a letter of protection to Sir John Lyon, the son of the royal favourite who had been killed by Sir James Lindsay in 1382.[99] Lyon was to be taken under the king's charge in order to avoid wardship during his minority. The letters wrested control of the Lyon estates from John's stepfather, the Douglas/Carrick adherent Sir James Sandilands of Calder, who had been one of the earl of Douglas's force at Otterburn.

By November 1388 Archibald the Grim and his close associate Sir James Douglas of Dalkeith were gaining the upper hand in the struggle over the Douglas inheritance. On 8 November Sir James Douglas was given temporary possession of the baronies of Westerkirk and Stable Gorton, and perhaps also the lordship of Liddesdale, which were in the king's hands by the death of James, 2nd earl of Douglas.[100] Dalkeith was to hold the baronies until the rightful heirs of the earl recovered sasine. The problem here was that Sir James undoubtedly regarded himself as a man with strong claims to the ownership of the two baronies, because Westerkirk and Stable Gorton were among the lands which had been resigned by Hugh Douglas, the brother of the good Sir James, to Sir William Douglas of Lothian, the 'knight of Liddesdale', Sir James Douglas of Dalkeith's uncle, in the 1330s and 1340s. Sir James had been declared his uncle's heir by entail, in other estates, shortly before Sir William's death at the hands of his godson William Douglas, the future 1st earl, who reclaimed all the estates alienated by Hugh Douglas. The death of James, 2nd earl of Douglas, without male heirs, allowed Douglas of Dalkeith to open a campaign to reclaim as much of his uncle's inheritance as possible, including the lordship of Liddesdale. Thus, in 1388, the Douglas feuds of the 1340s and 1350s were re-born.[101] The grant to Dalkeith in November 1389 was hedged with qualifications, and did not admit that Sir James had any rights to the baronies, but Dalkeith himself was likely to view the grant as a useful first step to permanent possession.

The grant of temporary fiscal rights in Westerkirk, Stable Gorton and Liddesdale to Douglas of Dalkeith may have been part of Carrick's desperate attempt to hold together his crumbling political affinity in late 1388. Before the death of the earl of Douglas at Otterburn, James Douglas of Dalkeith had clearly been an integral part of Carrick's political network, his son married to Carrick's daughter, and his brother, Sir Henry Douglas, one of Carrick's feed retainers. The conflicting territorial claims of Douglas of Dalkeith, Archibald, lord of Galloway, and Sir Malcolm Drummond to various elements of the Douglas inheritance tore apart the very heart of Carrick's regional power-base and forced key members of his affinity to look for a new political patron prepared to support their territorial ambitions. They had to look no further than Carrick's younger brother Robert, earl of Fife and Menteith.

On 1 December 1388, the politically isolated Carrick was forced to surrender the office of guardian during a general council in Edinburgh. Robert II opened the meeting with a declaration that he wished his son to subject himself to the will of the general council in regard to the administration of justice and the defence of the realm.[102] The king had thus gained some small measure of revenge for the treatment inflicted on him by his eldest son in 1384. Two arguments were apparently deployed to justify Carrick's replacement as guardian: the lax exercise of justice, especially in the north, and the manifest inability of Carrick to cope with the English invasion expected the following year. The general council of December 1388 complained that there had been defects in the governance of the realm for some time, because of the great age and indisposition of the king and the infirmity of his first-born son Carrick. This is the first official allusion to Carrick's lameness, said to have been produced by a kick from a horse which, ironically enough, belonged to Sir James Douglas of Dalkeith.[103] There is no chronicle record to suggest that Carrick accompanied either the western or eastern armies which invaded England in the summer of 1388, and it seems likely that Carrick's injury had occurred well before these campaigns. However, it is clear that Carrick's physical incapacity only became a political issue in the circumstances of the autumn of 1388 as Fife sought to remove his brother from power. Carrick's physical discomfort was, undoubtedly, another element in the propaganda battle which sought to portray Fife as the man best suited to defend the kingdom against the anticipated English invasion of 1389.[104]

The formal rhetoric of the general council explained the transfer of the guardianship and control of the kingdom to the earl of Fife, as it had to, in terms of the interests of the common weal, the defence of the kingdom and the dispensation of justice. But underlying these justifications was a set of stark political realities. Fife had made deals and promises to bring together a political coalition of sufficient strength and desperation to challenge and displace the heir to the throne. In the south, a Fife guardianship offered an effective defence of the kingdom and a favourable hearing for the claims of Archibald the Grim and James Douglas of Dalkeith to elements of the Douglas inheritance. In the north, Fife pledged to bring the earl of Buchan to heel, and to deliver justice on the unruly clans of the central Highlands, an attractive proposition to men such as David Lindsay, lord of Glen Esk, and John Dunbar, earl of Moray, who were, in other ways, natural supporters of the earl of Carrick.

Thus, in December 1388, the most capable and ruthless of Robert II's sons acquired real political power. The new guardian's armies would soon be on the march, not only south to carry war against the English, but also north to confront his brother Buchan. The collapse of Carrick's political power and the establishment of Fife's guardianship had profound consequences for the royal Stewart line represented by Carrick and his sons. The five years of the Fife guardianship would see the new guardian become the dominant political and territorial figure north of the Forth. In the south Fife's guardianship allowed the consolidation of Archibald the Grim's triumph in the struggle over the Douglas inheritance, a triumph which produced a unified Douglas establishment of immense power. When the Fife guardianship came to an official end in 1393, the royal Stewart line was faced by two entrenched magnate affinities whose position had been secured through their successful political opposition to the senior branch of the royal dynasty during and after 1388. It would be a long and hard road back to the full exercise of royal power for Carrick and his sons.

NOTES

1. *APS*, i, 500.
2. SRO Torphichen Writs GD 119/61; *RMS*, i, no. 759.
3. *CDS*, iv, no. 391.
4. *RMS*, i, nos. 762, 763.
5. SRO RH2/6/4, p. 103.
6. *ER*, ii, 67.
7. *RMS*, i, no. 764. Moray's claim may have rested on the 1312 grant by Robert I to Thomas Randolph, earl of Moray, John's maternal grandfather. Strath Nairn was not mentioned by name but it could have been argued that the lordship was encompassed in the general terms of the grant: *RRS*, v, 633–5.
8. *RMS*, i, nos. 765, 766.

9. *APS*, i, 553. This was a classic description of the cateran lifestyle from the lowland perspective, concentrating on their movement from one location to another and their forcible seizure of victuals and other goods. An act against caterans had been passed in the November 1384 council, which again stressed their seizure of goods through force and violence.

10. See A. Grant, 'The Wolf of Badenoch', 146–53, for a detailed discussion of Alexander's disputes with the bishop of Moray.

11. *APS*, i, 550–3. Urquhart seems to have been leased to Alexander Stewart shortly after it had been granted to Strathearn in 1371. At that stage Strathearn was still a minor.

12. SRO RH2/6/4, 103; SRO RH6/182, mentioning a grant by Strathearn of lands within his earldom to Sir David Lindsay's brother, Sir Alexander Lindsay.

13. Duke of Atholl's Muniments Box 2/Parcel 1, 5 March 1390: Euphemia is countess of Strathearn.

14. SRO RH6/184.

15. SRO GD 52/1035; *Moray Reg.*, 196–7.

16. SRO Fraser MacKintosh Collection GD 128/64/4/1. Chisholm had already resigned lands in Invermoriston to Alexander Stewart around 1384: *RMS*, i, no. 789.

17. SRO RH6/186. Farquhar's first territorial interest in Strathnaver was as the result of a grant from Buchan of the lands of Mellness and Hope confirmed by Robert II in 1379: RH6/174.

18. *Moray Reg.*, 196–7.

19. *APS*, i, 553.

20. Fraser, *Menteith*, ii, 260. In the early 1390s a John Logie, probably the same man, would act as chamberlain in the household of Carrick's son and heir David: *ER*, iii, 320, 325, 330, 331, 342, 353.

21. *ER*, iii, 118.

22. *Ibid.*, 117.

23. J. J. Palmer, *England, France and Christendom 1377–1399* (London, 1972), 51–2; Terrier de Loray, *Jean de Vienne* (Paris, 1877), Appendix, no. 89.

24. *APS*, i, 552.

25. *Chron. Fordun*, i, 383; *Chron. Wyntoun* (Laing), iii, 23; *Chron. Bower* (Goodall), ii, 399–400; *Froissart*, xi, 213; *Froissart* (Johnes) ii, 35; T. de Loray, *Vienne*, 189.

26. *Cartularium Comitatus de Levenax* (Maitland Club, 1833), 6–8.

27. SRO Glencairn Muniments GD 39/1/11.

28. Fraser, *Douglas*, iii, 399.

29. *Froissart*, xi, 254; *Froissart* (Johnes), ii, 48.

30. G. Crawford, *The History of the Shire of Renfrew* (Paisley, 1782), reprint of 1710, 25; W. Drummond, 1st Viscount Strathallan, *The Genealogy of the Most Noble and Ancient House of Drummond* (Glasgow, 1681), 8.

31. *APS*, i, 554–5.

32. *Foedera*, vii, 468–9.
33. *Froissart* (Johnes), ii, 36.
34. *Chron. Wyntoun* (Laing), iii, 24; *Chron. Bower* (Goodall), ii, 400–1; *Froissart* (Johnes), ii, 48–9.
35. *Foedera*, vii, 473; N. B. Lewis, 'The Last Medieval Summons of the English Feudal Levy', *EHR*, lxxiii (1958), 1–26; *Chron. Wyntoun* (Laing), iii, 28–9.
36. *Froissart* (Johnes), ii, 52–3; *Chron. Wyntoun* (Laing), iii, 29–31.
37. *Froissart* (Johnes), ii, 53.
38. *Rot.Scot.*, ii, 75; *Chron. Bower* (Goodall), ii, 401; *Chron. Fordun*, i, 383; *Chron. Wyntoun* (Laing), iii, 28–9.
39. *Froissart* (Johnes), ii, 56–7.
40. *Chron. Bower* (Goodall), ii, 401; *Chron. Wyntoun* (Laing), iii, 24–5. Bower has it that the French admiral departed from Scotland around 1 November 1385 after the French had run out of money: *Chron. Fordun*, i, 383.
41. *Rot.Scot.*, ii, 75.
42. *Foedera*, vii, 526–7; *Rot.Scot.*, ii, 93. The 1386 negotiations reached agreement on a renewal of the truce only four days before the existing truce was due to expire. The Scots may well have delayed until the last minute in order to see whether the threatened French armada against England would appear.
43. *Froissart* (Johnes), ii, 48.
44. *Foedera*, viii, 484–5.
45. SRO GD 25/1/21.
46. SRO GD 25/1/22: witnessed by Sir Robert Danielston, Sir Gilbert Kennedy and Sir Adam Fullerton.
47. *Melrose Liber*, ii, 466, 10 April 1386, crown confirmation of some of Melrose abbey's lands in Roxburgh to John Chatto on the forfeiture of the previous occupant, who had remained at the peace of the English.
48. *APS*, i, 553–4. See A. Grant, 'The Otterburn War', for an explanation of the terms under which Colville sought to recover his lands.
49. *RMS*, i, no. 773; *ER*, iii, 152, 192, 199, 240, 281. On 2 August 1386, while Robert II was at Selkirk, he confirmed grants made by James, earl of Douglas, to John Swinton, of lands in Clackmannan and Angus. Swinton had married the second earl's mother after the death of William, 1st earl of Douglas: SRO RH6/165.
50. Edinburgh University Library, John Maitland Thomson Collection of Photographic Negatives, no. 13. Carrick was attended by his adherents, Sir Thomas Erskine, Sir Robert Danielston, William Cunningham, Sir John Stewart of Innermeath, Sir Andrew Mercer, Adam Forrester and John Shaw, lord of Hayle. Most of these men had also witnessed a charter of 24 January 1387 by Carrick in favour of John of Park, of the office of sergeant of fee in Strath Gryfe: SRO Inventory of Craigans Writs, GD 148/4.

51. SRO GD 150/34.
52. On 20 October 1384 Henry Douglas received sureties for the ransom, 48 gold nobles, of William Chamberlain, Englishman, his prisoner: SRO GD 150/45. However, Sir Henry himself seems to have been captured by the English during 1384: *Chron. Knighton*, ii, 203, 297–8. In 1385 Sir Henry received 33 livres tournois from the French war chest.
53. SRO GD 150/50; *Mort.Reg.*, ii, 158–9. At around this period Carrick issued a charter of lands in his earldom of Carrick to Thomas Kennedy for Kennedy's service to David Stewart. The witnesses included Sir Henry and Carrick's brother-in-law Sir Malcolm Drummond, Thomas Erskine, Adam Forrester and John and James Shaw: Laing Charters, no. 68.
54. E.g., Viscount Strathallan, *Genealogy of the House of Drummond*, 82–3. An obligation by John, earl of Carrick, Robert of Fife and Menteith, and Alexander lord of Badenoch to defend the natural sons of Robert II by Marion Cardeny in the lands specified in the king's charters granted to them, 'that they nor none of them shal sustaine any injurie in the possession of the saids lands, or violence wherethrough they may be hindered to freely use and enjoy the same notwithstanding of any estate we may possibly come to': Edinburgh, 21 June 1382.
55. *Cartularium Comitatus de Levenax* (Maitland Club, 1833), 8–9.
56. On 8 June 1387 the king issued a precept of sasine in favour of Logie in the lands of Logie and Strath Gartney, narrating that the lands had been resigned by Fife in the presence of the king and Carrick: Fraser, *Grandtully*, i, 141*. Sasine was delivered by Walter Stewart of Railston, sheriff of Perth, on 4 July following. On 8 October, at Kilwinning, Robert II issued a confirmation of David II's 1368 grant of Logie in regality: Fraser, *Grandtully*, i, 140*–141*; *Ibid.*, 142*; *Menteith*, ii, no. 43; Fraser, *Grandtully*, i, 138*. The settlement of the Logie/Strath Gartney issue in favour of John Logie, after at least ten years of litigation, illustrates Carrick's political ascendancy in 1387.
57. *RMS*, i, no. 753.
58. *RMS*, i, no. 751; *ER*, iii, 200.
59. *RMS*, i, nos. 756, 767.
60. *Rot.Scot.*, ii, 92; *War and Border Societies in the Middle Ages*, edd. A. Goodman and A. Tuck, 'Introduction', 26, no. 42; Argyll Transcripts, vol. i, at date.
61. SRO Haddington Burgh Records B30/21/3.
62. Despite his title of earl of Orkney, Henry Sinclair, as lord of Roslin and other lands and lordships in East Lothian, had extensive political and social ties in the region. He was at Dirleton castle, the chief stronghold of his half-brother Sir John Haliburton, on 24 July 1388, shortly before the major Otterburn campaign of July/August 1388: SRO GD 122/1/144.

63. *Rot.Scot.*, ii, 93.
64. *Froissart* (Johnes), ii, 361–2; A. Grant, 'The Otterburn War', 47. The men attending the council certainly included the earls of Fife and Douglas, the bishops of St Andrews and Dunkeld, Sir James Lindsay and Sir Patrick Graham of Kincardine, who were all in Edinburgh on 6 May 1388: SRO Haldane of Gleneagles GD 198/8.
65. Goodman, Introduction, 13–16.
66. A. Grant, 'The Otterburn War', 47–50.
67. Goodman, Introduction, 17–18.
68. *Chron. Wyntoun*, iii, 24; H. Summerson, 'Responses to War: Carlisle and the West March in the later Fourteenth Century', in *War and Border Societies*, 155–77, esp. 159–60; Goodman, Introduction, 18.
69. *Chron. Wyntoun* (Laing), iii, 32; *Froissart* (Johnes), ii, 372.
70. Goodman, Introduction, 16; *The Westminster Chronicle 1381–1394*, edd. L. C. Hector and B. Harvey (Oxford, 1982), 344–5.
71. On 27 July 1388 the earl of Douglas was at Edybredschelis near Selkirk with his brother-in-law, Sir Malcolm Drummond, Sir John Swinton, John Towers, Murdoch of Glassary and Henry Weddall: *Melrose Liber*, ii, 465–6; *Chron. Wyntoun* (Laing), iii, 34–9; *Froissart* (Johnes), ii, 361–72, esp. 369–71.
72. *Froissart* (Johnes), ii, 368.
73. *Chron. Wyntoun* (Laing), ii, 369–70.
74. *Ibid.*, iii, 29–30.
75. *Ibid.*, iii, 32–4.
76. *Ibid.*, iii, 34.
77. *Chron. Bower* (Goodall), ii, 405.
78. *Chron. Wyntoun* (Laing), iii, 34.
79. *Ibid.*, iii, 36.
80. *Ibid.*, iii, 35–6.
81. *Froissart* (Johnes), ii, 363.
82. *Chron. Wyntoun* (Laing), iii, 35.
83. *Ibid.*, iii, 37–8.
84. *Ibid.*, iii, 39.
85. *Ibid.*, iii, 30.
86. A. M. McKim, 'James Douglas and Barbour's ideal of Knighthood', in *Forum for Modern Language Studies*, xvii, (1981), 176–7.
87. *Froissart* (Johnes), ii, 372.
88. *Ibid.*, ii, 376.
89. *Chron. Wyntoun*, iii, 45.
90. *Ibid.*, iii, 42.
91. *Ibid.*
92. *Froissart* (Johnes), ii, 376.
93. *Charters of the Friars Preachers of Ayr* (Ayr and Wigtown Archaeological Association, 1881), 27–8.

94. *Froissart* (Johnes), ii, 373–4.

95. SRO RH6/190; *APS*, i, 555.

96. NRAS Lauderdale Muniments, Writs and Titles of Lauder 1359–1402, Deed Box C136/44/36.

97. *Liber S. Marie de Calchou* (Bannatyne Club, 1846), ii, 408.

98. SRO RH6/197.

99. NRAS, no. 885, Glamis Charters, Box 1.

100. *Mort. Reg.*, ii, 161–2.

101. *Mort. Reg.*, 89–91; *Chron. Fordun*, i, 370, and note 12.

102. *APS*, i, 555–6.

103. *Chron. Bower* (Goodall), ii, 414.

104. At first Richard II had intended to respond immediately to the reverse at Otterburn with a campaign against the Scots in the autumn of 1388, but a great council at Northampton on 20 August deferred the expedition to the summer of 1389. An English parliament of January 1389 laid out plans for Richard personally to head an invasion of Scotland in August 1389. The Scots, therefore, had every reason to suspect that their kingdom would need a vigorous war leader in 1389: *Foedera*, vii, 594; *Westminster*, 350–1, 375–9.

6

Brothers Divided: The Guardianship of the Earl of Fife and Menteith, 1388–93

When Robert, earl of Fife and Menteith, became guardian of the kingdom in December 1388, he was faced by a three-headed political crisis which had, with no little help from Fife himself, overwhelmed the political skills of the earl of Carrick. Firstly, the Scottish kingdom was at war, facing a formidable military threat from England, where Richard II had committed himself to an invasion of Scotland in order to expunge the humiliation of the defeat at Otterburn and to punish the Scots for their invasions of northern England during 1388.[1] Fife's new task of organising the defence of the realm was complicated by the political rivalries which had split the nobility of southern Scotland in the wake of the death of James, 2nd earl of Douglas. In December 1388 the title of earl of Douglas and possession of the castles and lordships of the Douglas inheritance were a matter of open dispute between Archibald Douglas, lord of Galloway, and a disparate collection of kinsmen and adherents of the 2nd earl clustered around the figure of Sir Malcolm Drummond, the dead earl's brother-in-law. The third area of political crisis was the north of Scotland, where the activities of Fife's brother, Alexander, earl of Buchan, had been the subject of long-standing complaint.

These interrelated problems seemed likely to prove an insurmountable hurdle to a man exercising authority under severe restrictions, and whose right and ability to rule were likely to be constantly questioned by supporters of his brother Carrick. Moreover, Fife's political authority was further weakened by the inevitability of Robert II's death and the accession of Carrick to the throne. Charters dealing with the alienation of royal lands or revenues still required the express consent of Carrick as heir to the throne, so that Fife's exercise of power held out no long-term guarantees to the beneficiaries of his patronage and policies. Remarkably, through a combination of immense personal energy, propaganda, and political astuteness, Fife would maintain his political hold on the kingdom, in various forms and despite many challenges, for the next thirty-two years.

The physical campaign against Buchan's interests in the north could hardly begin until Fife had achieved some form of resolution of the dispute over the Douglas inheritance and had ensured that the Scottish kingdom would be adequately defended against English invasion. The various political dogfights over the vast Douglas inheritance remained largely unresolved at the start of Fife's guardianship in December 1388, and the new guardian himself appears to have made no immediate or dramatic intervention in the dispute on his appointment. But over the winter of 1388/9 a clear community of interest began to develop between Fife, Archibald Douglas, lord of Galloway, and Sir James Douglas of Dalkeith. One dispute which involved Fife himself was brought to a speedy conclusion. As we have seen, in August 1388 letters were sent to Alan Lauder, the constable of Tantallon, ordering him to deliver the fortress into Fife's custody. Lauder evidently ignored these instructions, and on 7 January 1389 further royal letters had to be sent to the recalcitrant constable.[112] Robert II's renewed appeal, no doubt made more compelling by Fife's promotion to the guardianship, brought an almost immediate response. On 20 January Fife and Margaret, countess of Mar, came to an agreement at Tantallon by which Fife guaranteed that the countess would not be ejected from the castle while Fife, as superior of the barony of North Berwick, exercised the wardship, nor by 'any that sal enter that castel throch ws'. The countess had evidently feared that the guardian would seek to remove her and her men from the fortress, in which she had resided since 1379, in favour of one of the heirs of the 2nd earl.[3] Fife also promised to 'manteyn hir, hir men, hir landys and al hir possessons aganys ony that wald wrang thaim'.

The January agreement secured the countess and her household a temporary and non-heritable right of occupation, while allowing Fife access to, and use of, the strategically important castle. By 29 January Fife was in Tantallon issuing letters as governor of the kingdom in favour of Alan Lauder, the constable who had resisted his claims to the East Lothian fortress for the last five months of 1388, in a dispute between Lauder and Sir James Sandilands of Calder. Fife's transactions in Tantallon were witnessed by, amongst others, Sir Malcolm Drummond.[4] Drummond, the second earl of Douglas's brother-in-law, was the heir to the rights of possession enjoyed by earl James in the barony of North Berwick and he was certainly one of those who could have threatened Margaret Stewart's occupation of Tantallon. Drummond's presence suggests his grudging approval for the deal between Fife and countess Margaret which adversely affected his own claims to the East Lothian properties of the Douglas earls. Although Drummond had been associated with Alan Lauder and other adherents of countess

Margaret after Otterburn, Margaret's alliance with Fife marked the beginning of a breakdown in her relationship with Sir Malcolm, a process which greatly undermined Drummond's chances of success in the wider dispute over the Douglas inheritance.[5] Fife's alliance with countess Margaret, the political focus for a powerful group of East Lothian Douglas adherents, and her men, effectively ended their involvement in Drummond's larger conflict with Archibald, lord of Galloway, and Sir James Douglas of Dalkeith.

As 1389 progressed, Fife's political relationship with Margaret Stewart and her adherents grew closer, while Drummond's fortunes experienced a rapid nose-dive. When the 2nd earl of Douglas's affinity made its final stand in the summer of 1389, Fife's political astuteness ensured that John Sinclair of Herdmanston, countess Margaret's half-brother, the man who had carried the 2nd earl's banner to victory at Otterburn, and the rest of Douglas's East Lothian affinity would not be supporting their former allies.

Fife's temporary control of Tantallon also gave the new guardian, for the first time, an independent and secure base south of the Forth rivalling Carrick's castle in Edinburgh, from which he could co-ordinate, and be seen to be personally leading, the defence of the realm. East Lothian had probably been subject to a *chevauchée* by English forces in December 1388; any further attacks in 1389 would be met head-on by the new guardian.[6] Fife was a politician of no little skill and experience, and he knew that his guardianship would stand or fall on his success in leading the nation in arms; the anonymous pro-Fife chronicler was probably already at work producing propaganda which placed the earl at the heart of the Scottish war effort of the 1380s, and portrayed him as a natural and established leader of the 'young' chivalry of southern Scotland.[7] But men were not won over by propaganda alone, and for the preservation of his political authority within Scotland, for the fulfilment of his personal ambitions, and, in the last analysis, for the defence of the realm, the guardian would have to be seen to command the Scottish war effort from the front during 1389.

Between the end of January and a general council of April 1389, the claims of Archibald Douglas, lord of Galloway, to the title and entailed estates of the late earl of Douglas seem to have gained the support of Fife. There were a number of reasons why Fife would have found Archibald's claims more attractive than those of Sir Malcolm Drummond or any other heirs by blood to the 2nd earl. Firstly, Drummond was politically aligned with Fife's brother and rival, Carrick, while Archibald Douglas's support in November/December 1388 had probably been crucial in allowing Fife to displace his brother as guardian. If the anonymous chronicle can be relied upon, Fife and Sir Archibald had a long record of military and political co-operation during the 1380s.[8] Moreover, and especially important in the context of 1389, Sir Archibald was not only the son of Bruce's companion and Barbour's archetypal loyal knight, the 'Good Sir James', but he had also built his own intimidating reputation as a war leader, acknowledged even by Froissart, which was unequalled by any of the other contenders for the Douglas inheritance.[9] The reputation was backed up by Douglas's personal command of a formidable affinity from the south-west which could have, and perhaps already had, delivered effective control of many of the contested lordships and estates to the lord of Galloway. In terms of the guardian's wider remit of defending the realm, Archibald Douglas's personal prestige and very real military power made him a much more attractive ally than Drummond and the shattered fragments of the 2nd earl's affinity. If the defence of the Scottish kingdom was the official *raison d'être* of the Fife guardianship, then it was also the mission and justification of the earls and earldom of Douglas.

The eclipse of Sir Malcolm Drummond's ambitions was illustrated at the very start of the April general council, when, on 2 April, letters of sasine which had been issued in Drummond's favour for Selkirk forest were declared null and void.[10] On 7 April the council ratified an entail of 29 May 1342 by which the bulk of the Douglas estates were to descend to the lord of Galloway, declaring that Sir Archibald was legally infeft in the estates named in the entail and that any letters of sasine issued in violation of the entail were to be of no avail. The entail covered the lands of Douglasdale (from which the earl took his title), Carmichael, the forest of Selkirk, Lauderdale, Bedrule, Eskdale, Stable Gordon, Buittle in Galloway and the ferme of Rutherglen.[11] Three days after the confirmation of the charter of entail, on 10 April, Archibald Douglas first appears as earl of Douglas, eight months after the death of the previous earl.[12]

Archibald's triumph in the general council was reflected in changes in the political composition of the King's privy council. The witnesses to the charter in which Archibald first appeared as earl included two men, Matthew Glendinning, bishop of Glasgow, and Sir James Douglas of Dalkeith, who had not previously been regular witnesses to the king's great seal charters. Glendinning's familial connections and early ecclesiastical career lay in the western and middle Marches, and the bishop had a record of crown service in Anglo-Scottish diplomacy.[13] The new prominence of Sir James Douglas of Dalkeith was a more worrying development for Sir Malcolm Drummond. Sir James was the nephew of Sir William Douglas, the knight of Liddesdale, who had obtained possession of Liddesdale in February 1342 in a series of dubious deals with Robert the Steward, which saw control of the earldom of Atholl transferred to the Steward. In August 1353 the knight of Liddesdale had been ambushed and killed by his godson, William Douglas (later 1st earl).[14] After Sir William's death the lordship of Liddesdale was confirmed in the possession of William Douglas, the future 1st earl, in a royal grant of 12 February 1354.[15] The title 'lord of Liddesdale' was used by both the 1st and 2nd earls, with James being styled lord of Liddesdale before he succeeded to the earldom in 1384.[16] After the 2nd earl's death in 1388, Douglas of Dalkeith revived his claims to the unentailed Liddesdale lordship as heir to his uncle, the one-time knight of Liddesdale. The knight of Liddesdale's only daughter and heir, Mary Douglas, had died in 1367 without issue, and Douglas of Dalkeith had already been declared as her heir in the lands of Preston and Buittle in Galloway.[17] In 1388/9 it seems that James Douglas of Dalkeith received, at first, a grant of the relief due to the crown from Liddesdale, and then letters of sasine delivering possession of the lordship as the result of an inquiry presided over by the earl of Fife, which discussed the recognition of Liddesdale and other lands.[18]

Fife had thus come down in favour of Douglas of Dalkeith's claims to be the knight of Liddesdale's heir in the great border lordship. Sir James set out to secure the political allegiance of his new tenants in Liddesdale against rival claimants to the lordship through indentures and bonds of service.[19] His occupation of Liddesdale undoubtedly had the support of the new earl of Douglas, who had no rival claim to the unentailed lordship and, more importantly, had a long and close personal association with Douglas of Dalkeith.[20] Besides Liddesdale, it seems that Drummond was also being challenged over possession of the sheriffship of Roxburgh, with the general council deciding that a grant previously made to Drummond of the sheriffship could be annulled and the office granted to someone else.[21]

In short, the general council of April 1389 saw the complete territorial and political triumph of the lord of Galloway and Douglas of Dalkeith in the struggle over the Douglas inheritance.

Another notable feature of the council was the strengthening of the position of Margaret Stewart, countess of Mar and Angus, and her illegitimate son George, the bastard son of William, 1st earl of Douglas. Margaret had already secured an understanding with Fife over her occupation of Tantallon and North Berwick in January. On 8 April, at the council in Edinburgh, Margaret issued a charter 'with the deliberation of her council' in favour of Sir Richard Comyn, a man with strong links to the guardian. If Margaret's council is indicated by the men witnessing this timely concession to a Fife adherent, then it included her Sinclair half-brothers, Sir John (of Herdmanston), Sir James and Sir Walter, and Sir William Borthwick.[22] On the following day, in the general council, the countess resigned the earldom of Angus and the lordship of Abernethy in Perthshire and Bunkle in Berwickshire in favour of her illegitimate son George and his heirs, whom failing Elizabeth Stewart, the countess's sister, and any heirs produced by her marriage to Sir Alexander Hamilton.[23] The grant received Robert II's confirmation on 10 April, in a charter witnessed by the earl of March.

On the same day Robert II confirmed a grant by the countess to her sister and her husband of Innerwick, and lands in Abernethy, with an entail in favour of George Douglas.[24] The grant was clearly designed to compensate Alexander Hamilton and his wife for their abandonment of claims to half the Angus inheritance. The countess's original undated and unplaced charter is significant, because it was witnessed by Fife, the Dunbar earls of March and Moray, the countess's Sinclair kinsmen, Alan Lauder, the constable of Tantallon, and Henry Weddale.[25] It would seem that Fife had engineered an agreement with the countess and her adherents, probably in Tantallon itself, between January and April 1389, which would secure her bastard son, earl James's brother, as earl of Angus. The presence of the Dunbar earls would seem to indicate that they were offering their support to the countess of Angus and the rump of the Douglas affinity retained in her service. For political and military reasons Fife could not afford to alienate either Margaret Stewart's men or the Dunbar earls, of whose political allegiance he was by no means assured. The concessions over Angus no doubt ensured the acquiesence of this powerful combination of Lothian and Berwickshire noblemen to the wider settlement in favour of Archibald, lord of Galloway.

The general council thus dealt a crushing blow to the claims of Sir Malcolm Drummond as heir, through his wife, to the great Douglas estates in the south of Scotland although, in reality, Drummond's political defeat had been secured long before the council met. Sir Malcolm evidently knew what to expect from the assembly and declined to attend, claiming that he would not do so because the guardian Fife had failed to provide him with letters guaranteeing his physical safety. Drummond's reluctance to appear in Edinburgh without a safe conduct suggests a deep mistrust of the guardian, and an overwhelming fear of Archibald the Grim and James Douglas of Dalkeith, who seem to have been engaged in a number of physical confrontations with Drummond and his allies during 1389.[26] The bulk of the Douglas inheritance was to go to Archibald the Grim as the new earl of Douglas, with the unentailed lordship of Liddesdale and perhaps also the sheriffship of Roxburgh passing to Archibald's ally Douglas of Dalkeith, who became a member of the king's council in April 1389. The unentailed lands of the barony of North Berwick and the castle of

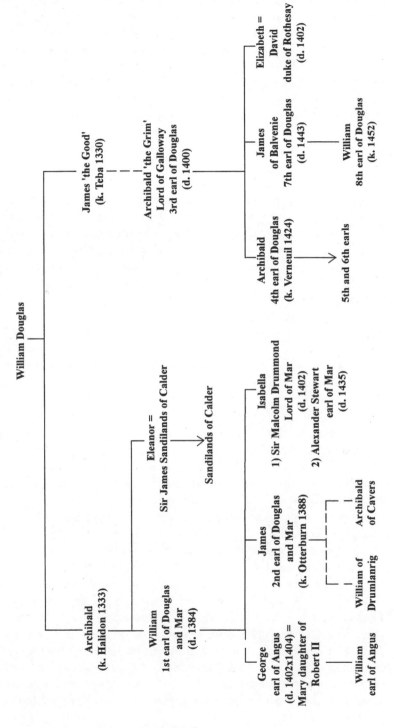

4) THE DOUGLAS INHERITANCE

Tantallon were already indefinitely in the hands of Margaret Stewart, the countess of Angus, who headed the only part of the old Douglas affinity to emerge from the wreckage of the 2nd earl's lordship in 1388–9 with their fortunes secured, if not enhanced. The settlement engineered by Fife in the winter of 1388/9 was a dazzling example of *realpolitik*. The earldoms of Douglas and Angus were secured in the hands of bastards whose affinities were politically and militarily loyal or indispensable to the guardian, both for the preservation of his personal authority within Scotland and in his wider task of defending the realm.

The April general council took place against a background of increasing military activity on the Anglo-Scottish border. Richard II's determination to launch a massive reprisal against the Scots for the indignities inflicted on the English in 1388 was apparently unabated. A great council at Westminster on 20 January decided that the king himself would invade Scotland on 1 August 1389.[27] The Scots themselves, however, were also keen to renew hostilities. In February or March 1389, Scottish forces raided the English west March.[28] The man behind the Scottish raid in the west was probably Archibald the Grim, who thereby gave a timely demonstration of his willingness and ability to lead the Scottish war effort during 1389. In retaliation Lord Beaumont, one of the English wardens of the west March, raided into Scotland apparently as far as Falkirk, although this may be a misrendering of 'Hawick'. The unusual choice of route for this raid may have been intended to threaten the interests of the new guardian around Stirling.[29] On 25 June serious hostilities recommenced with an English invasion of the Scottish east March, headed by Thomas Mowbray, earl of Nottingham, and Ralph, lord Neville.[30] The English force was reduced in size and effectiveness by disputes between various northern noblemen, and was eventually forced to retreat after encountering a much larger Scottish army under the personal command — so the anonymous chronicler triumphantly informs us — of Fife and the new earl of Douglas. At least some elements of the Scottish force bypassed Nottingham's army, crossed the border on 29 June, and raided through Northumberland to Tynemouth.[31]

The English expedition of June 1389 was undoubtedly encouraged by the continued political discord within Scotland. The disaffected members of the old Douglas affinity, who had been so comprehensively defeated by Fife and Archibald the Grim in April 1389, had evidently been in contact with the English court and its representatives for some time. On 19 June 1389, only a week before Nottingham's invasion, Richard II issued safe conducts in favour of Sir Malcolm Drummond, Sir James Sandilands, Sir John and William Haliburton, and their retinues to a combined total of 140 men. More strikingly, on the same day, the English king took under his protection, for half a year, the estates of Drummond and his associates. The lands and lordships assigned over by Drummond to Richard II's protection included his own Perthshire estates but also, and more importantly, all the lordships Drummond claimed as heir to the 2nd earl of Douglas and which were actually in the possession of Archibald, 3rd earl of Douglas, James Douglas of Dalkeith, and Margaret Stewart, countess of Angus.[32] Having lost the struggle within Scotland, Drummond and his allies evidently hoped to press their claims with the support of the English king.[33] If Drummond was anticipating that Nottingham's expedition of June 1389, combined with Richard II's promised August campaign, would deliver possession of at least some of the contested Douglas lordships to himself and his associates, under the English king's protection, he was to be sorely disappointed. Not only was Nottingham's expedition successfully resisted by Fife and the new earl of Douglas, but on 18 June 1389, the day before Drummond received his safe conduct and letters of protection, a three-year truce was concluded between England and France. Despite the protests of the English negotiators, the Scots were to be offered the option of inclusion in the truce.[34]

It was thus, ironically enough, the collapse of English plans for military intervention in the south of Scotland which delivered the final political blow to the old Douglas affinity in 1389.

Fife and Archibald, earl of Douglas, on the other hand, were likely to see considerable political benefits, both for themselves and the kingdom, in accepting inclusion in the truce. For Fife, peace in the south would free him to tackle the political problems in his own area of interest and influence north of the Forth. For Archibald the Grim a truce would remove the possibility of English intervention in support of rival claimants to the title and estates of the earldom of Douglas, and allow Archibald to consolidate his political hold on his new earldom. More generally, the two men could argue that, regardless of their remarkable run of military success in 1388–9, the Scots could hardly hope to reject the truce and conduct a sustained military campaign over three years alone and unaided against the might of the English kingdom.

Despite these considerations, at least one English chronicle suggests that there was some opposition within Scotland to the settlement of the truce from those who were keen to participate in plundering raids on the north of England.[35] The account provided by the anonymous Scottish chronicler of the truce negotiations which ensued with French envoys and representatives of the English crown in July/August 1389 may have been intended to counter popular criticism that the Fife regime had entered a truce which secured no material gains for the Scottish kingdom, at a time when the Scots were still enjoying a period of military ascendancy.[36] The English and French envoys were received by Robert II in Dunfermline, where the king was attended by all the major figures in the recent Scottish war effort, including George, earl of March, and the recently released James Lindsay of Crawford.[37] The anonymous chronicle presented Robert II's acceptance of inclusion in the truce as a decision which the king made largely to answer the entreaties of the English and French envoys, and generally portrayed the whole affair as a diplomatic triumph for the Scottish king and kingdom. If there was a political danger for Fife and Archibald Douglas in appearing too eager to conclude a truce which did not secure any of the Scots' original war aims of 1388, then the anonymous chronicler's account of the truce negotiations within Scotland at least partly absolved the two men of responsibility for the decision by emphasising Robert II's role.[38]

By September 1389 peace of a sort had been secured on the Anglo-Scottish border, and Fife was free to turn his attention elsewhere. Fife's own interests, and those of the men who had supported or acquiesced in the creation of the Fife guardianship, demanded an effective political/military intervention in the north. The hour of reckoning had finally arrived for the 'Wolf of Badenoch', Alexander Stewart, earl of Buchan.

FIFE IN THE NORTH: LEADER OF THE PACK

The first indication of the new political agenda being pursued by Fife in the north came in late 1388. On 11 December, within ten days of his appointment as guardian, Fife removed his brother Alexander Stewart, earl of Buchan, from the office of justiciar north of the Forth. In a frank condemnation of Buchan's record, it was noted that he had been 'useless to the community' in the exercise of the office of justiciary.[39] The loss of the justiciarship was simply the opening shot of a formidable co-ordinated assault against Alexander's position as the chief representative of royal power in northern Perthshire and the central and northern Highlands, and as a major landowner and officeholder in the north.

The political restraints under which Fife was operating in late 1388 are, however, indicated by his treatment of the justiciary after Buchan's enforced removal from the office. There was, apparently, no immediate attempt to appoint a successor to Buchan as justiciar, although Fife clearly favoured his own son, Murdoch, for the office. Fife was evidently not confident enough in his political authority to provoke open opposition by promoting Murdoch's claims in December 1388. Sir David Lindsay of Glen Esk, for example, whose political support Fife was courting late in 1388, appears to have lodged a claim to the office on the basis of his father's term as justiciar before 1382.[40] In these circumstances Murdoch Stewart's appointment to the justiciarship was delayed until 2 April 1389, when it was formalised in the general council which also saw the resolution of the dispute over the earldom of Douglas. In the council of April 1389 the office of justiciar north of the Forth, which had apparently lain vacant since the previous December, was granted to Fife's son Murdoch Stewart for one year.[41] Some of the members of the general council seem to have been concerned that Murdoch lacked the territorial and political power to exercise the office effectively, and it was stipulated that his father, Fife, was to assist his son in the execution of the office.

This was the prelude to a relentless attack by Fife and his son on the political and territorial interests of Buchan and his family and allies in Highland Perthshire. By early 1390 Murdoch was using the title Lord of the Appin of Dull.[42] The lordship of the Appin of Dull covered much of the western half of the earldom of Atholl, and encompassed Strath Tay, Fortingall and Glen Lyon. Murdoch's territorial and jurisdictional expansion into northern Perthshire in 1389 directly supplanted his uncle, the earl of Buchan, who had probably acted as royal justiciar in the Appin of Dull since 1372, and who had clearly been the dominant political and territorial lord in the area after 1371.[43] The promotion of Murdoch as lord of the Appin of Dull roughly coincided with the resignation by Isabella, countess of Fife, of her claims to the barony of Strathord with the lands of Strath Braan, Discher and Toyer (that is, the north and south sides of Loch Tay) and the isle of Loch Tay, in free regality, in favour of Murdoch's father, Fife, on 12 August 1389 at Dunfermline.[44] Isabella's resignation and the opening of Fife's assault on Buchan's interests in Perthshire were thus clearly tied to the entry of the Scots to the three-year Anglo-French truce, a decision finalised at Dunfermline in early August 1389.

At around the same time Fife obtained possession of another lordship in northern Perthshire through a grant of the lands of Fortingall.[45] Isabella's resignation and the acquisition of Fortingall meant that Fife and his son Murdoch sought to exercise control over a bloc of territory in Atholl and northern Perthshire stretching north and east from the barony of Glen Dochart which Fife had had in his possession since 1374. Much of this area, including Fortingall, seems to have been at the centre of a long-running dispute involving Fife, Buchan, and the Clann Donnchaidh or Robertsons of Atholl. Fife's new claims to the Perthshire lands of Duncan, 10th earl of Fife, many of which seem to have been occupied by the Clann Donnchaidh for the previous forty years, thus directly threatened the position of the Clan in Fortingall, Strath Braan and Loch Tay, where Fife became the new feudal superior.[46]

Alexander earl of Buchan's position in northern Perthshire had been greatly enhanced around 1379 by a substantial resignation of lands in the southern part of Strath Tummel and Garth and Bolfracks in his favour by a Janet Menzies.[47] The identity of this Janet Menzies is uncertain, but she was at the centre of a web of conflicting territorial claims to estates in northern Perthshire which probably underlay the political tension between Fife and his brother Buchan.[48]

Fife's personal territorial ambitions in Perthshire and the south-western and central Highlands were clearly considerable; and they were further reflected in Fife's agreement with Duncan, earl of Lennox, in February 1392 by which Fife's son Murdoch was to marry Duncan's eldest daughter and become heir to the earldom of Lennox.[49] The agreement meant that Robert's heir would personally control a huge contiguous lordship embracing the earldoms of Lennox and Menteith, Glen Dochart, Loch Tay, Fortingall, Strath Tay, Strath Braan and Strathord.

Fife's machinations against Alexander Stewart in Perthshire and beyond were supported, late in 1389, by physical campaigning on the part of Robert and his allies. Shortly after the resignations made by the countess of Fife in Dunfermline in August 1389, the guardian headed north accompanied by a powerful collection of his own retainers from Fife. Robert II, in contrast, headed west to the Stewartry lands in Ayrshire and the islands of the Firth of Clyde. By 27 October 1389, Fife, as guardian of the kingdom, was in Inverness arbitrating a dispute between John Dunbar, earl of Moray, and Alexander Bur, bishop of Moray. Fife's council on this occasion included John Swinton, the newly established lord of Mar, Sir David Lindsay of Glen Esk and his brother Alexander, and a mix of local lairds and the guardian's own adherents from Fife, notably Alan Erskine, sheriff of Fife, Sir John Hay, Sir George Leslie, lord of Rothes, Thomas Sibbald of Balgonie, Robert Livingstone, John Lindsay of Wauchope, John Ramornie, Walter Tulloch and William Chalmers of Aberdeen.[50] The bishop of Moray, as we have seen, had a long-running dispute with Alexander Stewart over the latter's imposition of caterans on church lands in Badenoch and Strathspey. Fife's arbitration of the dispute between the bishop and earl of Moray was probably being encouraged as a means of co-ordinating action against Buchan. In the following February, when the guardian was once again in Inverness, the bishop completed an indenture with the earl of Moray's son, Thomas Dunbar, sheriff of Inverness, in which the bishop complained of the devastation of the church's lands and gave them over to Thomas's protection. Dunbar was especially enjoined to defend the bishop's lands against 'all malefactors and caterans'.[51] This was a clear invitation for the earl of

Moray and his son to take on Buchan and his adherents in their strongholds of Badenoch and Strathspey.

Fife's visit to Inverness in October/November 1389 also allowed other moves to be made against Buchan. On 2 November 1389, just five days after the Moray arbitration, Alexander, bishop of Moray, and Alexander Kylquhous, bishop of Ross, presided over the apparent settlement of a marital dispute between Alexander Stewart and his wife, Euphemia, countess of Ross. The countess had complained that her marriage to the earl was a sham, and that Alexander was cohabiting with one Mairead, daughter of Eachann. The earl promised to return to Euphemia as her husband, to restore her property, and to cease making threats and employing his adherents against her.[52] Euphemia's boldness in initiating proceedings against Alexander in 1389 was no doubt derived from the fact that the new guardian of the kingdom was present in Inverness and was actively looking for ways to undercut Buchan's authority in the region. The guardian himself was attended by men who were committed to the defence of the rights of Euphemia and her son, Alexander Leslie, the heir to the earldom of Ross, in Ross. Fife's 'council' in Inverness on 27 October had included Alexander Leslie's cousin and uncle, Sir David Lindsay of Glen Esk, and George Leslie, lord of Rothes.[53] It is doubtful whether Euphemia and her son's kinsmen were looking for a genuine personal reconciliation between the countess and Buchan. If Euphemia's action resulted in a divorce, then Buchan's rights in the vast Ross inheritance would be annulled, and the reconstituted Lindsay/Leslie affinity would be able to take action to recover the territorial and political power lost to them in 1382. It was no accident that Euphemia and her son Alexander Leslie were to be closely associated with Fife during the remainder of his guardianship.

The opening years of the Fife guardianship thus saw a spectacular collapse in the position of the earl of Buchan. Buchan was removed from the justiciarship north of the Forth and his northern lieutenancy, while his territorial and political interests in Perthshire, the Appin of Dull and the earldom of Ross came under concerted attack. It was a collapse largely engineered by the new guardian and his son as they strove to advance their own territorial interests and those of their kinsmen and allies.

Within two months of Fife's tour of the north, in late January 1390, Robert II himself was to be found on a circuit of the north–east. The king's itinerary was probably meant to bolster the new political settlement in the north, but it may also have hastened the monarch's death. At the end of March Robert II returned to the Stewartry, and on 19 April he died in the castle of his Stewart ancestors at Dundonald.[54]

Robert II's demise in the modest but impressive castle of Dundonald, 'in his cuntré', may seem to symbolise what most historians have regarded as a kingship of limited ambition, achievement, energy and political authority. In personal terms the judgement is unduly harsh, for it seems unlikely that the most successful, ambitious and ruthless Scottish magnate of the 1340s and 1350s suddenly awoke on 23 February 1371 as a man unable to deal with the political hurly-burly of the Scottish kingdom. While later chroniclers and historians saw Robert II's age at the time of his accession as one of the key factors in explaining the king's inability to govern effectively, it seems that a much more important element was the political legacy of the last ten years of David II's reign, during which David created a royal establishment, overwhelmingly centred in Lothian, Angus and the north-east of Scotland, which regarded Robert II with fear and suspicion. It was this situation which set real limits on Robert II's authority in key areas of the kingdom after 1371. However, Robert II's response to opposition in the early years of his reign was largely successful, as hostile magnate affinities were mollified by marriage alliances into the new royal house and the granting away of considerable royal patronage. The grants must have seemed a small price to pay for the consolidation of the Stewarts' claim to be the kingdom's new royal dynasty. Alongside this process the Stewarts' political stranglehold on the kingdom was tightened by the promotion of the king's sons as regional magnates. It is doubtful whether Robert II or any of his contemporaries saw the dreadful portents of future political disaster which fifteenth-century chroniclers identified so easily in the growing influence of the royal offspring. Instead, the lieutenancies of Carrick in the south, and Buchan in the north, must have appeared as a natural means by which Robert II could extend the political reach of the royal dynasty into areas outwith the king's own territorial and political heartland in Perthshire and the Stewartry.

In the end, the Buchan lieutenancy was to prove the source of many of the most serious political problems of Robert's reign. The repeated and largely unanswered complaints to the king's council about Buchan's imposition of caterans on secular and ecclesiastical estates seem to have received a less than sympathetic audience from a monarch well versed in the realities of political power in the central Highlands.[55]

The ousting of Robert II from the exercise of most of the functions of kingship by his son Carrick in 1384 was to some extent based on discontent over Buchan's exercise of lordship in the north, but the core of Carrick's political support lay in Scotland south of the Forth, an area where Robert II had never exercised personal political influence outside the Stewartry. The propaganda employed by Carrick and the southern aristocracy to justify their move against Robert II added further weight to the traditional view of the aged king as an inadequate monarch.

Froissart's influential picture of a king who spent a great deal of his time in 'la sauvage Escose' and who was not personally involved in border warfare is, essentially, correct, but this situation was not the product of the king's increasing failure to exert control over, or give military leadership to, the aristocracy involved in border warfare, but rather the result of Robert II's own very early and deliberate decision to use his son Carrick to discharge most of the functions of royal government in the south.

Ironically, Robert II's success in laying the foundations of a strong royal dynasty was further obscured by the political disasters which overwhelmed his son and heir Carrick in 1388, and which brought the king a modest recovery of his personal political influence. If the 2nd earl of Douglas had emerged unscathed from the Otterburn campaign of 1388, then there is little reason to doubt that there would have been no Fife guardianship, and that John earl of Carrick's accession to the throne in 1390 would have produced a kingship with an unchallengeable political hold on the south of Scotland. The reality of Carrick's exercise of power in Scotland in the wake of Robert II's death would be somewhat less impressive.

ROBERT JOHN FARANYEAR: THE ACCESSION OF ROBERT III

Robert II's demise raised a host of practical and theoretical political problems. The most obvious difficulty facing the king's eldest son and designated heir, John, earl of Carrick, was that he had already been declared incapable of governing the kingdom as a royal lieutenant in December 1388. Since that date, Carrick's younger brother, Fife, had effectively run the kingdom. However, the death of Robert II raised rather more political dangers for Fife, whose position as guardian of the kingdom for his father had obviously terminated on the king's death.[56] In 1390 Fife and his allies faced the unattractive prospect of Carrick, the man they had ousted from power in 1388, attaining and exercising unrestricted royal authority. Despite Carrick's removal from the lieutenancy in 1388 there was no suggestion that he had thereby surrendered his position as heir apparent, and he continued to confirm alienations of crown land between 1388 and 1390. Moreover, the terms of Fife's appointment as guardian in 1388 had included specific provision for Carrick's reclamation of the office if a general council decided that he had recovered the ability to govern.[57] If Carrick, politically strengthened by his undeniable status as heir to the deceased Robert II, could gather enough support to refuse any renewal of Fife's guardianship and to recover full jurisdiction within his kingdom, then the Fife-inspired settlements of 1388–90, in both the north and south, would be seriously threatened. Thus, Fife and Archibald, earl of Douglas, and their political associates needed to obtain some guarantee of their hold on royal policy and power before Carrick succeeded to the throne.

The conflicting ambitions and hopes of Fife and Carrick no doubt contributed to the confused political situation in the spring and summer of 1390, which saw a remarkable four-month gap between Robert II's death and Carrick's coronation as Robert III on 14 August 1390. Bower's description of Robert III's coronation is interesting:

> 'Once the body of . . . King Robert II had been placed in its tomb and the kingdom had been entrusted to the guardianship of his son (that is Robert his second son), John, earl of Carrick, the first born son of the dead king was crowned at Scone in the royal manner . . . He was thereafter with the consent of the estates known as King Robert III.'[58]

The crucial point in Bower's description is that Robert, earl of Fife's position as guardian was confirmed before Carrick's coronation. It seems unlikely, in fact, that all these events occurred as late as August 1390. Certainly, Carrick appears to have taken the name Robert III by 20 May 1390, when he issued a privy seal letter in favour of his illegitimate son John Stewart of Auchingowan at Linlithgow.[59] The preservation of the Fife guardianship may well have been decided by a council meeting at Linlithgow shortly before the issuing of this letter.

The continuation of the Fife guardianship for a 53-year-old king who was patently not senile, during a period of truce between England and Scotland, was no doubt hard to justify. The anonymous chronicle, perhaps a product of late 1390 or early 1391, reflected Fife-inspired propaganda which had probably been used during 1390. The thrust of the chronicle emphasised the leadership qualities of Fife as commander of the nation in arms, in co-operation with Archibald, earl of Douglas, in the period 1384–8, and as warden of the kingdom after 1388. After describing Robert III's coronation, the anonymous chronicler expresses the pious hope that the new king would

> . . govern and wphald his land
> In na ware state, na he it fand;
> . . . .
> For qwhen his fadyr endyt wes,
> Off Scotland wes na fute off land
> Owte off Scottis mennys hand[60]

The picture of Robert III inheriting a political legacy of sound government and Scottish success in war and diplomacy from his father's reign, chiefly secured by the effort and skill of the earl of Fife, amounted to a powerful justification for the preservation of the Fife guardianship.

One major figure who would have been bitterly opposed to any limitation on the new king's power through the continuation of Fife's guardianship was Alexander Stewart, earl of Buchan. Alexander may well have anticipated the reversal of at least some of the policies pursued by the Fife regime in 1388–90, particularly as Carrick's lieutenancy in 1384–88 had seen Buchan attain the height of his territorial and jurisdictional power. If, as seems to have been the case, Fife's guardianship was confirmed in May 1390, this would have represented a crushing blow to Buchan's hopes of rescuing his pre-eminent role in the political affairs of the kingdom north of the Forth. It was at the end of May that Buchan began to make his own rather more direct contribution to the constitutional debate with a devastating attack on the burgh of Forres while, shortly afterwards, on 17 June, Elgin and its cathedral were also given to the flames. The attacks into Moray by Buchan and his adherents, identified by Wyntoun as 'wyld, wikkit, heland men', played an important part in securing the earl's ferocious and unenviable historical reputation and his by-name the Wolf of Badenoch.[61]

The attacks were spurred by two factors. Firstly, on the local level, there was the spectacularly ill-timed decision of John Dunbar, earl of Moray, and David Lindsay, lord of Glen Esk, to attend a lavish tournament at the court of Richard II. Moray had been in Elgin on 1 May 1390, alongside the bishop of Moray, but had journeyed to London by 30 May.[62] Both Moray and Glen Esk, key figures in Fife's undermining of the Wolf in 1388–1390, were in England when the great storm which had been building in Badenoch broke upon the Moray coastal plain. The fact that both men thought it appropriate to leave Scotland in May 1390 is perhaps another indication that Fife's position as guardian, and by implication the political settlement he had established in the north, was confirmed some time in that month. One of the targets of the raids on Forres and Elgin was Alexander Bur, bishop of Moray, a cleric who had played an important role in the events of 1388–90. The bishop had encouraged the earl of Moray and his son to interfere in Buchan's heartland of Badenoch and Strathspey by giving over church lands in these areas to their protection. In addition, the bishop had played a crucial part in the early stages of Euphemia countess of Ross's attempts to obtain a divorce from Buchan.[63] When Dunbar, Lindsay and their retinues headed south in the summer of 1390, an opportunity undoubtedly existed for the Wolf to avenge himself on at least one of the men who had brought his great northern lordship to the edge of collapse.

To concentrate on these local factors, however, is probably to underestimate Buchan's aims and ambitions in 1390. The attacks on Elgin and Forres may, in fact, be only the best recorded (because the most politically damaging) elements in a much wider campaign launched by the Wolf in May/June 1390. In attacking Moray, Alexander was unleashing war against the Fife settlement of the north established in 1388–90, and directly challenging the newly reconstituted Fife guardianship. If Buchan could show that control of the north was impossible without his co-operation, then he might hope for political and territorial concessions from a new king who was not likely to view Fife's aggrandisement in the north with any great favour.

The seriousness of the crisis which enveloped the north of the kingdom in the summer of 1390 is shown in the fact that Robert II remained unburied, and Robert III uncrowned, until August. In the intervening months Robert III, surrounded by Fife and his allies, was based in Perthshire, probably engaged in punitive action against Buchan. On 16 July the king was in Perth, ratifying the terms of the Anglo-Scottish truce which had been established in the last year of his father's reign. The men named as conservators of the truce included the two Dunbar earls of March and Moray, the latter, no doubt, having sped north from London when he received the news that his earldom had been overrun by Buchan's caterans. On 23 July the king was at Logierait, the old administrative centre of the earldom of Atholl, apparently attempting to find some solution to the conflict in the north between his two younger brothers.[64] Alexander's attack on Elgin and Forres had resulted in his excommunication by Alexander Bur, bishop of Moray. Buchan's release from excommunication by Walter Trail, bishop of St Andrews, at Perth, in the presence of the king, Fife, William Keith, Malcolm Drummond, lord of Mar, and Thomas Erskine, on the provision that he agreed to provide some compensation to the bishop of Moray for the assault on Elgin and Forres, may have occurred shortly before or during Robert III's coronation ceremony at Scone.[65] Certainly by 13 August 1390 the political position had stabilised sufficiently for Robert II to be buried at Scone and, on the following day, for the earl of Carrick to receive his formal coronation as Robert III at the traditional inauguration site for Scottish kings.[66]

John earl of Carrick's change of name to Robert in 1390 was regarded, by the sixteenth century, as a means of avoiding comparison with the disastrous reigns of John Balliol and John II of France, whose political careers were distinguished by military and political failure in their struggles with the English crown.[67] The change also circumvented any practical difficulties over the numbering of a king John following on Balliol's brief reign. The historical perspective of the Bruce/Stewart dynasty heaped doubt on the legality of Balliol's original claim to the crown.[68] In these circumstances any attempt to style the new king John II would have given belated credence to the claims of John I's descendants to be Scotland's true royal dynasty. By 1390 the Balliols had disappeared as dynastic rivals to the Bruce/Stewart line, but in 1356 Edward Balliol, as pro-Bruce chronicles were keen to point out, had resigned all his claims to the Scottish crown in favour of Edward III.[69] The Scots would have been understandably reluctant to give the claims residing with the English royal family any greater authority.

The driving force behind the highly unusual decision that the heir to the throne should change his name before becoming king is uncertain. It may well have been Carrick himself, eager to bolster his tenuous political authority by associating his kingship with that of Robert I. In a situation where those supporting Fife's political control of the kingdom were making direct comparisons between the guardian's martial prowess and that of Robert I, Carrick would hardly wish to saddle himself with a name which, in a fourteenth-century Scottish context, was hung about with clouds of shame and military failure. The change of name may thus have been intended to make a number of points about the continuity of royal authority and the king's place and suitability as the new defender of the Scottish kingdom. As the anonymous chronicle remarked, 'the thryd Robert thus crownyd was', placing the new king in a seamless line derived from Robert I.[70]

The years after 1390 were to see a gradual, piecemeal, and painstaking recovery of political authority on the part of Robert III and his family. The long-term effect of this process was the slow undermining of support for the Fife guardianship. In the short term, however, Fife remained hugely influential in the formulation and execution of royal policies, especially in his own area of interest north of the Forth, so much so, indeed, that by the time of its official demise, in early 1393, the guardianship was no longer politically necessary even for those, notably Fife and Archibald, 3rd earl of Douglas, who had been most committed to its creation in 1388 and its continuation in 1390.

Once Fife had re-established his guardianship in 1390, the earl's policies and ambitions were bound to dominate Scotland north of the Forth. The violent attempt, in the summer of 1390, by Alexander, earl of Buchan, to shake loose Fife's control of the region, had been almost wholly unsuccessful. Fife retained his position as guardian of the kingdom and his son Murdoch continued to exercise the office of justiciar north of the Forth.[71] Buchan's demonstration of his local power and desperation may, however, have delayed Fife's plans to inconvenience the Wolf in areas such as Ross and Urquhart. Otherwise, the years after 1390 were distinguished by a relentless expansion of Fife's interests in the central and south-western Highlands.

Late in 1391 Fife embarked on the second phase of his assault on the position of Buchan and his allies in the region. On 12 October 1391 Thomas Chisholm was entered into Urquhart castle as a salaried royal custodian while the king was touring in Atholl.[72] As we have seen, possession of Urquhart had been disputed for some time by Buchan and his younger brother David, earl of Strathearn, before the latter's death on a date between 1385 and 1390. After David's death the defence of the rights of his young daughter and heiress, Euphemia Stewart, to the barony and castle of Urquhart was conducted by Euphemia's uncles and tutors, David Lindsay of Glen Esk and Walter Stewart of Brechin, Strathearn's younger brother, with Walter becoming chief justiciar within the regality of Strathearn.[73] Men committed to upholding the claims of Euphemia Stewart played a prominent role in the Highland campaign of late 1391, which saw Urquhart delivered into the hands of a salaried royal constable. Walter Stewart of Brechin, for example, received payments for his expenses in remote parts during 1391 and 1392. Brechin also collected the sums owed to his cousin, Sir Walter Stewart of Railston, the sheriff of Perth, who was similarly employed in remote parts in 1391–93. Stewart of Railston had been a feed retainer of the earl of Strathearn during the 1380s and both he and Walter Stewart of Brechin were members of earl David's council in 1381.[74]

The chief target of the 1391 campaign in which Stewart of Brechin and Stewart of Railston were involved was, clearly, Urquhart castle. The new royal custodian, Thomas Chisholm, received possession of Urquhart on 12 October 1391.[75] The political and military conditions in the Great Glen, and the magnitude of the task facing the new castellan, were revealed in the payments made to Chisholm by the crown in February 1392 for four months' custody and provisioning of the castle of Urquhart at a rate 'pro mensem quator decim libriis de voluntate Regis'. This was obviously an emergency rate, which would have resulted in a huge annual payment of £168, more than four times the pension given to Robert Chisholm for the custody of Urquhart in David II's reign.[76] Thomas Chisholm had previously displayed some level of social and political attachment to Buchan, but by October 1391 he was clearly being employed directly by the Fife regime.[77]

The right by which the crown reclaimed control of Urquhart is unclear. The insertion of a royal constable could have been justified by the overriding need of the crown to control the strategic fortress during a period of noted political unrest in the central Highlands, or as the recognition of a property which was the subject of a dispute between Buchan and Euphemia, the young countess of Strathearn. It seems more likely, however, that the Fife regime had moved into Urquhart explicitly to protect Euphemia's property rights, and that Thomas Chisholm's entry into Urquhart in October 1391 indicated yet another area where Alexander Stewart's power in the central Highlands was undermined during the Fife guardianship. In November 1391 Buchan made a rare appearance at the royal court, perhaps to present his views on Urquhart and other issues directly to Robert III.[78] If so, the attempt to garner political support was an abject failure, for Fife was now turning his attention to the final destruction of Buchan's increasingly tenuous hold on Ross.

The political situation in Ross had probably been highly confused since late 1389, when Fife had encouraged Euphemia, countess of Ross, to open proceedings against Buchan over his treatment of the countess and her property. There may well have been a local power struggle between those obeying Buchan as lord of Ross, and those remaining loyal to the countess and her young son, Alexander Leslie, the heir to the earldom. The struggle remained unresolved until 1392. In June of that year the bishops of St Andrews, Glasgow and Aberdeen were given a papal mandate to investigate Alexander's marriage to Euphemia which, it was claimed, had given rise to 'wars, plundering, arson, murders and many other damages and scandals, and it is likely that more will happen if they remain united in this union'.[79] It seems likely that Fife was directly involved in obtaining this commission, because the papal dispensation for the marriage of Fife's son Murdoch to the earl of Lennox's daughter was issued on the same date. Euphemia submitted a further petition to the pope before 5 December 1392, on which date Clement VII gave permission for her separation from Alexander and for the restoration of her extensive lands and goods.[80] By this stage Fife's support for Euphemia and Alexander Leslie was obvious. On 1 October 1392, for example, Euphemia issued a charter in Fife's castle of Stirling which was witnessed by Murdoch Stewart, Fife's son and heir, and to which Alexander Leslie gave his consent using the seal of Fife as guardian of the kingdom.[81]

Fife's links with the Leslies were safeguarded by George Leslie, lord of Rothes, a Fife adherent who had accompanied the guardian's northern expedition of 1389. George Leslie was Alexander Leslie's cousin or uncle, and he witnessed and received several grants from Alexander Leslie and Euphemia, countess of Ross, during the 1390s.[82] Sir Richard Comyn, a former adherent of Sir Walter Leslie, Alexander's father, also maintained close links with Fife.[83] Fife's political backing for the resurgent Leslie interest in Ross was confirmed by the marriage of his daughter, Isobel, to Alexander Leslie, the young heir to Ross, before 1398.[84] By 4 May 1394, Euphemia, countess of Ross, was issuing charters from her castle of Dingwall, with the consent of her son and heir, Alexander Leslie, surrounded by her own men. Buchan's hold on Ross had been effectively destroyed.[85] The Lindsay/Leslie affinity had, with Fife's support, triumphed in their long-running struggle with Buchan, and had reduced Robert II's 1382 settlement of the north to ruins.

In the midst of this catalogue of disaster for Buchan and his adherents, two of the earl's sons were involved in a great plundering raid in early 1392, perhaps on and around 18 January, into the lowlands of Angus, headed by Clann Donnchaidh and involving a number of kindreds from Atholl and northern Perthshire. The raiders were overtaken as they returned to Atholl by a force of knights and men-at-arms drawn from Angus. The ensuing pitched battle in Glen Brerachan or Glasclune ended in near-disaster for the Angus men. Sir Walter Ogilvy, sheriff of Angus, the first to engage the raiders, was killed alongside his half-brother and a number of lairds attached to his household. David Linday of Glen Esk arrived in time to assist Sir Walter, but, like Sir Patrick Gray, had to be taken from the field severely wounded.[86] Wyntoun saw the incident as part of a long-running dispute between the Clann Donnchaidh and Lindsay of Glen Esk over the Glen Esk inheritance. It was also an extraordinary gesture of political defiance a little less than four months after the crown had recovered control of Urquhart, and Robert III had personally toured Atholl and northern Perthshire.

Sir David Lindsay, whom Wyntoun identifies as the principal target of the 1392 raid, was a long-standing opponent of Buchan and had been heavily involved in Fife's highland campaigns of 1389 and 1391. The Glen Brerachan raid may simply have been one of many raids on Angus during the troubled early years of Robert III's reign, but it also has the appearance of a concerted politico-military response to Lindsay's involvement in the wider campaign conducted by Fife and his allies against the earl of Buchan and his adherents in Atholl and elsewhere.[87] The battle also demonstrated the formidable military capacity and organisation of the Atholl kindreds, and the fact that Buchan and his family had retained their political and military leadership of the major Gaelic kindreds in northern Perthshire. In one version of Bower's chronicle Buchan's son Duncan was described, in specifically military terms, as the 'armiductor' of the cateran forces who descended on Angus in 1392.[88] In the end, the political effect of the raid was probably counter-productive as far as Buchan was concerned, for it allowed his opponents to identify him even more closely with a type of Gaelic lordship which was increasingly seen as wild and lawless, justifying the earl's exclusion from royal office and favour. Certainly the royal council of March 1392 which outlawed Buchan's sons and their adherents for their part in Ogilvy's death drew a sharp distinction between the 'evil doers' who resided in the Highland parts of the realm, and the king's faithful subjects.[89]

At the same time as Fife and his son presented themselves as upholders of justice and the defenders of the kingdom's 'faithful subjects' against the caterans who disturbed Moray, Angus and Perthshire, the guardian was busily promoting his own political and territorial interests as a great lord in the Gaelic society of the southwestern Highlands. In fact, Fife's guardianship saw a revolution in the balance of territorial and political power within the Lennox/Argyll region which fundamentally altered the established political framework of Gaelic Scotland.

Fife's ambitions in the region were made manifest in the terms of a marriage indenture of February 1392 between the guardian and Duncan, earl of Lennox. The indenture specified that Fife's eldest son Murdoch would marry Lennox's eldest daughter Isabella, to whom the right to the entire earldom of Lennox was to descend (the earl of Lennox having produced no male heirs). Isabella's two younger sisters were to be married with Fife's approval, presumably to men who could be trusted not to contest the descent of the earldom. On 8 November 1392 Robert III gave his consent to the entailing of Lennox in favour of Murdoch Stewart and his heirs.[90] Fife, whose earldom of Menteith bordered Lennox, had enjoyed a good relationship with the neighbouring comital family throughout the 1370s and 1380s.[91] That close relationship bore fruit in 1392 in the deal which apparently ensured that Fife's heir would one day become earl of Menteith and Lennox.

Fife's move to secure this formidable inheritance in the southwestern Highlands for his eldest son was part of a wide-ranging extension of the guardian's political and territorial control over the region. His marriage policy in the 1390s provided his son Murdoch with links to two important families in Argyll and Lennox. Firstly, Murdoch's sister Marjory married Duncan Campbell, the son and heir of Sir Colin Campbell, lord of Loch Awe and, since 24 May 1382, hereditary lieutenant of Argyll between Loch Gilp and Loch Melfort.[92] The close connection between Fife and Duncan Campbell and, indeed, the burgeoning power of the Clan Campbell within Argyll, was demonstrated on 6 July 1395 when Duncan took part in a perambulation of lands in Fife led by the earl. In this document Campbell was described as the son and heir of Colin Campbell, 'dominus de Ergadia'.

The use of the title 'lord of Argyll' indicated that by 1395 the Campbell chief regarded himself as regional overlord in Argyll, and as the heir to the political hegemony which had been exercised by the Macdougall 'lords of Argyll' before their eclipse in the wars of independence.[93]

Although the Campbells had steadily expanded their political and territorial control in mid-Argyll and Cowal throughout the fourteenth century, their open promotion of a claim to regional overlordship throughout Argyll was a highly significant development. The title 'dominus de Ergadia' was clearly derived from the term customarily employed in Gaelic society to denote the overlord of the province of Argyll, that is *Regulus* of Argyll, or *Rìgh Airir Goidel*.[94] From the twelfth century onwards, use of the title *Rìgh Airir Goidel* had been confined to the heads of the three major kindreds, the Clan Donald, Clan Dugall and Clan Ruari, descended from Somerled, who had established himself as *Regulus* of Argyll and as *Rìgh Innes Gall*, 'king of the Hebrides', before his death in 1164.[95] Bannerman argues that for most of this period the title *Rìgh Airir Goidel* had been 'subsidiary to *Rìgh Innes Gall* and normally held by the same person'.[96] Sir Colin Campbell's claim to be 'lord of Argyll' thus not only broke the customary link between the *Rìgh Innes Gall* and *Rìgh Airir Goidel*, but meant that for the first time in two centuries the monopoly exercised by Somerled's descendants over regional lordship in Argyll was being openly challenged. Sir Colin Campbell's bid for recognition as provincial overlord in Argyll was clearly being backed and promoted by Fife. The marriage of Campbell's heir to Fife's daughter tied the fortunes of the emerging Campbell lordship in Argyll to the growing regional power of the guardian's family in Menteith and Lennox.

The timing of all these developments was significant, for in the late 1380s and early 1390s the three kindreds which had traditionally exercised overlordship in the Isles and Argyll were in no position to respond to the Campbell/Fife challenge. The Clàn Ruari had disappeared as a functioning political unit after the assassination of the head of the clan, Ranald MacRuari, in 1346.[97] In contrast, the Clan Donald had prospered under their head, John of Islay, 'lord of the Isles', a title reflecting his status in the Gaelic world as *Rìgh Innes Gall*. But John died in or around 1387, and the political cohesion of the Clan Donald was disrupted by a series of territorial disputes amongst John's sons.[98] At almost exactly the same time, and certainly before April 1388, the head of Clan Dugall, John Macdougall, lord of Lorn, died without direct male heirs, with the feudal right to the lordship of Lorn being transferred in 1388 to John Stewart of Innermeath, the husband of John Macdougall's daughter Isobel.[99] John Macdougall's death not only prevented the Lorn-based Clan Dugall from contesting Campbell's claim to be *Rìgh Airir Goidel* but also threatened the political and territorial hold of the clan on their own heartland, with Fife and his allies in Lennox and Argyll apparently planning a co-ordinated expansion into Lorn in support of John Stewart.[100] John Stewart's links to Fife were strong: John was present alongside Duncan Campbell on the Fife perambulation of 1395, and he and his son witnessed several charters issued by the earl in Fife. Shortly after 27 September 1397 John's son, Robert, married Fife's daughter Johanna.[101]

The Fife guardianship thus saw a dramatic expansion of the earl's territorial influence in the south-western Highlands. By 1397 Murdoch Stewart was the heir by entail to the earldom of Lennox, and the brother-in-law of Duncan Campbell, heir to the Campbell lordship which dominated the bulk of Argyll on Lennox's western flank, and Robert Stewart, heir to the lordship of Lorn in northern Argyll reaching to the southern shores of Loch Linnhe. Murdoch and his immediate kinsmen thus looked set to dominate the west coast between the northern shores of the Firth of Clyde and Loch Linnhe, forming an impressive territorial bloc to the north of the ancient Stewartry lands held by the royal line. When Murdoch's position as justiciar north of the Forth, heir to the earldom of Menteith and the lordships of the Appin of Dull, Glen Dochart, and keeper of Stirling castle is also taken into account, the regional dominance established by Fife and his family becomes apparent.

In fact, there remained only one lonely and defiant figure of any political significance in the area to the north of the Firth of Clyde whose first allegiance was not to the earl of Fife. The mighty castle of Dumbarton, perched high above the tidal waters of the Clyde, was held for the crown by Sir Robert Danielston, sheriff of Dumbarton, a man whose family had a long record of personal service to Robert III. Fife's guardianship undoubtedly increased the local pressure on Danielston's position in Dumbarton. After 1392, Fife had a vested interest in augmenting the territorial and jurisdictional power of Duncan, earl of Lennox, in the expectation that the ultimate beneficiary of this patronage would be his own son Murdoch. Lennox thus found himself the recipient of several important grants in the early 1390s.[102] More importantly, the earls of Lennox had long-standing but politically dormant claims to Dumbarton castle and the sheriffdom of Lennox. The support of Fife, as a powerful figure within the royal administration, for the earl of Lennox's ancient claims to the royal stronghold which dominated the south of his earldom and the sheriffship which overlapped so extensively with his own jurisdiction would become critical after the death of Sir Robert Danielston, the royal custodian of the castle, in 1396–7.[103]

While Fife successfully consolidated his regional control in Argyll and Lennox, it soon became evident that the political and territorial consequences of the guardian's assault on the earl of Buchan's Highland lordship were almost wholly disastrous. The stramash in the Great Glen lordships had seen a rapid territorial advance by Alexander of the Isles, lord of Lochaber, whose forces pushed north and east into areas of the Great Glen over which Buchan had previously exercised lordship. By 25 September 1394 the lord of Lochaber's political influence had reached the northern end of the Great Glen. On that date Thomas Dunbar, the hapless and hopeless earl of Moray, was forced to buy Alexander's 'protection' for the lands of the regality of Moray, against caterans and other men, for a period of seven years. For this singular service Moray was to give Alexander 80 merks annually, 60 merks of which were to be raised from the lands of Bona and Essich at the northern end of Loch Ness. The lands and castle of Bona had, of course, been given to Buchan by Thomas's father John, earl of Moray, only eight years previously.[104] The earls of Moray, who had helped to bring Buchan down, had once again displayed their almost complete inability to defend their own earldom. It is difficult to know whether the lord of Lochaber had simply seized control of the areas where Buchan's lordship had collapsed after 1388, or if Moray and Fife actually regarded Alexander of the Isles as a dependable ally in their struggle against Alexander Stewart in Urquhart and Ross, and as a man who could control raiding into Moray and the area around Inverness. Lochaber certainly excepted his prior allegiance to the earl of Fife in the agreement with Moray in 1394, and there is some evidence that the guardian arranged Alexander of the Isles' marriage to the earl of Lennox's daughter in the early 1390s, presumably in an attempt to draw the lord of Lochaber into Fife's political network.[105]

If the guardian intended to involve the lordship in the politics of the central Highlands and to utilise its military power against Buchan, it was a policy of short-term expediency rather than long-term wisdom. In the years after 1388 the lordship's 'standing army' in Lochaber, under the leadership of the guardian's own cousin, may have been viewed by Fife as the vital western arm of the great coalition he had pieced together in order to undermine Buchan's personal lordship. But as Fife and his northern allies were soon to discover, the lord of Lochaber followed no political agenda other than his own. In destroying Buchan's royal lieutenancy in the north, Fife had sown the wind, and he and his friends were about to reap the whirlwind.

The years of the Fife guardianship nevertheless saw the earl attain a predominant position in the political and territorial settlement of Scotland north of the Forth. Fife's son Murdoch became justiciar north of the Forth, lord of the Appin of Dull and heir by entail to the earldom of Lennox. Fife's sons-in-law were the heirs to the earldom of Ross and the lordships of Argyll and Lorn. Fife's young niece, Euphemia Stewart, heiress to the earldoms of Strathearn and Caithness and the lordship of Urquhart, was in the ward of Walter Stewart, lord of Brechin, Fife's younger brother and a man wholly committed to the guardian's Highland policy. Before 1400 Euphemia was to be engaged to Patrick Graham, the son of Patrick Graham of Kincardine, one of Fife's adherents.[106]

Through his own immediate kinsmen and clients Fife had established a formidable political network north of the Forth. Fife's later advancement to ducal rank, as duke of Albany in 1398, used the ancient name for Scotland north of the Forth, simply re-emphasising and reflecting the political position he had built up in 1388–1393.[107] Curiously, the only significant reverse experienced by Fife in the years after 1390 occurred in the very heart of his territorial power. As we have seen, the lordship of Strath Gartney, bordering Fife's earldom of Menteith, had been a matter of debate between Fife and John Logie, a kinsman and adherent of Fife's brother John, earl of Carrick. During the Carrick lieutenancy Logie had recovered control of Strath Gartney and the lands of Logie in Strathearn. The position changed dramatically after 1388 when, with the benefit of his new status as guardian, Fife attempted to reclaim Logie and Strath Gartney. On 5 May 1389 John, earl of Carrick, was required to make a formal attestation that Fife had resigned the lands of Logie and Strath Gartney to John Logie, as had been specified in an arbitration of the dispute in 1385. The renewed threat to Logie is made clear in a letter of 22 March 1391 by Fife to the inhabitants of Strath Gartney, narrating that, although he had previously ordered them not to obey Logie as their lord, they were now to do so.[108] In the late 1380s, then, the dispute between Logie and Fife acted as a political barometer with Logie ascendant during the Carrick lieutenancy, Fife seeking to reverse Logie's gains during the guardianship of 1388–90 and, perhaps most significantly, Logie being restored after the earl of Carrick became king as Robert III in 1390. While Fife could safely ignore Logie's claims in 1388–90, it was a different matter to defy the wishes of Robert III after 1390. The revival in Logie's fortunes after Robert III's accession was a minor inconvenience for Fife, for Logie was one of the king's few committed supporters north of the Forth. The earl of Carrick's real power base, before he became king as Robert III, had been south of the Forth. It was in this area that Robert III could most effectively use his enhanced status as king to reconstruct his political authority. It was thus Carrick's political adversaries from 1388 in this region, principally Archibald, 3rd earl of Douglas, who had most to fear from a resurgence in the fortunes of Robert III's adherents after the king's accession.

NOTES

1. *Westminster*, 350–1, 376–9.
2. SRO RH6/190; NRAS 832 Lauderdale Muniments, Writs and Titles of Lauder 1359–1402, Deed Box C136/44/36.
3. Fraser, *Douglas*, iii, 32–3; SRO RH1/2/141.
4. SRO RH6/190; GD 212 Maitland Thomson Notebooks Box 1/Book 10 p. 25. The others were Walter Stewart, lord of Brechin, Sir William Lindsay of the Byres, Sir Robert Stewart of Innermeath, Sir William Borthwick and Sir Andrew Mercer. Lindsay and Borthwick were adherents of the deceased 2nd earl of Douglas who had remained in the service of Margaret Sinclair after Otterburn, Borthwick being named as one of those who had held Tantallon in late 1388.
5. *CDS*, iv, no. 391; SRO RH6/197: An undated agreement between Alan Lauder and Alexander Montgomery, brother of John Montgomery of Eaglesham, an adherent of the 2nd earl. The witnesses included Drummond, Sir William Lindsay of the Byres, Sir William Borthwick, John Liddell, Adam Forrester and William Napier.
6. *Westminster*, 375.
7. *Chron. Wyntoun* (Amours), vi, 316–7, 320–325; *Chron. Wyntoun* (Laing), iii, 24, 29–34. See A. Grant, 'The Otterburn War', 45–6, where the chronicler's promotion of Fife as a war leader is noted.
8. *Chron. Wyntoun* (Laing), iii, 24, 29–34.
9. *Froissart* (Johnes), ii, 376.
10. *APS*, i, 557.
11. *APS*, i, 557–8; Fraser, *Douglas*, iii, 357: From an extract drawn up at the instance of the 3rd earl on 8 March 1391/2. The entail had been issued by Hugh Douglas, the brother of the Good Sir James, in favour of his nephew William Douglas, the future first earl, and his heirs male, on the failure of whom to William Douglas, lord of Liddesdale, and his heirs male, whom failing to Archibald Douglas, son of Sir James. The entail was issued at a time when Sir William Douglas of Liddesdale was achieving control over a large part of the Douglas inheritance through resignations made by Hugh, and the document was probably more concerned with securing a place for the knight of Liddesdale in the Douglas inheritance than ensuring the succession of William Douglas to the estates possessed by his uncle Hugh.
12. SRO RH6/195. Although other documents issued on the same day still style Archibald simply as lord of Galloway.
13. D. E. R. Watt, *Dictionary*, 220–223.
14. *Chron. Fordun*, i, 370.

15. Fraser, *Douglas*, iii, 360–1.
16. *RMS*, i, no. 647; RH6/155.
17. Douglas of Dalkeith's perception of himself as the heir to the knight of Liddesdale's vast estates was reflected in the foundation he made in 1406 of six chaplainries in the chapel of St Nicholas of Dalkeith. Masses were to be sung for the kings of Scotland, Sir James's immediate family and for William of Douglas, lord of Liddesdale, his uncle, and Mary his daughter: SRO Calendar of Dunbeath Muniments GD 97/ Section 2/3.
18. SRO GD 150/178.
19. *Ibid.*; A. Grant, 'The Otterburn War', 51.
20. In 1367 Archibald the Grim had knighted the young James Douglas shortly before he fought in a judicial duel with Thomas Erskine over lands which had belonged to James's cousin, Mary Douglas: *Chron. Fordun*, i, 370, note 12. Sir James had accompanied the lord of Galloway on his embassy to France in 1371. In 1383 Sir James was named as a member of the lord of Galloway's justiciar court sitting in Dumfries: *Liber Melrose*, ii, 455–7. In September 1390, the apparently hypochondriac James Douglas of Dalkeith drew up a will which declared that on his death the tutelage or wardship of his son or grandson should be held by Archibald, 3rd earl of Douglas and lord of Galloway: *Mort.Reg.*, ii, 170–6.
21. *APS*, i, 558.
22. Fraser, *Douglas*, iii, 33–4.
23. Fraser, *Douglas*, iii, 364–5; *APS*, i, 565–6.
24. SRO RH6/195.
25. SRO GD 90/1/30; *A.B.Ill.*, iv, 161.
26. *APS*, i, 557–8.
27. *Westminster*, 376–9.
28. *Chronicon Henrici Knighton*, ed. J. R. Lumby (London, 1895), ii, 308–9; *Westminster*, 383–5.
29. *Knighton*, 308–9; Goodman, *War and Border Societies*, 19.
30. *Westminster*, 396–7.
31. *Ibid.*; *Chron. Wyntoun* (Laing), iii, 40–1.
32. *CDS*, iv, no. 391.
33. There is some evidence to suggest that the adherents of Sir James Sandilands and Sir James Douglas of Dalkeith were in open conflict by mid-1389: SRO GD 150/178.
34. *Westminster*, 402–5.
35. Walsingham, *Hist.Angl.*, ii, 182–3.
36. *Westminster*, 398–9; *CDS*, iv, no. 395; *Rot.Scot.*, ii, 98–9; *Chron. Wynton* (Laing), iii, 41–3.
37. *Chron. Wyntoun* (Laing), iii, 41–3; SRO Sempill of Craigievar Muniments GD 250/Box 1/no. 174; *A.B.Ill.*, ii, 30.

38. *Chron. Wyntoun* (Laing), iii, 41–3.

39. *APS*, i, 556.

40. *APS*, i, 556–7. Fife was keen to make concessions to David Lindsay in late 1388. Lindsay was given a grant of the superiority of the barony of Guthrie on 8 December 1388: SRO GD Guthrie of Guthrie MSS, GD 188/Box 1/1/1.

41. *APS*, i, 557.

42. John Stuart (ed.), 'The Errol Papers', in *Spalding Club Miscellany II* (Spalding Club, 1842), 319; W. Fraser, *History of the Carnegies, Earls of Southesk, and of their Kindred* (Edinburgh, 1867), ii, 498–99.

43. SRO RH1/2/134; *ER*, ii, 425.

44. SRO RH6/196. On the same day Isabella resigned her claims to the baronies of Coull and O'Neill in Aberdeenshire, formerly held by her father, in favour of the guardian.

45. *RMS*, i, App. 2, no. 1744; Robertson, *Index*, p. 139.

46. In 1345 Duncan Andrewson, the then head of *Clann Donnchaidh*, was the chief forester of Strath Braan, by the grant of Robert the Steward as the earl of Fife's bailie, and in 1347 was to be found concluding indentures at Dull. Duncan Andrewson also seems to have received a grant of the earl of Fife's lands to the north and south of Loch Tay, incorporated within the barony of Strathord, a grant later confirmed by David II. This gift may have reflected *Clann Donnchaidh*'s advance into these Perthshire lordships during the Steward's period of control of the lands. In 1358, Duncan Andrewson's son Robert was identified as occupying various lands in Atholl and Fortingall: *ER*, ii, 555, 558; SRO GD 121/Box 4/Bundle 10/3; Fraser, *Grandtully*, i, 2–3; *RMS*, i, App. 2, no. 1396. Like Alexander Stewart's adherents in Badenoch and Strathspey, the *Clann Donnchaidh*'s territorial success seems to have been based on a style of lordship which their lowland neighbours regarded as innately lawless.

47. *RMS*, i, no. 676.

48. Janet Menzies may have been the wife of Alexander Menzies of Fortingall, and the daughter and heiress of the senior figure in *Clann Donnchaidh*, Robert Duncanson of Atholl and his wife, herself a daughter and heiress of Sir John Stirling of Glen Esk: J. A. Robertson, *Comitatus de Atholia* (Perth, 1860), 25. David II confirmed a grant by Robert Duncanson of Atholl in favour of Alexander Menzies, apparently on the occasion of Menzies' marriage to Jean, Robert's daughter, who is described as the heir to Glen Esk: *RMS*, i, App. 2, no. 1395; Robertson's *Index*, p. 51, no. 46. Robertson speculates that Jean's (*recte* Janet's) liaison with Alexander Menzies produced one daughter, also Janet, who was married to Buchan's son Robert, and that this marriage explained the resignation made by Janet senior in favour of Alexander Stewart in 1379. Alexander Menzies, lord of Fortingall, was

dead by 5 June 1381, when his daughter and heiress, Janet, who had been married and widowed before that date, was to be found in Fife's castle of Doune in Menteith: *A.B.Ill.*, ii, 389; iv, 83. If the younger Janet had been briefly married to one of Buchan's sons between 1379 and 1381 and produced children, then their claims to Alexander Menzies' inheritance were brushed aside by Fife, who had already secured his claim to Alexander Menzies' barony of Glen Dochart in 1375/6 and who would later secure title to Fortingall. Even if Janet had produced no heirs, there was likely to be tension between Buchan and *Clann Donnchaidh* on the one hand, and Fife on the other, over the status of any lands, including the Strath Tummel lands granted to Buchan in 1379, to which Janet had right as the granddaughter of Robert Duncanson of Atholl.

49. Fraser, *Lennox*, ii, 43.
50. *Moray Reg.*, 197–201.
51. *Ibid.*, 201–3.
52. *Ibid.*, 353–4.
53. *Ibid.*, 197–201.
54. *Chron. Wyntoun* (Laing), iii, 44.
55. The Stewart interest in the lordships of northern Perthshire and Strathspey had been established by the king himself during the 1340s and 1350s.
56. *APS*, i, 555–6.
57. *APS*, i, 555–6.
58. *Chron. Bower* (Watt), viii, 2–5. Bower adds a seemingly picturesque story about the granger of the monastery of Scone complaining to the new king about the damage done to the monastery's crops because of the great multitude of men and horses gathered for the coronation. The story is perhaps given greater weight by a grant made by the king on 15 December 1393 specifically intended to compensate the monastery of Scone because of its use as the site for the king's coronation, and those of his predecessors, and for the many and frequent meetings held there, causing inconvenience and great expense: NLS Ch. A8.
59. *HMC Report*, iv, App. 528; Strathclyde Regional Archives, Mitchell Library, Shaw Stewarts of Ardgowan, T-Ard 1/6/11/1.
60. *Chron. Wyntoun* (Laing), iii, 45.
61. *Ibid.*, iii, 55; *Moray Reg.*, 381–2; *Chron. Bower* (Goodall), ii, 416.
62. *The Records of Elgin* (New Spalding Club, 1903–8), ii, 454; *Ane Account of the Families of Innes* (Spalding Club, 1864), 66–7; *Rot.Scot.*, ii, 103, 104, 106.
63. A. Grant, 'The Wolf', 151–3. By 19 August the new king had, unsurprisingly, released the bishop of Moray from his obligation to pay for Thomas Dunbar's spectacularly unsuccessful protection of the bishop's lands and possessions: *Moray. Reg.*, 204.

64. *Foedera*, vii, 683; *RMS*, i, no. 802.

65. *Moray Reg.*, 381–3.

66. *Chron. Bower* (Watt), viii, 2–5; *Chron. Wyntoun* (Laing), iii, 44–5, 50–1, 54–5.

67. Bellenden, *Chronicles*, 354, where it is suggested that the Scots considered John an 'unchancy' name.

68. *Barbour's Bruce* (STS, 1980), ii, 7; *Chron. Fordun*, i, 313–4, 373–4.

69. *Chron. Fordun*, i, 373–4; *Chron. Wyntoun* (Laing), ii, 485.

70. *Chron. Wyntoun* (Laing), iii, 45. The change may not have had its desired effect, for Robert III also seems to have acquired the nickname Robert John 'Fernyear', or farneyeir, Robert who was John last year. The references to his nickname occur in very late Highland chronicles: *Reliquiae Celticae*, ii, 158–9; *Highland Papers*, ii, 93, 95, note 1.

71. NLS, Fleming of Wigtown, Ch.no.15821.

72. *ER*, iii, 277.

73. On 5 March 1390 Glen Esk and Brechin were styled Euphemia's uncles and tutors: Duke of Atholl's Muniments, Blair Castle, Blair Atholl, Box 2/Parcel 1. During a justiciary court held in Strathearn in 1391 Brechin was referred to as chief justiciar. Stewart's jurisdiction was almost certainly confined to the regality of Strathearn, as there is no evidence to suggest that there was an office of chief justiciar of Scotland at this stage: SRO GD 24/5/17.

74. *ER*, iii, 17, 274, 290, 310; BM Campbell Charters, xxx, no. 19.

75. *ER*, iii, 274, 277, 317.

76. *ER*, ii, 143, 187.

77. In 1389 Chisholm had stood as one of the sureties for Buchan's compliance with the terms of the settlement between the earl and his wife Euphemia, countess of Ross: *Moray Reg.*, 353–4. Chisholm was probably the nephew of Alexander de Ard, the man who had resigned his extensive property rights in Caithness, Strathearn and elsewhere in favour of Buchan and his younger brother David during the 1370s: B. E. Crawford, 'The earls of Orkney-Caithness', 30–1, 214.

78. SRO Brown-Pullarton Documents GD 1/19/1.

79. *CPL Clement VII*, 174.

80. *Ibid.*, 181.

81. NLS, Fleming of Wigtown, Ch.no.15821.

82. SRO Rothes Cartulary GD 204/4 and 701; GD 297/179.

83. Chapter 3 *supra*; SRO GD 297/229; NRAS No. 885, Glamis Charters, Box 3/nos. 54, 56.

84. *SP*, i, 149.

85. SRO GD 93/15.

86. *Chron. Wyntoun* (Laing), iii, 58–60; *Chron. Bower* (Watt), viii, 7; *APS*, i, 579–80, where a list of those against whom action was to be taken for their involvement in the raid is laid out.

87. For a slightly different interpretation of the significance of the Glen Brerachan raid, see A. Grant, 'The Wolf', 154–5. In July 1389 the monastery of Coupar Angus was allowed to appropriate the revenues of the parish church of Torref because of the reduction in the monastery's revenues as a result of the wars, 'which for many years have been waged in those parts', as well as for the expenses incurred through hospitality: *CPL Clement VII*, 147–8.

88. *Chron. Bower* (Watt), viii, 7, note f; *Extracta*, 203; *APS*, i, 579–80. Bower's Coupar Angus Manuscript tends to employ technical military terms to describe Highland chiefs and their adherents: *Chron. Bower* (Watt), viii, 363, note 28.

89. *APS*, i, 579. The contrast between Gaelic- and English-speaking societies in terms of adherence to the norms of the common law and feudal tenure was a subject of increasingly hostile comment in the chronicles and documentary records of lowland Scotland.

90. Fraser, *Lennox*, ii, 43–5, 49–51; *RMS*, i, no. 862.

91. The papal dispensation for the marriage of Murdoch and Isabella, issued on 9 June 1392, revealed that Lennox had acted as godfather at Murdoch's baptism: *CPL Clement VII*, 174.

92. The exact date of Marjory's marriage is uncertain, but the only son of the union, Archibald, was considered old enough to give his consent to his father's grant of lands in Craignish in 1414, suggesting a date for his parents' marriage in the 1390s: *RMS*, ii, no. 2128; SRO RH1/2/87; SRO RH6/244.

93. See S. Boardman, 'Gaelic Kindred, Feudal Power: Campbell Lordship in Medieval Scotland', in *Alba; Celtic Scotland in the Middle Ages* eds. A. MacDonald and E. J. Cowan (forthcoming, 1996). Aside from the direct ties established between Murdoch and the Campbells through Marjory's marriage, Murdoch's bride-to-be, Isabella of Lennox, was Duncan Campbell's cousin.

94. Boardman, 'Gaelic Kindred'; K. A. Steer and J. W. M. Bannerman, *Late Medieval Monumental Sculpture in the West Highlands* (RCAHMS, 1977), Appendix 2, 201–4.

95. Bannerman, *Monumental Sculpture*, 201–2.

96. *Ibid.*

97. *Chron. Wyntoun* (Laing), ii, 472; Bannerman, *Monumental Sculpture*, 204.

98. Bannerman, *Monumental Sculpture*, 101, 162–3.

99. Argyll Transcripts, ii, at date. John's brother Robert, who appears to have been married to Isobel's sister, Janet, resigned his claims to the lordship of Lorn in favour of his brother in exchange for a grant of the barony of Durisdeer.

100. At some point between 1385 and 1393 Ivar Campbell of Strachur granted Duncan, earl of Lennox, lands in Lorn and Benderloch,

including the Macdougall heartlands of Dunollie and Ardstaffnage, which had been granted to Ivar's ancestor Arthur Campbell by Robert I. The original grant seems to have been made while the Macdougalls of Lorn were in political exile, but it seems likely that the recovery of Macdougall power in Lorn in the mid-fourteenth century meant that the Campbells of Strachur had never actually obtained possession of the lands. Ivar's resignation seems to have been intended to take advantage of the new situation in Lorn after the death of John Macdougall, lord of Lorn, in or shortly before 1388. The Strachur Campbells were tenants of Fife in Glen Dochart, and the resignation in favour of Duncan, earl of Lennox, if made after 1392, would ultimately have been to the benefit of Fife's son Murdoch, as heir to Lennox. With Archibald Campbell of Loch Awe witnessing the resignation, the stage was set for a successful assertion of political control in Lorn by the Stewarts of Lorn, supported by the Campbells of Loch Awe and the earls of Lennox; all three families had·established political links to Fife by the mid-1390s: *Highland Papers*, iv, 17–18; G. W. S. Barrow, *Bruce*, 290.

101. *CPL Benedict XIII*, 75.

102. The 1392 marriage treaty stipulated that Lennox was to have half the profits of the justiciary courts of Dumbarton and Stirling where they were derived from the earldom, for as long as Fife himself had the right to these revenues. Fife also granted to Duncan, and his heirs under the terms of the entail of 1392, the office of coroner in the earldom of Lennox in a charter which is misdated 1400 and which probably belongs to 1392–3: Fraser, *Lennox*, ii, 43–5; *Lennox Cart.*, 95.

103. On 14 July 1321 Robert I granted to Malcolm, 4th earl of Lennox, the earldom of Lennox, including the sheriffship of Dumbarton and the custody of Dumbarton castle. The charter explained that Alexander III had taken control of Dumbarton castle from Maldouen, 3rd earl of Lennox, in the thirteenth century, during a period when the ownership of the fortress was being hotly contested by the king and the earl. Even Robert I's grant of the castle and sheriffship to Malcolm in 1321 was highly conditional, with the addition of a clause asserting that if the king and his heirs retained the sheriffship and castle, then they would pay 500 merks annually from the royal customs to Malcolm and his heirs. Dumbarton remained a 'royal' fortress throughout the reigns of David II and Robert II in the keeping of salaried royal custodians, with no indication that the earls were receiving their 500 merks compensation from the king's customs: Fraser, *Lennox*, ii, 20–22.

104. *Moray Reg.*, 354–5; SRO RH 6/184.

105. A. B. W. MacEwan, in *SWHIHR Notes and Queries*, xiv, 6–8; *Highland Papers*, iv, 16. As Fife had an effective veto on the marriages

of Lennox's younger daughters after 1392, we may assume that any
marriage between the lord of Lochaber and Elizabeth of Lennox was
arranged by, or had the full approval of, Fife.

106. SRO GD 160/1/6.

107. *Chron. Bower* (Watt), viii, 13, 154 n. 45; J. W. M. Bannerman, *Studies
in the History of Dalriada* (Edinburgh, 1974), 118–19. Fife's standing in
the north is illustrated by chronicle accounts written from two very
different perspectives. The English chronicler Walsingham described
the political system of Scotland in the early fifteenth century as
operating on the basis that the earl of Douglas governed the south,
and the duke of Albany those areas north of the Scottish Sea. In the
Black Book of Clanranald John lord of the Isles' marriage to Robert
the Steward's daughter Margaret is described thus: 'he (John)
proceeded to the mouth of the river of Glasgow, and had threescore
longships with him, and he married Margaret, the daughter of
Robert Stuart, whom we call King of Scotland, but the real person
(i.e. the real power in the land) was Robert, earl of Fife, that is the
brother-german of old Robert Fearingiora, that is the king, and he
was governor of Scotland': *Reliquiae Celticae* (Inverness, 1894), ii,
159.

108. Fraser, *Menteith*, ii, 265; *A.B.Ill.*, iii, 133.

7

Ghosts of the Past, Visions of the Future: Robert III, 1390–98

In the autumn of 1390 the 53-year-old Robert III, despite his accession to the throne, appeared a man broken physically and politically. Robert's subjects had already delivered two resounding votes of no-confidence in their new king's capacity to govern and defend the kingdom with his removal from the guardianship in 1388, and the extension of Fife's exercise of the same office in the summer of 1390 after Robert II's death.[1] An impression of the weakness and ineffectiveness of the Scottish royal dynasty had travelled across Europe as far as the Po valley by the mid-1390s, where Thomas, 3rd Marquis of Saluzzo, could write of a dream visit to the court of a Scottish king who was unable to defend his kingdom against the English without the assistance of the French, and who feared for the safety of his own crown.[2] The king's personal political prestige was certainly no match for that of his remarkable younger brother, the guardian Fife, who was managing to present himself as both an active focus for the chivalry of southern Scotland in the defence of the Scottish marches, and as the dominant political personality in the affairs of the kingdom north of the Forth.

However, Robert III and the political allies who remained with him after the débâcle of 1388 were playing a long and cautious game in which they had control of two priceless assets, namely the king's young sons David and Robert. In 1390 the elder of the king's sons and the heir to the throne, David, was twelve years of age. David's progression towards adulthood and an active role in royal government after 1390 would, inevitably, make Fife's continued control of the kingdom as guardian harder and harder to justify. It was thus equally predictable that from an early stage in his career David became a vehicle for Robert III's reassertion of his political authority over the kingdom, and that the prince's household became the focus for those men seeking to overturn certain aspects of the political settlement engineered by Fife in 1388 and to even old scores with the guardian and his allies.

One of the features of Robert III's kingship which has been noted and decried by some modern historians as symbolic of the collapse of royal authority after 1390 was the king's granting of heritable pensions to various noblemen in return for their retinue service to himself and to David his first-born son.[3] In fact, the purpose of the pensions granted out in the early 1390s seems to have been twofold. Firstly, they were part of Robert III's attempt to reconstruct an affinity, exclusively loyal to himself and his son and heir David, from the wreckage of the Carrick/Lindsay/Douglas faction which had been the dominant political grouping in the kingdom during most of the 1380s. Secondly they rewarded and supported men who were at the heart of the working affinity growing up around the heir to the throne as he began to play an active role in royal government. The earliest grants of heritable pensions as retaining fees were made to Sir David Lindsay of Glen Esk, Sir John Montgomery of Eaglesham, Sir William Lindsay of the Byres, Sir William Stewart of Jedworth, Sir William Danielston and the earl of Moray.[4] All of these men had been politically associated, directly or indirectly, with Robert III or the 2nd earl of Douglas prior to 1388.[5] It was unsurprising that they were the men to whom Robert III looked in order to re-establish his influence in government after 1390.

The identity of Robert III's pensioned retainers confirms that the king's slow recovery of political power after 1390 was based in his old heartland south of the Forth. The cutting edge of this recovery was the household of the king's precocious son David, who had been created earl of Carrick on his father's accession to the throne. Carrick's personal retinue was dominated by adherents of Robert III and the 2nd earl of Douglas, who were returning to positions of political influence and favour after 1390. The emergence of the young prince as an active figure in the royal administration can probably be dated to 1392, when David was only fourteen years of age. Early in that year the young earl received a huge annuity of £640 from royal customs revenue, a grant which established the financial independence of Carrick's household.[6] However, the identity of David's financial officers confirms that, in political terms, the prince's establishment was a carefully controlled and nurtured offshoot of the royal household. Carrick's first two chamberlains, for example, were William Drummond and John Logie, both kinsmen of the young earl's mother Queen Annabella.[7] Carrick's huge annuity not only increased the patronage available for those men in the service of the young prince, but also implied that Carrick's household was the centre of considerable social and administrative activity. It was no coincidence that the first reference to Carrick's personal involvement in the conduct of royal government dates from 1392, with the young prince attending a justiciary court in Lanark, nor that Robert III was actively recruiting men to serve himself *and* his son David in 1391 and early 1392.[8] The king's development of his son's household as an active agency of royal government clearly undermined Fife's position as guardian. The situation was made more disturbing for Fife and Archibald, 3rd earl of Douglas, by the fact that the young prince's affinity was dominated by one-time members of the old Douglas establishment. The ghosts of Otterburn were refusing to rest, and the loyal retainers of James, 2nd earl of Douglas, were once again gathering in the service of a young and vigorous lord.

The dominant personality in Carrick's household by 1393 was James Lindsay, lord of Crawford, a man noted for his strong political links with Robert III and James, 2nd earl of Douglas. Lindsay had fought at Otterburn in 1388 where, according to Froissart, he had had the misfortune to be captured by the bishop of Durham whilst pursuing an English knight, Sir Mathew Redman, from the field.[9] Lindsay was certainly in the custody of Henry Percy, earl of Northumberland, on 25 September 1388, shortly after Otterburn.[10] Sir James was thus languishing in England during the critical months in 1388/9 when Fife became guardian of the kingdom and Archibald the Grim established himself as earl of Douglas. One English chronicler suggests that Lindsay was eventually released in the summer of 1389, in part exchange for the sons of the earl of Northumberland, Sir Henry Percy and his brother Ralph, who had been captured by the Scots at Otterburn; and Sir James had certainly returned to Scotland by early August 1389.[11] Lindsay was very much a member of the old Douglas affinity which had been defeated by Archibald the Grim in the contest for control of the Douglas inheritance, and on his return to Scotland he was immediately associated with the other key figures whose political fortunes had collapsed after Otterburn, Sir Malcolm Drummond, Sir James Sandilands of Calder, Sir John Haliburton of that Ilk, and William Douglas of Drumlanrig.[12] Sir James Lindsay re-emerged as a man of political influence in the wake of Robert III's accession to the throne, appearing as an auditor at the first exchequer session of Robert III's reign in February 1391 and serving alongside his cousin, William Lindsay of Rossie, as one of the Scottish sureties for the observance of an extension of the truce of Leulighem in July 1392.[13]

The growing political influence and activity of the Robert III loyalists gathered around the heir to the throne was no doubt the critical factor in the termination of the Fife guardianship in early 1393. On 4 February the auditors of the exchequer allowed what turned out to be the final payment to Fife for his exercise of the guardianship. Four days later Robert III granted pensions of 200 merks and 100 merks respectively to Fife and Murdoch, his son, in return for their retinue service to David, earl of Carrick, the king's heir or, on David's death, Robert Stewart, the king's second son.[14] The pensions may well have been intended to provide some level of financial compensation to Fife for the loss of the thousand merks per annum associated with the guardianship, and they clearly differed in scale and purpose from earlier retaining fees granted by Robert III in 1390–2. The political symbolism of the displaced guardian and his son pledging their loyalty and service to the heir to the throne is unmistakable, both in terms of the immediate political control of the kingdom and the long-term dynastic ascendancy of Robert III's family.

Fife's exercise of the guardianship had been, from his appointment in 1388 onwards, regarded as finite and under constant review. It had been justified by the incapacity of Robert III and the tender years of the king's sons and, in terms of political necessity, the threat posed to the kingdom by imminent English invasion. By early 1393 the Anglo-Scottish truce established through the treaty of Leulighem had held firm for four years and showed no sign of imminent collapse. The removal of the likelihood of renewed warfare with England weakened the case for the retention of the Fife guardianship, but the most pressing reason for its abolition in early 1393 was undoubtedly the increasingly assertive role of David, earl of Carrick, in the great affairs of the kingdom. Fife's demission of the office of guardian in 1393 was achieved with little political friction and rancour, probably because the earl's territorial and jurisdictional power in the north was left unchallenged. The guardianship was, in fact, the only office lost to Fife and his son in 1393, with Murdoch retaining the justiciarship north of the Forth, and the two men received a substantial compensation in the combined pension of 300 merks for their service and loyalty to Carrick.

With the ending of the Fife guardianship in February 1393 Robert III had recovered nominal control of his kingdom. It soon became clear, however, that most of the active functions of kingship would be discharged by Carrick and his retainers, the men spearheading the reassertion of the authority of the royal lineage south of the Forth. Even before February 1393 the young prince had been personally involved in a justice ayre in Lanark, although in what capacity is not clear.[15] Politically, the 15-year-old earl seems to have been alarmingly precocious. Early in 1394 he was named alongside the king in a joint supplication to Clement VII with regard to the abbot of Newbattle. Rather strikingly, the supplication recorded that the king and the earl were willing to undertake the restoration of the monastery of Newbattle, which had been badly damaged in the English invasions of the 1380s, but that they would not do so until Abbot John was replaced because he was 'exceedingly ungrateful *to the earl* [my italics] and hateful to him'.[16]

At this stage Carrick's household was dominated by Robert III's long-standing ally, Sir James Lindsay, and Sir James's cousin Sir David Lindsay of Glen Esk, who had been the recipient of a pension for his 'retinue service' to Carrick since 1391.[17] The relationship between the Lindsays and Carrick was both political and romantic, for Carrick was involved in an affair with Euphemia Lindsay, Sir David's sister.[18] The growing political and administrative role of the young earl in the south relied heavily on the established influence of the Lindsay kin in the area. Carrick, Sir James and Sir David Lindsay began to feature in Anglo-Scottish diplomacy, all being named as conservators of the Anglo-Scottish truce on 29 September 1394, while James Lindsay was named on the same day as a commissioner to negotiate a permanent peace between the two kingdoms.[19] On 27 December 1394 David, styled earl of Carrick and lord of Nithsdale, appeared in Dumfries confirming a charter involving lands in the burgh. Carrick's charter was witnessed by Sir James Lindsay, styled lord of Buchan, Sir David Lindsay of Glen Esk, Sir John Hamilton of Fingalton, Sir William Lindsay of Rossie (Sir David's half-brother), and Walter Hamilton, men who would remain members of Carrick's household until his death.[20] The charter suggests that Carrick had reclaimed the lordship of Nithsdale after the death of William Douglas, the illegitimate son of Archibald the Grim, in 1392.[21]

Carrick's reclamation of Nithsdale and his appearance in Dumfries in the company of Sir James Lindsay must have been a worrying development for Archibald, 3rd earl of Douglas. Nithsdale gave the heir to the throne a territorial interest in Douglas's heartland in the south-west, which combined with his control of Carrick to the north of Douglas's lordship of Galloway and Sir James Lindsay's own extensive political and territorial interests to form a powerful counter-balance to the earl of Douglas's influence in the region. The emergence of Carrick as an active figure in the politics of southern Scotland, with his extensive political and familial ties to Archibald's enemies from the old Douglas affinity, thus seemed to represent a genuine political challenge to the new earl of Douglas's ascendancy in the region. Archibald may even have felt that the territorial gains which he and his family had secured in 1388/9 were by no means irreversible; the earl certainly thought it worthwhile to have a notarial copy of the entail which underpinned his claims to the bulk of the Douglas inheritance drawn up in early 1391, perhaps in anticipation of a legal challenge to his hold on these estates.[22]

Alongside Carrick's insertion into Nithsdale, the heir to the throne's supporters from the earldom of Carrick may also have been making life uncomfortable for the earl of Douglas in the lordship of Wigtown. A highly unreliable traditional account of the Clan Kennedy claimed that

Alexander Kennedy (in fact effective head of Clan Kennedy only after 1408) triumphed in a confrontation with the 'Erll of Wigtone Douglaise . . . quha wes ane werry gritt manne', which the chronicler places in the fourth year of Robert III's reign, that is, according to the chronicle itself, 1390 (recte 1394).[23] Despite the general inaccuracies of the chronicle, the clash between the Kennedies, the chief kindred in the heir to the throne's earldom of Carrick, and Archibald, earl of Douglas, could well be dated to the early 1390s as Robert III, Carrick and Sir James Lindsay challenged Douglas's political supremacy in the south. Similar shadowy evidence for royal disruption of Archibald Douglas's political control of the south-west exists in the chronicle history of the Agnew lords of Lochnaw, where it is suggested that the Agnews, having been forced into exile by the activities of Archibald the Grim in the 1370s, were able to return to their ancestral estates during Robert III's reign, partly because of the political support given to them by members of the royal family.[24]

If Sir James Lindsay's influence in Carrick's household was a source of political annoyance for the earl of Douglas, it was also worrying for the earl of Fife, for by 1395 Lindsay was embroiled in a series of disputes with Fife's political allies. Most seriously, Lindsay became involved in a feud with Robert Keith, the grandson of Sir William Keith the Marischal. The conflict between the two men disrupted the north-east, with one brief Latin chronicle suggesting that 'destructa fuit pro majore parte tota patria inter Dee et Spee propter discordiam inter Jacobum de Lyndesay et Robertum de Kethe'.[25] Wyntoun's more detailed description records a pitched battle at Bourtrie in the Garioch in 1395 as Sir James Lindsay led a force of 400 men to relieve his wife, who was besieged in Lindsay's castle of Fyvie by her own nephew, Robert Keith. Robert Keith and his adherents were defeated with the loss of around 60 men.[26] Aside from disrupting the politics of the north-east, the Lindsay/Keith feud undoubtedly exacerbated political tensions at the national level, because Sir James Lindsay was the senior member of the earl of Carrick's household, while the Keiths were very closely associated with Carrick's uncle, the earl of Fife.[27]

Tension between Lindsay and Fife over the Fyvie issue would have been complicated by Lindsay's long-standing claim to the lordship of Buchan. Sir James's claims to Buchan had made little headway during the 1380s when his chief protagonist had been the dominant political figure in the north, Alexander Stewart, earl of Buchan. The collapse of Alexander's power in 1388–92 allowed Lindsay to establish effective control of the barony of Kingedward, the only significant property associated with the title of Buchan. On 21 October 1391 Lindsay, as lord of Buchan, confirmed various transfers of land in Kingedward.[28]

In 1392, however, Euphemia, countess of Ross, successfully completed her divorce from the discredited Alexander Stewart. The countess's independent rights to the barony of Kingedward were, thereafter, vigorously supported by her ally Fife, who was no doubt eager to protect the hereditary rights of the countess's son, Alexander Leslie, who was, or was soon to be, Fife's son-in-law. In August 1392 the Kingedward lands whose transfer had been ratified by Sir James Lindsay in 1391 were sold to Sir David Fleming. Fleming sought confirmation of the transaction from the countess of Ross rather than Lindsay, the countess issuing her confirmation on 1 October from Fife's castle of Stirling.[29] Lindsay was styling himself lord of Buchan in 1395 and, presumably, was still contesting possession of Kingedward with the countess.

The political tensions engendered by Sir James Lindsay's influence in the heir to the throne's household were brought to a sudden end by Lindsay's death between 5 April 1395 and 6 March 1396.[30] Lindsay's career after 1390 had illustrated that control of the young earl of Carrick was a precious political commodity. It is hardly surprising that, after Sir James's death, the romantic and political affiliations of the heir to the throne became a matter of open political dispute.

The first man off the mark was George Dunbar, earl of March. By August 1395 the bishops of St Andrews and Brechin had been given a papal mandate to allow Carrick to marry Elizabeth Dunbar, the earl of March's daughter.[31] At first sight the proposed marriage seems to have been a sensible extension of Robert III's established policy of providing his son with powerful allies south of the Forth from amongst the men who had been politically aligned with the old Douglas affinity. March was one of the most influential figures in the south of Scotland, an earl with a large following and a proven record in Anglo-Scottish warfare and diplomacy. Moreover, March's nephew, Thomas, earl of Moray, son of the earl of Moray who had played such a prominent part in the Otterburn campaign, was already the recipient of a retaining pension for his service to the king and Carrick.[32] Carrick's marriage to Moray's cousin would have meant that the prince's political affinity, which already included Sir David Lindsay of Glen Esk, would have begun to rival Fife's network of kinsmen and allies in the north. In 1395–6 Berwickshire landowners associated with March were to be found in Carrick's service and household alongside Sir David Lindsay and his brother Sir William of Rossie.[33]

However, from the very start of Carrick's liaison with Elizabeth Dunbar, there were doubts about the level of royal support for their marriage. There was no indication that Robert III had supplicated the pope on behalf of the young couple, and the marriage was evidently rushed through before the papal dispensation was made known in Scotland and certainly before the important matter of the heir to the throne's marriage was discussed by a parliament or general council.[34] Robert III's actions during 1396 certainly suggest that he had not given his approval to the match, which may also have caused tension within Carrick's own household.[35]

The difficulties which Robert III's kingship endured in the wake of what seems to have been a piece of straightforward opportunism on the part of the earl of March were exacerbated by the long-term damage inflicted on the king's prestige by the worsening of the political situation north of the Forth. In this area, as in the south, royal authority was maintained after 1393 by the earl of Carrick in conjunction with, or in most cases instead of, the king himself. The young heir to the throne took a leading role in a royal expedition to the north and north-east in 1395–6 which may have been partly concerned with the suppression of the Lindsay/Keith feud. Carrick certainly received compensation for the expenses he had incurred 'apud Aberden circa promocionem rei publice' and elsewhere 'in partibus borealibus'.[36] Carrick's involvement in the north from 1395/6 onwards may have reflected the shifting regional balance amongst his closest supporters. After Sir James Lindsay's death the senior figure in the heir to the throne's household was David Lindsay of Glen Esk, whose chief territorial and political interests lay in Angus. The political concerns of Sir Malcolm Drummond, Carrick's maternal uncle, had also shifted from the south of Scotland with his acquisition of the 'frontier' lordship of Mar in 1390. By 1395 both Glen Esk and Drummond, the most loyal and influential of Carrick's political associates, may have been encouraging him to intervene in the north.

The state of the central Highlands was a source of particular concern. The long-term consequences of the destruction of the earl of Buchan's central Highland lordship during the Fife guardianship were now becoming painfully apparent. As we have seen, Alexander, lord of Lochaber's territorial and political interests had spread rapidly north and east through the Great Glen in the early 1390s. The agreement of September 1394, by which the earl of Moray assigned lands at the northern end of Loch Ness to the lord of Lochaber in return for Alexander's obligation to defend the earldom from cateran raids, left Thomas Chisholm, the royal custodian of Urquhart castle since 1391, in the unenviable position of defending Urquhart with the land and water routes to the north and south of the fortress under the control of Alexander of the Isles.[37] It was a hopeless task, especially given the fact that the maintenance of professional mercenary troops now gave great Gaelic lords such as Alexander of the Isles the capacity to mount and sustain prolonged sieges.[38]

Chisholm seems either to have abandoned the fight and gone over to Lochaber's service, or to have been displaced by Alexander's adherents between 1395, when he received his last recorded payment as custodian, and April 1398, when a parliament largely concerned with co-ordinating an expedition against Alexander of the Isles discussed the need to place a trustworthy constable in Urquhart until the kingdom was pacified.[39] The expanding political influence of Isles-based lords and kindreds in the Great Glen was exemplified in the advance of a cadet branch of the MacLeans of Lochbuie (known as the *Siol Eachainn*, 'descendants of Eachann' by reason of their descent from Hector (Gaelic *Eachann*) MacLean, the first of the Lochbuie MacLeans) into mainland Morvern in the late fourteenth century. From their new territorial base in Kingairloch the *MacEachan* kindred followed Lochaber's advance into the Great Glen. Traditional accounts suggest that they took on the role of hereditary custodians of both Urquhart and Bona castles for the lords of the Isles, and it is certain that by 1440 Hector, son of Tearlach, the great-great-grandson of the progenitor of the clan, was acting as steward of Urquhart.[40]

Apart from the advance of the lord of Lochaber, the central Highlands were suffering from the effects of a serious feud between two Gaelic kindreds, the 'Clan Kay' and 'Clan Qwhele', which lowland chroniclers saw as destabilising 'a large part of the north of Scotland beyond the mountains'.[41] The crown response to this feud, as in so much else, was led by Carrick. At some stage between April 1396 and May 1397 Carrick was in northern parts for 'negociis regis', taking money from the custumars of Montrose and Aberdeen to finance his expedition.[42] One of the results of Carrick's appearance in the north was probably the infamous 30-a-side clan fight of September 1396 on the North Inch of Perth, a judicial conflict, presided over by the king, designed to bring the long-running dispute between the two kindreds to an end. The mutual bravery and butchery of the Highland kindreds involved in the struggle on the North Inch both horrified and impressed near-contemporary lowland chroniclers such as Wyntoun and Bower.[43] It also had its effect on later writers, with the episode providing one of the key dramatic moments in Sir Walter Scott's *The Fair Maid of Perth* where, however, the central hero of the affair became the hammer-handed Perth armourer Henry Smith, 'Henry of the Wynd', champion of the civic values of the industrious and law-abiding burghers of Perth.[44] The picturesque details of the 30-a-side contest are thus well known, although the actual identity of the two clans involved has never been satisfactorily established, despite much learned debate.[45] From the crown's point of view the spectacle at Perth was clearly intended as a response to repeated complaints about the ineffectiveness of royal justice in the north, and as a display of the royal line's ability to exercise lordship over the Gaelic kindreds of the central Highlands. Here the king could be seen personally presiding over a vicious and bloody form of dispute settlement which, according to Bower, had the desired effect in that 'for a long time the north remained quiet'.[46] While the brutal duel on the North Inch was a public relations triumph for Robert III, the men who had actually engineered the submission of the two clans to this form of dispute settlement were identified by Bower as Sir David Lindsay of Glen Esk and Thomas Dunbar, earl of Moray. Both of these men had probably accompanied the earl of Carrick's northern expedition in 1396.[47]

The autumn of 1396 did, however, see Robert III make a startling personal intervention in the south of Scotland, with a sudden move against his son's marriage to Elizabeth Dunbar, the earl of March's daughter. Late in 1396 the king personally initiated an attempt to invalidate the union. Between 26 April 1396 and 3 June 1397, but probably in the autumn of 1396, Robert III arrived at Haddington with a large army of 'genitibus suis' with the aim, so Bower informs us, of besieging the castle of Dunbar, 'in connection with the irregular marriage of his son and a daughter of the earl of March'.[48] George, earl of March, seems to have found the political situation within Scotland in the winter of 1396/7 rather uncomfortable, and on 26 February 1397 he obtained a six-month safe conduct from Richard II for himself and a hundred of his men.[49] At around the same time Walter Trail, bishop of St Andrews, initiated ecclesiastical proceedings against the marriage on the grounds that David and Elizabeth had failed to wait for the papal dispensation of August 1395 before marrying. The political and ecclesiastical assault on the validity of the Dunbar marriage in late 1396 explains the plea for absolution delivered by David and Elizabeth to Benedict XIII in the winter of 1396–7. On 10 March 1397 Benedict issued a dispensation to Gilbert Greenlaw, bishop of Aberdeen, the abbot of Kelso, and the dean of Dunbar, narrating that David and Elizabeth had applied for absolution, and granting that they should be allowed to marry after a suitable period of separation.[50]

The reasons underlying Robert III's attack on March in late 1396 are obscure, but its result may have been a fracturing of the close political relationship between the king and his son, for there is every indication that Carrick himself still favoured a marriage to Elizabeth Dunbar. The papal dispensation of March 1397 certainly suggests that Carrick had been personally involved in supplications to save the match.

In launching an attack on Carrick's Dunbar links, Robert III may have been seeking to re-assert his political control over the behaviour and political alliances of the 19-year-old prince, who was already displaying a disturbing propensity for aggressive independent action. Royal disruption of a match apparently supported by the heir to the throne was followed, in the exchequer audit of May 1397, by open criticism of Carrick for his raising of subsidies directly from the custumars of Edinburgh on his own authority, and without any mandate from the king and his officers.[51]

The exact status of Carrick's relationship with Elizabeth Dunbar after 1397 is uncertain. It may well be that the king, Carrick and March agreed on a prolonged separation of the couple, under the terms of the papal dispensation of March 1397, before their eventual re-marriage. Certainly there is no indication that Carrick and Elizabeth lived together after 1397, but the earl of March's furious reaction to the news, in early 1400, that Carrick was about to set aside Elizabeth and marry the earl of Douglas's daughter suggests that at that stage Dunbar still expected his daughter's delayed union with the heir to the throne to be carried through.[52]

In mid-1397 Robert III concluded a significant marriage settlement with a major southern magnate. On 24 May, in Edinburgh, King Robert reached agreement with Margaret Stewart, countess of Mar and Angus, that her son George, lord of Angus, would marry one of the king's daughters.[53] Amongst the extensive grants made by the king to the couple were obligations to confirm, under the great seal, any gifts or entails to be made by Isabella Douglas, countess of Mar, in favour of George, her half brother, and entails already made by Sir James Sandilands of Calder. Sandilands' grants in favour of George Douglas had been drawn up in April and May 1397, and were striking in their extent and intent. Sandilands, with the counsel and consent of his 'friends', had given over to George, earl of Angus (significantly described as the son of Sandilands' lord and uncle William, earl of Douglas and Mar), all his potential claims to the barony of Cavers, the sheriffship of Roxburgh, the forest of Jedworth, the lordship of Liddesdale, the town of Selkirk, the regality of Buittle and Drumlanrig and other lesser Douglas estates after the death of Isabella, countess of Mar, George's sister.[54] Sandilands' grant thus laid stress on George's position as the son of William, 1st of earl of Douglas (with no mention of his illegitimacy), and gave over to him Sir James's powerful claims to inherit all the unentailed Douglas estates on the death of Isabella Douglas, countess of Mar, George's half-sister, whose long marriage to Sir Malcolm Drummond had produced no heirs. The 'friends' who had counselled Sandilands' resignation included Sir David Lindsay, lord of Glen Esk, William Lindsay of the Byres, John Lindsay of Wauchope, Thomas Erskine, John Haliburton of that Ilk and Sir William Borthwick. This group was a mix of former or current adherents of Robert III, Carrick and Margaret, countess of Angus.

Sandilands' resignation and the subsequent marriage settlement between Robert III and the Angus Douglases represented the carefully co-ordinated culmination of the king's policies in the south since 1390. From the first, Robert III had surrounded the heir to the throne with adherents and kinsmen of the first two earls of Douglas, or men drawn from the wider Douglas/Lindsay affinity which had been Robert's own powerbase during the 1380s. These men had generally sought to restrict or reverse the territorial aggrandisement achieved by Archibald, 3rd earl of Douglas, and Sir James Douglas of Dalkeith during the Fife guardianship. In 1397 the powerful claims to all the unentailed Douglas estates and lordships vested in Sir James Sandilands were transferred to George Douglas, illegitimate son of William, 1st earl of Douglas, already the political focus for his father and brother's adherents in East Lothian. George was guaranteed royal support in his prosecution of claims to the wider Douglas inheritance as part of the marriage contracted to the king's daughter in 1397. The advance of George Douglas represented a clear threat to all those, particularly the 3rd earl of Douglas and his long-time friend and ally, Sir James Douglas of Dalkeith, who were occupying unentailed Douglas lordships on the basis of titles established or allowed during the Fife guardianship.

By the mid-1390s, George Douglas, earl of Angus, was emerging as one of the most important and active regional lords in the political affairs of southern Scotland. Early in 1398, according to Wyntoun, he was attending March Days alongside the earl of Carrick, 'A young Prynce plesand and mychty', Fife, Douglas, Moray and Sir David Lindsay of Glen Esk.[55] After the royal marriage contract of 1397, it was inevitable that Angus, backed by the crown, would mount a challenge to Archibald the Grim and Douglas of Dalkeith's exercise of lordship in Liddesdale and the other unentailed Douglas lordships. The growing political tension in East Lothian between Angus and Douglas of Dalkeith spilt over into open confrontation in 1398, with George Douglas and his adherents, notably his mother's kinsmen, the Sinclairs of Hirdmanston, launching a series of devastating raids on Dalkeith's estates during that year.[56] For at least the next four years, Douglas of Dalkeith's scattered property interests came under attack from George Douglas and his allies, who included Henry Sinclair, earl of Orkney, William Lindsay of the Byres, Sir James Sandilands, William of Newbigging and Davy Fleming.[57]

The Angus marriage of 1397 coincided with the emergence of Carrick as a regular member of his father's privy council, and the disappearance of Mathew Glendinning, bishop of Glasgow, who had been brought into royal government in April 1389, during the general council which had seen the triumph of Archibald the Grim and

Douglas of Dalkeith in the struggle over the Douglas inheritance. Another governmental change in the summer of 1397 saw Duncan Petyt replaced as chancellor by Gilbert Greenlaw, bishop of Aberdeen.[58] It may be significant that Greenlaw was one of the clerics who had supported Carrick's papal supplication for the preservation of his marriage to Elizabeth Dunbar.

The cumulative evidence suggests that in the summer of 1397 the settlement of the Douglas inheritance imposed during the Fife guardianship was under direct attack from the kinsmen and adherents of George Douglas, earl of Angus, with the full backing of Robert III and David, earl of Carrick. At the same time Carrick assumed a far greater prominence in the affairs of the royal government and shrugged off his father's attempt to control his political alliances and activities.

By the end of 1397 Carrick's extensive role in the political life of the kingdom was striking. The heir to the throne was newly established as a member of the king's council and served as the king's chief representative at Anglo-Scottish March Days and truce negotiations.[59] Carrick's robust denial of Percy claims to Jedworth forest during negotiations with the duke of Lancaster in March 1398, which was approvingly recorded by the chronicler Wyntoun, seemed to confirm the young prince's credentials as a forceful defender of the rights of the Scottish kingdom.[60] Besides the earl's role in Anglo-Scottish diplomacy, Carrick and his retainers had also been involved in punitive military/judicial expeditions into the central Highlands in 1395 and 1396.[61] Here, clearly, was a young man of immense energy, who was, probably quite self-consciously, intent on establishing his personal reputation in the two areas of royal activity which were regarded as crucial by the crown's subjects in the late fourteenth century: the defence of the status and integrity of the kingdom against the English monarchy, and the vigorous imposition of political and military lordship over the Gaelic lords of the west and central Highlands.

The young prince's leading role in both these spheres of royal government was revealed early in 1398, for immediately after his meeting with the English commissioners on the border in March 1398, Carrick travelled north to attend a general council, at Perth in the following month, which arranged for the heir to the throne or his uncle, Fife, to lead a large royal army against the lord of the Isles and his brothers during the summer of 1398.[62] The Perth Council reflected Carrick's growing power and influence, and the declining political authority of the king, in a number of other ways.

On 28 April 1398 Carrick received a very real indication of his growing importance inside the realm with his creation as duke of Rothesay in a ceremony at Scone. On the same day Rothesay's uncle,

Fife, was made duke of Albany. A week before the creation of the two royal dukedoms, Sir David Lindsay of Glen Esk, a principal member of Rothesay's household, had been made earl of Crawford, taking his title from the south-western lands he had inherited from Sir James Lindsay rather than any of his more established estates north of the Forth.[63] The foundation of the royal dukedoms has been ascribed to a desire on the part of the Scots government to have commissioners of equivalent status to those of the English king during Anglo-Scottish March Days and truce negotiations.[64] The fact that the newly created Rothesay, Albany and Crawford were regular participants in Scottish diplomacy, and had all been involved in negotiations with John, duke of Lancaster, in the previous month, might support this view. However, the Scots had happily dealt with the duke of Lancaster during the 1380s without feeling any pressing need to have commissioners to match his rank. Moreover, the creation of the dukedoms of Rothesay and Albany and the earldom of Crawford took place during an extended general council at Perth, where the king in particular, and the royal house in general, were being directly confronted with complaints about the political situation in the north.

The principal crown response was the organisation of a military expedition which was to move against Donald, lord of the Isles, and his brothers Alexander, lord of Lochaber, and John, lord of Dunivaig and the Glens, and the 'perdones et vastatores' in their service.[65] The army was to be headed by one or other of the two new royal dukes, and it seems to have been their impending leadership of royal forces destined for the central Highlands and the Hebrides which underlay the choice of ducal titles. Certainly, Fife's new title of Albany appears to have been a deliberate revival of the ancient Gaelic description for all of Scotland north of the Forth and Clyde.[66] Albany's title expressed the duke's aspiration to regional lordship over the area north of the Clyde in a way which was acceptable and understandable to the duke's allies and adherents in the Gaelic society of the south-western Highlands. Similarly, the title Rothesay, derived from the ancestral Stewart stronghold on the Isle of Bute, re-affirmed in the heir to the throne the Stewart family's status as active regional lords in the Firth of Clyde, and located the centre of that lordship in a fortress which was, in the context of 1398, a front-line defence against the lordship of the Isles' political influence in Kintyre, Knapdale and Cowal.

Rothesay's title may also have been designed to have other reso-nances for the Gaelic lords who were to support the crown's 1398 expedition. The fourteenth-century lowland chronicler, John of For-dun, incorporates into his *Chronica Gentis Scottorum* a curious tale concerning the origin of the name Rothesay, claiming that it derived from Euthacius or Eugenius Rothay, whom Fordun identifies, in a chapter entitled 'The first King of the Scots inhabiting the Islands of Albion', as a great-grandson of Simon Brek, and as the first leader of the Scots who crossed from Ireland to the 'islands of Albion'.[67] The provenance of the Eugenius Rothay legend is highly uncertain; it does not have any place in the origin legends of the Scots produced within Gaelic Scotland or Ireland.[68] However, depending on how widely the mythic origin of Rothesay's name was known or accepted in the Gaelic west, the heir to the throne's use of the title was potentially very useful in the political context of 1398, for it implicitly associated the prince with the first Gaelic lord of the western Isles, a figure whose authority in the Hebrides predated the hegemony established by Somerled and his descendants from the twelfth century onwards.

The adoption of the titles Albany and Rothesay thus seems to have been part of a crown propaganda drive accompanying the political and military campaign to be waged against the lordship of the Isles by the royal dukes during the summer of 1398. The political justification of the 1398 expedition to the Isles was to be framed in the context and terminology of Gaelic Scotland. If Donald, lord of the Isles, was stressing his position as *Rìgh Innes Gall*, descendant of Somerled and leader of the Gaelhealtachd, then the crown responded in terms which the Gaelic kindreds in royal service would understand. The titles Albany and Rothesay invoked the royal dynasty's Gaelic origins and its claim to the exercise of an ancient authority throughout Gaelic Scotland, and used them to contest Donald of the Isles' pretensions to the social and political leadership of the Scottish Gael. When Albany and Rothesay issued from Dumbarton in the summer of 1398 to carry war against the Isles, the two dukes were presenting themselves as the leaders rather than the persecutors of the Gael. It could hardly be otherwise, for war in the Hebrides would rely on the support of Albany's network of powerful allies in the west, including the earl or mormaer of Lennox and Sir Colin Campbell of Loch Awe, pretender to the title of *Rìgh Airir Goidel*, men whose place in the Gaelic world was confirmed in the collection of clan genealogies made up around 1400 and preserved in the enigmatic Gaelic Manuscript 1467 in the National Library of Scotland. It is tempting to suggest that the compilation of MS. 1467 must, in some way, have been inspired directly by the contemporary political and propaganda struggle between the crown and the lordship of the Isles.[69]

The near-simultaneous creation of an earldom for Sir David Lindsay of Glen Esk, already established as the effective military leader of the Angus lowlands, who had been heavily involved in military and judicial campaigns in the north throughout the 1390s, would seem to reinforce the view that the ducal titles were part of an attempt to reimpose royal authority in the north and west through the granting of an enhanced regional status to the heir to the throne and his uncle, encouraging the growth and consolidation of two active 'royal' lordships lying north and south of the Clyde whose holders had the local power and prestige to compete with the lordship of the Isles for the leadership of the Gaelic kindreds of the western Isles and Central Highlands.

Although the new titles do not seem to have been accompanied by any additional grants of land or jurisdictional power, there was clearly a delegation of royal authority and prestige implicit in the creation of the two dukedoms. The ducal titles were conferred during a ceremony conducted at Scone, the traditional centre for the investiture of kings, and the foremost prelate in the realm, Walter Trail, bishop of St Andrews, played a leading role in the proceedings. Bishop Trail led a mass and then preached a sermon on the 'state of the realm' before the king and queen.[70] The sermon no doubt reflected the 'multis punctis et articulis necessariis pro negociis regni et rei publice' which were under discussion in the general council of April/May 1398.[71]

Trail's sermon was unlikely to provide much comfort for Robert III, for the council seems to have been dominated by entreaties and complaints about the deteriorating situation in the north, and resentment and distrust of the king. Robert III's own response to the advances made by Clan Donald was clearly regarded as inadequate. As late as October 1397 he was apparently intent on dealing with the lordship through the establishment of more social and political ties between the king's allies in the west and the ruling house of Clan Donald, petitioning in that month in favour of a marriage between Robert Duncanson Lamont, chief of the Lamonts in Cowal, and Anna, daughter of Donald, lord of the Isles.[72]

The principal area of concern for the council of April 1398 appears to have been the position of Alexander, lord of Lochaber, in the central Highlands. As we have already seen, the lord of Lochaber and lordship kindreds associated with him had advanced rapidly into the Great Glen in the years after the destruction of the earl of Buchan's lordship in the area. The lord of Lochaber's eastern neighbours soon found him an even less congenial figure than Alexander Stewart. Lochaber had clearly ignored the terms of his 1394 indenture with Thomas, earl of Moray, by which Alexander was to suppress cateran raids into the earldom and the lands of the bishopric of Moray. By 1398 Lochaber was assigning church lands to his own adherents, and the clerical establishment in Moray seems to have regarded the political situation in the region as desperate. A brief chronicle in the Register of Moray

5) HIGHLAND CONNECTION: ALBANY AND THE LORDSHIP OF THE ISLES

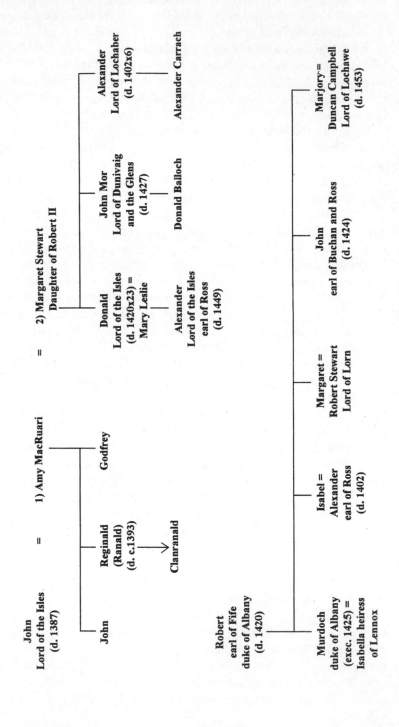

records the creation of the dukedoms of Rothesay and Albany in April 1398, and then, apparently talking of the same period, asserts that

'In those days there was no law in Scotland, but he who was stronger oppressed him who was weaker and the whole realm was a den of thieves; murders, herschips and fireraising and all other misdeeds remained unpunished; and justice, as if outlawed, lay in exile outwith the bounds of the realm.'[73]

William Spynie, at that stage only recently confirmed as the bishop of Moray after the death of Alexander Bur, certainly brought the complaints of his new diocese to the general council of April/May.[74] It seems certain that Spynie would have sympathised with — and may personally have promoted — the general council's preparation of an expedition against the lord of Lochaber and his brothers, and the additional demand that Urquhart castle in the Great Glen should be put into the hands of a good and sufficient captain until the kingdom was pacified.[75]

The general council combined its evident concern for effective royal action against the forces of the lordship with an open distrust of, and contempt for, the king. The council articles insisted that Robert III was not to be allowed to issue åny remissions to the rebels without the express consent of the council. This concerted criticism of the king in the April/May general council encouraged and emboldened the estates to protest against the king's policies in areas unrelated to the crisis in the north. One of the articles noted that it had been decided to cancel a grant made by the king to his long-time adherent John Shaw of the receivership of certain customs, because it was said to be against the 'good of the realm'. It was significant that the council chose Sir Patrick Graham, a well-known Albany adherent, as Shaw's replacement.[76]

Although Robert III appears to have escaped from the council of April 1398 with his power and authority undiminished, in reality the king's prestige had suffered a mortal blow. In the midst of consistent complaints about the ineffectiveness of the royal administration in the north, two royal dukes, the king's son and brother, had been created to lead the Scottish host against the lordship of the Isles. The same council had openly revoked and reversed royal patronage. While there had been no direct attempt to restrict the king's authority through the appointment of a guardian, Robert III must have known that his tenuous hold on power was slipping. The slow haemorrhaging of political support from a king facing relentless criticism of his personal inability to deal with the persistent strategic problems of the central Highlands gathered pace during 1398, and the obvious beneficiary was the heir to the throne.

Rothesay's political ascendancy seems to have had the implicit backing of some of the king's immediate family and household, including his queen, Annabella Drummond. Sometime in 1398, according to Bower, it was Queen Annabella, rather than the king, who arranged a tournament in Edinburgh for twelve knights, 'among whom the leading figure was her son the prince of the realm David Stewart. This occasion for the conferment of knighthood on him was staged close to the north side of the town of Edinburgh'.[77] Annabella's promotion of her son in the 1398 tournament may have been designed to mark Carrick's advance to a new political and social status, and to focus the loyalty of his knightly companions, and their families, on the young prince.

The intended base for the royal campaign against Donald of the Isles and his brothers during the summer of 1398 was Dumbarton. Amongst the first of the noblemen gathering in the royal burgh in late July 1398 was the west-coast magnate contesting Clan Donald's overlordship in Argyll, Albany's ally, Sir Colin Campbell, lord of Loch Awe, and his kinsman Arthur Campbell of Menstrie.[78] By early August the aspiring *Rìgh Airir Goídel* had been joined in Dumbarton by the king himself, along with the 'leading men and important nobles in the kingdom'.[79] Dumbarton's usefulness as the centre for the Highland expedition of 1398 must, however, have been affected adversely by a dispute between the king and the unofficial constable of the royal castle of Dumbarton, the militant and secularised cleric Walter Danielston, who had seized control of the fortress late in 1397, after the death of his brother Sir Robert Danielston.[80] Danielston's occupation of Dumbarton was a matter of interest to Albany, as well as to the king, for the jurisdiction of the custodian and the sheriff of Dumbarton was enmeshed with that of the earldom of Lennox, to which the duke's son was heir. The king and Albany may, in fact, have been supporting different solutions to the problem of finding a replacement for Sir Robert Danielston in Dumbarton after 1396.[81] Walter's seizure of the royal castle, apparently with significant local support, provoked a bitter reaction from Robert III. As Wyntoun recounts, Danielston

> The Castell tuk off Dunbertane.
> That Lithcow menyt in Louthiane,
> And syndry uthir landis sare
> Menyt, that evyr he gat in thare
> Set it plesit nocht to the King
> That hous he held till his endying.[82]

The final two lines provided a damning comment on Robert III's political impotence. Whatever Danielston's motives, the fact that one of the kingdom's principal royal fortresses was being held in open defiance of the crown must have contributed to the general dissatisfaction with Robert III's governance of the realm. The arrival of royal forces in Dumbarton *en route* to the Isles allowed the king to organise a siege of the fortress. For at least three months, between early August and the end of October 1398, Robert III was at Dumbarton with a considerable army which required substantial supplies of iron, wood and foodstuffs for its activities in the Isles and around the royal castle.[83] The scale of the operation is shown in the three-year hiatus in the rendering of accounts by the bailies of the burgh of Dumbarton between 1397 and 1400, in which latter year the burgh was allowed to give in a reduced burghal ferm because of 'guerre de uno anno trium annorum'.[84] Robert III's attempts to remove Danielston from Dumbarton in the summer and autumn of 1398, while Albany and Rothesay were moving against Donald of the Isles, were ultimately unsuccessful. The failure of the royal siege is hardly surprising given the description of the fortress by the Englishman John Harding in the fifteenth century:

> . . . no man may that strong castell assayle.
> Upon a rocke so hye the same doth stande,
> That yf the walles were beaten to the rocke,
> Yet were it full harde to clymbe with foot or hand,
> And so to wynne, yf any to them approche,
> So strong it is to get without reproche,
> That without honger and cruell famyshemente,
> Yt cannot bee taken to my judgemente.[85]

Yet in 1398 the failure of Robert III's siege of Dumbarton must have seemed symptomatic of the king's personal ineffectiveness and his crumbling political authority. Rothesay's territorial and political position, in contrast, continued to advance. On 6 September 1398 at Dumbarton, in the midst of the campaign against the lordship, Robert III assigned control of the royal earldom of Atholl to Rothesay.[86] The grant of Atholl, along with his co-leadership of the royal armies moving against the lordship, confirmed Rothesay's emergence as the man exercising personal lordship in the north on behalf of the senior Stewart line. Although Albany and Rothesay's campaign against Donald of the Isles achieved only limited success, by the autumn of 1398 the heir to the throne had clearly established himself as the political, military and judicial representative of the Scottish crown in Anglo-Scottish diplomacy and in the imposition of control over the Gaelic lords and kindreds of the West.[87]

Robert III, in his five years of personal rule, had displayed a dangerous reliance on his son and his retainers to implement royal policy. His own contribution to the governance of the realm, undoubtedly restricted by illness, seems to have involved long spells of relative inactivity broken by occasional and usually ineffective bursts of aggression.[88] Political discontent with the king, clearly running high in the general council of April 1398, became well-nigh unstoppable in the aftermath of the 1398 expedition to the Isles. Robert III's personal exercise of power was probably effectively ended during an informal gathering of noblemen at the duke of Albany's manor of Falkland on and around 14 November 1398, only two weeks after the close of the royal campaign in the west.[89] Albany's guests included Walter, bishop of St Andrews, Gilbert, bishop of Aberdeen and chancellor of the kingdom, the king's son David, duke of Rothesay, Archibald, earl of Douglas, and Albany's son Murdoch, justiciar north of the Forth. This assembly of the most powerful magnates and prelates in the kingdom had two recent precedents, from 1384 and 1388, for the way in which an unsatisfactory king or guardian could be sidelined, and effective power transferred to the nearest adult male within the royal dynasty. With Robert III's government regarded as a manifest failure, Albany and Douglas were evidently negotiating with Rothesay, the 20-year-old heir to the throne, in an attempt to recast the royal administration in a more effective and amenable form. Albany had little cause to support his brother, but he had built up a working relationship with his nephew during the Highland campaigns of 1397–8. Moreover, many of Albany's northern affinity and key members of Rothesay's household enjoyed close political, social and familial links and shared almost identical political and strategic goals in the region north of the Forth. David Lindsay, earl of Crawford, in particular, provided a crucial political link between the two royal dukes.[90]

Archibald, 3rd earl of Douglas, on the other hand, had faced and survived the political hostility of Robert III and his associates throughout the 1390s, including the crown-inspired assault by George, earl of Angus, on Archibald's friend and associate, James Douglas of Dalkeith, during 1398. Archibald would thus have felt little loyalty to Robert III, a man whom he had already helped to displace from power in 1388. However, late in 1398 Douglas was presented with an opportunity to transform the fraught political relationship between his family and the royal house. The earl's backing for any attempt which the heir to the throne might make to restrict his father's authority would, despite Rothesay's earlier involvement with Archibald the Grim's political adversaries, place the young prince in Douglas's debt. An agreement with Rothesay held out the prospect of a settlement of the political animosity which had been the key feature of the relationship between the royal dynasty and the earl of Douglas after 1389. Rothesay, like many members of the old Douglas affinity, had abandoned the vengeful ghosts of the Otterburn campaign and had reconciled himself to the reality of the 3rd earl's power in the south.[91]

The result of the Falkland negotiations was made apparent during a general council of January 1399 in Perth which saw Robert III's demission of power and the creation of a three-year lieutenancy for Rothesay. The duke was to govern the realm with the advice of a council of twenty-one named men, a list which included Albany and Douglas.[92] Within a year the new political relationship between Rothesay and the earls of Douglas would be cemented by the prince's marriage to the 3rd earl's daughter.[93]

Since 1390 Robert III had consistently sought to support and advance the interests of his own dynasty in the person of his first-born son David, duke of Rothesay. For most of this period Rothesay's growing political power and assertiveness must have been regarded by the king as an indication of his own triumph over his adversaries from the 1380s. By 1398, largely as a result of Robert III's own inadequacies, Rothesay was co-operating with his father's principal political opponents in order to remove the king from power; the young prince had been transformed from a symbol of the king's success to an agent of his downfall.

NOTES

1. Above, pp. 152, 174–5.
2. *Notices et extraits des Manuscrits de la Bibliothèque Nationale et autres Bibliothèques*, v, 564: from *Le Chevalier Errant* by the Marquis of Saluzzo, who died in 1416. Saluzzo's account could have been influenced by the unflattering picture of Robert II in Froissart's Chronicle, which was published in 1393, although at no stage does Froissart suggest that Robert II's hold on the crown was under threat. It seems most likely that Saluzzo was reflecting a contemporary French view that the Scots were dependent on French diplomatic support, and that Robert III's political authority within his own kingdom was very weak.
3. Nicholson, *Later Middle Ages*, 211–2, where the pensions are viewed as part of a Europe-wide breakdown in the efficacy of the feudal contract, with the crown paying for the loyalty of men whose service as tenants-in-chief should have been rendered automatically.
4. *ER*, iii, 251–2, 280, 287, 292, 295, 316, 340–1, 471, 488; *Charters and Documents Relating to the City of Edinburgh, 1143–1540* (Scottish Burgh Record Society, 1871), 44; *RMS*, i, nos. 811–2: pensions to William Stewart and William Lindsay (2 January and 27 March 1392), 2 January 1391 for Sir David Lindsay.

5. Montgomery, Stewart of Jedworth, Lindsay of the Byres and the earl of Moray had all fought alongside the 2nd earl of Douglas at Otterburn, where Montgomery was reputed to have captured Sir Henry Percy: *Froissart* (Johnes), ii, 362, 371; *Chron. Wyntoun* (Laing), iii, 36. William Danielston was the brother of Sir Robert Danielston, who had been a regular charter witness for Robert III throughout the 1380s.

6. *ER*, iii, 290–1. The pension was clearly intended to be a permanent alienation to Robert III's own immediate family. Its terms, to some extent, ran counter to the great entailing of the crown in 1373. The pension was to be held by David and his heirs, whom failing Robert Stewart, his brother and his heirs, whom failing their sisters produced between the king and queen Annabella 'in suam promocionem viris maritandis, quibus deficientibus viris et legitimis heredibus regis'.

7. *ER*, iii, 286, 288, 291–93, 296, 298, 300–1, 303, 320, 325, 330–1, 342, 353. John Logie was probably the queen's cousin, and the man involved in the long-running dispute with Fife over the lordship of Strath Gartney. Carrick's teacher and schoolmaster was a Thomas Mauchane or Mather, who had served as Robert III's chaplain in the 1380s: *CPP*, i, 578.

8. *ER*, iii, 311.

9. *Froissart* (Johnes), ii, 373–74.

10. *CDS*, iv, no. 384.

11. *Westminster*, 400–1. The English sources lay great emphasis on Lindsay's political importance within Scotland before his capture, an impression confirmed by the large payment of 2,000 livres tournois made to Sir James from the war subsidy distributed to Scottish noblemen by the French crown in 1385. Lindsay's share was surpassed only by the sums given to the earls of Carrick, Douglas, Fife, and March, and the lord of Galloway: *Foedera*, vii, 484–5.

12. SRO Lothian Muniments GD40/3/234: an undated and unplaced charter which was probably issued in the autumn of 1389 at Calder castle. Lindsay was a witness to the charter, which was issued by Sir James Sandilands and Sir John Haliburton of that Ilk in favour of Sir Thomas Cranston, of the lands of Falnash (Roxburghshire) and ten merklands in Longniddry. The charter was certainly issued after 1384, and probably after the 2nd earl of Douglas's demise in 1388. Lindsay's fellow-witnesses included Sir Malcolm Drummond, William Haliburton, William of Newbigging, William Douglas, lord of Drumlanrig, a natural son of the 2nd earl of Douglas, and Simon Murray, constable of Calder. Both of the granters had sought safe conducts from Richard II in June 1389 and had placed their lands, including Falnash and Longniddry, into the English king's protection. At least

two of the principal charter witnesses, Drummond and William Haliburton, had also applied for English safe conducts.

13. *ER*, iii, 219. In the company of William Stewart of Jedworth, another Douglas loyalist later recruited as one of Carrick's pensioned retainers: *CDS*, v, no. 2055.

14. *ER*, iii, 317; *RMS*, i, nos. 868, 869. It seems significant that the retaining pensions gifted to Fife and his son did not specify any service to Robert III.

15. *ER*, iii, 311. The identity of the justiciar south of the Forth is uncertain, although it seems most likely that Fife had secured Archibald, 3rd earl of Douglas, as justiciar after 1388. By 1393 Carrick had either replaced Douglas as justiciar or was accompanying the earl on his judicial progress.

16. *CPL, CLement VII*, 198.

17. *ER*, iii, 251, 359, 361, 386, 388.

18. *Chron. Bower* (Watt), viii, 41.

19. *Foedera*, vii, 788. David Lindsay had established a cross-border reputation with his exploits in a tournament held by Richard II in London in 1390: *Chron. Wyntoun* (Laing), iii, 47–50; *Chron. Bower* (Watt), viii, 13.

20. John Stuart (ed.), *Spalding Club Miscellany V* (Spalding Club, 1852), 230.

21. Wiliam Douglas had received the royal lordship of Nithsdale possibly as a result of his marriage to Robert II's daughter, Egidia, on or shortly before 26 December 1387: *RMS*, i, no. 753. The grant of Nithsdale followed shortly thereafter, certainly before 10 February 1390, and probably during the Fife guardianship: *ER*, iii, 207, where Douglas is styled 'de Niddesdal'; *Chron. Wyntoun* (Laing), iii, 30–1; Fraser, *Douglas*, iii, 399–400. William Douglas's military exploits in both Ireland and England during 1388 were reported in great detail in the anonymous account which reflected political propaganda produced by supporters of Fife and Archibald the Grim between 1388 and 1390. With the proclamation of the Anglo-Scottish truce in 1389, William Douglas's considerable personal energy was diverted to Prussia, where he hoped to join the crusades of the Teutonic Knights against the heathens. Douglas was in Bruges by December 1390, but was killed in 1391 in Königsberg in a quarrel with crusading English knights: *Chron. Wyntoun* (Laing), iii, 32–4; SRO AD 1/27. Douglas's companions in Bruges included Sir Robert Stewart of Durisdeer, the man who had fought alongside Douglas in the raid on Ireland in 1388: Macquarrie, *Crusades*, 85–7.

22. *RRS*, vi, 93–5; Fraser, *Douglas*, iii, 357.

23. NLS 'Historie of the Kennedies', in Adv. MSS., 33.3.28; *Historical and Genealogical Accounts of the principal families of the name of Kennedy, from*

an original manuscript, ed. R. Pitcairn (Edinburgh, 1830), 5. The chronicle regularly conflates various generations of the Kennedy family and has a hopelessly confused chronology.

24. A. Agnew, *The Hereditary Sheriffs of Galloway* (Edinburgh, 1843), 51–2.

25. *Edinburgh University Library; Catalogue of Manuscripts*, Appendix iv, 329 (MSS 27).

26. *Chron. Wyntoun* (Laing), iii, 62–3. The castle of Fyvie and the thanage of Formartine in which it stood had been held by Sir James Lindsay since 1382: *Abdn.Reg.*, 138. In 1389 Lindsay was released from English custody in exchange for Henry and Ralph Percy. On 28 September 1390 Robert III granted Sir Henry Preston all the barony of Formartine, except the castle of Fyvie and some named estates, on the resignation of James Lindsay: RMS, i, no. 801. The grant was said to be for the ransom of Sir Ralph Percy, suggesting that Sir James Lindsay was having to compensate those who had been due a share of Percy's ransom from his own resources. Preston seems to have pressed for control of Fyvie castle, the chief residence of his new barony of Formartine, and the estates remaining in Lindsay's possession. At some stage between 1393 and 1396 a settlement was attempted when Preston married Sir James Lindsay's sister, and the couple were given the Formartine lands which had been excluded from the 1390 grant with the exception, yet again, of Fyvie castle: NRAS no. 523: Fyvie Castle Muniments, no. 4. Preston enjoyed the support of Sir William Keith, the Marischal, and the Marischal's son and grandson, both named Robert, who witnessed the various transactions between Preston and Lindsay.

27. The Robert Keith involved in the battle of Bourtrie was Fife's nephew; he appeared as a witness to a grant by Fife in Stirling on 18 February 1399, and plans were made for his marriage to a daughter of William Graham, a Fife adherent: *RMS*, i, App. 1, no. 155.

28. *Charter Chest of the Earldom of Wigtown* (SRS, 1910), 50 (nos. 843–46).29. *Ibid.*, nos. 847–9; NLS Fleming of Wigtown Collection, Ch. nos. 15821, 16086.

30. ER, iii, 361; Fraser, *Douglas*, iii, 365–6.

31. *CPL, Benedict XIII*, 45. The March marriage must have been contracted almost immediately on the death of Sir James Lindsay, who was still alive in April 1395 (assuming that Euphemia Lindsay could not have been set aside while Sir James remained active in Carrick's household).

32. ER, iii, 316, 340–1, 348, 371.

33. *Ibid.*, iii, 384, 405.

34. *CPL, Benedict XII*, 70; *Chron. Bower* (Watt), viii, 31.

35. *Chron. Bower* (Watt), viii, 41, for the suggestion that Carrick's

rejection of Euphemia Lindsay annoyed her brother William Lindsay of Rossie.

36. *ER*, iii, 388, 402, 458.

37. *Moray Reg.*, 354–5.

38. K. Simms, *Kings to Warlords*, 127.

39. *ER*, iii, 376; *APS*, i, 570.

40. J. W. M. Bannerman, *Monumental Sculpture*, 129–31 (no. 54); A. M. Sinclair, *The Clan Gillean* (Charlottetown, 1899), 276–80; SRO Rose of Kilravock GD 125/Box 14; C. Innes (ed.), *A Genealogical Deduction of the Family of Rose of Kilravock* (Spalding Club, 1898), 131.

41. *Chron. Bower* (Watt), viii, 7.

42. *ER*, iii, 412, 415, 441, 442.

43. *Chron. Bower* (Watt), viii, 7–11; *Chron. Wyntoun* (Laing), iii, 63–4.

44. Sir Walter Scott, *The Fair Maid of Perth* (Edinburgh, 1828), 408–25.

45. A. M. Shaw, *The Clan Battle at Perth in 1396* (Wimbledon, 1874); W. F. Skene, *Celtic Scotland* (Edinburgh, 1890), iii, 307–18; J. Neilson, *Trial by Combat* (Glasgow, 1890), 251–5. The 'Clan Qwhele' had been involved in the great Glasclune raid of 1392.

46. *Chron. Bower* (Watt), viii, 10–11; *ER*, iii, 418.

47. *ER*, iii, 412, 415.

48. *Chron. Bower* (Watt), viii, 5, 31; *ER*, iii, 428.

49. *Rot.Scot.*, ii, 136.

50. *CPL, Benedict XIII*, 70.

51. *ER*, iii, 407–8.

52. *Chron. Bower* (Watt), viii, 31–33.

53. Fraser, *Douglas*, iii, 38–9.

54. *Ibid.*, 35–6. On 27 April 1397 Sandilands made further resignations in favour of the countess of Angus and her son, including a five-year lease of Sandilands' castle of Calder: *Ibid.*, 37–8.

55. *Chron. Wyntoun* (Laing), iii, 65–6. Wyntoun's description has Carrick defending the rights of the Scottish kingdom in emphatic fashion, proving his ability to rule. Wyntoun's overall assessment of the prince is remarkably positive. Note, however, that Carrick's defence of the rights of Archibald, earl of Douglas, to reside with his men in Jedworth must be seen against the background of the transfer of a claim to Jedworth to George Douglas.

56. NLS Morton Chartulary MS.72. ff. 33r, 36r.

57. *Ibid.*, ff. 34v, 39r.

58. SRO RH6/205, 14 January 1397, Petyt still Chancellor; J. Anderson (ed.), *Calendar of the Laing Charters 854–1837* (Edinburgh, 1899), no. 83.

59. *ER*, iii, 378; *Chron. Wyntoun* (Laing), iii, 65–6; *Rot. Scot.*, ii, 138; *CDS*, iv, nos. 492–3, 502. Carrick's pensioned retainers also played a prominent role in the diplomatic sphere, particularly Sir David Lindsay, Sir William Lindsay of Rossie, and Sir William Stewart of Jedworth.

60. *Chron. Wyntoun* (Laing), iii, 66.
61. *ER*, iii, 402, 412, 415, 441, 442, 458.
62. *APS*, i, 570.
63. *Chron. Wyntoun* (Laing), iii, 69–70; *Chron. Bower* (Watt), viii, 11, 13; *Moray Reg.*, 382.
64. E. W. M. Balfour-Melville, *James I, King of Scots 1406–1437* (London, 1936), 13–4; R. Nicholson, *Later Middle Ages*, 213–4.
65. *APS*, i, 570.
66. J. W. M. Bannerman, *Studies in the History of Dalriada* (Edinburgh, 1974), 118–19.
67. *Chron. Fordun*, i, 24–5, 301–2; W. W. Scott, 'John of Fordun's Description of the Western Isles', *Scottish Studies*, xxiii (1979), 1–13, at 11.
68. Cf. W. W. Scott, 'John of Fordun's Description', 11, for the suggestion that the story is essentially Fordun's own invention in order to gratify the new Stewart king whose lordships included Bute.
69. One recent interpretation suggests that MS. 1467 was, in essence, a list of the kindreds over which the lord of the Isles claimed some form of overlordship: J. W. M. Bannerman, *Monumental Sculpture*, 205; M. D. W. MacGregor, 'A Political History of the MacGregors before 1571' (unpublished Ph.D. thesis), Edinburgh, 1989, Appendix 13: The Dating and Composition of MS 1467, 414–420. Several of the kindreds whose descent is given, notably the Mormaers of Lennox, the Campbells of Loch Awe and the MacNabs of Glen Dochart, were demonstrably in the service of the duke of Albany.
70. *Chron. Bower* (Watt), viii, 13; *Chron. Wyntoun* (Laing), iii, 69–70. Wyntoun suggests that Carrick and the Stewartry were annexed to the title of Rothesay which was, thereafter, to be held by the king's eldest son.
71. *ER*, iii, 460.
72. *CPL, Benedict XIII*, 79.
73. *Moray Reg.*, 211, for complaints against Lochaber for giving over the bishop's lands of 'Kynmily' to Ranald MacAlexander, John Chisholm of the Ard, and John White; *Ibid.*, 382; R. Nicholson, *Later Middle Ages*, 209–10.
74. On 3 May Alexander Stewart, earl of Buchan, was ordered to restore the castle of Spynie, which the earl seems to have held, quite legitimately, during the vacancy of the see, to the new bishop: *Moray Reg.*, 208.
75. *APS*, i, 570. Aside from the problems in and around Moray and the Great Glen, other branches of the ruling dynasty within the lordship made extensive gains elsewhere in the kingdom. Godfrey of the Isles, an elder half-brother of the lord of the Isles, is reputed to have launched a huge seaborne campaign against Skye, nominally held

by Albany's young son-in-law, Alexander Leslie, during the 1390s, a campaign beaten off by the MacLeods: I. F. Grant, *The MacLeods: The History of a Clan, 1200–1956* (London, 1959), 45–6. By 1401 Godfrey's son Angus had established himself on the northern mainland, with the power to intervene in territorial disputes in Strathglass, Strathnaver, Sutherland and Caithness.

76. *APS*, i, 571.

77. *Chron. Bower* (Watt), viii, 11.

78. *Highland Papers*, iv, 18–19.

79. NLS Fleming of Wigtown Collection, Ch. no. 15730 (4 August 1398); *HMC Report*, xv (viii), 51 (10 August).

80. Walter had seized control of the royal fortress on the Clyde after the death of his brother, Sir Robert, between 26 April 1396 and 8 May 1397. Sir Robert had succeeded his father, Sir John Danielston, as sheriff and keeper of Dumbarton, so that by 1397 the Danielstons had held the fortress continuously for at least 37 years, and probably considered that they had a hereditary right to the constableship of the castle and its associated offices: *ER*, iii, 422, 425; *ER*, i, 572, 574, 582; *Cartulariam Comitatus de Levenax* (Maitland Club, 1833), 58–9. Sir Robert had no sons but did have two daughters, married respectively to Sir William Cunningham of Kilmaurs and Sir Robert Maxwell of Pollock: T. F. Donald, 'The Dennistons of Denniston', *SHR*, xv (1917–1918), 241.

81. In December 1396, probably shortly after Sir Robert Danielston's death, Murdoch Stewart and Lennox seem to have concluded an agreement with one of Sir Robert's sons-in-law Sir William Cunningham, the younger, of Kilmaurs, perhaps in the expectation that he would succeed to Sir Robert's estates and offices: SRO Glencairn Muniments GD 39/1/13, a charter of 8 December by which Robert III confirmed a grant by Murdoch Stewart to Sir William Cunningham of the lands and barony of Redhall. Duncan, earl of Lennox, must have approved of this deal, since Redhall was the barony which had been given to Murdoch Stewart and the earl's daughter on their marriage in 1392. Robert III, on the other hand, may have been promoting the claims of Patrick Danielston, Walter's young nephew. Patrick was the son of the deceased Sir William Danielston, who had served as one of Robert III's pensioned retainers in the early 1390s. In 1398 Patrick was in the care of Robert III's illegitimate son James Stewart of Kilbride. As a cleric Walter had no children of his own, but he may have hoped to secure parts of his brother's inheritance either for his young nephew Patrick, or his nieces. It is possible that Danielston had the tacit support of Albany and Lennox in the capture of Dumbarton, for Walter had been personally appointed by Duncan, earl of Lennox, to the hospital of Polmadie in the early 1390s.

82. *Chron. Wyntoun* (Laing), iii, 76. Linlithgow's displeasure would seem to be based on the fact that the keeper of Dumbarton was due an 80-merk pension from the burghal fermes. Although there is no evidence that Danielston ever successfully collected this payment, he may have made some attempt to uplift the pension in 1398.

83. NLS Fleming of Wigtown Collection, Ch. no. 15730 (4 August); *HMC Report*, xv, part viii, 51 (10 August); SRO GD 124/1/525 (11 August); BM Harleian MSS. no. 4694 f. 13r–v (9 September); SRO GD 124/1/422 (29 October); *ER*, iii, 465–6, 490.

84. *ER*, iii, 502.

85. P. Hume Brown, *Early Travellers in Scotland* (Edinburgh, 1973), 21.

86. BM Harleian MSS, no. 4694, f. 13r–v, issued at Dumbarton.

87. The Albany/Rothesay expedition forced Donald to take his brother Alexander of Lochaber into custody and give assurances for his future behaviour. By November 1399 Donald had reneged on the deal and released Alexander: *APS*, i, 575.

88. The king was certainly ill in the winter of 1392/3: *ER*, iii, 306.

89. *RMS*, i, no. 886.

90. Crawford was one of Rothesay's pensioned retainers and a regular charter witness for the prince. However, the earl had also been involved in Albany's northern campaigns against the Wolf of Badenoch in the period 1388–93, and continued to maintain a close contact with Albany and his adherents. Duke of Atholl's Muniments, Blair Castle, Blair Atholl, Box 7/ Parcel iv/ Innermeath: Lindsay appears as a witness alongside Murdoch Stewart to a pre-1398 charter by Albany (as earl of Fife and Menteith), to John Stewart of Innermeath of lands in earldom of Fife. On 20 April 1398 at Perth, the day before his creation as earl of Crawford, David Lindsay, *lord of Crawford*, witnessed a charter by Robert Stewart, lord of Durisdeer, which was also witnessed by Fife, his son Murdoch, John, lord of Lorn, Thomas Kirkpatrick and William Lindsay of Rossie: NRAS Buccleuch Muniments, Drawer 3 (lands in the barony of Durisdeer).

91. Richard Hangangside, for example, was one of the men who had held Tantallon in 1388 for Margaret Sinclair, the mistress of William, 1st earl of Douglas. On a date before December 1400 Hangangside was providing for masses for the souls of his deceased lords William and James, 1st and 2nd earls of Douglas, and for the soul of his current lord Archibald, 3rd earl: *Kelso Liber*, 410–12.

92. *APS*, i, 572–4.

93. *Chron. Bower* (Watt), viii, 31.

8

Comets and Shooting Stars:
The Lieutenancy of the Duke of Rothesay,
1398–1402

The general council which met in Perth in January 1399, within three months of the conclusion of the Albany/Rothesay campaign against Donald of the Isles and his brothers, saw the end of Robert III's brief period of personal rule. The council's criticism of the king's ability to govern his realm was direct, brutal and final. The 'mysgovernance of the realm and the defaut of the keiping of the common law' were to be 'input to' the king and his officers, 'sen it is welesene and kennyt' that the king 'for seknes of his person may nocht travail to governe the Realme na restrygne trespassours and rebellours', a criticism clearly derived from the events of the previous year. Because of the king's incapacity, it was 'sene to the consail maste expedient that the duc of Rothesay be the kingis lieutenande generally throch al the Kynrike for the terme of thre yher'.[1]

It has been suggested that the appointment of Rothesay was a thinly veiled attack on the position of the duke of Albany.[2] Certainly, the general council gave leave to the king to summon his officers before the council to answer for their failings 'and thair ansuere herde the consail sal be redy to juge thair defautes, syn na man aw to be condampnyt qwhil he be callit and accusit'.[3] This clause may have been directed against Albany's son Murdoch, who was justiciar north of the Forth, or against the duke himself, who had clearly been given some form of special responsibility for the enforcement of the legislation of a general council held in Stirling in 1397 intended to improve the effectiveness of criminal justice. It seems strange, however, if the aim of the general council was indeed to downgrade the status of Albany and Murdoch and to promote Rothesay at their expense, that neither man had been officially summoned to the January council to answer for their deficiencies. Even if Albany and Murdoch were among the royal officers to be judged by the council when, and if, Robert III made his formal complaint against them, this could not have reversed the decision to give the duke of Rothesay effective control of royal government. It is likely that accusations were made against certain royal officers during the course of the council, probably by the king in his own defence, but it seems clear that the council had been called primarily to remove Robert III from power, a bloodless coup finalised during the meeting of Albany, Douglas and Rothesay the previous November.[4]

There were several figures who may have played a key role in encouraging some measure of political co-operation between Albany, Douglas and the heir to the throne during 1399. Queen Annabella, Rothesay's mother, received a glowing epitaph from the chronicler Bower for her work, alongside Walter Trail, bishop of St Andrews, who had attended the November 1398 meeting at Falkland, in raising 'high the honour of the kingdom as it were by recalling to amity princes and magnates who had been roused to discord'.[5] An even more important personality in ensuring a stable relationship between Rothesay and Albany in 1398–9 was David Lindsay, the newly created earl of Crawford. David Lindsay was an integral part of Rothesay's household, but also enjoyed a good relationship with Albany and his northern allies. Crawford's closeness to Albany and his northern interests was confirmed in one of the first royal grants of the Rothesay lieutenancy. On 5 February 1399, at Perth, Robert III granted the barony of Fitkill in Fife to Sir George Leslie on the resignation of Alexander Leslie, earl of Ross.[6] The earl's resignation was made during the general council which had seen Rothesay created lieutenant, and the men employed by Ross to resign Fitkill to the crown were his cousin David Lindsay, William Dalziel and Sir John Ramornie.[7] Alexander and George Leslie were both attached to Albany's affinity, Alexander being the duke's son-in-law, while Crawford and Ramornie were members of Rothesay's household.

The close co-operation between men attached to Rothesay and Albany early in 1399 hardly supports the notion that the prince's lieutenancy was part of an attempt to destroy Albany's political influence, nor is such a view advanced by the various conditions imposed on Rothesay's exercise of the powers of lieutenancy by the 1399 council. One of the restrictions was that Rothesay was to govern using the advice of a council of twenty-one designated wise men.[8] The secular element of this council was dominated by northern interests and Albany adherents. Rothesay's 'special council' was to include Albany himself, his brother Walter Stewart of Brechin, Alexander Leslie, earl of Ross, Albany's son-in-law, Thomas Dunbar, earl of Moray, David, earl of Crawford, Sir William Keith, the Marischal, Albany's father-in-law, Sir Patrick Graham, and Sir John Ramornie, who had extensive ties to Albany's son Murdoch. Albany and his allies thus dominated the 'council' assigned to advise the young lieutenant, and the remaining conditions imposed by the general council ensured that it would be difficult, if not impossible, for Rothesay to bypass this body in formulating and executing royal policies and distributing patronage. Furthermore, there was no indication of any attempt by Rothesay to undermine Albany's position in the kingdom in the early months of the lieutenancy, with Murdoch Stewart continuing to act as justiciar north of the Forth.[9] In political terms, then, 1399 saw Robert III displaced from power by a powerful aristocratic coalition, headed by the king's long-term political rivals Albany and Douglas, which had flung its support behind the promotion of the heir to the throne as a means of addressing widespread concern over the ineffectiveness of the royal administration. Rothesay thus became a royal lieutenant under strict conciliar control, a situation designed to preserve the political influence of Albany and his allies and to exclude Robert III from any meaningful role in government.[10]

Aside from the Ross grant of February 1399, there were further indications of the promotion of Albany's interests in the early months of 1399, and of some measure of co-operation between the duke and men associated with Queen Annabella and Rothesay. On 18 February 1399, at Stirling, Albany issued a charter of the baronies of Coull and O'Neill in Aberdeenshire to his son John Stewart.[11] The first named witness to the charter was Sir Malcolm Drummond, Lord of Mar, brother of Queen Annabella Drummond and Rothesay's maternal uncle. Drummond had a long-standing claim, through his wife Isabella Douglas, to possession of Coull and O'Neill, so that his appearance as a witness to the Albany grant was doubly significant, because it meant that the queen's brother was abandoning a long-running dispute with Albany within three weeks of Rothesay becoming lieutenant. Queen Annabella's interests were also directly addressed during the January 1399 council, which stipulated that the queen was to receive the 2,000-merk pension which had been assigned to her in 1391 without any interference from the chamberlain, Albany, and his deputies.[12] It would seem that the queen, her brother Malcolm Drummond, and her son Rothesay had effectively abandoned Robert III late in 1398, and had reached an accommodation with Albany.

At first sight, the Rothesay lieutenancy seemed to offer a new dawn for the Stewart monarchy. Royal power was to be exercised by a young and vigorous prince who had already established himself as an active participant in Anglo-Scottish diplomacy and as a leader of military expeditions into the central Highlands and the Hebrides. Moreover, Rothesay's lieutenancy was founded on a policy of co-operation rather than confrontation with the two most powerful magnates in the kingdom, Albany and Douglas, a fact which held out the prospect of a more effective implementation of crown policy than had been the case during Robert III's personal rule. However, the high promise of early 1399 was not to be fulfilled, and by the autumn of that year the fates were already beginning to conspire against Rothesay's regime, with a significant worsening of the Scottish kingdom's political relationship with the English crown.

In July 1399 Henry Bolingbroke, son of John of Gaunt, duke of Lancaster, returned from exile to lead a successful revolt against his cousin, Richard II. By 30 September 1399 Richard II had been forced to abdicate, and on 13 October Henry Bolingbroke was crowned as Henry IV.[13] The new usurper king was understandably eager to confirm the existing Anglo-Scottish truce. On 6 October 1399 Robert III replied to a letter from Henry, claiming that he was willing to confirm the truce which had been negotiated earlier in that year with Richard II, but that his parliament and council would have to meet to consider the matter.[14] Despite Robert III's diplomatic reply, it is clear that some Scots were already exploiting the confused political situation within England and mounting large-scale raids into the English northern counties. Shortly before 13 October 1399 one of these forays surprised, captured and wrecked Sir Thomas Grey's castle of Wark.[15] On 2 November Robert III wrote again to Henry IV (still styling him duke of Lancaster – a fact which clearly annoyed the English king) in a conciliatory but evasive manner.[16] Henry IV's undated reply to Robert's letter makes plain that the English king was irritated not only by the Scots' refusal to accord him the title King of England, but also by the activities of the elder sons of the Scottish wardens, probably Archibald Douglas, son of the 3rd earl of Douglas, and George Dunbar and his numerous brothers, sons of the earl of March, who were causing 'very great and horrible outrages . . . within our kingdom, through the making of war'.[17] Despite this, Henry suggested that deputies of the wardens of the Marches should meet at Kelso on 5 January 1400 to decide on a suitable meeting place for envoys to arrange a truce. Henry IV's attitude towards the Scots was expressed in a more bellicose manner to an English parliament on 10 November 1399, where the king announced that he would personally punish the Scots for their attack on Wark.[18]

The likelihood of an English military intervention in Scotland was greatly enhanced by the extraordinary conflict which broke out in the early months of 1400 between the two most powerful Scottish border families, the Douglasses and the Dunbars. The dispute centred on the issue of the duke of Rothesay's marriage to Elizabeth Dunbar. Despite the uncertain status of the marriage after 1397 George, earl of March, seems to have continued to hope for the implementation of the papal dispensation of March 1397, which allowed for the re-marriage of

Elizabeth and Rothesay after a suitable period apart. Early in 1400, however, March saw the prize of a prestigious and politically influential match for his daughter disappear with Rothesay's betrothal to Mary Douglas, the daughter of March's fellow warden and rival for influence in the borders, Archibald, 3rd earl of Douglas.

A Douglas marriage would have been attractive to Rothesay for a number of reasons, not least because it rewarded earl Archibald for his support in the creation of Rothesay's lieutenancy in 1399, and further identified the most powerful magnate family south of the Forth with the political fortunes of the heir to the throne. The chronicler Bower claims that on hearing of Rothesay's impending marriage to Mary Douglas, March approached Robert III and demanded that the king should ensure that 'the marriage between the lord of Rothesay and his daughter be [fully] carried through, or he should at least repay to him the money which had been handed over'.[19] Disappointed by the king's reply, March issued threats, 'saying that either the king should keep his agreement with him, or he would arrange for something unheard of and unusual to be done in the kingdom'. The nature of March's threat soon became apparent. On 18 February 1400 the earl wrote to Henry IV from his castle of Dunbar, complaining that Rothesay had greatly wronged his daughter by marrying another 'as it ys said' (a phrase which suggests that March did not yet know for certain that the Rothesay/Douglas marriage had taken place), and requesting a safe conduct from the English king, which Henry IV issued on 8 March 1400 for the earl and a hundred of his men.[20] March also asked for Henry's 'holp and suppowall fore swilk honest service as i may do efter my power to yhour noble lordship, and to yhour land'. If the English king could reach an understanding with the disgruntled Scottish earl, then the possibility existed for an English force to cross into the Scottish eastern march and on into Lothian largely unopposed, and on 14 March Henry IV wrote to the earl of Westmorland instructing him to meet and negotiate with March as the Scottish earl had requested.[21] On the same day Robert III replied to a letter which he had received over two months previously from Henry, and explained the failure of the Scots to meet with English commissioners at Kelso on 5 January.[22]

The Scots' evasion of meaningful negotiation and the possibilities opened up by March's disaffection with the royal lieutenant seem to have convinced Henry of the desirability of an English military expedition against Scotland in the summer of 1400.[23] Whatever the result of George Dunbar's negotiations in England in March 1400, the earl had returned to his castle of Dunbar by 8 May, attended by his brother Sir Patrick Dunbar, his nephew Sir Robert Maitland, his cousin Sir Robert Lauder and Sir Patrick Hepburn, 'bachilario nostro'.[24] At this stage Rothesay and his council seem to have been unaware of the import of Dunbar's dealings with the English king, and on 17 May 1400 March's heritable pension from the customs of Dunbar was paid as usual.[25] However, the Scots became thoroughly alarmed in June 1400, when the seriousness and the scale of Henry IV's expedition against them became apparent. Towards the end of May the English king had ordered his army to assemble at York on 24 June, and at the same time opened negotiations with Donald of the Isles and his brother John. Presumably this was an effort to involve the Islesman — who had been on the receiving end of military action by Rothesay and Albany only two years before — in a co-ordinated attack on the Stewart monarchy during the summer of 1400.[26] By early June it must have been clear to Rothesay and his new father-in-law, Douglas, that they had made a massive miscalculation in their belligerent treatment of Henry IV.

On 4 June came the first indication of Rothesay's preparations for war, a life grant to his brother-in-law Archibald Douglas of the keepership of Edinburgh castle with an annual pension of 200 merks, twice the amount paid to previous custodians.[27] The grant seems to have been the final straw for George Dunbar. By 21 June 1400 Henry IV had moved north to Pontefract, to oversee the mustering of English forces at York, and from there issued a safe conduct to March and fifty of his men, allowing the earl to attend an interview with the English king.[28] March's wish to meet the English king while the latter was gathering an army to invade Scotland suggests treason of the highest order. George Dunbar's support for, or acquiescence in, the English invasion would have seen Henry IV's army meeting little or no sustained resistance in the eastern march. If March allowed English forces to operate from his strongholds in Berwickshire and Lothian, the most important of which was Dunbar, barely 40 miles from Edinburgh, then many of the hard-won territorial gains made by the Scots in southern Scotland during the 1380s would have been jeopardised.

It was while March was with the English king in late June or early July that Rothesay and his brother-in-law, Archibald, master of Douglas, took decisive action against the earl's interests in Scotland and forestalled any possibility of Dunbar being used as a centre for a hostile garrison. Archibald, master of Douglas, descended on March's castle of Dunbar and obtained possession of the stronghold through the acquiescence or active support of the earl's nephew, Sir Robert Maitland, who may have been acting as custodian of Dunbar while March was in England.[29] The accounts of the episode given by Wyntoun and Bower are curiously sympathetic towards George Dunbar. Both chroniclers suggest that March was the victim of unwarranted rumour, '. . . fenyeit fals suspiciownyis, . . . all unpro-

vabyll be resownyis', as Wyntoun has it, in the wake of his confrontation with Rothesay over the lieutenant's marriage, and that Douglas's
seizure of Dunbar was treacherous and precipitate, forcing March to
commit himself to Henry IV.[30] Both accounts tend to fly in the face of
documentary evidence, which shows the earl to have been engaged in
near-treasonable negotiations with Henry IV from February 1400
onwards. It seems likely that the full nature of March's English
negotiations was revealed to Rothesay and Douglas by men within
the earl's own affinity in late June. Certainly March's nephew, Sir
Robert Maitland, handed Dunbar castle over to Douglas in highly
dubious circumstances, while Sir Patrick Hepburn, who had been
witnessing March's charters as late as 8 May 1400, seems to have
become a particular target for the earl's hatred after 1400.

The turning of key members of March's affinity and Douglas's
seizure of Dunbar left the earl marooned in England with few realistic
political options; on 2 August the earl and his entire family, including
the jilted Elizabeth, obtained year-long safe conducts from the English
king, with March having promised Henry IV, on 25 July, that he would
renounce his allegiance to Robert III before 23 August.[31] The speci-
fication of Monday, 23 August as the deadline for March to transfer his
allegiance to the English king was highly significant, for it seemed to
tie in with a change in emphasis in Henry IV's prosecution of his
campaign against the Scots during 1400. On 6–7 August, while at
Newcastle, Henry sent out letters to Robert III and the magnates of
Scotland. Henry's letter to Robert III reminded the Scottish monarch
of the English crown's ancient claims to superiority and overlordship
over Scotland 'from the time of Locrinus son of Brutus', and therefore
of Henry's own right to receive the liege homage and fealty of Robert
and the great magnates of the Scottish kingdom. In light of these claims,
the English king formally summoned Robert III to deliver the homage
he owed to Henry for the Scottish realm at Edinburgh on Monday, 23
August.[32] Henry's letter to the 'dukes, earls and other magnates of the
realm of Scotland' informed them of the summons made on their king,
and asked them to ensure his appearance at Edinburgh or, if Robert
refused to follow their advice, to offer their own homage to the English
king on the specified date. Henry's arrangement with March ensured
that at least one Scottish nobleman would be present at Edinburgh to
acknowledge the English king's claims to overlordship on 23 August,
and may have been designed to encourage others in the proposed path
of the English advance to follow suit.

Henry IV's letters presented the English king as an aggrieved
overlord denied his legitimate rights, anxious to avoid the shedding
of Christian blood, with no interest in the wanton destruction of the

Scottish kingdom, hoping for a favourable response to his summons 'as an alternative to our being provoked into stretching out the arm of our power following your defiance and rebellion in this matter'. The sentiments expressed in King Henry's letters seem to be more than cynically pious statements designed to justify a military attack on the Scottish kingdom and to give some legitimacy to the political defection of the earl of March. The huge English army, numbering between 15,000 and 20,000 men, which Henry IV led into Scotland on 14 August, moved swiftly north to Leith, encountering no significant resistance from the Scots and behaving in a remarkably restrained fashion, with little raiding and harrying of the country through which it passed.[33] Henry IV had clearly abandoned any plans to use his forces in a destructive punitive raid. Instead Bower's account of the 1400 expedition, probably based on his local knowledge of the area around Haddington, stresses Henry's generosity in granting protection to castles, monasteries and villages in the path of his army.

Henry's benevolence was no doubt largely inspired by the wish not to alienate existing or potential supporters of George Dunbar in Lothian and Berwickshire, but it also reflected what the king seems to have regarded as his own family's long political association with the Scottish kingdom. According to Bower, Henry granted protection to the monks of Holyrood because of the hospitality afforded by the monastery to his father, John of Gaunt, during his brief period of exile in Scotland in 1381, but also because Henry himself was 'half a Scot . . . having the blood of the Comyns in my veins [on my mother's side]. As for coming here as an enemy, I call the Almighty to witness that I have been provoked.[34] The long service of Henry's father, John of Gaunt, as Lieutenant of the Marches for Richard II had maintained the family's social links with the nobility of southern Scotland throughout the 1380s and 1390s. In the 1370s and 1380s Sir John Swinton had been one of Gaunt's most loyal pensioned retainers, and on 7 July 1400 the same John Swinton obtained a safe conduct to come to the court of king Henry, the son of Swinton's former lord, as he gathered his forces at York.[35]

Thus, for a number of cogent political and personal reasons Henry IV may have been disinclined to conduct a devastating *chevauchée* through southern Scotland. The campaign of August 1400 clearly involved an element of intimidation, a demonstration of the English king's capacity to ravage southern Scotland if he wished, but it was accompanied by a considerable propaganda effort in which Henry was at pains to avoid being seen as an enemy to the Scottish kingdom. Henry portrayed himself as an overlord, by blood half a Scot, whose rightful claims were being unjustly denied, and he took the trouble to justify his arguments directly to the nobility of southern Scotland. From the viewpoint of English historians, Henry's behaviour in 1400 was 'naïve' and his expedition not only costly, but 'utterly futile'.[36] The effectiveness of the expedition is certainly to be doubted, but it does seem to represent a relatively sophisticated attempt by the English crown to consolidate the expansion of its political influence in southern Scotland which followed logically from March's defection. Henry's propaganda utilised not only the well-rehearsed arguments for the English crown's ancient and historical claims to superiority, but also exploited what was portrayed as Henry's own personal affiliation with the Scottish kingdom.

Effective leadership of the political and military response to the English campaign was in the hands of the duke of Rothesay, whose father, Robert III, seems to have remained in Bute for the duration of the invasion.[37] Rothesay, and his brother-in-law, Archibald Douglas, were sensibly not prepared to meet the immense English force in open battle, and retreated to the relative safety of Edinburgh castle along with other southern noblemen.[38] Bower suggests that a considerable Scottish force was mobilised under the duke of Albany, who advanced to Calder Moor to the west of Edinburgh, but that this army withdrew because of 'certain animosities which had previously arisen between the duke of Rothesay' and Albany — although it seems more likely that Albany was simply unwilling to risk a confrontation with the English army. The nature of these animosities is not explained, but it may be that Albany had not supported Rothesay's annulment of the Elizabeth Dunbar marriage, nor the lieutenant's subsequent treatment of the earl of March. Wyntoun certainly suggests that Albany never agreed to March's exile.[39] In these circumstances Albany could have been forgiven for believing that Rothesay and his new Douglas kinsmen had needlessly brought Henry IV's invasion down upon their own heads.

With Albany unwilling or unable to take the field, and Rothesay and Douglas holed up in Edinburgh, Henry IV's invasion simply petered out, his army troubled by a lack of supplies.[40] From Leith on 21 August, Henry vainly repeated his demand for homage. Rothesay replied with a belligerent letter from the safety of Edinburgh castle, agreeing with Henry's wish to avoid the spilling of Christian blood and therefore offering a combat between the noblemen of the two kingdoms to the number of 100, 200 or 300 a side to settle the disputes between them.[41] Rothesay may also have responded to Henry IV's deployment of the Brut legend to support his claim to exercise an ancient superiority over Scotland by invoking the Scottish kingdom and royal dynasty's own well-developed origin myth which justified and sustained the Scottish kingdom's existence as an independent political entity.[42] In the end, Henry appears to have been forced to accept simply a promise from the Scots to consider the issue of homage, and on 29 August, a little over two weeks after entering Scotland, the English king and his army recrossed the border, having received few tangible benefits from their expedition.[43]

March's defection and the English invasion of 1400 seem to have had little immediate effect on the duke of Rothesay's political position within Scotland, but they did leave a dangerous legacy. The earl of March's exile and his ongoing feud with the Douglas family dangerously destabilised the political situation in the south of Scotland and proved to be a formidable obstacle to the establishment of any effective Anglo-Scottish truces. The chronicle accounts also suggest that many in Scotland felt some sympathy for March, and were alarmed at the way in which he had been treated by the royal lieutenant.

However, there was no sign of impending crisis in Rothesay's exercise of power during a parliament held in Perth/Scone in February/March 1401. The parliament introduced a raft of measures to improve the exercise of criminal and property law, legislation which indicated a vigorous and active administration at odds with the chronicle accounts which portray Rothesay as a dissolute and frivolous figure.[44] The parliament also provided evidence, despite Bower's assertion of a rift between the royal dukes in the previous August, of a continuing association of the principal members of Rothesay's household with Albany and his northern allies.[45] Yet despite this interaction between the Rothesay and Albany affinities, the broad political consensus which had brought about and sustained Rothesay's lieutenancy since 1399 began to break down in the second half of 1401, with the relationship between the lieutenant and his uncle collapsing completely. The political estrangement is presented by Bower, who is generally sympathetic to Albany, as a result of Rothesay's return to unruly and irresponsible behaviour after the death of his mother, Queen Annabella Drummond, in the harvest time (perhaps September or October) of 1401.[46]

Bower had no doubt that the death of Annabella had a profound effect on Rothesay: 'on the death of . . . his noble mother, who used to curb him in many things, it was as if a noose had become worn: he hoped to free himself and, spurning his council of honourable men, gave himself up to his previous frivolity'.[47] More generally, Bower saw the deaths of Queen Annabella, Walter Trail, bishop of St Andrews, and Archibald the Grim, 3rd earl of Douglas, as having a destabilising effect on the politics of the kingdom. The three deaths entailed more than simply the removal of respected figures who had played a key role in maintaining a measure of political unity during the Rothesay lieutenancy. The demise of Trail and Annabella Drummond, in particular, gave rise to specific political problems which increased the tension between Rothesay and Albany.

There is little doubt that in the autumn of 1401, shortly after the death of his mother, Rothesay began to exploit his political and financial rights as royal lieutenant in a much more vigorous and aggressive manner. In particular, the young prince made a determined intervention into the confused situation surrounding the bishopric of St Andrews in the wake of Bishop Trail's death.[48] Trail was dead before 1

ys chapter elected Thomas Stewart, arch-
lf-brother of Robert III and Albany, as his
confirmation of Stewart's position was
f Benedict XIII, who was besieged in his
ch forces between 1398 and March 1403.[49]
say's counsellors encouraged the duke to
n the king's behalf until a new bishop was
ertain that the lieutenant was active in the
ate 1401, organising a siege of Reres castle
r Elie.[50] The owner of Reres, Sir John
ns to have had his lands taken into royal
say's attack on Wemyss probably resulted
o the lieutenant's attempts to occupy the
, for Sir John and his sons had served as the
castle since 1383.[52] The siege engines
Reres were actually constructed in St
hat the assault on the personal stronghold
ws coincided with, and reinforced, a siege
late 1401. That there was local resistance
implied in Bower's comment that at some
2 the castle there was 'ready to surrender
ies around St Andrews and Reres in the
y to please his uncle Albany, for although
n, sanctioned the payments for the lieu-
n Wemyss was, in fact, one of the duke's

o occupy the bishop's castle by force and
copal revenues was symptomatic of the
ial policies adopted by the lieutenant in
drews was a particularly attractive target,
in the kingdom, with an annual income
es at £3,507 in 1366.[55] The diversion of
o the lieutenant's own coffers directly
crown's principal financial officer, the
ay also have been some unease amongst
ct, Thomas Stewart, over how long
control the castle and the episcopal

revenues given the ongoing difficulties in procuring confirmations from the papal court. Although Albany would eventually support the claims of a rival candidate to the bishopric of St Andrews, Wyntoun noted that the royal duke 'lovit his persone [Thomas Stewart's] tendirly'.[56]

The political tensions created in and around St Andrews after Trail's death were exacerbated by Rothesay's decision to make an increased use of the right to uplift royal customs revenue directly, a power which had been granted to him as part of his commission of lieutenancy in January 1399. In the months after May/June 1401, Rothesay visited a number of east-coast burghs — Edinburgh, Dundee, Montrose and Aberdeen — and took money directly from their custumars.[57] In Montrose and Dundee the custumars were persuaded to hand over the required sums through the application of physical violence by Rothesay and his adherents. In Montrose, John Tyndale was abducted and imprisoned by Rothesay until he handed over £24, despite the fact that Tyndale and his fellow custumar had already given over all the customs revenue which they had received to Albany's deputy chamberlain, Walter Tulloch.[58] Rothesay's assertive east-coast tour may also have seen the lieutenant attempt to gain control of the crown lands and 2,500-merk pension which had been held by his mother. The prince issued at least one charter after the queen's death, disposing of lands which she had owned in Angus and Fife to Richard Spalding, a Dundee burgess.[59]

Rothesay's increasingly independent behaviour in late 1401 was undoubtedly alarming for his uncle Albany, who could hardly ignore the fact that the lieutenant was simply bypassing the chamberlain's office to take revenue as he required directly from the royal burghs. The chronicler Bower saw the political instability of late 1401 as a result of the young prince's return to unruly and frivolous ways, a lifestyle which caused the council assigned to supervise and regulate the Rothesay lieutenancy in 1399 to resign in despair.[60] It seems more likely that around the middle of 1401 Rothesay simply rejected the political constraints placed on him by this Albany-dominated council. Rothesay had good reason for confidence about his political position in 1401: he was young, he had exercised the office of lieutenant and run the kingdom for close on three years. He had a powerful ally in his brother-in-law Archibald, earl of Douglas, and he was the heir to the throne. Robert III, Rothesay's aged and incapacitated father, already twice declared incapable of governing his kingdom, was hardly in a position to replace or curb his son; indeed the general council of January 1399 had specifically stated that the king could not countermand the lieutenant. The king was old and ill; sooner rather than later the duke of Rothesay would be David III; and his future gave him prestige and power.

Albany, the most able of Robert II's sons, remained a powerful and well-connected figure in the north and at the royal court, but his hold on authority and power was slipping in 1401. As the events of 1388 and 1399 had proved, he was capable of decisive political action, but as long as Rothesay remained alive, Albany did not represent a viable political alternative, for he could not regain the guardianship or become lieutenant while the 24-year-old heir to the throne was politically active. And Albany was old, almost as old as his brother Robert III. In 1403 he was considering the possibility that he might die before the king, whereas time was clearly on Rothesay's side. From the middle of 1401, confident of his future, Rothesay simply ignored his father's court and Albany's allies on the council, and began to behave like the king he expected to become.

The increased political tension caused by Rothesay's bid to free himself from the conciliar restrictions on his authority was reflected in the rumours which began to circulate in Scotland during 1401. It was suggested that Rothesay's counsellors were encouraging the young duke to arrest his uncle in order to 'remove him forthwith from the scene'.[61] In reality, however, it was Albany who was carefully priming a decisive political blow against his nephew.

Rothesay's forceful visits to Dundee, Montrose and Aberdeen in the autumn of 1401 seem to have been crowned with the arrival of encouraging news from Fife. The holders of the episcopal castle had apparently agreed to surrender the fortress to the lieutenant. Rothesay headed south accompanied by Sir John Ramornie and William Lindsay of Rossie and, perhaps, David, earl of Crawford, Sir John Hamilton of Fingalton and Walter Hamilton.[62] Most of these men had witnessed the young duke's first recorded charter in 1394, and had served the prince for at least eight years. But there was black treachery in the very heart of the prince's household, for after crossing the river Eden at the ford of Nydie Rothesay was 'arrested' by Sir John Ramornie and Sir William Lindsay of Rossie on the road between the ford and Strathtyrum, on the outskirts of St Andrews.[63] The seizure of Rothesay, frustratingly undated in Bower's account, would have occurred between 22 February and 18 March 1402 if the chronicler's incidental observation that the duke was at liberty in Edinburgh when a strange and striking comet appeared in the heavens, and that he had been made captive by the time the comet faded, is correct.[64] However, there are several pieces of 'negative' evidence which suggest that Rothesay's capture must have occurred late in 1401. It is striking, for example, that the prince failed to witness any royal charters issued in the autumn/winter of 1401 and did

witnessing charters issued by the 4th earl of Douglas in Dunbar castle in 1401, little over a year after performing the same role for the earl of March.[76]

From 1400 onwards, then, the 4th earl of Douglas's political outlook was dominated by two clear and interrelated aims: firstly, the consolidation of his tenuous hold on the lordship of Dunbar, and secondly the pursuit of his cross-border feud with the earl of March. It was these political concerns which Albany would have to address if he wished to secure Douglas's support for his arrest of the earl's brother-in-law.

It seems probable that the earl of Douglas was not involved in the initial arrest and imprisonment of Rothesay in St Andrews. If the move against the heir to the throne had been pre-planned by Albany and Douglas, then there would have been little need for the council held by Albany and, apparently, attended by Douglas, at Culross a few days after Rothesay's arrest, while the heir to the throne was still imprisoned in the episcopal castle. The use of Culross, in the west of Fife, may indicate that Albany and Douglas met as the latter moved north towards St Andrews, probably on receiving news of Rothesay's arrest, either to support his brother-in-law or to strike a deal with Albany. Albany would seem to have taken a calculated political gamble in seizing his nephew, knowing that he would have to reach some form of agreement with Douglas if his coup was to be successful. The council at Culross thus took shape as a meeting between the two most powerful magnates in the kingdom, discussing the future of the heir to the throne.

Bower insists that the 'weak and decrepit' Robert III had written to Albany sanctioning Rothesay's arrest and temporary imprisonment.[77] It is clear, however, even if this were true, that the king had no political control over, nor any direct involvement in, the meeting at Culross. For most of the previous three years Robert III had been more or less permanently resident in the Stewarts' Ayrshire lands or on the islands of the Firth of Clyde, and it was a measure of the king's political impotence that he remained in that region during the critical months of 1401/2.

Douglas had two options after Albany's seizure of the heir to the throne. Continued support for Rothesay would have involved the earl in a long and costly struggle with Albany and his numerous allies, a conflict which Douglas could not be confident of winning and which would have disrupted the earl's policies and ambitions in his own sphere of influence in the south. A rapprochement with Albany, on the other hand, offered both men tangible political benefits. For Albany, the chief benefit was, clearly, the neutralisation of the most powerful figure who might have remained loyal to Rothesay. In return for Douglas's acquiescence, Albany could offer the earl substantial and unrestrained support for Douglas interests and policies in the east March, and more belligerent campaigning against the exiled earl of March and his English backers. If, as seems likely, Rothesay's arrest took place in late September or early October 1401, then the adoption of a whole range of aggressive foreign policy initiatives by the Scots in October–December 1401 may well have reflected the need for Albany to make major policy concessions to Douglas in order to ensure that the earl did not intervene on Rothesay's behalf.

The most striking development in October 1401 was the territorial dismemberment of the earldom of March. The chief beneficiary of this process was the earl of Douglas, who by 20 October had been created lord of Dunbar, a lordship which clearly included possession of the chief stronghold of the earldom of March and made any meaningful reinstatement of the exiled earl virtually impossible.[78] The exact status of the earldom of March after George Dunbar's expulsion in 1400 is uncertain. One piece of parliamentary legislation from February 1401 may suggest that the earldom had been forfeited to the crown by that stage, and that Douglas and his new adherents holding land within March were pushing for the break-up of the earldom as a unified territorial unit and the creation of a number of individual lordships and baronies to be held directly of the crown.[79] Rothesay, for a number of reasons, seems to have failed to deliver the anticipated territorial bonanza to Douglas and his men. An entry in royal records from 1455 suggests, in fact, that the prince may have taken the title of March for himself.[80] If this late and isolated evidence is accurate, then it would mean that Rothesay had a very real interest in maintaining March as an effective earldom in the years after 1400, and in preserving the rights of the earl to the lands and fortress of Dunbar. Rothesay's enforcement of his own rights in the earldom would have been typical of the prince's policies during 1401, but would have left a disgruntled Archibald Douglas with little permanent reward for his role as the captor and defender of the castle of Dunbar and the earldom of March during and after 1400.

Rothesay may also have been disinclined to sanction the break-up of March because of the restrictions which it would place on his conduct of Anglo-Scottish diplomacy. The implacable opposition of the earl of Douglas and former March tenants to the restoration of George Dunbar was clear enough, but any permanent destruction of March's earldom would have made Anglo-Scottish negotiations for a truce or peace treaty, which had to deal with the position of the exiled earl, almost impossible.[81] It is striking, therefore, that shortly before planned Anglo-Scottish negotiations at Kirk Yetholm in October 1401 a series of royal grants began to dismantle the earldom of March and to create a number of lordships and baronies to be held directly of the crown.[82]

None of these charters was witnessed by Rothesay, and it is tempting to assume that by this stage the lieutenant was already in Albany's custody. The destruction of March and Douglas's acquisition of the lordship of Dunbar thus seem to have been part of the price paid by Albany in order to secure the earl's acceptance of the coup which had removed Rothesay from power.

The closing of the door on any restoration of March was symptomatic of the earl of Douglas's domination of Scottish foreign policy in late 1401, a period which saw an aggressive escalation of hostilities with the English crown. The chief Scottish representatives at the Anglo-Scottish negotiations of 17–20 October were the earls of Douglas and Angus, with the remainder of the commission being men firmly attached to the Douglas interest. The negotiations broke up in acrimonious fashion on 20 October, at least partly because Douglas appeared on the Scottish side of the Tweed for the day's debate at the head of a small army. After the collapse of the talks Douglas rode north to the castle of Dunbar where, later the same day, he issued charters of land in his new lordship of Dunbar in favour of Sir John Swinton.[83] Henry IV later blamed Douglas personally for the break-up of the October meeting with no truce established, and the English king's assessment was probably entirely accurate, for Douglas and the men of March loyal to him wanted and were prepared for war, sweeping into Northumberland shortly after the inconclusive meeting at Kirk Yetholm and burning the town of Bamburgh.[84]

At around the same time the Scots seem to have committed themselves to a major military venture against the English king in the following summer. In November or December 1401 the earl of Crawford left Scotland, apparently in order to secure French military support against the English. Certainly by 1 January 1402 the earl was in Paris, entering into a bond of service to the duke of Orléans. By 22 March 1402, Henry IV was aware of Crawford's presence in Harfleur, where the French were gathering a fleet to assist the Scots. At the end of March Crawford and the French naval force put to sea, but did not head directly for Scotland, opening instead a full-scale campaign against English merchant shipping in the Channel. On 8 May 1402, some five weeks after putting to sea, Crawford and at least some of the French fleet were stationed in Corunna Bay.[85]

Crawford may have tried to entice the French into supporting a military campaign against Henry IV by delivering the startling news that Richard II was not, in fact, dead, but had cunningly escaped from Henry IV's imprisonment; had been discovered working in the kitchens of Donald, lord of the Isles; and was now in the care of the Scottish court.[86] It is certain that in late 1401 the Scots began to make political use of a Richard II impostor. By March/April 1402 Jean de Creton, a French knight who had served in Richard II's household, was planning to travel to Scotland in order to ascertain whether the Scottish 'Richard II', of whom he had only recently received news, was, in fact, his old lord. It seems likely that the bearer of the glad tidings was indeed Crawford, who had arrived in France in December 1401, and was using the 'mammet' or pretender in an effort to persuade the French to provide military and political support for 'Richard' in his dynastic struggle to remove the usurper Henry IV from the English throne. Jean de Creton may well have sailed alongside Crawford on the fleet which journeyed to Scotland in the summer of 1402, and he had certainly returned to France from a visit to Scotland by October 1402, sadly convinced that the Scottish 'Richard II' was indeed an impostor.[87]

It thus seems clear that in late 1401 Scottish diplomacy and foreign policy were, in effect, being dictated by the earl of Douglas. The dismemberment of the earldom of March, the deployment of the Richard II impostor, and the search for French military aid all signalled a new and manifestly aggressive intent on the part of the Scottish government towards the English king. The policies hardly originated with Albany, largely preoccupied with the affairs of the kingdom north of the Forth, whom Wyntoun identifies as having been opposed to March's exile in 1400, and who was named by Rothesay in March 1401 as being in favour of negotiations for a truce or permanent peace between Scotland and England.[88]

Douglas's acceptance of Rothesay's arrest at the Culross council, made in return for the promotion of the earl's regional interests and control over the future conduct of Anglo-Scottish diplomacy, confirmed Albany's political triumph. The agreement between Albany and Douglas left the two men with the awkward political problem of how they should deal with the royal lieutenant and heir to the throne, and how they could justify their actions.

During the meeting at Culross, Albany and Douglas evidently agreed to move Rothesay from St Andrews to Albany's own castle of Falkland.[89] The arrangement seems rather ominous, especially given the fact that the young duke was forced to wear russet robes and to ride on a mule, indicating either that Douglas and Albany hoped to hide the duke's whereabouts from his adherents by disguising him as a cleric, or that they were engaging in a deliberate act of humiliation. Neither interpretation would suggest that a rapid or reasonable political compromise was likely. In England, russet was 'regarded by some as fit only for hermits or the corpses of the humble', while Lollard knights 'specified in their wills the use of russet for their grave-clothes as a sign of their humility'.[90] Bower's report of Rothesay's ignominious journey from St Andrews to Falkland, involving as it did a very obvious degradation of the duke's status, bears a strange resemblance to some of the chronicle accounts of the arrest, deposition and death of the English king Richard II in 1399/1400. After his arrest Richard was conveyed to London on a small horse, which the king's supporters regarded as a deliberate act of mockery and dishonour. Further, when the deposed king was taken from the Tower of London to Leeds castle in Kent in October 1399 he was disguised as a woodcutter. Richard's ultimate destination was Pontefract castle, like Falkland for Rothesay, one of the personal strongholds of his chief political enemy.[91]

The justifications offered by Albany and Douglas for Rothesay's arrest and continued imprisonment are reflected in Bower's description of the prince's behaviour shortly before his arrest as unruly and intemperate. This view of Rothesay as a moral degenerate was widely circulated, given that the contemporary English chronicler John Shirley (1366–1456), who does not appear to have had access to Bower's work, followed a remarkably similar line in his brief treatment of Rothesay's career in his chronicle account of the assassination of James I, *The Dethe of the Kynge of Scotis*.[92] According to Shirley, the young duke, encouraged by his father's decline into dotage, 'began unlaufully to take uppoun him the roialle governaunce', through which presumption and pride 'he wex fulle viceous in his liveing', despoiling young maidens and breaking the order of wedlock.[93] The cumulative effect of Bower's criticism of Rothesay, employing rather more restrained language than Shirley, also justified Albany's move against the royal lieutenant. In Bower's account Rothesay specifically rejected 'his council of honourable men', and 'gave himself up to his previous frivolity'. Moreover, Rothesay's romantic affiliations caused Bower to misapply a quotation, actually referring to David II, which suggested that

> It is the riotous living and convivial acts of David which will be celebrated.
> Because he regards [other] wives as superior to his own wife, royal morals will be lacking, he will lose respect.[94]

The chronicle tradition represented by Bower and Shirley portrayed Rothesay as a ruler who had rejected wise council, arbitrarily seized royal power, and was unable to control his slide into moral corruption. These observations would have had a strong resonance for the contemporary audience, for it was a commonplace of mediaeval political theory that a prince who followed a 'viscious' lifestyle, in the sense of indulging his vices, would bring ruin on himself and his kingdom.[95] Shirley, indeed, explicitly observed that because of the 'vicious lyving of the saide duke of Rossayae', the nobles of Scotland were 'soare dreding yf he hadde regned aftur his fadur, that many inconveniences, infortunes, and vengeances myght owe fyllonye and fallen uppon al that region by cause of his lyff soo opnly knowen vicious'.[96]

Thus both Bower and Shirley presented Albany and Douglas as men concerned to rescue the Scottish kingdom from the potentially disastrous effects of Rothesay's governance. This seems to mirror Albany and Douglas propaganda produced during and after 1402, for it is certain that the royal duke and his ally claimed to have acted to protect the 'common weal' when they were called to account for their arrest of Rothesay in a general council of May 1402.[97]

However, even if Albany's arguments justifying Rothesay's arrest were accepted, there remained severe theoretical and practical problems for the duke and the earl of Douglas to overcome if they were to derive any permanent political advantage from their seizure of the royal lieutenant. The successful transfers of royal power to guardians or lieutenants in 1384, 1388 and 1399 had all been justified by concentrating on the infirmity through age or illness of the then king or guardian, and his resulting inability to perform the basic functions of kingship in terms of protecting the realm from invasion and maintaining law and order.[98] In each case, power had been transferred to the nearest adult male within the royal family. These arguments could hardly be deployed against the 24-year-old Rothesay who, in late 1401, with the siege of Reres and the tour around the east-coast burghs, had displayed considerable, and for some rather alarming, vigour. It seems doubtful, in fact, whether Albany and Douglas could have justified before any representative assembly a prolonged or permanent transfer of power from the young heir to the throne to his aged uncle, and this no doubt explains why there was no attempt to seek the approval of a parliament or general council for any formal recasting of the royal government during the prince's imprisonment.

The political deadlock in the months after Rothesay's arrest, with the royal lieutenant incarcerated and no replacement appointed, raises the issue of Albany's intentions towards his nephew. Bower generously suggests that the duke's aim was that his nephew should be 'put into custody for a time until, after punishment by the rod of discipline, he should know himself better', implying that the young prince would be released once he had seen the error of his ways.[99] Bower's account reflects not only his fondness for Albany, but also seems to conform to a wider political conservatism in Scottish writings of the fifteenth century, which 'prevented the open discussion of the removal of a bad king by his subjects'.[100] Shirley, perhaps influenced by the more radical political theories of continental writers such as Jean de Gerson, had no qualms in seeing Albany's imprisonment of Rothesay as part of a deliberate, and justifiable, plan to do away with an inadequate and tyrannical ruler by starving him to death in custody. Shirley's appraisal of the situation seems to have been shared by Albany and Douglas, who must quickly have realised that Rothesay was simply too young, active and capable to accept political marginalisation in the way that his father and grandfather had done. While Rothesay lived, an Albany lieutenancy, the only effective guarantee for the political interests of the men who had conspired against the prince, was unobtainable. If, as seemed more than likely, Rothesay outlived his ailing 65-year-old father and succeeded to the throne as David III, Albany and Douglas would find it almost impossible to hold the new, and no doubt vengeful, king in captivity, or force him to respect any political or constitutional restraints which they had managed to place on him in 1401/2. In these circumstances it seems that Albany and Douglas reached the inescapable conclusion that Rothesay, like Richard II in England in 1400, was simply too dangerous to be allowed to live.

On 25–27 March 1402 David, duke of Rothesay, died in his uncle's castle of Falkland, and was swiftly laid to rest in the nearby monastery of Lindores. Bower claimed that the prince had passed away from the effects of dysentery, although he acknowledged that many asserted that the real cause was starvation.[101] The controversy over Rothesay's death dominated a general council of 16–20 May 1402, the first recorded piece of royal business for close on six months, during which Albany and Douglas attempted to justify the heir to the throne's arrest, imprisonment and death. Both men applied for, and received, a royal indemnity for themselves and any of their men and adherents who had been involved in the prince's capture. The terms of the indemnity suggest that many of their contemporaries were directly accusing the two men of Rothesay's murder, with the king's pardon asserting that Rothesay had died 'by divine providence, and not otherwise', and ordering that no-one should 'murmur against' the duke and earl.[102]

That Rothesay's demise was divinely ordained seemed to be confirmed by Bower's tale of the appearance, shortly before the prince's arrest as he claims, of a 'wonderful comet . . . emitting hairy rays towards the north'. Perturbed by this strange and dreadful sight, the young prince consulted with astrologers before prophetically declaring that the star heralded 'the death or removal of some prince or the destruction of some country'. After Rothesay's arrest 'the star at once returned to its previous state as God willed'.[103] In reality, Rothesay was already warded in Falkland when the comet of 1402 climbed into the heavens, and if the prince heard tell of the fiery star floating in the skies above Fife he must have suspected that it carried news of his own doom.

In fact, Albany and Douglas's political triumph had probably been secured well in advance of the general council. Since only a parliament had the power to try men for treason, it seems clear that Albany and Douglas had not been summoned to face specific charges in May 1402. Moreover, the council had been called in Edinburgh, a town dominated by the earl of Douglas since 1400, when he became keeper of the royal castle. The presence of Douglas and his adherents in Edinburgh castle limited the likelihood of an outspoken and effective opposition to the earl and Albany during the general council.[104] Albany, too, was well attended by his supporters, with many witnessing the proceedings of a chamberlain court held by the duke in Edinburgh on 19 May.[105] It seems likely that the council had been summoned not to prosecute Albany and Douglas, but to confirm their political ascendancy through the granting of a commission of lieutenancy to Albany as Rothesay's successor.[106] Since Robert III had already been declared incapable of running the kingdom on two occasions, in 1388 and 1399, and Rothesay's younger brother James was only seven years old in 1402, the office of lieutenant or guardian clearly had to be returned to the king's nearest adult male relative, his brother Albany. Opposition to Albany on the basis of the duke's part in Rothesay's demise was clearly not strong enough to disrupt the hold on power exercised by the Albany/Douglas coalition.

In 1399 Robert III had been set aside, and Rothesay's lieutenancy established, on the basis of political co-operation between Albany, Rothesay, and the 3rd earl of Douglas. In late 1401 Rothesay had abandoned the policy of co-operation with the Albany and Douglas affinities, and attempted to establish an independent and less restricted political authority based on the aggressive exploitation and assertion of royal rights. The lieutenant's move to establish his political primacy was premature. Once again Albany and a Douglas earl (this time the 4th earl) worked together to protect their own interests within the king-dom, and brought about Rothesay's political downfall. Rothesay's death and the transfer of political power back to Albany was made acceptable by the fiction that the prince had died of natural causes, and that his demise illustrated God's judgement on the duke's personal moral and political failings, a situation which required no detailed political justification.

The ease with which Albany and Douglas accomplished their destruction of the heir to the throne provided a sad commentary on the duke of Rothesay's short political career, and seemed to deliver a further shattering blow to the prestige and power of the royal Stewart line. But Albany and Douglas would have little time to enjoy their triumph, for the comet of early 1402 had cast its baleful light over many men besides Rothesay, and the months after the prince's death would be filled with individual and collective disaster for the Scottish aristocracy. In particular, late 1402 saw the bloody culmination of the aggressive foreign policy to which the new lieutenant had committed himself in order to win Douglas support. By March 1402 the English were aware of the increased threat from the Scots, for Crawford had been sighted on board the French fleet assembling in Harfleur, while in the following month rumours were spreading through the English shires north of London that Richard II was alive in Scotland and would invade England at midsummer.[107] On 9 May royal officials in Northumberland, Cumberland and Westmorland were ordered to arrest anyone who claimed that Richard II was still alive.[108] The use of the Richard II impostor as a dynastic threat to Henry IV went hand-in-hand with an increase in cross-border raiding co-ordinated by the earl of Douglas. One of these raids, led by Patrick Hepburn of Hailes, met with disaster on Nisbet Muir on 22 June 1402 when Hepburn's force was routed by March's adherents from Berwickshire, and men of the earl of Northumberland. The response of Albany and Douglas was to send a large army, largely recruited from their own affinities, into northern England in September 1402, where it was overwhelmed by English forces at Humbleton on 14 September. The Scots experienced huge losses through death or, more particularly, capture by the English. The list of prestigious prisoners included the earl of Douglas himself, and Murdoch Stewart, Albany's son and heir.[109] Albany's heavy repayment to Douglas for the earl's support in 1401/2 is obvious in the commitment of a large number of the duke's adherents under the command of his son and heir Murdoch to the campaign of September 1402. It may well be that Albany's own participation was prevented only by a renewed crisis in the north where, on 3 July 1402, Alexander of the Isles, lord of Lochaber, launched an attack on Elgin.[110]

In many ways Humbleton, much more than Rothesay's death, marked the end of an era. The battle, and more especially the loss through capture of Murdoch Stewart, justiciar north of the Forth, the earls of Douglas, Moray, Angus and Orkney, along with Sir Thomas Erskine and other lesser figures, had a profound effect on the internal politics of the Scottish kingdom and combined with the deaths in 1402 of the duke of Rothesay, earl of Carrick and Atholl and Steward of Scotland, Alexander Leslie, earl of Ross, and Malcolm Drummond, lord of Mar, to produce a huge political vacuum both north and south of the Forth, leaving few adult earls or important regional lords capable of playing a role in the politics of the kingdom. In the south, two previously insignificant figures, Henry, earl of Orkney and lord of Roslin, and Sir David Fleming of Biggar (who were both captured at Humbleton but quickly ransomed), rose, taking advantage of the temporary eclipse of Douglas power to become the key figures in the conduct of war and diplomacy on the Anglo-Scottish border. In the north, the earldoms of Ross, Moray and Mar lay without active male earls to protect and defend them, while the justiciar of the north languished in an English prison. In the years 1402–6 the lieutenant Albany was forced to find new means and personnel to protect his many interests in the north, and this included a belated and grudging rapprochement between Albany and his brother and former arch-rival in the region, Alexander, earl of Buchan, and Buchan's formidable son, also Alexander, who was to wrest control of the earldom of Mar from the lieutenant's allies in 1404.

1402 also had a devastating effect on the status of the royal court and the prestige of the royal line. It became increasingly clear in the years 1402–4 that the royal court was no longer, in any sense, the political focus of the kingdom. Robert III's great seal charters were issued in traditional centres of Stewart power in the west, and served simply to ratify the aggrandisement of the new lieutenant and his allies. The witness lists to the king's charters bore no relation to the settled lists of powerful and influential magnates which had been the norm, even during the Rothesay lieutenancy. The composition of the group of men attending the king varied wildly; charter witness lists came to be dominated in numerical terms by low-status members of the king's immediate household, chaplains and clerks, and by men attached to Albany. Rothesay's death and Robert III's apparently final retreat into the west left the vulnerable seven-year-old James Stewart as the last hope for any revival in the fortunes of the royal dynasty; on the continent the French openly discussed the possibility of the extinction of the royal Stewart line; in the north, Donald of the Isles viewed the vacant earldom of Ross with a covetous eye; in the south Scotland lay largely undefended against the ambitions of the English king, his great border lords, and the exiled earl of March. Overall, the closing years of Robert III's undistinguished rule held out the promise of interesting times.

NOTES

1. *APS*, i, 572.
2. R. Nicholson, *The Later Middle Ages*, 214–5.
3. *APS*, i, 572.
4. A. A. M. Duncan, 'Councils General, 1404–1423', *SHR*, xxxv (1956), 139–40.

5. *Chron. Bower* (Watt), viii, 37.
6. SRO GD 204/4.
7. *HMC Report*, iv, App. 494 (No. 9). Dalziel was a Crawford adherent who had accompanied Lindsay on his chivalric trip to the English court in 1390: *Chron. Bower* (Watt), viii, 15. The resignation was confirmed in the presence of 'plurium regni nostri procerum baronium, militum et nobilium', clearly men who had been attending the general council.
8. *APS*, i, 572.
9. SRO GD 204/701.
10. This interpretation differs substantially from that offered by the author in an earlier, intensely dull, article on the duke of Rothesay's career: 'The Man who would be King: The Lieutenancy and Death of David, Duke of Rothesay, 1378–1402', in *People and Power in Scotland*, eds. R. Mason and N. Macdougall (Edinburgh, 1992), 1–27. The present chapter entirely supersedes that article.
11. *RMS*, i, App. 1, no. 155.
12. *APS*, i, 574.
13. A. Steel, *Richard II* (Cambridge, 1962), 260–288; A. Tuck, *Richard II and the English Nobility* (London, 1973), 221–225.
14. F. C. Hingeston (ed.), *Royal and Historical Letters during the Reign of Henry the Fourth* (London, 1860), i, 4–5.
15. *CDS*, iv, 542; *Hist.Ang*, ii, 242.
16. Robert offered a meeting of commissioners at Haddenstank on the border in order to arrange a truce and suggested that, in the meantime, the wardens of the Marches should hold a March Day: Hingeston, *Letters Henry IV*, i, 8–10.
17. *Ibid.*, i, 11–14.
18. Wylie, *Henry IV*, i, 21–3.
19. *Chron. Bower* (Watt), viii, 31.
20. BM. Cotton MSS., Vespasian F viii, no. 18; *Nat. MSS. Scot.*, ii, no. 53; *CDS*, iv, no. 539.
21. Hingeston, *Letters Henry IV*, i, 28–30.
22. *Ibid.*, i, 25–7.
23. Henry was also encouraged by a meeting of the English council in March 1400 to go to the border in person to take action against the Scots: *Proc. of Privy Council*, i, 124–6.
24. *Melrose Liber*, ii, 490–1.
25. *ER*, iii, 499.
26. A. L. Brown, 'The English Campaign in Scotland, 1400', in *British Government and Administration: Studies presented to S. B. Chrimes*, eds. H. Hearder and H. R. Loyn (Cardiff, 1974), 42; *Rot.Scot.*, ii, 155.
27. *ER*, iii, 515.
28. *CDS*, iv, no. 546; *Foedera*, viii, 149.

29. *Chron. Bower* (Watt), viii, 33; *Chron. Wyntoun* (Laing), iii, 78. Bower has Maitland as custodian of the castle, Wyntoun as March's treacherous nephew who 'Tuk the castell wyth a slicht'.

30. Bower's account portrays the earl's dealings with the English as a result rather than a cause of Douglas's action. Wyntoun's estimation of the earl of March was very positive:

> Worschipful, and al wertuous,
> A nobill lord and rycht famous;
> Happy in till were he wes,
> And off gud gowernale in pes:

Chron. Wyntoun (Laing), iii, 78. Both Wyntoun and Bower were writing after March had been restored to his earldom in 1409, and this may partly explain their positive gloss of George Dunbar's actions during 1400.

31. *Foedera*, viii, 153; *CDS*, iv, nos. 551–2.

32. *Ibid.*, iv, nos. 553–4; *Foedera*, viii, 156; *Chron. Bower* (Watt), viii, 311–13; E. L. G. Stones, 'The Appeal to History in Anglo-Scottish relations between 1291 and 1401', *Archives*, ix, 1969–70. Besides justifying his claims to overlordship in Scotland through the mythical division of Britain between the sons of Brutus, Henry's letter also made reference to several historical examples of Scottish kings rendering homage to the English crown, namely William I to Henry II and John I, Alexander III to Henry III and Edward I, and John de Balliol to Edward I.

33. A. L. Brown, 'The English Campaign', 43; *Chron. Bower* (Watt), viii, 35–7; *Chron. Wyntoun* (Laing), iii, 77.

34. *Chron. Bower* (Watt), viii, 37. Henry's Scottish descent had been noted in the preparations for the contentious parliament of 1364 as one of the arguments in favour of accepting John of Gaunt, Henry's father, as heir presumptive to the Scottish throne, and the earl of March's appeal for Henry's assistance in February 1400 had begun with a declaration of the earl's kinship to the king: *supra*, Chapter 1; BM. Cotton MSS., Vespasian F viii, no. 18; *Nat. MSS. Scot.*, ii, no. 53; *CDS*, iv, no. 539.

35. *CDS*, iv, nos. 549, 550.

36. A. L. Brown, 'The English Campaign', 40, 44.

37. SRO GD 1/19/2. There are indications that Henry initially planned to send forces to the west coast, perhaps to confront Robert III directly: A. L. Brown, 'The English Campaign', 52.

38. *Chron. Bower* (Watt), viii, 35.

39. *Chron. Wyntoun* (Laing), iii, 79.

40. A. L. Brown, 'The English Campaign', 52; cf. *Chron. Wyntoun* (Laing), iii, 77, which suggests that Henry's army was steadily diminished by desertion.

41. *CDS*, iv, no. 557; *Foedera*, viii, 157.

42. It is certainly the circumstances of Henry's IV's 1400 expedition which provide the background for the events of the curious vernacular poem, 'The Ring of the Roy Robert'. The poem describes the reply of Robert II (*recte* Robert III) to a written demand for his homage from Henry IV. The details of the Scottish king's reply as given in the poem correspond exactly with the points raised by Henry's letters of 6–7 August 1400. The Scottish king's rejection of Henry's right to superiority as the descendant of Locrine, eldest son of Brutus, rests squarely on the Scota legend:

> Scotland evir yit hes bene fre
> Sen scota of egipt tuik the see.

The final element of the Scottish king's reply is to offer a combat of 60, 40 or 20 a side, mirroring Rothesay's actual response to Henry's demands for homage in August 1400. It thus seems possible that 'The Ring of the Roy Robert' contains, in a rather garbled form, a genuine record of the Scottish response to Henry's demands in 1400.

43. *Proc. Privy Council*, i, 169; *Chronicon Adae de Usk*, ed. E. M. Thompson (London, 1904), 47. Even an attempt to force the surrender of Dalhousie castle had been repulsed: *Chron. Wyntoun* (Laing), iii, 77.

44. *APS*, i, 575–6.

45. On 27 February 1401, at Perth, the earl of Crawford witnessed a charter by his cousin Alexander Leslie, earl of Ross, in favour of George Leslie of Rothes in the company of Albany, Murdoch Stewart, and a number of Ross and Albany adherents: SRO GD 204/701.

46. *Chron. Bower* (Watt), viii, 39; *Chron. Wyntoun* (Laing), iii, 81. As the harvest date in the early fifteenth century was generally considerably later than at the present day, it would seem that Queen Annabella died in late September, October, or even early November. I should like to thank Dr I. Whyte of the University of Lancaster for information concerning harvest dates.

47. *Chron. Bower* (Watt), viii, 39.

48. Watt, *Dictionary*, 542.

49. *Chron. Wyntoun* (Laing), iii, 80.

50. *Chron. Bower* (Watt), viii, 39; *ER*, iii, 559–60.

51. *RMS*, i, no. 53; Fraser, *Wemyss*, ii, 44.

52. Sir John was given a grant of the office of constable in June 1383, and seems to have held the post until July 1400, when he gave his second son, Alexander, various lands near St Andrews along with (added as an interlineation) the constabulary of an unspecified 'castal'. The castle was probably St Andrews, because in August 1440 Alexander's son John received a charter of the same lands which incorporated the constableship of the episcopal castle: Robert Douglas, *Baronage of*

Scotland (Edinburgh, 1798), 553; SRO Paterson of Denmuir Writs GD 1/34/1; *RMS*, ii, no. 244.

53. *Chron. Bower* (Watt), viii, 39.

54. As earl of Fife, Albany was Wemyss' feudal superior. In November 1399 the duke had stood as a surety for Wemyss' good behaviour during a parliamentary lawsuit, Sir John was an occasional witness to charters issued by Albany, while the duke had witnessed the arrangements for the marriage of Sir John's eldest son, Duncan, to a daughter of Sir Thomas Erskine: Fraser, *Wemyss*, ii, 38–42; *APS*, i, 574; Fraser, *Douglas*, iii, 31–2; Fraser, *Keir*, 207; SRO GD 124/1/1055: Undated charter but c.April 1398xJuly 1401.

55. *APS*, i, 498–501.

56. *Chron. Wyntoun* (Laing), iii, 80.

57. *ER*, iii, 546, 549, 552, 559.

58. *Ibid.*, iii, 549–50.

59. *RMS*, ii, no. 181.

60. *Chron. Bower* (Watt), viii, 39.

61. *Ibid.*, viii, 41.

62. These men had all witnessed Rothesay's grant to Richard Spalding, issued shortly before the duke's appearance in Fife: *RMS*, ii, no. 181.

63. *Chron. Bower* (Watt), viii, 39.

64. The exact duration of the comet's appearance in 1402 can be gleaned from highly accurate Chinese, Japanese and Korean observations which show that the comet was visible in the Far East on 20 February 1402 and faded from sight on 19 or 20 March. Given Scotland's northerly latitude, the comet probably became visible there a day or two later, and disappeared a day or two earlier, than in Japan and Korea: *Chron. Bower* (Watt), viii, 41; Ho Peng Yoke, 'Ancient and Medieval Observations of Comets and Novae in Chinese sources', *Vistas in Astronomy*, 5 (1962), 200. I should like to thank Dr F. R. Stephenson, Department of Physics, University of Durham, for this reference.

65. SRO Stair Muniments GD 135/No. 375 (17 September 1401 — Isle of Cumbrae); *HMC Report*, i, 15, App. viii, 33 (11 October 1401 — Renfrew); NLS Fleming of Wigtown Collection, Ch. No. 15821 (1 December 1401 — Rutherglen); *Chron. Bower* (Watt), viii, 39.

66. Albany was the superior of Sir William's lands of Rossie in Fife. Between 1398 and 1402 Lindsay had been present at the duke's castle of Falkland to witness Albany's confirmation of an agreement involving Sir John Ramornie, Lindsay's co-conspirator in the arrest of Rothesay: *RMS*, i, no. 938; SRO GD 212/Box 1/Book 6, 178.

67. *ER*, iii, *ad indicem*.

68. In 1389 Ramornie was named as a member of Albany's council, and had acted as a financial receiver for Albany's son Murdoch, in his capacity as justiciar north of the Forth: *Moray. Reg.*, 197–201; *ER*, iii, 266.

69. In 1400 Walter Hamilton, apparently a member of Rothesay's household, acted as a receiver of Drummond's pension from the burgh of Haddington: *ER*, iii, 387, 412, 414, 442, 443, 468, 475, 496.

70. *Chron. Wyntoun* (Laing), iii, 87–8.

71. *Ibid.*; *ER*, iii, lxxix; *RMS*, ii, no. 1239.

72. On 8 November 1402 Isabella, as a widow, issued a charter at Kildrummy which was witnessed by Gilbert Greenlaw, bishop of Aberdeen, the royal chancellor, William Keith, the Marischal, and Keith's son Alexander. Alexander Keith was Albany's brother-in-law and both he and his father were allies of the royal duke. On 18 March 1403 Isabella issued another charter at Kildrummy, in favour of the bishop of Aberdeen, on the advice of Albany and David, earl of Crawford, who were described as members of the countess's 'consilio nostro speciali'. It was thus Albany and his associates who obtained control of Kildrummy and the earldom of Mar after Malcolm Drummond's death, and it was the Keiths, Lindsays, the bishop of Aberdeen and Albany himself who were the immediate beneficiaries of Isabella's patronage: SRO RH6/211; *SP*, iv, 37; Fraser, *Wemyss*, ii, 39: 17 June 1400, William Keith the Marischal and his son, Robert, witnessing a notarial instrument in Albany's castle of Falkland: *Abdn. Reg.*, 207; SRO GD 124/7/3; SRO GD 124/1/118 & 119; *A.B.Ill.*, ii, 372; *Maitland Miscellany*, I, prt. ii, 358.

73. The 3rd earl was certainly dead before 9 February 1401: *Chron. Wyntoun* (Laing), iii, 77–8; SRO GD 12/14 & 15.

74. *Supra*, 10–15.

75. *Chron. Bower* (Watt), viii, 33.

76. SRO GD 12/16; *Melrose Liber.*, ii, 490–1; *Laing Charters*, no. 81.

77. *Chron. Bower* (Watt), viii, 39.

78. SRO GD 12/16; SRO RH6/210.

79. The legislation asserted that any lands granted away by the crown from within earldoms or lordships temporarily in royal control should continue to be held directly of the crown, even if the earldom or lordship was subsequently regranted with the service of tenants and tenandries. The legislation may not have been inspired by the situation in March (the earldoms of Ross, Caithness and Strathearn had all been settled on new individuals shortly before February 1401), but it would certainly have been attractive for Douglas and former March adherents: *APS*, i, 575–6.

80. *ER*, vi, 55, where it is suggested that Rothesay was in legal possession of the earldom when he died.

81. In March 1401 Rothesay had to write to Henry IV asking for the transfer of a meeting of commissioners proposed by the English king from Carlisle to Melrose, partly because the earl of Douglas, who dominated the Scottish western March, was opposed to the confer-

ence. Rothesay claimed that he and Albany were, in contrast, keen to conclude an agreement. On 16 May 1401, Douglas did arrange a temporary truce with the earl of Northumberland to last until Martinmas of the same year, and agreed to a meeting at Kirk Yetholm in October 1401 in order to reach a more permanent arrangement. It was clear, however, given Henry IV's instructions to his commissioners in October 1401, that George Dunbar had been specifically excluded from the truce negotiated by Douglas for May–November 1401: *Rot.Scot.*, ii, 157; H. Nicolas (ed.), *Proceedings and Ordinances of the Privy Council of England* (London, 1834), i, 127; F. C. Hingeston (ed.), *Royal and Historical letters during the Reign of Henry the Fourth* (London, 1860), i, 52–56.

82. Six days before the meeting with the English commission, on 11 October 1401, at Renfrew, Robert III issued a charter to Sir Robert Maitland of the lands of Tibbers in the earldom of March, which were in the king's hands because of the forfeiture of the earl of March, with the lands to be held directly of the king. On the same day the king confirmed a charter of 28 April 1401, issued at the castle of Dunbar by the earl of Douglas in favour of Maitland. The grants rewarded the man who had handed Dunbar castle over to Douglas in 1400, and their timing suggests that Douglas was seeking to guarantee the position of his adherents within March before the meeting with the English commissioners, who were under strict instructions to have George Dunbar included in any truce: *HMC Report*, xv, App. viii, 33; *APS*, vii, 159; *RMS*, i, App. 2, no. 1769. Gordon and Fogo to Adam Gordon: Robertson's *Index*, 147. Ellem to Thomas Erskine: E. L. G. Stones (ed.), *Anglo-Scottish Relations 1174–1328: Some Selected Documents* (Oxford, 1965), 173–182.

83. Swinton, one of Douglas's fellow commissioners, also received a grant of Cranschaws near Haddington from the earl: SRO GD 12/16; SRO RH6/210.

84. Hingeston, *Letters Henry IV*, i, 52–6, 58–65.

85. Archives Nationales, K 57 No. 9/12; NLS Crawford and Balcarres Collection (Personal Papers 75/1/1–4); C. J. Ford, 'Piracy or Policy: the Crisis in the Channel, 1400–1403', in *T.R.H.S.*, xxix (1979), 71–2; Alexander Lindsay, Lord Lindsay, *Lives of the Lindsays: or a Memoir of the Houses of Crawford and Balcarres* (London, 1849), i, 99.

86. *Chron. Bower* (Watt), viii, 29.

87. J. J. N. Palmer, 'The Authorship, Date and Historical value of the French Chronicles of the Lancastrian Revolution', in *Bulletin of the John Rylands Library*, lxi (1978–9), 151–154.

88. Nicolas, *Proc. of Privy Council*, i, 127; *Chron. Wyntoun* (Laing), iii, 78–9.

89. *Chron. Bower* (Watt), viii, 39; *APS*, i, 582–3.

90. I. M. W. Harvey, *Jack Cade's Rebellion of 1450* (Oxford, 1991), 20; K. B.

MacFarlane, *Lancastrian Kings and Lollard Knights* (Oxford, 1972), 211. The marked association of the wearing of russet with Lollard sympathies in England may indicate a veiled condemnation of Rothesay's activities in the bishopric of St Andrews in 1401; M. Aston, *Lollards and Reformers: Images and Literacy in late Medieval Religion* (London, 1984), 16–7.

91. L. D. Duls, *Richard II in the Early Chronicles* (The Hague, 1975), 161–4; A. Steel, *Richard II*, 286.

92. M. Connolly, ' "The Dethe of the Kynge of Scotis": A New Edition', *SHR*, lxxi (1992), 46–69.

93. *Ibid.*, 49.

94. *Chron. Bower* (Watt), viii, 39, 41, 167.

95. S. Mapstone, 'The Advice to Princes Tradition in Scottish Literature, 1450–1500' (unpublished D.Phil. thesis, Oxford 1986).

96. M. Connolly, 'The Dethe', 49.

97. *APS*, i, 582–3.

98. *Supra*, Chapters 4, 7.

99. *Chron. Bower* (Watt), viii, 39.

100. S. Mapstone, 'Advice to Princes', 81.

101. *Chron. Bower* (Watt), viii, 41.

102. *APS*, i, 582–3.

103. *Chron. Bower* (Watt), viii, 41.

104. Douglas issued a charter in Edinburgh on 21 May witnessed by Sir John Swinton, Sir William Stewart of Teviotdale, Sir William Borthwick and William Crawford, the constable of Edinburgh castle: SRO GD 15/332.

105. SRO RH2/2/13 no. 52.

106. A. A. M. Duncan, 'Councils General, 1404–1423', *SHR*, xxxv (1956), 136.

107. H. Maxwell-Lyte (ed.), *Calendar of Patent Rolls Henry IV 1401–5* (London, 1905), 99–100.

108. *Ibid.*, 125.

109. *Chron. Bower* (Watt), viii, 43–9; *HMC Report*, x, App. vi, 77–8; *Chron. Wyntoun* (Laing), iii, 85–7.

110. *Moray Reg.*, 382–3.

9

Contempt of Court

In the wake of the duke of Rothesay's death, the promotion of Albany to the lieutenancy, and the battle of Humbleton in September 1402, Robert III endured an almost complete political and geographical marginalisation. For most of the next two years the king was physically, and perhaps forcibly, confined to his family's ancestral west-coast heartland of the Stewartry and the islands of the Firth of Clyde, his court dominated by supporters of his brother Albany and low-status members of the royal household. The king was clearly a spent force, bereft of policy, purpose and ambition, a man broken by old age, ill health, repeated personal political humiliation, and the early deaths of two of his three sons. With king Robert apparently facing a slow and miserable physical and political decline, and utterly incapable of resisting or challenging the ambitions of his brother and lieutenant, the future of the royal Stewart line, now vested entirely in the person of the king's young and vulnerable son James, was hemmed in by uncertainty. The duke of Albany, in contrast, was a man in overdrive, sweeping through the political wreckage generated by the events of 1402 with characteristic energy and opportunism, principally to advance his own family's interests, but also to provide the kingdom with some semblance of royal government.

The first charters to be granted by Robert III after the general council of May 1402 confirmed the king's withdrawal into the Stewartry, Albany's domination of royal patronage, and, it seems, the physical control of the royal court by the lieutenant's adherents. On 8 November 1402 king Robert was at Southannan on the Ayrshire coast, a dwelling place associated with the Semples of Eliotston, a Renfrewshire family with long-standing connections to the old baronial Stewarts.[1] From Southannan the king issued a grant in favour of John Barclay of Kippo, an Albany adherent from the earldom of Fife, in the presence of, amongst others, the king's brother Walter, earl of Caithness, and Sir John Wemyss of Reres.

The earl of Caithness, the youngest of the king's legitimate brothers, was gaining a new political prominence in the years around 1402, apparently as a trusted ally of the lieutenant. Bower certainly identifies Caithness as 'the principal adviser' in the killing of Rothesay, which would suggest a close political link between Walter and Albany during 1402.[2] Walter's comital title, granted to him between 31 May 1401 and July 1402, may well have been intended to reward him for his role in Rothesay's downfall.[3] Sir John Wemyss of Reres was another man intimately involved in Albany's eradication of Rothesay in 1401/2, and Sir John's appearance at the king's court in Southannan confirmed the Fife laird's remarkable political revival after the besieging of his castle and the forfeiture of his lands by the ill-fated prince the previous year.[4] Robert III was still at Southannan at the end of November, granting a charter to another Fife man connected with Albany, Thomas Dischington of Ardross, a gift witnessed by Caithness, and John Barclay of Kippo, the recipient of the 8 November grant.[5] The two Southannan grants were symptomatic of the total collapse of king Robert's personal political influence late in 1402, with the king isolated in the Stewartry, attended by politically unimportant members of his own household, but also by men who were clearly agents of the lieutenant Albany. It was probably the intended role of Caithness and the Fife lairds, who had suddenly appeared in the king's household in the autumn of 1402, to regulate and control the political activity of the royal court while their true patron was engaged in discharging his extensive duties elsewhere in the kingdom. It would be the policies and ambitions of Albany which would dominate the realm for the next two years, as the lieutenant sought to respond to the regional crises which beset Scotland north and south of the Forth.

DANCING WITH WOLVES: THE LIEUTENANT IN THE NORTH

Albany's political predominance in the months after his creation as the king's lieutenant was reflected in the rapid advance of the territorial interests of the duke and his allies north of the Forth. Perhaps the most important breakthrough for Albany's affinity involved the royal fortress of Dumbarton, which had been held by the political maverick, Walter Danielston, since 1397.[6] Shortly after becoming lieutenant, Albany reached a startling agreement with Danielston, by which the low-ranking and highly secularised cleric agreed to leave Dumbarton 'gyve that he, Mycht Bishop off Sanctandrewis be'.[7] The St Andrews bishopric was still technically vacant, following the death of Walter Trail in 1401, due to the problems experienced by the bishop-elect, Thomas Stewart, in obtaining papal confirmation of his position. The lieutenant's eagerness to secure Danielston's removal from Dumbarton saw Albany meet with his half-brother Thomas, at Abernethy, probably in May or June 1402. Albany persuaded Thomas to resign his claims to the bishopric, and arranged for a new assembly of the St Andrews cathedral chapter to elect Danielston in his stead.[8] Unsurprisingly, the insertion of Danielston into the kingdom's most prestigious ecclesiastical office was not universally popular, and Wyntoun claimed that it was

> Agane conscience of mony men:
> Bot like it wes to stanch then
> Wykkit dedis, mony and fell,
> Be the stuff oysit off that Castell [Dumbarton].[9]

Danielston's controversial episcopal career was short-lived, for the new bishop of St Andrews died around Christmas 1402.[10]

Albany's ambitious plans for the vacated 'royal' fortress of Dumbarton became clear on 15 May 1403, when Robert III confirmed the transfer of the keepership of the castle and the associated office of sheriff of Lennox to Walter Buchanan of that Ilk.[11] The royal charter, in fact, merely confirmed an agreement (the text of which does not survive) which had already been finalised between Buchanan and Duncan, earl of Lennox. Although Robert III's ratification of the deal was made 'reservande till us and till our ayris sic as pertenys til our ryal Majeste', the clear implication was that in early 1403 the earl of Lennox, rather than the king, had disposed of the offices of custodian and sheriff of Dumbarton. The new keeper of Dumbarton, Walter Buchanan, was a Lennox adherent with strong links to Albany and his son Murdoch Stewart.[12] By mid-1403, with his allies in control of the great fortress on the Clyde, the lieutenant's ascendancy in the south-western Highlands was almost complete. For the first time since the thirteenth century, the massive stronghold at Dumbarton and the authority of the sheriff of Lennox were held by men politically dependent on, and aligned with, the comital house of Lennox, a legacy of undisputed local control to which Murdoch Stewart was seemingly destined to succeed. Dumbarton also dominated the land and sea routes to and from Argyll, increasing the influence of the Albany Stewarts in a region already largely under the sway of the lieutenant's kinsmen, the Campbell lords of Lochawe.

With the settlement of Dumbarton on Buchanan in 1403, the lieutenant's territorial and jurisdictional interests extended in an almost unbroken swathe across central Scotland, stretching from the North Sea shores of Fife in the east to Loch Fyne and the Atlantic coast of Argyll in the west, and taking in two of the kingdom's three most important royal castles, Stirling and Dumbarton. In the years after 1402 Albany, the man discharging most of the duties of royal government, may also have tried to centre some of the economic functions of the crown within this hugely impressive personal lordship, for sometime shortly after 1400 a royal mint was established in Dumbarton.[13] The use of the west-coast burgh as a regional mint was a novel and short-lived experiment and, while it has been suggested that Walter Danielston founded the mint late in 1402 through the franchisal right of the bishops of St Andrews to mint royal coins, it seems most likely the mint was established and developed by the lieutenant once the burgh's castle had been secured in the hands of men committed to Albany/Lennox interests in the area.[14]

Buchanan's acquisition of Dumbarton was simply one element of the patronage directed towards Albany's allies in the Lennox.[15] The king made three visits to Dumbarton in 1403/4, almost the only appearances made by the monarch outside the Stewartry in the two years after the council of May 1402; all three expeditions were personally supervised by Albany and culminated in substantial royal grants to members of the lieutenant's affinity.

While Albany's hold on his political heartland in the south-western Highlands grew ever tighter, the lieutenant faced a rather more formidable challenge in attempting to uphold crown interests, and to impose a political settlement amenable to himself, over the rest of Scotland north of the Forth. The exercise of local lordship in the entire region had been badly disrupted by the deaths, in 1402, of the men who had enjoyed title to the earldoms of Ross, Mar and Atholl, and by the capture of the earl of Moray and Murdoch Stewart, who had served continuously as justiciar of the north for thirteen years, at Humbleton. Albany himself, despite his advancing years, took over his son's role as justiciar and drove the northern ayres with a vengeance.[16] The other breaches in the duke's established network of kinsmen and allies in the north were not so easily repaired.

The most grievous blow for Albany's northern interests was undoubtedly the death, on 8 May 1402, of the lieutenant's son-in-law Alexander Leslie, earl of Ross, in his castle of Dingwall.[17] Leslie's death left his young daughter Euphemia, Albany's granddaughter, as heiress to the vast Ross estates. The lieutenant moved swiftly to obtain physical control of Euphemia and the Ross inheritance, and by 15 November 1403 Albany and his brother-in-law, Alexander Keith of Grandon, were certainly in effective control of the Aberdeenshire barony of Kingedward.[18] Dominating the earldom itself, and other Highland lordships held by the comital family, would be a less easy task, although by 11 July 1405 Albany was able to issue charters from

Dingwall castle, styling himself 'lord of the ward of Ross', dealing with the constabulary of the castle of Nairn and its associated sheriffship.[19]

The lieutenant's authority in Ross and the other lordships claimed by his granddaughter was, in reality, far less secure than the charter evidence suggests, for the royal duke faced a formidable rival claimant to the northern earldom. Shortly after Alexander Leslie's death in 1402, Donald of the Isles, who was married to Alexander's sister Mariota, Euphemia's aunt, began to press his wife's claims to Ross. The regional political and military power of the lordship ensured some measure of success, and on a date between 1405 and 1411 physical control of Dingwall castle fell to the Lord of the Isles and his spouse.[20] The contest between Donald of the Isles and Albany for command of the earldom, which would eventually culminate in the infamous Battle of 'Red Harlaw' in 1411, exacerbated the steady decline in comital authority within Ross which had been a feature of the second half of the fourteenth century. It appears likely that Albany's direct political influence as 'lord of the ward of Ross' was intermittent and restricted to the areas around eastern comital centres such as Dingwall, while effective lordship over central and western Ross was contested by a number of powerful rival kindreds, MacKenzies, Mathesons and the Rosses of Balnagowan.[21]

Albany's personal involvement in the political struggle in Ross was just one part of the lieutenant's expanding workload in the north. In September 1403 the duke's established role in central Perthshire was augmented by a royal grant of the earldom of Atholl, in free regality, for the duration of Robert III's life.[22] The earldom of Atholl had reverted to Robert III's control after Rothesay's death, and the grant of regality powers to last for the king's lifetime was clearly intended to allow the lieutenant and his agents to exercise effective political control in Atholl without prejudicing the hereditary rights of the royal dynasty to the earldom. However, shortly before 28 April 1404 Albany arranged what seems to have been a permanent alienation of Atholl to Walter Stewart, earl of Caithness, the duke's brother, political ally, and a long-standing supporter of the lieutenant's strategic interests in Perthshire.[23] Walter Stewart's acquisition of Atholl was one of a number of transactions which must have disturbed the dwindling band of men who were prepared to uphold the interests of Robert III and his young heir. Having already gained effective control of Dumbarton castle, an important element of the 'formal' royal establishment, Albany and his allies were now making substantial territorial gains from within the patrimony of the royal Stewart line.[24]

Despite Albany's formidable personal energy, the lieutenant's attempt to reconstruct a network of reliable agents to protect his interests in the north could not surmount some of the long-term strategic and political problems of the region. The situation in the earldoms of Moray and Mar was particularly problematic for the royal duke. The vulnerability of Moray to raid from the west had been underlined on 3 July 1402 when the burgh of Elgin was attacked and burnt by the forces of Alexander of the Isles, lord of Lochaber.[25] The motivation for the raid is unclear, although Lochaber may have been seeking simply to use the hiatus in local and royal government arising from the deaths of the duke of Rothesay and the earl of Ross in early 1402 to extend his own particular form of overlordship into the Moray coastal plain. Alexander of the Isles was swiftly excommunicated by William Spynie, bishop of Moray, and the lord of Lochaber and his captains came into Elgin to seek forgiveness and absolution from the bishop on 6 October 1402, presumably after some persuasion by the secular arm in the shape of the royal lieutenant. The ceremony probably did little to allay the long-term fears of the canons and burgesses of Elgin, for the lord of Lochaber turned up at the head of a 'great army' to make his redress. It seems surprising, in view of the attack on Moray in July 1402, that Thomas Dunbar, earl of Moray, chose to commit himself to the Humbleton campaign in August and September of the same year. Although both Thomas and his father John had displayed a rare talent for leaving Moray totally unprotected at critical junctures, there seems little doubt that Dunbar's capture at Humbleton was a further blow to Albany's hopes of maintaining political control and stability in the north through a system of proven allies.

Despite Albany's securing of the lord of Lochaber's submission in Elgin in October 1402, the events of that year had left the lieutenant with no great regional ally in the north capable of withstanding the local political, territorial and military ambitions of Donald of the Isles in Ross, or Alexander of the Isles and his 'great army' in Moray. In these circumstances Albany was forced to reach an accommodation with a former bitter adversary, whose lordship was flourishing in the political vacuum produced by the catastrophes of 1402, and who possessed the local power, prestige and military might necessary to bring some measure of political stability to the north. Thus it was that in the years after 1402 the forgotten man of the Stewart dynasty, Alexander Stewart, earl of Buchan and lord of Badenoch, 'the Wolf', and his dangerous brood of warlike sons returned to the service of the crown. The modest revival of the Wolf's career as an agent of crown policy was underway by July 1404 when Buchan attended an exchequer session in Perth and received payment for his expenses 'for the common good'.[26] On 8 July 1404, while at Perth, Hugh Fraser, lord of Lovat, assigned various lands in Inverness-shire to Buchan in return for

£75 and a promise of the earl's 'help and counsel'.[27] The fact that Fraser of Lovat, whose main estates lay to the west of Inverness, was seeking the protection of the Wolf indicates that Buchan's personal political lordship was being extended to adherents of the absent earl of Moray in the area around Inverness. A more formal indication of Buchan's expanding role in this region came with a royal grant of the castle hill of the burgh of Inverness, a gift which implied that Alexander was also to act as custodian of the strategic royal castle, replacing the earl of Moray who had probably been custodian of the castle since 1390.[28]

Buchan's apparent reconciliation with the lieutenant during 1404 was put to the test in the month after the Perth exchequer session by events in the earldom of Mar, for in August 1404 Buchan's eldest son, Alexander, mounted a spectacular political coup against the Albany placemen who had dominated Mar since the death of Malcolm Drummond, lord of Mar, in 1402.[29] On 12 August 1404 Drummond's widow, Isabella, countess of Mar and Garioch, gave over the earldom of Mar, the lordship of Garioch, the forest of Jedworth, a 200-merk pension from the royal customs and all her other lands, rents and possessions to Alexander Stewart, Buchan's 'natural' son, according to the terms of a contract of marriage concluded between them. The descent of the earldom given in the charter is especially significant, for Mar and the other lordships were to descend to the heirs produced by Alexander and Isabella (a rather unlikely occurrence given Isabella's age and her inability to produce a child with her first husband), whom failing to Alexander's heirs and assignees.[30] This arrangement would have seen the extensive Mar inheritance pass permanently into the possession of the Wolf's 'natural' son and his heirs.

The circumstances behind Isabella's proposed marriage and the consequent catapulting of Buchan's natural son into the first rank of the Scottish nobility are unclear. Nineteenth-century historians favoured the view that Alexander engineered the death of Malcolm Drummond, lord of Mar, in 1402, and obtained the earldom through the kidnap of the widowed Isabella and the forcible occupation of the earldom's principal fortress, Kildrummy.[31] In fact, Alexander was entirely blameless in the matter of Drummond's death, and was in possession of neither the countess nor Kildrummy castle in the immediate aftermath of the lord of Mar's demise. Between November 1402 and early 1404 the earldom of Mar and the countess's council were dominated by Albany and his kinsmen and allies, David, earl of Crawford, and the family of Albany's father-in-law William Keith, the Marischal.[32] Albany, Crawford and the Marischal shared an identical long-term aim in Mar, for all three men were committed to supporting the claims of Sir Thomas Erskine and his son Sir Robert

to both Mar and Garioch after the death of the childless countess
Isabella. The Erskine interest in Mar rested on Sir Thomas's marriage to
Janet Keith, who claimed to be countess Isabella's nearest heir in Mar
and Garioch as the great granddaughter of Donald, earl of Mar, who
had died in 1297. The Erskine claim had long enjoyed the support of
Janet Keith's half-brother, William Keith the Marischal, and the
Marischal's son-in-law Albany. Albany and the Marischal had both
been involved in Sir Thomas Erskine's successful attempts to obtain
royal recognition of, and protection for, his wife's rights in Mar and the
Garioch during the 1390s.[33] The Erskines' prospects in Mar received
another substantial boost in November 1400, when the earl of
Crawford bound himself to aid Sir Thomas and his son Robert in
the prosecution of their claim to the earldom after the death of countess
Isabella.[34]

The Erskines had been unable to establish any personal influence
inside Mar as countess Isabella's heirs after Malcolm Drummond's
death, because both Sir Thomas and his son Robert were captured
by the English at Humbleton. Yet this scarcely seemed to matter, for
control of the earldom rested in the hands of a powerful combination of
Erskine's allies, the royal lieutenant, the earl of Crawford, and the
Marischal. These men clearly intended to secure an Erskine succession
to Mar by ensuring that countess Isabella remained in their hands, and
unmarried, until her death.

The reaction of Albany, Crawford and the Marischal to the news
that Alexander Stewart was in Kildrummy and preparing to marry
countess Isabella under terms which would permanently disinherit the
Erskines must have been one of shock and anger. The descent of the
Wolf's son into Mar in July or early August 1404 had destroyed the
long-laid plans of the lieutenant and his allies in the region. While it
seems likely that Alexander gained access to, and control over,
Kildrummy castle and countess Isabella by force, it was equally clear
that the intervention of the Wolf's son in Mar had the full backing of
several important local families. The 12 August charter, which would
have seen Mar given over permanently to Alexander Stewart and his
heirs and assignees, was witnessed by Alexander Waghorn, bishop of
Ross, Sir Andrew Leslie, Sir John Forbes, Forbes' son and heir
Alexander and his kinsman Duncan, Alexander Irvine of Drum and
William Chalmers the elder. Alexander Waghorn, an enigmatic figure,
seems to have been associated with the Wolf's son for some time before
1404 and had, presumably, been brought to Kildrummy by Alexander
in order to bless his union with countess Isabella.[35] However, the
remaining charter witnesses were all from well-established families in
the earldom of Mar or lordship of Garioch, while William Chalmers

was, most likely, a burgess and one of the custumars of Aberdeen.[36] These local men had been excluded from the countess Isabella's council by the intrusion of Albany's allies in 1402, and had no good reason to support the lieutenant's policy of keeping the earldom without an active male lord in order to accommodate the Erskines at a time of noted unrest and lawlessness in the north. Some of the local lairds may have entertained more specific grievances against the lieutenant's agents in Mar. This was certainly true of Alexander Irvine of Drum, who at this stage was engaged in a bitter feud with William Keith, the Marischal, and his family.[37] The group gathering around Alexander Stewart in August 1404 illustrates that there was significant support within the earldom for the adoption of Alexander as lord of Mar and the setting aside of the Erskine claims. Such a prospect was simply unacceptable to Albany, the earl of Crawford and the Marischal, and a major political and military confrontation in the north-east seemed imminent.

The gathering storm in the north and Alexander Stewart's open defiance of the lieutenant in the late autumn of 1404 brought about an unanticipated revival in Robert III's political influence. By 26 November the king and the royal court had emerged from the Stewartry and had moved north to Perth, clearly to play some part in bringing the dispute in Mar to a conclusion.[38] It may be that Albany had requested the king's presence in Perth in order to support the lieutenant's position in Mar with the full weight of royal authority, but it seems more likely that Robert III had come north as the only man acceptable to Alexander Stewart, the king's nephew, as an arbitrator of the dispute between Alexander and his uncle, the royal lieutenant who controlled the formal mechanisms of royal patronage and justice.

The men with the king in Perth in late November included David, earl of Crawford, and Walter Ogilvy of Carcary. Ogilvy was the brother of Sir Alexander Ogilvy of Auchterhouse, sheriff of Angus, and a son of the Walter Ogilvy who had been killed fighting alongside the earl of Crawford, then lord of Glen Esk, against forces led by Alexander Stewart's brothers at the battle of Glen Brerechan in 1392. Walter Ogilvy, the son, retained this close association with Crawford, while he held his lands of Carcary from John Erskine of Dun, the brother of Sir Robert Erskine.[39] Crawford and Ogilvy, both apparently dedicated to upholding Erskine rights in Mar, left the royal court at Perth in late November, and by 1 December had journeyed to Kildrummy castle, where countess Isabella gave Ogilvy a grant of the lands of Tullicurran in Strathardle, the castle of Glenatnay in Perthshire, and the kirkton of Eassie in Angus.[40] Crawford and Ogilvy had clearly been sent to Kildrummy in early December 1404, direct from the royal court, in order to negotiate and supervise a settlement between those backing the Erskines' claims in Mar and the, mainly local, families supporting Alexander Stewart. Crawford returned south to the king and lieutenant at Perth also immediately, apparently bringing with him details of a suitable compromise, while Ogilvy remained in Kildrummy with the countess.[41]

The nature of the agreement became clear during a curious ceremony acted out before the gates of Kildrummy on 9 December (misdated 9 September in the notarial instrument which recorded the events of the day) while countess Isabella was holding a meeting 'pro utilitate rei publica et gubernatione patria', that is 'for the good of the realm and the governance of the country (in a local sense)', with her council, named as Alexander, bishop of Ross, Andrew Leslie, lord of Sydie, Walter Ogilvy of Carcary, William Chalmers, Richard Lovell and Thomas Gray, and attended by the free tenants of the earldom and 'all the people of the country'.[42] Into this stage-managed occasion came Alexander Stewart, who handed over to the countess the castle of Kildrummy with its charters and silver vessels, whereupon Isabella 'chose' Alexander to be her husband and gave to him in free marriage the earldom of Mar, the lordship of Garioch, and her other lands in Scotland. The crucial feature of the new grant of Mar to Alexander Stewart in December 1404 was the adjustment of the descent of the earldom from that which had been proposed in the charter of the previous August. Under the terms of the December marriage contract, Mar and the other lordships were to be held by Alexander and Isabella in liferent and, following their deaths, by any heirs produced between them. However, if the couple failed to produce children (as seemed highly probable), then the earldom was to descend not to Alexander's heirs, as had been stipulated in the August settlement, but to the nearest heirs of countess Isabella, a position claimed by Robert Erskine. The alteration in descent was re-emphasised in a series of charters issued by Isabella to Alexander on the same day as the ceremony outside Kildrummy.[43] The new descent reserved and protected the Erskines' hereditary claim to Mar, which was, in effect, being deferred for Alexander Stewart's lifetime, whilst guaranteeing Stewart's uncontested liferent of the earldom.

The presence of the lairds of Mar and Garioch and 'all the people of the country' at Kildrummy, the chief fortress of Mar, to witness the ceremony of 9 December 1404 which saw Alexander Stewart established as earl suggests that, in Mar at least, the open acclamation and approval of all the free tenants of the earldom were seen as an integral part of the creation of a new earl, a feature which sanctioned and legitimised comital authority. In 1351 William, earl of Ross, had laid similar stress on the support of all the free tenants of the earldom of Ross for his proposed entailing of the earldom in favour of his brother Hugh.[44]

In 1404 a number of factors may have inclined the free tenants of Mar to support the claims of the Wolf's son to be their earl. Alexander Stewart certainly seems to have been able to exploit a local backlash against the domination of the earldom in the years 1402–4 by Albany assignees from Angus and the Mearns. Initially, local resentment may well have been aroused by the circumstances surrounding the death of Malcolm Drummond, lord of Mar, in 1402. Albany's subsequent policy of keeping the earldom without an effective local lord in order to secure the succession to Mar for a family with little political and social influence in the region seems to have caused further antagonism. The great gathering outside Kildrummy on 9 December was said to have been discussing not only the good of the kingdom, but also the 'governance of the country'. The distinction between national and local needs may have been deliberately drawn, because the royal lieutenant's view of how Mar should be governed had been openly rejected by many local families when they offered their support to Alexander Stewart.

The attractions of Alexander Stewart as a local lord in Mar were powerful and immediate. Just west across the hills from Kildrummy lay Badenoch, the very centre of the territorial and military lordship which had been built up by Alexander Stewart's father. From the strongholds of Badenoch the Wolf's son and his men could either defend or denude western Mar. The lowland chronicler Bower saw Alexander Stewart as a man who underwent a miraculous social and political conversion, for he was 'in his youth . . . very headstrong and wild and the . . . leader of a band of caterans. But later he came to his senses, and, being changed into another kind of man, ruled with acceptance nearly all the country north of the Mounth'.[45] In reality, it was precisely Alexander's established ability to control and direct the activities of the substantial cateran forces in the lordships west of Mar which made Stewart's political protection attractive to the Aberdeen burgesses and Mar families, such as the Forbes, whose lands lay in the west of the earldom. Alexander Stewart offered the local community strong and effective lordship, backed up by the necessary sanction of considerable military force. However, in the years after 1404 the new earl of Mar also earned the unstinting praise of lowland chroniclers, and cultivated the support of the chivalry of Mar, Angus and the Mearns through a series of chivalric exploits and, in particular, his heroic defence of the north-eastern lowlands against the encroaching forces of Donald of the Isles at the battle of Harlaw in 1411.[46] Mar was not about to repeat the political mistakes of his father, whose northern lieutenancy had eventually been seen as a cultural and political threat to the lowland communities and lordships whose interests it was meant to defend and protect. In terms of the lordship which sustained his political authority, Mar was not really 'another kind of man', for he clearly continued to employ the methods which had underpinned his father's power. However, the political application of Mar's military strength was largely seen to serve the interests of the earl's adherents within Mar and, in the long term, to uphold the strategic concerns of the royal lieutenant. Moreover, the earl's career as the crown's regional agent in the north after 1404 flourished in a sympathetic political environment, for the inhabitants of Moray, Mar, Angus and the Mearns, as well as the lieutenant Albany, came to regard Alexander Stewart as the last effective bulwark against the advancing political and territorial influence of the lordship of the Isles. Thus, as father gave way to son, the historical reputation of the Badenoch Stewarts experienced a remarkable transformation, with the ravening wolf replaced by a bristling but dependable guard dog.

In the short term, however, Alexander Stewart's acquisition of Mar in 1404 represented a considerable setback for Albany's interests, and graphically illustrated the geographic and political limits of Albany's lieutenancy in the north. Even with the resources of the lieutenancy and justiciarship behind him, Albany had been unable or unwilling to impose his own preferred solution in Mar. Given his problems elsewhere in the north, Albany could hardly afford to become involved in a long-drawn-out struggle with Alexander Stewart, his family, and the local landowners in Mar. Instead, the lieutenant contented himself with obtaining long-term guarantees for the Erskines' position in the earldom, and worked to establish a tolerable working relationship with the new earl. Crown confirmation of the new settlement in Mar was, on this occasion, not long delayed. On 15 and 21 January 1405 Robert III ratified nearly all the territorial arrangements of 9 December, except for refusing any claims Alexander might advance to the barony of Cavers in Roxburghshire.[47] Before long Albany, ever the pragmatist, was seeking to harness and exploit the regional power of Buchan and his son, the new earl of Mar, to suppress local disorder and to assist in the lieutenant's wider struggle with the Clan Donald in Ross, Moray and the central Highlands. The employment of Buchan and Mar in the defence of 'royal' interests in the north was quickly made clear in the grant of the castle hill of Inverness to Buchan in late 1404 or early 1405. The grant was apparently made in entail, suggesting that the earl of Mar was expected to succeed his father as custodian of the fortress and as the defender of the royal burgh which it protected.[48]

While Albany was fully engaged in the maintenance of his own variety of political order in the north, it was inevitable that the lieutenant's ability to participate in the affairs of the kingdom south of the Forth, to guide Anglo-Scottish diplomacy or lead localised warfare on the borders, would be limited. It was not the case that Albany had no interest in the conduct of diplomacy — it could hardly be otherwise with his son Murdoch in English captivity — simply that it was not likely that Albany could provide the same measure of personal leadership in the south of Scotland that he could in the north.

SOUTH OF THE BORDER?: ALBANY, DOUGLAS, THE PERCIES, AND THE COCKLAWS CAMPAIGN

The situation in the south of Scotland after 1402 was, in most respects, even worse than that north of the Forth in terms of the loss, temporary or permanent, of effective local leaders. Amongst the many men who had failed to return from the Humbleton campaign, the most signi-ficant figure was Archibald, 4th earl of Douglas, head of the family which had dominated the border since 1388. Douglas's capture at Humbleton, along with George, earl of Angus (who died of plague while a prisoner of the English), and Thomas Dunbar, earl of Moray, combined with the exile of George, earl of March, to produce a situation where the Scottish marches were undefended by an active nobleman of comital rank. The position was exacerbated by the large-scale loss through death or capture of many of the most experienced political and military leaders of the border aristocracy below the rank of earl during 1402. The dreary roll-call included Sir Patrick Hepburn (killed at Nesbit Muir), Sir John Swinton and Sir Adam Gordon (both killed at Humbleton), Sir William Stewart of Jedworth (executed by the English after Humbleton), and Sir James Douglas of Dalkeith the younger (captured at Humbleton). Well could the chronicler Bower lament that 'The flower as it were of the fighting men of the whole realm of Scotland was captured and ransomed'.[49]

Thus, in late 1402 and early 1403 the south of Scotland seemed open to a concerted territorial advance by Henry IV and his great northern lords, the earls of Northumberland and Westmorland, supported by the Scottish earl of March. The English king fired the opening shots in just such a campaign on 2 March 1403, with a grant of the lands of the captured earl of Douglas, that is, the earldom of Douglas, Eskdale, Liddesdale, Lauderdale, the lordship of Selkirk, Ettrick forest and Teviotdale to Henry Percy, earl of Northumberland. At the same time the earl of Westmorland received a grant of the lordships of Galloway, Annandale and the town and castle of Roxburgh.[50] Bower

suggests that, with the help of the earl of March, the earl of Northumberland's son Henry Percy 'Hotspur' intended to 'subject Scotland
as far as the Scottish sea [the Forth] to his will'.[51]

In the spring of 1403 Henry Hotspur opened the great offensive with
a siege of Cocklaws tower near Ormiston in Teviotdale, presumably in
an attempt to implement the grant of Douglas lands given to his father,
before coming to an accommodation, sometime before 30 May 1403,
with the captain of the fortress, John Grymslaw, by which the castle
was to be surrendered to Percy on 1 August 1403 if it was not relieved
by a Scottish force beforehand.[52] Henry Percy, buoyed by the
comprehensive triumph of English arms at Humbleton, may have
hoped to provoke a second decisive full-scale military confrontation
with the depleted and dispirited forces of the Scottish crown around
Cocklaws in the autumn of 1403. Hotspur's grand design was diverted,
and the south of Scotland saved from further military action, by the
well-known and much-discussed rebellion of the earl of Northumberland and his fiery son against Henry IV in July 1403, a revolt which
ended in Hotspur's defeat and death in battle against the king's army at
Shrewsbury on 21 July.[53] The view of the Scottish chronicler, Bower,
was that Hotspur abandoned the siege of Cocklaws in May 1403 and
made the arrangement for relief or surrender with its garrison intending
to use the impending confrontation with the Scots in August 1403 as a
cloak to recruit men who were eventually to be deployed in rebellion
against Henry IV.[54] Bower's interpretation implies that the Percy
rebellion involved early and sustained political duplicity. This is a
view that has been vigorously challenged in a recent examination of the
Percies' political aims during 1403, which suggests that the attack on
Cocklaws tower, a strongpoint in the heart of Teviotdale, one of the
Douglas lordships assigned to the earl of Northumberland, represented
a genuine attempt by Hotspur to enforce his father's claims to Douglas
estates and lordships.[55] The same study argues that the Percies continued to think in terms of the annexation of the Douglas estates
throughout May and June 1403, although increasingly exasperated by
Henry IV's unwillingness to allocate sufficient resources to their
campaign, and that the family's continuing concern with the defence
of Cocklaws tower and the north of England actually contributed to
the eventual failure of their rebellion, because the men raised by
Hotspur and his father to defend the English border were still deployed
in that area, fulfilling exactly that role, during the course of Henry
Hotspur's rebellion.[56] This 'positive' assessment of Percy actions during
1403 seems to receive indirect support from the Scottish chronicle
accounts, for neither Bower nor Wyntoun gives the slightest hint of
collusion between the Percies and the Scottish lieutenant, Albany; both

record that Albany mobilised a Scottish army in the autumn of 1403 to relieve Cocklaws, and that this force fully expected to meet with Percy's army in Teviotdale.

There remain, however, several unanswered questions in relation to Scottish involvement in Percy's rebellion and the chronicle treatment of Albany's expedition to relieve Cocklaws. The most problematic area is the behaviour of Archibald Douglas, 4th earl of Douglas, who had apparently been held as a captive of the earl of Northumberland since Humbleton, but who fought alongside Henry Hotspur against Henry IV at the battle of Shrewsbury on 21 July 1403.[57] The willingness of Douglas and his fellow Scottish captives to fight for the Percies against the English king has never been satisfactorily explained. Although Bower and Wyntoun ascribe the appearance of the captured Scots to a general eagerness to be involved in a conflict which was guaranteed to result in huge English losses, it is unlikely that earl Archibald would have been willing to risk his own life, and those of his men, in support of former enemies, without a tangible political incentive.

Northumberland and his son could offer Douglas and his adherents some important concessions in return for their military support during 1403. Firstly, it seems likely that Hotspur and his father guaranteed the release of their Scottish captives, and perhaps the waiving of the substantial ransoms owed by earl Archibald and his retainers, in the event of Henry IV's overthrow. The political and military co-operation of Hotspur and Douglas during July 1403 also implies that the Percies had effectively abandoned any pursuit of the claims to Douglas lordships which had been granted to them in March 1403. It may, however, have been a third consideration which finally saw earl Archibald ride to war in the Welsh Marches in the company of Hotspur. If the Percies succeeded in ousting Henry IV with the assistance of earl Archibald, then the position of Douglas's bitter adversary, George Dunbar, earl of March, whose family and adherents were entirely dependent, physically and politically, on the continued goodwill of the English crown, would have become impossible. The earl of Douglas had already acquiesced in the elimination of a Scottish prince of royal blood, his own brother-in-law, in his relentless pursuit of Dunbar's downfall; Archibald was unlikely to blanch at the thought of consigning a usurper English king to a similar fate.

If co-operation with Northumberland and Hotspur offered Douglas a number of potential political advantages, it is less clear why the Percies should have been willing to make any substantial concessions to secure the service of a handful of captive Scottish knights, estimated as less than twenty in number by Wyntoun. Earl Archibald, of course, commanded a considerable military following within Scotland, and one later chronicle account asserts that Douglas was paroled by the earl of Northumberland shortly before the battle of Shrewsbury in order to recruit troops within the northern kingdom to assist the Percy rebellion.[58] The suggestion that Douglas was allowed to travel to Scotland in the summer of 1403 is flatly denied by the contemporary chronicler, Andrew Wyntoun. Wyntoun explains Douglas's role at Shrewsbury by claiming that the earl had little option since

> Frethit he wes nocht off presowne,
> Fra he was takyn at Homyldone[59]

Despite Wyntoun's certainty, at least two charters seem to indicate that earl Archibald may have been in Scotland shortly before the outbreak of the Percies' rebellion, although Douglas's 'appearance' as a witness to a royal charter dated 5 May 1403 is unlikely, and probably resulted from a scribal error or miscopying.[60] No such dubiety surrounds a charter issued by earl Archibald himself, clearly dated 10 July 1403, and apparently granted from Edinburgh.[61] The charter, which gave over the lands of Tulliallan to Sir John Edmonstone, was witnessed by a number of important border knights, including Sir John Seton, Sir William Abernethy, Sir William Hay and Sir William Borthwick, and William Crawford, who was the earl's constable of Edinburgh castle. Of these men, Edmonstone, Seton, Abernethy and Hay had all been captured with Douglas at Humbleton.[62] The charter suggests that Douglas and at least some of the Scottish knights held by the Percies after Humbleton were, in fact, in Scotland when the great rebellion against Henry IV began.[63] Douglas, perhaps now at the head of a force hastily recruited within Scotland, would have had to sweep south like the wind from Edinburgh on 10 July 1403 in order to join with Henry Hotspur, who had begun the raising of Cheshire in rebellion on or about 9 July.[64] Earl Archibald was noted as accompanying some of Sir Henry Percy's recruiting drives from Chester into North Wales, which took place between 9 and 17 July, while Henry IV was certainly aware of, and exploiting for propaganda purposes, the presence of Scots in Hotspur's army by 18 July.[65]

If Douglas was indeed in Scotland on and around 10 July 1403, gathering men to assist a Percy rebellion against the English crown, it must have been quite obvious to Albany that there would be no English force arriving to accept the surrender of Cocklaws tower on 1 August 1403. Yet both Bower and Wyntoun portray the lieutenant's organisation of an expedition to relieve Cocklaws in July/August 1403 in the most heroic light.[66] Bower reports that many of the Scottish noblemen who gathered at a council, held by Albany at Falkland in May or June

1403, to discuss the arrangements made by the garrison of Cocklaws with Sir Henry Percy, were understandably reluctant to risk an open battle with the English 'in support of such a little tower', but that the 64-year-old Albany had delivered a stirring speech: 'i vow to God and St Fillan that if i am spared i shall be there on the appointed day even if no one comes with me save my boy Patrick as rider of my warhorse'. Roused by the example of Albany's personal bravery and defiance, the rest of the assembly vowed to support a campaign to relieve Cocklaws.[67]

The reference to St. Fillan in Albany's speech, otherwise clearly invented by Bower, may have reflected a genuine association between the lieutenant and the cult of St. Fillan, for Fillan was particularly identified with Glen Dochart, a lordship held by Albany since 1374. Aside from the local connection, Bower may have been making a wider propaganda point on Albany's behalf. Robert I, whose career as a defender of the Scottish kingdom against English aggression had already achieved a mythic status by the late fourteenth century, had been a noted patron of St. Fillan.[68] On the eve of Bannockburn Bruce had invoked the assistance of St. Fillan, and Bower may have been deliberately attempting to associate Bruce's preparations before that famous battle with Albany's before the anticipated battle of Cocklaws.

In the end, of course, there was to be no English army for Albany to confront, although in his account of the lieutenant's rather curious expedition to relieve Cocklaws Bower insists, perhaps rather defensively, that Albany was relishing the opportunity to meet the Percies in open battle at Cocklaws: 'There was not one indeed, . . . who did not believe that there was to be a clash between the governor [*recte* lieutenant] and Percy: they had every reason to believe that he had assembled a large force at that time', and that Albany 'was approaching the castle hoping for nothing else than a battle'.[69] Albany's reported eagerness for battle might appear a little strange, even perverse, given the Scots' recent disastrous experience of full-scale warfare at Humbleton. But while Albany may have committed the Scots to the relief of Cocklaws in May or June 1403 in the expectation of having to meet and defeat an English army in Teviotdale, it seems inconceivable that the lieutenant was still labouring under that misapprehension when his forces actually took to the field around mid-July. The nature of Albany's campaign suggests, in fact, that the Scots were confident there would be no effective military intervention from south of the border, for the duke began his offensive with determined and prolonged sieges of English garrisons established in strongholds which had fallen to the enemy after Humbleton.[70] After recapturing Innerwick castle in East Lothian, the lieutenant moved on towards Cocklaws, where Albany secured a risk-free propaganda victory by allowing his host to go through the charade of surrounding the fortress, although by this stage, as even Bower admits, Albany had been made aware of Hotspur's defeat and death at Shrewsbury. Albany had thus symbolically fulfilled his oath, and the Scottish chroniclers dutifully wrote up the Cocklaws campaign as a conspicuous example of the bravery, daring and effectiveness of the lieutenant and the Scottish host in the defence of the kingdom. Wyntoun and Bower were certainly not men to hold back in their praise of the lieutenant, and Bower's description of Albany's decisive speech during the council at Falkland, in particular, was clearly intended to reflect personal credit on the duke as a man committed to the defence of the realm. Wyntoun, whose chronicle was completed while Albany was governor of the kingdom and whose principal patron was the duke's adherent Sir John Wemyss of Reres, displayed his own positive estimation of Albany in a 72-line oration in praise of the duke's character.[71] More generally, the elaborate chronicle presentation of what was a huge non-event was surely meant to suggest that the Scots retained the capacity and determination to defend their kingdom and to engage in full-scale warfare with the English despite the disaster of Humbleton.

The truth was rather less reassuring, for in reality the Scottish kingdom had escaped from a major political and military crisis south of the Forth during 1403 through sheer good luck. Overall, in fact, the events around Cocklaws tower tended to confirm the inability of the lieutenant's regime, heavily preoccupied with the concerns of the north, to offer an effective defence of the south of Scotland against the ambitions of the English crown and border aristocracy after 1402. The entire affair, after all, resulted from the fact that in May 1403 the beleaguered Scottish garrison in Cocklaws could not be relieved; there was simply no prospect of the appearance of a Scottish force strong enough to defend the tower and break Hotspur's siege. The regional political and military lordships which protected the south of Scotland had effectively collapsed with the loss, through death, imprisonment or political exile, of the great lords who led and mobilised the chivalry of Lothian and the borders. Wyntoun's description of the force led by Albany to the 'relief' of Cocklaws confirms the paralysis of military and political leadership in the south, for the troops who stormed Innerwick castle and made their empty gesture of defiance around the walls of Cocklaws tower were raised largely from the lieutenant's own heartland in Scotland north of the Forth.[72]

The political and military situation in the south of Scotland in early 1403 had seemed to make widespread territorial and political advances by the English crown and its representatives almost inevitable. The confidence of Henry IV and his northern lords was displayed in the grants of Douglas estates to the Percies and the earl of Westmorland, and in George Dunbar's clear anticipation of the recovery of at least some of his strongholds and lands within Scotland.[73] The Scots, in the aftermath of Nesbit Muir and Humbleton, seem to have had little heart for further military confrontation. Even Bower's report of Albany's rousing speech to the council at Falkland implies that the majority opinion, before the lieutenant's eloquent outburst, was that Cocklaws should be quietly abandoned to the Percies.[74] In the end, however, the English crown, beset by rebellion in Wales and in the north, was unable to derive any permanent advantage from the desperate political state of southern Scotland. Abbot Bower thankfully and reverentially asserted that the hand of a merciful God lay behind the diversion of the political energies of the English crown and the Percies into the internecine conflict which culminated at Shrewsbury. 'For that war which was expected and dreaded by the Scots . . . he transferred happily at the appointed time . . . like a rushing river to the south to be fought at Shrewsbury on the borders of Wales'.[75]

The lieutenant, embroiled in the affairs of the north, made little effort to take advantage as the threat of English military action in the south receded. Instead, a bid for the political and social leadership of the nobility of the south of Scotland emerged from a rather unlikely source. By the summer of 1404 it was obvious that a remarkable revival was under way, for after two years of utter obscurity, the disregarded and broken king was shuffling his way back into the political arena. As Robert III came in from the west to spend prolonged spells in Linlithgow and Edinburgh, the Albany placemen around the royal court melted away, to be replaced by the king's own adherents. Robert's recovery of relative political independence coincided with an attempt by the king and his supporters to assert the authority of the royal house throughout the south of the kingdom. The political future of the dynasty would be determined by the success or failure of that attempt.

NOTES

1. SRO RH 1/1/2; *RMS*, i, 490; SRO GD3/1/Bundle 15/3. John Berclay's father, Hugh, had been described as 'oure lufit squier hwichon the Berclay lord of Kyppow' by Albany in a letter of 1 May 1380: GD 90/1/29. Between 1402 and April 1404 Robert III issued charters from Dumbarton, Rothesay, Dundonald, Southannan, Eliotston, Christwell and Renfrew.

2. The charter was also witnessed by five chaplains and clerks of the king's household: *Chron. Bower* (Watt), viii, 301.

3. On 31 May 1401 Walter was still simply lord of Brechin: *ER*, iii, 515. Before July 1402 Walter's niece, Euphemia, resigned her claim to the earldom of Caithness in favour of her uncle: *SP*, i, 437.

4. That the attack on Wemyss had been very much Rothesay's personal policy is indicated by the swift rehabilitation of Sir John after the prince's death. By 24 May 1402 Wemyss' lands had been restored to him, an arrangement made probably in the general council of May which had confirmed the promotion of Wemyss' patron, Albany, to the lieutenancy: Fraser, *Wemyss*, ii, 44.

5. *RMS*, i, Addenda, no. 1. The charter was also witnessed by four of the five household clerks who had attested the 8 November charter.

6. *Supra*, Chapter 7.

7. *Chron. Wyntoun* (Laing), iii, 83.

8. *Ibid.*, iii, 83. When Danielston died around Christmas 1402 it was claimed that he had held the bishopric for a little over half a year, suggesting that Thomas Stewart's resignation and Danielston's promotion occurred in May or June 1402: *Ibid.*, iii, 84.

9. *Ibid.*, iii, 83.

10. *Ibid.*, iii, 84.

11. NLS, Adv. MSS. 34.3.25, 63.

12. Buchanan was a major landowner in the earldom of Lennox, and a frequent witness to earl Duncan's charters. In 1392 Buchanan had twice been associated with Albany and Murdoch in charters issued from Stirling: Fraser, *Lennox*, ii, 37–9, 45; *Lennox Cart.*, 58, 59, 64, 72, 73; NLS Fleming of Wigtown, Ch.no.15821. A Walter Buchanan, either this man or his son, took part in the Humbleton campaign of 1402 in the service of Murdoch Stewart, and was captured alongside Murdoch by the English on 14 September 1402. The younger of the two Walter Buchanans eventually married Murdoch's daughter Isobel: *HMC Report*, x, App.vi, 78; Fraser, *Menteith*, i, 280.

13. I. Stewart, 'The Scottish Royal Mints' in *Mints, Dies and Currency: Essays in Memory of A. E. G. Baldwin*, ed. R. A. G. Carson (London, 1971), 165–273, at 184 and 231–2.

14. V. Smart, *The Coins of St Andrews* (St Andrews University Library, 1991), 30–1. The surviving Dumbarton coins, all Robert III groats, indicate that the operation there involved several issues of coinage. This suggests that the mint was active for a far longer period than the six months in 1402 when Danielston may have been both bishop of St Andrews and in effective command of Dumbarton castle.

15. In February 1403 the king, at Dumbarton, granted various lands in Glendaruel to a Duncan McDowell. The lands were part of the barony of Cowal, an important component of the Stewartry, which had reverted to Robert III's nominal control after Rothesay's death. The charter favoured the earl of Lennox and Lennox's designated heir,

Murdoch Stewart, with an entail of McDowell's Cowal lands if the latter should die without heirs. In February 1404 the king assigned the lucrative ward of Sir Adam Gordon's heirs to the new Albany/Lennox custodian and sheriff of Dumbarton, Walter Buchanan: SRO Bruce and Kerr WS, GD 240 Box 9/Bundle 1; BM Harleian MSS, no. 4693, f.9v.

16. *ER*, iii, 644.

17. *The Calendar of Fearn: text and additions, 1471–1667* (SHS, 1991), 86.

18. *Abdn.Reg.*, i, 208: the lieutenant issuing precepts to his brother-in-law, Alexander Keith of Grandon, as Albany's bailie in the barony of Kingedward, ordering him to pay the second tenths due to the bishop of Aberdeen from the ward of Kingedward.

19. *The Book of the Thanes of Cawdor* (Spalding Club, 1859), 5.

20. K. Steer and J. W. M. Bannerman, *Monumental Sculpture*, 148–50 (no. 80), 205; *Chron. Bower* (Watt), viii, 77.

21. W. Matheson, 'Traditions of the MacKenzies', *TGSI*, xxxix–xl (1942–50), 193–228; 'Traditions of the Mathesons', *TGSI*, xlii (1953–9), 153–181; K. Steer and J. W. M. Bannerman, *Monumental Sculpture*, 205.

22. BM Harleian MSS., no. 4694, f. 15v–16v. The charter also stipulated that if Albany should die before the king, then his son John would hold the earldom for the remainder of the king's life. It was entirely in keeping with Robert III's itinerary at this stage that this charter was issued from Christwell in Renfrewshire.

23. A. A. M. Duncan, 'Councils General, 1404–1423', *SHR*, xxxv (1956), 136.

24. Aside from the major example of Atholl, Albany's associates were the beneficiaries of a number of smaller grants from within the Stewartry, notably in the barony of Cowal.

25. *Moray Reg.*, 382–3.

26. *ER*, iii, 600.

27. SRO GD 124/1/1128.

28. *RMS*, App. 2., no. 1936.

29. *Supra*, Chapter 8.

30. *RMS*, ii, no. 1239.

31. P. F. Tytler, *The History of Scotland*, iii, 123.

32. William Keith, the Marischal, and his son Alexander witnessed a charter issued by countess Isabella, from Kildrummy, in November 1402. In March 1403 Albany and Crawford were identified as members of the countess's special council. Albany, Crawford, Alexander Keith of Grandon and the bishop of Aberdeen all received substantial grants from Isabella during this period: SRO RH6/211; *Abdn. Reg.*, 207; *A.B.Ill.*, ii, 372; *Maitland Miscellany I*, pt. 2, 358.

33. SRO GD 124/1/118, 119.

34. SRO GD 124/7/3.

35. D. E. R. Watt, *Dictionary*, 562.
36. *ER*, iii, *ad indicem*.
37. Lieut-Col. J. Forbes-Leslie, *The Irvines of Drum and Collateral Branches* (Aberdeen, 1909), 25 (note 5), 30, 36–9.
38. Fraser, *Carnegies*, ii, 505–6.
39. Fraser, *Carnegies*, ii, 502. On 26 November Robert III issued two great seal confirmations of land deals in which Walter was involved: Fraser, *Carnegies*, ii, 505–6; SRO Inventory of Airlie Muniments GD 16/3/4.
40. SRO GD 16/24/199; Fraser, *Douglas*, iii, 732.
41. Ogilvy witnessed charters issued by Isabella on 5 and 8 December: SRO GD 124/1/122; *A.B.Ill.*, iii, 576.
42. SRO GD 124/1/123. Countess Isabella's 'council' was, in reality, a mix of men supporting either Alexander Stewart or the Albany/Crawford/Erskine position in Mar. The bishop of Ross, Andrew Leslie and William Chalmers had been with Alexander Stewart in Kildrummy in August 1404, while Walter Ogilvy clearly represented the interests of the Erskines and their backers. A dating of 9 September for the events around Kildrummy is impossible because the ceremony involved countess Isabella's marriage to Alexander Stewart, while on 10 November and 1, 5, and 8 December 1404 the countess was still issuing charters 'in her widowhood': Fraser, *Douglas*, iii, 730; SRO GD 16/24/199; SRO GD 124/1/122; *A.B.Ill.*, iii, 576. The formal grant of the earldom, issued on 9 December, was said to have been witnessed by 'all our [the countess'] tenants outside the castle of Kildrummy': SRO GD 124/1/124.
43. SRO GD 124/1/124–126. All these charters and precepts are dated 9 *December*, confirming the date of the ceremony outside Kildrummy, and contain specific guarantees for Alexander's liferent of Mar and the other lordships.
44. SRO GD 297/163.
45. *Chron. Bower* (Watt), viii, 293.
46. *Chron. Wyntoun* (Laing), iii, 102–116; *Chron. Bower* (Watt), viii, 75–7, 293.
47. GD 124/1/125–6.
48. *RMS*, App. 2, no. 1936.
49. *Chron. Bower* (Watt), viii, 47–9.
50. *Rot.Scot.*, ii, 163–4; *Foedera*, viii, 289.
51. *Chron. Bower* (Watt), viii, 49–51.
52. *Ibid.*, viii, 51, 173.
53. J. M. W. Bean, 'Henry IV and the Percies', *History*, xliv (1959), 212–227.
54. *Chron. Bower* (Watt), viii, 53.
55. P. M'Niven, 'The Scottish Policy of the Percies and the Strategy of the Rebellion of 1403', in *Bulletin of the John Rylands Library*, lxii (1979), 498–530.

56. P. M'Niven, 'Policy of the Percies', 516.

57. *Chron. Bower* (Watt), viii, 59; *Chron. Wyntoun* (Laing), iii, 90–1.

58. David Hume of Godscroft, *History of the Houses of Douglas and Angus* (Edinburgh, 1644), i, 222–3.

59. *Chron. Wyntoun* (Laing), iii, 90.

60. The charter was issued by Robert III, at Rothesay, in favour of his illegitimate son John Stewart of Auchingoune. Besides Douglas the charter witnesses included Sir Thomas Erskine, also captured by the English at Humbleton. The date is supplied by a fifteenth-century copy of the charter, the original having the calendar date and regnal year obscured by staining: SRO RH1/1/2. This is a photocopy of the original from the Earl of Mansfield's Muniments in Scone Palace: Strathclyde Regional Archives, Mitchell Library, Glasgow. Shaw Stewarts of Ardgowan, T-ARD 1/6/11/3 (fifteenth-century copy).

61. SRO Cardross Writs GD 15/333.

62. *Chron Bower* (Watt), viii, 49; *HMC Report*, x, Pt. 6, 77.

63. The possibility remains that the Douglas charter is misdated and that it was issued in July 1402, shortly before Douglas and his adherents took part in the ill-fated Humbleton campaign.

64. P. M'Niven, 'Policy of the Percies', 517.

65. *CDS*, iv, nos. 633, 646. I should like to thank Dr Philip Morgan, Department of History, University of Keele, for his clarification of Sir Henry Percy's movements in and around Chester in July 1403.

66. *Chron. Wyntoun* (Laing), iii, 89; *Chron. Bower* (Watt), viii, 55.

67. *Ibid.*, viii, 55.

68. G. W. S. Barrow, *Robert Bruce*, 318.

69. *Chron. Bower* (Watt), viii, 55–7.

70. *Ibid.*, 55; *Chron. Wyntoun* (Laing), iii, 90; *ER*, iii, 644.

71. *Chron. Wyntoun* (Laing), iii, 99–101.

72. *Ibid.*, iii, 89–90.

73. *Rot.Scot.*, ii, 163–4; *Foedera*, viii, 289; *CDS*, iv, no. 634.

74. *Chron. Bower* (Watt), viii, 55.

75. *Ibid.*, viii, 53.

Endgame: King, Bishop, Castle, Knight

When, on 28 April 1404, Robert III personally attended the opening of a general council in Linlithgow, the assembled estates probably did not regard the rare appearance of their sovereign at the centre of administrative affairs as a portent of any significant change in the political balance within the kingdom.[1] The king was in Linlithgow because the lieutenant required him to be present to deal with two important issues. Firstly, Albany's commission of lieutenancy, which was due to expire in May 1404, needed to be formally renewed with the consent of the king and the three estates. Secondly, with the conspicuous and sustained failure of Scottish political and military efforts to destabilise the resilient Henry IV's regime, the lieutenant had apparently decided on a change of diplomatic tack and was seeking to establish a more amicable relationship with the English king. Negotiations with the English monarch would need to be conducted on a sovereign-to-sovereign basis.

The Linlithgow council swiftly approved the renewal of Albany's lieutenancy for two years from Whitsunday (18 May) 1404, citing the king's 'great age and weakness' to explain the continuance of the office. The estates must also have discussed the diplomatic situation, for in the following month, on 23 May, Robert III issued a commission to Sir David Fleming of Biggar and Cumbernauld and Sir William Murehede to negotiate for the ransom and the release from English captivity of Albany's son Murdoch and Archibald, earl of Douglas, the latter having been taken into Henry IV's custody after the defeat of Douglas and Hotspur at Shrewsbury on 21 July 1403.[2] Albany's personal interest in the success of the mission is displayed in the thoroughly obsequious letter which the lieutenant sent to Henry IV from Falkland on 2 June.[3]

The political background of Sir David Fleming suggests that he was a man trusted both by the king and the lieutenant. Although Fleming, who was to play an increasingly important role in the politics of the kingdom in the last two years of Robert III's reign, had been closely associated with the duke of Albany during the 1390s, he also enjoyed a considerable reputation as a royal favourite. Sir Malcolm Fleming,

David's father, had served as the custodian and sheriff of Edinburgh for Robert III (then earl of Carrick) during the 1380s and, if an incidental chronicle reference is correct, the young David himself may have played a leading role in the political coup of 1384 which had established Carrick as guardian of the kingdom.[4] The chronicler Wyntoun certainly viewed Fleming as one of Robert III's personal favourites,

> . . . a knycht stout and bald,
> Trowit and luvit wel wyth the King.[5]

Fleming's cordial relationship with both the king and the lieutenant made him an ideal diplomatic envoy, and heightened his political status within Scotland, reflected in his appearance as the first named baron, after the earls of Atholl and Crawford, on the sederunt of the general council of April 1404.[6]

Fleming's diplomatic mission went well. On 6 July 1404 he and Murehede met with Henry IV and his commissioners at Pontefract castle, and arranged for a temporary truce to run to 19 April 1405, and for a full meeting to be held between representatives of the two kingdoms at Haddenstank on 8 October 1404.[7] Robert III re-appeared in Linlithgow in August 1404, having returned to the Stewartry for the summer, in order to appoint a straightforward mix of Albany and Douglas adherents, men who could be expected to negotiate with the interests of the earl of Douglas and Murdoch Stewart in mind, as his commissioners for the October meeting.[8] The commission included the bishop of Glasgow, Sir James Douglas of Dalkeith, and three adherents of the imprisoned earl of Douglas, Sir John Edmonstone, Sir William Borthwick and Master John Merton, along with Fleming and a prominent Albany supporter, John Stewart of Innermeath. On the same day Fleming received some tangible reward for his diplomatic efforts with a grant from Robert III of lands in the earldom of Carrick.[9]

Robert III seems to have been brought to Linlithgow in April/May and August 1404 largely to lend royal status to the diplomatic efforts of the lieutenant and the Douglas family to have Murdoch Stewart and earl Archibald released from imprisonment. However, while Robert III was in West Lothian in August 1404 the king's council experienced a quiet transformation with the emergence of a number of 'new' royal councillors, men who were not politically connected with, or dependent on, either Albany or Douglas. Amongst this group was Henry Wardlaw, the new bishop of St Andrews, who began to appear as a regular witness to the king's great seal charters in late August.[10] Wardlaw, whose ecclesiastical career had been based largely in Avignon, had been provided to the bishopric of St Andrews, after

Walter Danielston's death in late 1402, as a papal appointee, in opposition to the candidate supported by Albany and the St Andrews cathedral chapter, Gilbert Greenlaw, bishop of Aberdeen, and chancellor of the kingdom.[11] The potential animosity between the lieutenant and Wardlaw arising from Albany's support for Greenlaw's claim to St Andrews during 1403, and the new bishop's family background, seem to have inclined Robert III to view Wardlaw as a prospective political ally after his return to Scotland, which probably occurred in early 1404.[12] Henry was the nephew of cardinal Walter Wardlaw, bishop of Glasgow, who, before his death in 1387, had served as the chief diplomatic representative of the Scottish realm during Robert III's period as guardian of the kingdom.[13] The king evidently trusted Henry Wardlaw to the extent that the bishop received Robert III's son and heir James, earl of Carrick, for 'safe-keeping' in the bishop's castle of St Andrews on an unknown date between 1404 and 1406.[14]

On 24 August 1404 bishop Wardlaw was joined as a witness to the king's great seal charters by Henry Sinclair, earl of Orkney and lord of Roslin.[15] Henry Sinclair, despite his comital title, seems to have spent little time in his northern island-earldom. Instead, the earl's political and social life was centred on Lothian, where he possessed extensive estates and wide-ranging kinship ties and marital links to important local families, notably his mother's family, the Haliburtons of Dirleton, and the Sinclairs of Herdmanston.[16] It was undoubtedly because of their Lothian connections that Orkney and his father, also Henry, had maintained an active role in Anglo-Scottish warfare. The elder Henry, who otherwise seems to have spent a great deal of time in Orkney, had certainly participated in the Otterburn campaign of 1388 alongside his wife's kinsmen, the Haliburtons.[17] The younger Henry, who seems to have been resident in Lothian as lord of Roslin throughout the 1390s, succeeded to the comital title around 1400, after the death of his father, apparently during a defence of Orkney against a raiding English fleet. The new earl, however, remained in the south after his elevation to comital rank and participated in the disastrous Humbleton campaign of 1402, where he was one of the five Scottish earls made captive by the English (although he must have been ransomed fairly quickly after his capture).[18]

Humbleton, and the prolonged absence of the earls of Douglas, March and Angus after 1402, had created a destructive political vacuum in the south-east. From 1404 onwards Orkney, a man with an established territorial and political power-base in Lothian, attempted to assert his military and political leadership over the entire region. By mid-1405, Sinclair seems to have established himself as the principal military commander of the crown's forces in the south. It was certainly earl Henry who, shortly before 9 June 1405, led a Scottish force into Berwick castle to support a rapidly collapsing rebellion by northern English lords, led by the earl of Northumberland and lord Bardolph, against Henry IV.[19]

From late 1404 onwards, then, Orkney, Sir David Fleming and Henry Wardlaw formed a curious triumvirate around the king. All three men became more or less regular witnesses to the king's great seal charters, and were the recipients of direct royal patronage. All three men were also, at some stage, identified as custodians and guardians of the king's son, prince James.[20] It became increasingly clear that the king and prince were now attended by a group of loyal and ambitious councillors who were actively and aggressively pursuing their own and 'royal' interests, especially in the south of Scotland, and who were prepared to make use of the authority still attached to the king and, more particularly, to promote and exploit the potential political power of the ten-year-old prince James, the king-to-be. While this development represented a long-term threat to Albany's domination of the political life of the kingdom, Fleming and Orkney's sphere of interest precluded any immediate clash with the lieutenant, who was thoroughly engrossed with the affairs of the north. One man who could not afford indifference to the advance of Fleming and Orkney's influence in the south, however, was James Douglas of Balvenie, the brother of Archibald, 4th earl of Douglas, who had been left as the representative of Douglas power in Scotland after Humbleton. Although he retained the wardenship of all three Marches, Balvenie increasingly found that he was unable to direct crown domestic or foreign policy to serve the needs of the Douglas family, and the years after 1404 saw a dangerous escalation in political tension between James Douglas and the king's political agents south of the Forth.

The re-emergence of Robert III as a figure at the centre of political affairs was confirmed by the king's intervention in the dispute between Albany and Alexander Stewart over Mar late in 1404. While the settlement concluded outside Kildrummy on 9 December represented a clear defeat for the lieutenant's policies and personal interests in the north, the king and his councillors probably viewed Alexander Stewart and his father, the earl of Buchan, as potential allies. Buchan, in particular, had a long history of open hostility towards Albany, and a recent record of co-operation with the king's ill-starred son Rothesay, who had apparently employed earl Alexander as his bailie in the earldom of Atholl.[21]

The shaking of Albany's control of the north was immediately followed by another demonstration of the new assertiveness of the king in defence of his family's interests. On 10 December 1404, at Perth, in the presence of Albany, the earl of Crawford, and the king's three 'wise men', Orkney, Wardlaw and Fleming, Robert III created a huge regality for his son which encompassed all the lands of the Stewartry, that is, the baronies of Renfrew, Cunningham, Kyle-Stewart, and the islands of Bute, Arran, the two Cumbraes, along with Cowal, Knapdale, the lands and earldom of Carrick, and the baronies of Ratho and Innerwick in Lothian.[22] The grant of the Stewartry to prince James, and the effective removal of the royal dynasty's patrimony from normal crown administration, had two effects. Firstly, the lordships held in heritage by the royal line now became the personal property of the young prince, and could only be disposed of with the approval of James and his councillors. On a number of occasions after 1402 the king had been forced to make or confirm grants of royal lands in favour of Albany or his allies, or to reward men for their service to the administration run by the lieutenant from crown estates. Most seriously, early in 1404, Robert III had granted away the earldom of Atholl to his brother Walter Stewart. Atholl was a long-standing and integral part of the royal line's territorial inheritance and, having been held by the duke of Rothesay between 1398 and 1402, it should clearly have descended to the duke's younger brother prince James.[23] After December 1404 title to all the remaining lordships held by the royal dynasty was safely vested in the heir to the throne, and the door was firmly closed on any further temporary or permanent alienations of the prince's inheritance.

The second effect of the December grant was to remove a huge territorial lordship, which in the west stretched from the Firth of Clyde to the northern borders of the lordship of Galloway, from the jurisdiction of the justiciar south of the Forth. The identity of the southern justiciar throughout Robert III's reign is uncertain, but the most likely office holders were the earls of Douglas and, in the absence of the 4th earl after 1402, James Douglas of Balvenie. Robert III's grant of regality rights over the Stewart earldoms and lordships not only diminished Douglas influence in the south, but also gave the men actively exercising the prince's new rights, Fleming and Orkney, a wide-ranging regional authority which began to rival the established power of the Douglases.

In fact, the December settlement in favour of prince James marked the start of a concerted royal campaign to rebuild a coherent political lordship in the south. During the first half of 1405 Robert III's court was, in remarkable contrast to the years 1402–1404, almost permanently stationed in Lothian, either at Edinburgh or Linlithgow, while royal patronage was diverted away from the lieutenant and his friends and towards the king's 'new' regular councillors, Orkney, Fleming and

Wardlaw. Orkney received an early indication of royal favour in January 1405, when the earl was freed from the obligation of castle-guard duty due to the crown from his Lothian baronies, while in the same month the king's intervention in a dispute over the barony of Cavers in Roxburghshire eventually ended with a contentious grant of the barony to the king's favourite Sir David Fleming in August 1405.[24]

The king was still in Edinburgh on 30 January 1405, in the company of Orkney, Fleming and William Ruthven, the sheriff of the burgh of Perth, when he made a grant to the burgesses of Perth of eleven pounds from the burgh fermes for the upkeep of the bridge over the Tay.[25] The gift was said to be for the salvation of the souls of Robert II and Elizabeth Mure, queen Annabella Drummond, and the king's dead son, David, duke of Rothesay, and was one of a number of grants dating from late 1404 and early 1405 in which the king made formal provision for masses for his departed wife and son. The earliest of these, in favour of Crossraguel abbey in August 1404, was also the first occasion on which the earl of Orkney witnessed a royal charter.[26] The link may not have been coincidental, for Orkney's sister was married to John Drummond of Cargill, brother of queen Annabella and Sir Malcolm Drummond, Rothesay's uncle.[27] That Robert III and the men around him in early 1405 were thinking a great deal about Rothesay's fate is confirmed by the fact that, little over a week after the Perth charter, the king granted the chaplains of the altar of St Saviour in the parish kirk of Dundee 100 shillings from the Dundee customs with the provision that they should say masses for the duke's soul. Rothesay, queen Annabella, Robert II and Elizabeth Mure were also named as beneficiaries of prayer in a grant by the king to the monastery of Deer, which was probably made in early 1405.[28] Although Robert III's sudden interest in the welfare of the souls of his wife and son may have been stirred by his own physical condition and the thought that he might soon be rejoining his family, it is striking to note that royal recognition of Rothesay and queen Annabella coincided with the king's re-emergence from the west and the appearance of Orkney, Fleming and Wardlaw as royal councillors.

The king's belated display of paternal concern may have been accompanied by a rather more alarming development for the men who had been involved in the elimination of the duke of Rothesay in 1402, for the young prince's uneasy and vengeful spirit was not, apparently, ready to be ushered into paradise by the devout masses of the priests of Crossraguel, Dundee and Deer. Instead, at some stage shortly after Rothesay's death, a tradition began to emerge which depicted the duke as a royal martyr, murdered in horrific circum-stances, whose tomb at the isolated abbey of Lindores was the scene of

Locations of Royal Acts: Robert III

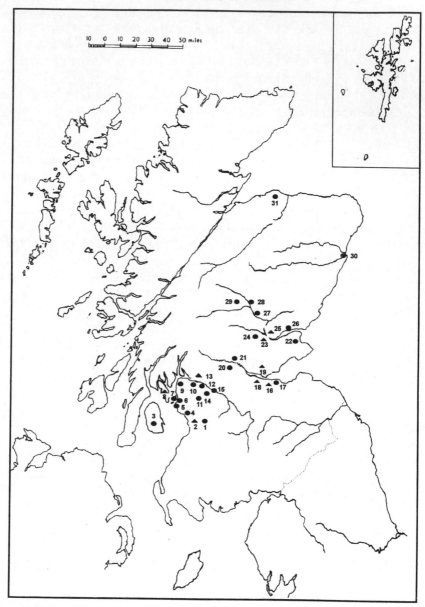

KEY: ● 1–10 Acts issued ▲ Over 10 Acts issued

KEY

STEWARTRY AND FIRTH OF CLYDE

(1)	Garvellan? (Muirkirk)	1
(2)	Dundonald	13
(3)	Isle of Arran	1
(4)	Irvine	6
(5)	Ardneil	1
(6)	Southannan	2
(7)	Cumbrae	1
(8)	Rothesay-Bute	16
(9)	Christwell	1
(10)	Finlaystone	3
(11)	Eliotston	1
(12)	Erskine	1
(13)	Dumbarton	13
(14)	Renfrew	4
(15)	Glasgow	4
	TOTAL	68

LOTHIAN

(16)	Edinburgh	53
(17)	Dalkeith	1
(18)	Linlithgow	55
	TOTAL	109
(19)	Dunfermline	15
(20)	Stirling	8
(21)	Cambuskenneth	1
(22)	Strathtyrum	1

PERTHSHIRE

(23)	Perth	42
(24)	Methven	1
(25)	Scone	20
(26)	Dundee	1
(27)	Dunkeld	1
(28)	Logierait	1
(29)	Cardeny?	1
	TOTAL	67
(30)	Aberdeen	1
(31)	Spynie?	1

miracles.[29] The use of 'miracle' stories as a means of preserving support for defeated causes and factions was a well-attested feature of four-teenth-century English political life. In 1323, for example, Edward II's government had to take action against men who were publishing stories of miracles occurring at the site of the hanging of the rebels Henry de Montfort and Henry Wylyngton in order, so royal corre-spondence alleged, 'to alienate the affection of the people from the king'.[30] The growth of tales which elaborated on the miserable circumstances of Rothesay's demise was clearly a huge political embarrassment for Albany and his allies, designed to 'alienate the affection of the people' from the royal lieutenant. The burst of crown patronage to secure masses in Rothesay's memory in 1404/5 may indicate that the king and the royal council were doing little to stop the spread of stories which depicted the duke as a prince cruelly and unjustly done to death.

The royal court's extended sojourn in Lothian during the early months of 1405 also witnessed a profound change in Scottish diplomat-ic policy, which was now under the direct control of the king's council. The Scots abruptly abandoned the negotiations with Henry IV which they had pursued during the previous year. An Anglo-Scottish meeting planned for 24 March 1405, in advance of the expiry of the truce on 19 April, collapsed when no representatives of the Scottish king appeared, and the truce was left to expire.[31] By May 1405 a small-scale naval war had broken out on the Irish sea, with Thomas Macculloch attacking English ports in Ulster before being captured in Dublin Bay, while a retaliatory raid from Ireland attacked Whithorn and Arran, where the captain of the royal castle of Brodick was captured and his son killed.[32] For the Scots the expiry of the truce may have seemed no bad thing: a year of patient diplomacy had brought them no closer to securing the release of Murdoch Stewart or the earl of Douglas, while Henry IV's increasingly serious domestic political problems held out the hope that the English king could be forced into concessions by a more belligerent stance.

On 28 May 1405 king Henry informed his council of a major northern rebellion involving the earl of Northumberland, Thomas, lord Bardolph, and Archbishop Scrope of York.[33] The Scots, and more particularly the men around Robert III, gave immediate support to Northumberland and Bardolph. On the same day as Henry IV delivered the news of Northumberland's rebellion to his council, Robert III was in Linlithgow issuing another grant in favour of Henry Wardlaw, bishop of St Andrews.[34] Those attending the king at Linlithgow on 28 May included the earl of Orkney. From the royal court at Linlithgow, Orkney must have moved south directly to bring aid to Northumberland and Bardolph, for by 9 June earl Henry was with the English rebels in Berwick castle.[35] Despite Scottish assistance Northumberland and Bardolph's rebellion was crumbling in the face of Henry IV's energetic and ruthless intervention in the north. On 8 June Northumberland's ally, archbishop Scrope, the metropolitan of York, was executed for his role in the rebellion. If king Henry was prepared to have the blood of the archbishop of York on his hands, Northumberland and lord Bardolph could expect little mercy, and on 11 June the earl began to negotiate for a safe haven in Scotland, apparently offering to surrender Berwick to the Scots.[36] Shortly thereafter Northumberland and Bardolph abandoned their precarious stronghold in Berwick, the burgh being given to the flames by Orkney's retreating Scottish force, and fled north of the border.

The close and personal involvement of Robert III and his councillors in supporting the English rebels, illustrated in Orkney's appearance in Berwick in early June 1405 direct from the royal court, was maintained in the negotiations which brought Northumberland and Bardolph into the care of the Scottish crown. Sir David Fleming, according to the English chronicler Walsingham, personally guaranteed the safety of the English earl and lord Bardolph, 'in fide sua suscepit', while the earl's son was given over to the safe-keeping of another favoured royal councillor, Henry Wardlaw, in his formidable episcopal castle of St Andrews.[37] Northumberland's heir would not be short of suitable young aristocratic company in St Andrews, for Wardlaw was already playing host to the Scottish king's son, prince James.[38] Wardlaw, like Fleming and Orkney, may actually have been on the border in June 1405, perhaps meeting with Northumberland at the priory of Coldingham.[39] By June 1405 it was clear that the Scottish kingdom had been committed to a policy of support for Northumberland and Bardolph which had been formulated at the royal court and implemented and sustained by the king's most trusted councillors.

The Scots' assistance to Northumberland brought an immediate response from the English, who attacked the exposed Douglas lordships of Teviotdale, Lauderdale and Ettrick forest. James Douglas of Balvenie, the warden of the Marches, and Henry IV entered into an animated correspondence in which each sought to establish that their adversaries had been responsible for the first infringement of the truce.[40] Although Douglas replied to the English king in a fairly defiant tone, it is unclear how far Balvenie could continue to support the position of Northumberland and Bardolph in Scotland, for it was a policy which could not obtain the release of James's brother from English custody once Henry IV had crushed the English lords' rebellion, and it had provoked massive English raids on Douglas estates in the south.

Aside from the breakdown in Anglo-Scottish relations, the summer of 1405 saw renewed difficulties for the royal administration in the North. On 2 July 1405 the king's lieutenant appeared at the royal court in Linlithgow, apparently bringing with him news of a looming crisis north of the Forth. The disquieting tidings from the north may well have concerned the ailing health and expected death of the king's brother, Alexander, earl of Buchan, the 'Wolf', who seems to have died around 20 July 1405. The imminent death of earl Alexander threatened widespread political disruption with the collapse of the personal lordship which defended crown interests in Ross and Moray. Albany may well have been anticipating an extensive political and military assault by Donald of the Isles on the troubled earldom of Ross and Moray coastal plain in the wake of Buchan's death, for the lieutenant charged north from his meeting with the king at Linlithgow to appear in Dingwall castle by 11 July.[41] Robert III, displaying his new-found political and personal dynamism, also moved north, for on 26 July James Douglas of Balvenie informed Henry IV that the king 'was passit in the northe partis of Scotlande', while the exchequer session which was normally held in Perth in June/July was cancelled.[42]

By 10 August the immediate emergency in the north had receded, and Robert III and Albany had returned south to Erskine on the river Clyde, where the king issued a grant of the barony of Cavers with its associated office of sheriff of Roxburgh to Sir David Fleming.[43] Amongst the men who reputedly witnessed the king's charter was Archibald, earl of Douglas, lord of Galloway. Douglas's unexpected appearance in Scotland during August 1405, if genuine, can only be explained in terms of his temporary release by Henry IV in order to achieve a specific diplomatic objective for the English king. The chronicler Walsingham supplies the probable motivation behind Douglas's mission when he reports that an exchange of the English exiles, Northumberland and Bardolph, for some of the Scottish prisoners held by Henry IV, undoubtedly Douglas himself and Albany's son Murdoch Stewart, was under active consideration in 1405/6.[44] The grant of Cavers to Sir David Fleming, who had been one of the key figures in offering Northumberland and Bardolph a safe haven, may have been intended to secure Sir David's agreement to the handing over of the two English lords to the tender mercy of Henry IV's judges and executioners. The grant was also significant in that it pushed Fleming into the middle of a long-running dispute over possession of the barony and the sheriffship of Roxburgh.

In January 1405 Robert III had excluded the barony of Cavers from his general ratification of the grants made by Isabella, countess of Mar, in favour of her new husband Alexander Stewart.[45] The arrangement probably reflected the fact that heritable possession of the barony was a matter of open contention before the king's council between countess Isabella's nephew Archibald Douglas, an illegitimate son of James, 2nd earl of Douglas, and James Sandilands of Calder, whose claims enjoyed the support of the kinsmen and adherents of the infant William Douglas, earl of Angus. Archibald Douglas had been given a grant of Cavers by countess Isabella on a date between late 1402 and December 1404.[46] James Sandilands' interest in the border barony rested on his position as the grandson of Eleanor Douglas, sister of William, 1st earl of Douglas, and his subsequent claim to be countess Isabella's nearest legitimate heir in all the estates, including Cavers, which she had inherited from her father, earl William. However, the real beneficiary of any successful prosecution of Sandilands' claim would have been the young earl of Angus, for in 1397 all the rights of the Sandilands family to lands held by countess Isabella had been assigned over to William's father George, earl of Angus, and his heirs.[47] By 7 February 1405, Sandilands and his allies from the Angus affinity seemed to be on the edge of victory when they obtained a formal acknowledgement from Robert III that he had promised, in indentures made in the summer of 1397, not only to confirm gifts made by countess Isabella to George, earl of Angus, and all the entails made in George's favour by Sir James Sandilands, but also to withhold royal approval for any resignation or heritable alienation made by Isabella to any others.[48] The royal judgement invalidated Isabella's grant of Cavers to Archibald Douglas, and the barony was instantly reclaimed by the crown because Isabella had granted it to her nephew without the king's permission.[49] Despite this success Sandilands and the Angus affinity had little cause for celebration, for it soon became apparent that the king and his councillors, having obtained control of Cavers and the sheriff-ship of Roxburgh, had no intention of regranting them to Sandilands.

The grant of both the barony and the sheriffship to the king's favourite Sir David Fleming in August 1405 was thus a devastating blow for Sandilands. It was also a major political mistake on the part of the king and his ambitious adherent, for it was a move which earned Fleming the enmity of the powerful Angus/Douglas family, headed in 1405 by the intimidating Margaret, countess of Angus, and her kinsman Sir William Sinclair of Herdmanston who acted as tutor to Margaret's grandson, earl William.[50] For countess Margaret, Robert III's grant of Cavers to one of his own councillors, which effectively disinherited her grandson, must have seemed a horrifying breach of the spirit, if not the letter, of the 1397 agreement she had made with the king. As the autumn of 1405 drew to a close, Fleming must have known that behind Tantallon castle's lofty walls he was not regarded with much favour.

Fleming did his best, however, to remain on amicable terms with the earl and countess of Mar, who had lost their superiority rights over Cavers. Two weeks after Fleming's acquisition of the lordship of Cavers and the office of sheriff of Roxburgh, Sir David compensated the earl and countess with a grant, at Perth, of possession of his lands of Monycabo for Isabella's lifetime.[51]

Robert III was also in Perth in late August/early September 1405, but by 28 October the king had returned to Dundonald, and was to remain in the west until his death in the spring of 1406.[52] Sir David Fleming journeyed to Dundonald with his king in October 1405, still high in royal favour, but the political future of the Lanarkshire knight, whose ambitions in the border area had already earned him the enmity of the Angus Douglases, was placed in severe doubt by his handling of Anglo-Scottish diplomacy in the autumn/winter of 1405/6. After Archibald, earl of Douglas's brief appearance in Scotland during August 1405, the Scots seem to have had an opportunity to secure the liberation of the earl and the other Scottish prisoners still held by Henry IV by arranging their exchange with the exiled English lords Northumberland and Bardolph. The prospects for Douglas's release were ruined, however, by the activities of Fleming, who apparently warned earl Henry and Bardolph of the plan to deliver them to the English, allowing the two men to flee to their allies in Wales.[53] The exact date of Northumberland and Bardolph's flight from Scotland is unknown, but by June 1406 there were complaints in the English parliament about the open collusion between the two men and the Welsh 'rebels'.[54]

The fact that Fleming was opposed to, and ultimately wrecked, a scheme designed to secure the release of the earl of Douglas was unlikely to impress earl Archibald's kinsmen and adherents within Scotland. For the earl's brother, James Douglas of Balvenie, warden of the Marches, custodian of Edinburgh castle, and probably justiciar south of the Forth in the earl's absence, it no doubt provided another reason to distrust and fear Fleming's burgeoning political authority in the south. In late 1405 Fleming, already perhaps acting as justiciar within the huge regality created for prince James in 1404, had added the sheriffship of Roxburgh to his personal lordship, encroaching eastwards into an area traditionally dominated by the earls of Douglas. Douglas political predominance in the south was also threatened by the emergence of Fleming's ally, Henry, earl of Orkney, as an alternative political and military focus for the lairds and barons of Lothian. The presence of a royal court, in which Fleming and Orkney wielded great personal influence, in Lothian during most of 1405 had also increased the pressure on Douglas's regional lordship. But by late 1405 Balvenie may already have been preparing his response to the slow undermining of Douglas authority in the south and his own exclusion from the councils of the king. The young James Douglas was the heir to a family tradition of decisive political action in defence of Douglas aims and interests. It was a political outlook, married to the prestige and strength of a great regional lordship, which had already seen James's father and elder brother play a critical role in the destruction of a succession of royal regimes which had ignored or opposed Douglas ambitions.

While resentment against Robert III's councillor Fleming was assuming worrying proportions in the south-east, there is little indication in the last months of 1405 of a political crisis of sufficient magnitude to explain the decision taken by the king and his advisers during the winter of 1405/6 to send Robert III's sole surviving legitimate son, James, earl of Carrick, to the continent for his own safety. Indeed, 1405 had seen a dramatic resurgence in the political power and influence of the king and the royal court, hardly the background to account for the disorganised, panic-stricken and incompetent efforts of the king's men to spirit the heir to the throne away to France in February/March 1406. Overall, the chronicle and record evidence suggests that the earl of Carrick's departure from Scotland was the result of a largely unforeseen emergency which overwhelmed the aged king and his supporters in the early months of 1406. The chronicler Bower, for example, asserts that the king 'with the matter of safety in mind *suddenly* [my italics] took the view that 'James, who was in the care of Henry Wardlaw, bishop of St Andrews, should be sent secretly with . . . Sir Henry de Sinclair, second earl of Orkney and a decent household in one vessel to his ally the lord Charles king of the French'. Once James had acquired 'good habits' he would return to Scotland 'in greater safety and govern his kingdom the more wisely'.[55] Wyntoun confirms some of the elements of Bower's tale. According to Wyntoun, Robert III

> Be preve counsele and ordinance
> Deliverit to send his son in France.[56]

Robert III's decision to send James to France was thus seen as a hasty judgment, forced on the king by immediate fears for his son's physical safety. This makes it unlikely that the departure of the king's secretary, Walter Forrester, for France before 28 October 1405 was connected with a long-term plan to convey the heir to the throne overseas, for the political situation in September/October 1405 was hardly desperate enough to warrant such a radical course of action.

The second point to emerge from Bower's account is that it was intended that James should not return to Scotland until he had reached manhood, when he could come back in 'greater safety', expressly identifying the remainder of James's minority as a period of danger for the young prince. An obvious contributory factor to any decision to get James out of Scotland could have been a realisation that Robert III was gravely, perhaps terminally, ill. The king had retired to the west in October 1405, possibly because of illness, and while Bower ascribes Robert III's death on 4 April 1406 to the shock of James's capture at sea by the English on 22 March, it may equally have been the result of a long-term physical decline which had actually precipitated James's flight in February 1406.[57] The king's imminent death would have raised the spectre of the young prince being given over to the tender care of his uncle Albany, the man who had already eliminated James's elder brother. The English chronicler Shirley, with his usual bluntness, asserted that James's flight from Scotland was inspired by his fear of Albany, while Bower's account, with its hint that the king was concerned with the issue of the prince's safety during his minority, implies that Robert III had little or no confidence in his son's likely guardian.[58] Given Rothesay's fate in 1402, a desperate attempt by a dying king to keep his remaining son out of Albany's hands in 1406 would not have been surprising.

A deep mistrust of the royal lieutenant and his allies would also account for the apparent secrecy surrounding the prince's movements during 1406. Both Bower and Wyntoun record, with just a hint of disapproval, that the judgment to send the heir to the throne to France was not taken by a general council or parliament, but by the king's 'preve counsele', who wished that James 'be sent secretly'.[59] Bower's implied explanation for this decision, that Robert III was concerned to provide his son with a French education, is clearly inadequate. It is difficult to envisage a parallel situation in any other fourteenth-century kingdom: the young heir of an old and weak king who was manifestly nearing the end of his life being committed to the care of a foreign ruler who was himself beset by internal political problems, without any consultation of the leading men of the kingdom through a general council or parliament. The flight of the young David II to France in the 1330s, for example, was clearly understandable in terms of the threat posed to the king by the armies of Edward Balliol and Edward III.[60] In 1406 there was no dynastic rival in arms against Carrick and his father, no English army threatening the sovereignty of the kingdom, yet James's position was still judged to be desperate enough to attempt to deliver the heir to the throne into an indefinite political exile.

Overall, however, an overwhelming fear of the duke of Albany's political ambition does not provide a satisfactory explanation of the behaviour of the king's men in January/February 1406. If the aim in early 1406 was to achieve a swift and inconspicuous transfer of the prince from his temporary quarters at St Andrews to the French court, then the whole operation must be regarded as an unmitigated shambles from start to finish. There are, moreover, several elements in the chronicle accounts which do not square with the notion of any preconceived plan to remove James secretly from the kingdom.

Firstly, the simplest scheme would surely have been for the prince to set sail directly from St Andrews. Bishop Wardlaw, James's guardian, was actively involved in shipping goods through the harbour nestled below his imposing cathedral, and may have maintained a number of his own vessels.[61] Instead, James was delivered into the custody of the earl of Orkney and Sir David Fleming, who took the prince from Fife into East Lothian. The prince's passage into Lothian was hardly likely to be unnoticed because, as Bower informs us, 'Sir David Fleming of Cumbernauld . . . accompanied the prince . . . along with a strong band of the leading men of Lothian'.[62] James's escort was presumably at least partly provided by the Lothian adherents of Henry, earl of Orkney. The notion that Carrick's appearance in Lothian with a considerable force was part of a secret plan to deliver the prince to the Bass Rock and a passage to France is fraught with problems. The Bass was certainly near one of the busiest sea routes in fourteenth-century Scotland for traders to and from Leith. But, while it offered a reasonable chance of an impromptu passage to France, the choice of the Bass confirms that there was no pre-arranged plan for a ship, French or otherwise, to meet the prince. Bower, indeed, says that the prince and his companions were waiting for the 'chance of a ship' and, after being rowed out to the Bass on or shortly before 14 February 1406, the heir to the throne had to wait over a month before a merchant ship from Danzig, the *Maryenknecht*, which had clearly been involved in a routine trading visit to Leith, picked up the prince, Orkney and the rest of James's companions.[63] All the evidence suggests that there was was no pre-planning of the prince's conveyance from the Bass to France.

Another strange feature of the heir to the throne's travels in 1406 is that East Lothian was hardly the safest place for the prince to be taken in the company of Sir David Fleming. Fleming was at odds with the families of the two most powerful magnates in the area, the earls of Douglas and Angus, whose kinsmen controlled the castles of Edinburgh and Tantallon, the latter overlooking the Bass Rock. The region was, in early 1406, probably the least secure in Scotland for any force headed by David Fleming, and would certainly not have been an intelligent choice as a safe route by which to take the prince out of the country. All of this suggests that the appearance of Carrick, Fleming and Orkney with a 'strong band' in East Lothian in early 1406 may not, initially, have been concerned with delivering the prince to the Bass, a task which could, in any case, have been accomplished with far more ease by ship from St Andrews. An expedition involving the 12-year-old heir to the throne, in an area where Orkney and Fleming faced considerable political hostility, may have been intended to act as a very obvious demonstration of royal support for the local ambitions of the men who controlled the prince's household. As a 14-year-old, James's elder brother, Rothesay, had been used in much the same way to advance the political interests of his then guardian, Sir James Lindsay of Crawford.

The king also had business to conclude in East Lothian. On 27 and 28 January 1406, a little over two weeks before Carrick, Fleming and Orkney appeared in Lothian, Robert III issued a number of charters from Dundonald in favour of his daughter, Mary Stewart, and her new husband James Kennedy.[64] Kennedy's marriage to Mary Stewart saw a strengthening of the ties between prince James and his new brother-in-law, a member of the foremost family in the prince's earldom of Carrick. The marriage was significant in another context, because Mary Stewart was the widow of George Douglas, earl of Angus, and mother of the infant William Douglas. Mary Stewart thus had extensive terce rights in the Angus earldom while Robert III, as William Douglas's grandfather and his nearest adult male relative, seems to have had a stronger claim to act as the young earl of Angus's tutor and to exercise control of the Angus estates and strongholds, including Tantallon, than Sir William Sinclair of Herdmanston, a relative of the earl's grandmother. It may thus have been to enforce the claims of his father and sister that James, prince of Scotland, accompanied the royal councillors Fleming and Orkney into Lothian.

If the presence of the prince and the assembling of a strong band from Lothian under the command of Fleming and Orkney was designed to intimidate the indomitable Margaret, countess of Angus, then the whole scheme was woefully ill-conceived. Moreover, there were others in East Lothian, besides the stubborn countess, unlikely to tolerate any further advance of Fleming and Orkney's influence in the region. With the prince's force in the vicinity of Tantallon, James Douglas of Balvenie and his adherents suddenly issued from Edinburgh's castle rock. Fleming and Orkney had overreached themselves, and now, isolated in the heartland of Douglas power, they were about to pay the price for their presumption. Wyntoun asserts that as the prince was rowed to the Bass from North Berwick, close to Tantallon,

> Schir Davy buskit hamwart sone
> Bot yong James of Douglace,
> That lord than of Balvany wace,
> Off ewill counsale and feloune
> Oure-tuke hym at Lang-hirdmanstoune.[65]

Bower agrees with Wyntoun that Fleming, pursued by Balvenie's force, was overtaken at Long Hermiston Moor on 14 February where, after a 'terrible fight', Sir David was killed.[66] Two others are known to have taken part in the battle, Sir Walter Haliburton of Dirleton and Sir William Sinclair of Herdmanston, although it is unclear on whose side they fought. Although both men were related to Fleming's ally, the earl of Orkney, it seems most likely that they were part of Douglas's force. Haliburton was Balvenie's brother-in-law, while Sinclair was the nephew and adherent of the countess of Angus.[67] In early 1406 there were considerable grounds for tension between Sinclair, as one of the countess's adherents, and the Fleming-led faction at the royal court which had possession of the heir to the throne. Fleming had obtained Cavers in August 1405 by overturning the Sandilands/Angus claim. In late 1405 Mary Stewart, the widow of George, earl of Angus, had married a member of the leading family in her brother's earldom of Carrick. If this was a prelude to the enforcement of Robert III's rights to custody of William Douglas and control of the Angus estates by Fleming, Orkney and Carrick in early 1406, then the appearance of Sinclair of Herdmanston at the battle of Long Hermiston Moor would have been quite understandable.

While both Bower and Wyntoun imply that the aim of the prince's East Lothian foray had always been the transfer of the heir to the throne to the Bass Rock, it seems more than likely that the decision to transport the king's son to the relative safety of the barren island in the Forth was only taken after Fleming and Orkney became aware of Balvenie's force, including Haliburton and Sinclair of Herdmanston, hurrying out from Edinburgh castle. With Balvenie blocking the lines of retreat west, Fleming's 'strong band' was penned in between Edinburgh and the sea. With the banners of the Black Douglas advancing down the coast towards them, and with no sanctuary to be found in the great castle of the Red Douglases at Tantallon, the prince's guardians would have been faced with a stark choice. While Orkney sailed the prince away from any involvement in an armed confrontation, Fleming began a long, desperate run for safety, driving south and west. Both chronicle accounts suggest that Fleming and his men were 'overtaken' by Douglas's force after a pursuit, rather than simply ambushed at Long Hermiston, a fact which would support the view that Fleming left the prince and Orkney at North Berwick on the same day as the battle (which Bower dated 14 February), and almost as soon as he and Orkney became aware of the threat posed by Balvenie's army. Fleming was unable to escape his pursuers. As Wyntoun lamented:

Quhat is thare mare to this to say?
Slane wes this knycht thare that day;
This ilke gud and gentyl knycht,
That wes baith manfull, lele, and wycht.[68]

Prince James and Orkney, meanwhile, were to remain on the Bass for
over a month after Fleming's demise, eventually embarking on the
Maryenknyght shortly before 22 March, on which date English ships
operating out of Great Yarmouth captured the Danzig trader and its
unlikely royal cargo in the North Sea off Flamborough Head.[69] It is
entirely conceivable that it was not until after the death of Fleming and
the prince's narrow escape from involvement in the confrontation with
Douglas of Balvenie that Robert III decided to send his son to France.
The events in East Lothian must have been a huge shock to the king, the
last shattering political reverse of a career mired in misfortune and
personal inadequacy. The king's favourite, one of the principal royal
advisers for the previous two years, had been killed while attempting to
enforce royal rights in the area, and another, Orkney, chased with
prince James on to the Bass. Here, quite clearly, was a situation in which
the king could entertain concern for the immediate and long-term
safety of his son. It seems that, as Bower suggests, the prince and
Orkney were indeed reduced to simply waiting for the chance of a ship.
The *Maryenknycht* probably put into Leith after the battle at Long
Hermiston, at a time when it may have appeared more sensible to
arrange James's passage to France rather than risk bringing the heir to
the throne back into a Scotland said by Walsingham to have been
wracked by civil war in the wake of Fleming's death, where those
upholding royal interests in the south had experienced a catastrophic
military defeat and where the north was dominated by the king's
powerful brother and lieutenant, Albany, who had already been
involved in the death of the king's eldest son.

The business of the kingdom seems to have been curiously mundane
during the heir to the throne's month-long stay on the Bass. Robert III
remained in the west, although moving from Dundonald to Rothesay,
from where he issued his last charters in February and March 1406.[70]
On 15 March, with the prince still on the Bass, the exchequer session
delayed since the previous summer began in Perth. While the most
important members of the political community were in Perth, the
Maryenknycht slipped out of Leith, called at the Bass to take on board
the prince, Orkney and the remainder of the royal household, and
headed out into the North Sea. The exchequer session was still running
on Monday 22 March when the *Maryenknycht* was intercepted by the
English.[71] Prince James had become a captive of Scotland's adversary,

Henry IV of England. The senior line of the Stewart dynasty established in 1371 was, by the end of Robert III's life, hanging by a thread. Of the king's three sons, only one remained; he was a minor, a prisoner in England, a refugee from immediate political violence in the south of Scotland and potential political violence in the shape of his own kinsmen, the Albany Stewarts.

On 4 April 1406, shortly after hearing the distressing news of his son's capture, Robert III died a lonely death in the castle of Rothesay on the Isle of Bute.[72] From this centre of Stewart power the king's body was taken, not to join his father in the traditional resting place of Scottish monarchs at Scone, nor to lie beside the wife who helped to remove him from power in 1399 in the royal chambers at Dunfermline, but to Paisley abbey which was, above all else, a Stewart creation. As Wyntoun lamented,

> His body wes had than to Paslay,
> And wes entyrit in that Abbay,
> The quhilk his elderis devotely,
> Fondyt, and dowyt rechely.[73]

Robert III evidently preferred to face eternity with the friendly ghosts of his long departed kinsmen rather than bed down in the company of illustrious strangers.

NOTES

1. A. A. M. Duncan, 'Councils General', 132–143.
2. PRO, E39/102/11; *CDS*, iv, no. 654; *Foedera*, viii, 359.
3. *Nat.MSS. Scot.*, ii, lvii.
4. *Chron. Pluscarden*, i, 347.
5. *Chron. Wyntoun* (Laing), iii, 94.
6. A. A. M. Duncan, 'Councils General', 134.
7. *Foedera*, viii, 359, 372.
8. *CDS*, iv, no. 664; *Foedera*, viii, 369.
9. *RMS*, i, App. 2, No. 1818.
10. *A.B.Ill.*, ii, 227.
11. *Chron. Wyntoun* (Laing), iii, 84–5; *Chron. Bower* (Watt), viii, 61; D. E. R. Watt, *Dictionary*, 564–69. Albany clearly anticipated the success of Greenlaw's candidature, and on 4 May 1403 arranged a royal grant of the personal goods of the deceased Walter, bishop of St Andrews (presumably a reference to Walter Trail, but perhaps to Walter Danielston), to the bishop of Aberdeen.
12. Wardlaw had certainly returned to Scotland by 24 April 1404: A. A. M. Duncan, 'Councils General', 134.

13. *Supra*, Chapter 4.

14. *Chron. Bower* (Watt), viii, 61.

15. SRO GD25/1/26. Copy of grant in favour of Crossraguel abbey, 24 August 1404.

16. Sinclair was lord of the baronies of Roslin, Pentland, Pentlandmuir, Cousland, Merton and Martonehill: *RMS*, i, Addenda 2; *SP*, iv, 333, ix, 102. The earl's mother, Jean, was the daughter of Sir Walter Haliburton of Dirleton. Henry was thus a nephew of the Sir John Haliburton who led attacks on the north of England during 1402 before being captured by the English at Nesbit Muir on 22 June, and cousin to Walter Haliburton, John's son, who succeeded to the family estates after his father's death shortly after his release from captivity: *Chron. Bower* (Watt), viii, 43; *RMS*, i, App. 2, no. 1923.

17. SRO GD 122/144. The earl was in Dirleton castle on 24 July 1388, shortly before Scottish forces advanced over the border.

18. B. E. Crawford, 'The Earls of Orkney-Caithness', 243–4; *CDS*, iv, Appendix, no. 19. Orkney witnessed a charter by Archibald, 4th earl of Douglas, from Lincluden sometime in late 1401 or 1402, alongside George Douglas, earl of Angus: W. Fraser, *Caerlaverock*, ii, 417.

19. *Royal and Historical Letters of Henry IV*, ed. F. C. Hingeston (London, 1860), ii, 61–2.

20. *Chron. Bower* (Watt), viii, 61 — Wardlaw and Sinclair; *Chron. Wyntoun* (Laing), iii, 94 — Fleming.

21. Fraser, *Wemyss*, iii, 44.

22. SRO GD124/1/129.

23. SRO GD 240 Box 9/Bundle 1; *RMS*, i, App. 2, no. 1818; Argyll Transcripts, ii. Walter Stewart was earl of Atholl by April 1404: A. A. M. Duncan, 'Councils General', 136.

24. *RMS*, i, Addenda 2. When Robert III confirmed Alexander Stewart in possession of the bulk of the Mar inheritance in January 1405 he rejected Alexander's claims to the barony of Cavers in Roxburghshire: SRO GD124/1/129; *RMS*, i, App. 1, no. 156.

25. Perth Burgh Records, Perth and Kinross District Archives, Sandeman Library, Perth. B59/23/10.

26. SRO GD25/1/26.

27. The fact that earl Henry collected a sum of money due to his brother-in-law, as heir to Sir Malcolm Drummond, from the customs of Aberdeen in 1404–5 suggests that the two men enjoyed a close political relationship: *ER*, iii, 630.

28. *ER*, iii, 626, 631; *Dundee Charters*, 26.

29. By the 1440s a pitiful description of Rothesay's slow starvation in Falkland had been incorporated into the account of James I's assassination produced by the English chronicler John Shirley. This part of the tale was clearly at odds with the 'official' Albany line, reproduced in

Bower, that the prince had died of natural causes, although Shirley's estimation of the heir to the throne's career otherwise mirrored Bower's hostile account. Bower's description of Rothesay's humiliating ride from St Andrews to Falkland also seems to be derived from an account which portrayed the prince in a sympathetic light. Hector Boece's early sixteenth-century *History of Scotland* retained the criticism of Rothesay's life, but enlarged on the pitiful circumstances of the duke's death and suggested that the prince had died 'with grete martirdome', and was the first chronicle to assert that his tomb at Lindores had acquired miraculous qualities. William Stewart's metrical version of Boece's work went even further, with Stewart self-consciously breaking away from Boece's account in an attempt to reconcile Boece's critical description of Rothesay with an obviously widely-held belief that the duke was a saint in his life as well as his death: Bellenden, *Chronicles*, ii, 361–2; W. B. Turnbull (ed.), William Stewart, *The Buik of the Croniclis of Scotland* (Rolls Series, 1858), iii, 473–8.

30. A. Goodman, *John of Gaunt*, 6; *CPR*, 1321–4, 578. The same reign saw the arrest, death and political martyrdom of Thomas of Lancaster, and the subsequent growth of a cult of St Thomas involving pilgrimages to his miracle-working tomb at Pontefract: *The Brut or The Chronicles of England*, ed. F. W. D. Brie, 2 vols., Early English Text Society (London, 1906–8), i, 217–31.

31. *Rot.Scot.*, ii, 173–4; *Foedera*, viii, 384–5; *CDS*, iv, no. 141.

32. *Wylie*, ii, 66; *Letters Henry IV*, ii, 73–6.

33. *Nicolas*, ii, 264–5.

34. *Liber Carta Prioratus Sancti Andree in Scotia* (Bannatyne Club, 1841), 414–6.

35. *Letters Henry IV*, ii, 61–3.

36. R. G. Davies, 'After the Execution of Archbishop Scrope: Henry IV, The Papacy and the English Episcopate, 1405–8', *Bulletin of the John Rylands Library*, lix (1976–77), 40–74; *Wylie*, ii, 263; *Rot.Parl.*, iii, 605.

37. Walsingham, *Hist.Angl.*, ii, 271; *Chron. Bower* (Watt), viii, 61; *Chron. Wyntoun* (Laing), iii, 92.

38. Exactly when Wardlaw became prince James's guardian is uncertain. The few references to James's personal expenses before 1406 indicate that these were being accounted for by officials of Robert III's own household until at least the middle of 1405, although the prince could have been placed in the bishop's safe-keeping at any stage after Wardlaw's return from Avignon in 1404: *ER*, iii, 617, 633; *Chron. Bower* (Watt), viii, 61.

39. *Priory of Coldingham* (Surtees Society, 1841), Appendix, lxxx.

40. *Letters Henry IV*, ii, 73–6.

41. SRO Seafield Muniments (Cullen) GD248/Box 718/1 (Linlithgow, 2 July); Buchan was certainly dead before 25 March 1406, while his

reconstructed tomb in Dunkeld cathedral gives the date of his death as 20 July which, if correct, can only refer to 20 July 1405: *ER*, iii, 634; *Cawdor Bk.*, 5 (Dingwall, 11 July).

42. *Letters Henry IV*, ii, 73–6.

43. *RMS*, i, App. 1, no. 156.

44. Walsingham. *Hist.Angl.*, ii, 273.

45. SRO GD124/1/125–6. Cavers should not, in any case, have been lumped in with the other estates in a grant with an eventual destination in favour of Sir Thomas or Sir Robert Erskine, for these men had absolutely no claim to countess Isabella's paternal inheritance. The exclusion may have been on that general basis, or perhaps because Sandilands had already raised a specific objection to the arrangement. The dispute produced a scramble by lay and ecclesiastical landowners within Cavers for crown confirmation of their holdings: NLS, Fleming of Wigtown Collection, Ch.no.15732; SRO, Brodie Writs GD1/17/3.

46. The August 1405 charter in Fleming's favour states that Isabella granted Cavers to her nephew while she was a widow, that is between Malcolm Drummond's death in 1402 and the countess's marriage to Alexander Stewart in 1404. Archibald Douglas had been in Kildrummy castle during the negotiations over the descent of countess Isabella's estates in early December 1404, and was thus in an ideal position to have his claims to Cavers protected in the final agreement fashioned between the earl and countess of Mar and the crown: *RMS*, i, App. 1, no. 156; Fraser, *Douglas*, iii, 732 (1 December 1404); SRO GD124/1/122 (5 December 1404).

47. In 1397 James's father, Sir James Sandilands of Calder, had assigned over to George Douglas, earl of Angus, all his rights to the unentailed Douglas estates held by the countess of Mar, including the barony of Cavers and the sheriffship of Roxburgh: Fraser, *Douglas*, iii, 35–6, 38–9.

48. SRO GD 119/163; *A.B.Ill.*, iv, 171.

49. The escheatment was detailed in the August grant in Fleming's favour: *RMS*, i, App. 1, no. 156.

50. Sinclair was probably personally involved in pursuing the Sandilands claim during 1405, for the 1397 agreement between George, earl of Angus, and Sandilands' father had seen the wardship of the young James given over to the earl. James Sandilands, who could only have been 19 in February 1405, was probably still under the guidance of Sinclair as the man exercising the wardship rights of the deceased George, who had died before November 1404 in English custody: Fraser, *Douglas*, iii, 39–40.

51. *A.B.Ill.*, iv, 172.

52. *RMS*, i, App. i, nos. 157, 158.

53. Walsingham, *Hist.Angl.*, ii, 273.

54. J. E. Lloyd, *Owen Glendower* (Oxford, 1931), 127.

55. *Chron. Bower* (Watt), viii, 61.

56. *Chron. Wyntoun* (Laing), iii, 94.

57. *Chron. Bower* (Watt), viii, 63.

58. M. Connolly, 'The Dethe', 49.

59. *Chron. Wyntoun* (Laing), iii, 94; *Chron. Bower* (Watt), viii, 61.

60. Balfour-Melville, *James I*, 29; R. Vaughan, *John the Fearless* (London, 1966), 31–7.

61. *St Andrews Liber*, 414–7; *Nat.MSS. Scot.*, ii, nos. lv–lvi.

62. *Chron. Bower* (Watt), viii, 61.

63. *Ibid.*; *CPR, Henry IV (1405–1408)*, 168.

64. SRO GD25/1/28. The lands of Dalrymple; *HMCReport*, v, 613. The 28 January grant saw the king, as tutor to his son and heir the earl of Carrick, give Kennedy the office of chief of his name, with the bailiary of Carrick and the leading of the men of the earldom.

65. *Chron. Wyntoun* (Laing), iii, 95.

66. *Chron. Bower* (Watt), viii, 61–3.

67. *Chron. Wyntoun*, iii, 95. In 1403 Haliburton had married Mary Douglas, widow of the duke of Rothesay and sister of James Douglas of Balvenie. From 1403 onwards Haliburton received the huge pensions due to his wife as Rothesay's widow, with James Douglas of Balvenie occasionally acting as his brother-in-law's deputy in the collection of the sums involved in the period 1404–6: *ER*, iii, 591, 594, 615, 616, 620. Haliburton was also to be found witnessing Balvenie charters in Edinburgh castle in January 1407: Fraser, *Douglas*, iii, 403.

68. *Chron. Wyntoun* (Laing), iii, 95.

69. Fleming's death is dated 14 February 1406 by Bower, and 'schir Davy' was certainly dead by 18 March: *ER*, iii, 615, 646; *CPR Henry IV*, iii, 168.

70. *HMC Report*, iv, 478 (No. 77); Perth Burgh Records B59/23/14.

71. *ER*, iii, 613.

72. *Chron. Bower* (Watt), viii, 63.

73. *Chron. Wyntoun* (Laing), iii, 98.

Conclusion:
The Kindly King

Looking back at Robert III's reign from the perspective of the 1440s, Walter Bower, abbot of the island-abbey of Inchcolm in the Firth of Forth, noted that it was an age characterised and marred by political unrest and instability, at the root of which lay the king's physical inability to dispense justice and to maintain order. There was, according to Bower, 'a great deal of dissension, strife and brawling among the magnates and the leading men, because the king, being bodily infirm, had no grip anywhere'.[1] Abbot Bower could point to a series of well known and spectacular outrages from Robert's reign — the brutal raid by the Wolf of Badenoch's caterans on the kirks of Elgin and Forres in the summer of 1390 or the death of the royal sheriff of Angus during the 'dulful dawwerk' of Glasclune in 1392 — to support his picture of political hardship and chaos descending on a kingdom and people deprived of an active and assertive king.

For Bower, the maintenance of royal power and public order alike depended on the vigorous intimidation, and in some cases the outright destruction, of those, no matter how great, who opposed or obstructed the king's will and laws. At the heart of Bower's conception of an effective and forceful royal government lay a personally dynamic king, capable of creating a climate of fear in which nobles and commoners alike were reluctant to defy the royal writ. The abbot thus naturally explains the political discord and disorder of Robert's reign in terms of the king's failure, through physical impairment, to create the intimidatory atmosphere necessary to maintain order and stability. Therefore in the absence of fear there was justification of the poet's saying:

> Under a slack shepherd the wolf fouls the wool, and the
> flock [is torn to pieces][2]

Andrew of Wyntoun shared abbot Bower's belief that 'Radure', the ability to inspire terror, was an essential and desirable part of successful kingship:

Raddour in prince is worthy thing;
For but raddour all governyng
Sall wyle worth and dispisit be;
And quhare that men may raddour se,
Men will dreid to trespas, and sa
A king peceable his land may ma.[3]

Bower's gloomy assessment of the state of the kingdom under Robert's shaky supervision seems to have been shared by the king's contemporaries. On at least four occasions between 1388 and 1404 Robert's subjects, assembled in parliament or general council, delivered their own unequivocal judgment on the king's abilities by declaring him incapable of governing the kingdom, and for ten of the sixteen years of Robert's reign royal authority was in fact exercised by an officially sanctioned guardian or lieutenant.[4] Robert III's ineptitude in discharging the basic functions of his office was attributed, in both official record and chronicle accounts, to his physical afflictions. References to the king's lameness, and what appears to be a recurring and debilitating illness, a 'seknes of his person', are numerous, and the king's infirmity even became part of a west Highland folk tale.[5]

As a consolation for Robert III's patent failure as a ruler of men, Bower allows the king the virtue of humility, a virtue demonstrated in the king's oft-quoted reply to his wife's perhaps rather impatient enquiry as to the monument and epitaph her useless spouse desired after his death: '. . . let these men who strive in this world for the pleasures of honour have shining monuments. I on the other hand should prefer to be buried at the bottom of a midden, so that my soul may be saved in the day of the lord. Bury me therefore, I beg you, in a midden, and write for my epitaph: "Here lies the worst of kings and the most wretched of men in the whole kingdom" '.[6] Bower's picture of an affable, gentle and fair-minded monarch, a man withdrawn from the competition for earthly glories and disarmingly aware of his own deficiencies, was reinforced by the chronicler's description of the king in old age. Robert was tall, 'with a luxuriant beard; he had the attractiveness of a snowy-white old age, with lively eyes which always spread good humour, and . . . ruddy cheeks blooming with every mark of handsome amiability'.[7] The impression of a benign and serene personality is further advanced by Bower's narration of two stories which display the king's generosity towards humble, although in one case highly impertinent, petitioners who had been financially inconvenienced by the activities of the royal court.[8]

The abbot's portrait of a king nearing the end of a long and ultimately dispiriting career undoubtedly places too much emphasis on Robert's sweet reasonableness and political apathy. In the brave years of his youth and until the catastrophic collapse, in the winter of 1388–9, of the political affinity which he led, there is every indication that the then earl of Carrick was an intensely ambitious man, heavily involved in the governance of the kingdom, and at the heart of the Scottish war effort in the south. Nor was there any sign of a particularly sweet or pacific disposition in 1384, when Carrick swept his father from power at the head of a coalition of noblemen seeking an intensification of the war with England.

Nevertheless, Bower's linkage of personal virtue and political inadequacy, with the former usually used to explain the latter, was taken up and developed by a succession of Scottish chroniclers, novelists and historians from the sixteenth to the twentieth century. For George Buchanan, Robert III was 'Blameless in domestic life . . . deficient in no virtue requisite for a private gentleman . . . he was a better man than he was a monarch'.[9] In the nineteenth century, the image of Robert III as an honourable, pious, and thoroughly incapable king presiding, with increasing bewilderment and horror, over the affairs of a violent, aggressive, self-seeking and arrogant nobility, was given a new vitality and pathos with Walter Scott's depiction of the king in *The Fair Maid of Perth*.[10] Scott's portrait fitted the intellectual prejudices of the age, which saw the late-medieval Scottish kingdom as being dominated by a grim battle between the crown and the nobility for political control of the realm. Thus, P. F. Tytler's *History of Scotland*, completed a few years after the publication of *The Fair Maid of Perth*, saw Robert III as a king whose 'sweet, pacific, and indolent nature . . . unfitted him to subdue the pride, or overawe and control the fierce passions and resentments of his barons'.[11] The more sober judgment of twentieth-century historians still nods in the direction of the Bower-derived view of Robert III as a man temperamentally unsuited to the task of medieval kingship, 'noted more for a natural kindliness and a dislike of injustice than for the ability and energy which alone could have given order and equity to his subjects'.[12]

Although Robert III's inability after 1390 to produce the dynamic and coercive personal lordship seen by Bower and Wyntoun as the essential core of competent kingship was clearly linked to the king's advancing years and ill health, there were other factors at work.

In the short term, the single most decisive event in shaping Robert III's ineffectual rule occurred, in fact, shortly before he became king. In early August 1388, in the bleak hills above Redesdale, Robert's brother-in-law and chief political ally James, 2nd earl of Douglas, flew into his final furious and fatal battle with Henry Percy's knights as they galloped into the earl's camp at Otterburn. In the wake of James

Douglas's death, the heir to the throne's long-cultivated regional supremacy south of the Forth fell apart in a rash of territorial disputes over the Douglas inheritance. As the political and territorial network which maintained his authority and status within the kingdom disintegrated around him, Robert was replaced as guardian of the kingdom by his accomplished and respected younger brother, the future duke of Albany. It was a blow from which the king-to-be never truly recovered. When his reign began in 1390, Robert III was already on the defensive, a king in name only, with Albany continuing to act as guardian of the realm. Robert was 53 when he ascended the throne, older than his five royal successors would be on the day of their deaths. The aggressive and energetic fifteenth-century Stewart monarchy of the five Jameses would be the product of youthful ambition and achievement. The new monarch's age, his various infirmities, the fact of his political humiliation in 1388 and the subsequent consolidation of Albany and Douglas influence in royal government, set tight constraints on the king's ability and inclination to recover and enhance his personal authority.

The establishment of the Albany guardianship in 1388 thus had profound consequences for the royal Stewart line and for the kingdom. Politically, the king was comprehensively eclipsed by his younger brother. Robert's physical and political weakness stood in stark contrast to the vigour of the guardian, with Albany establishing a significant reputation as a warleader in the south and as a bulwark against the forces of disorder in the north. The five years between 1388 and 1393 saw Albany and his son Murdoch make a series of spectacular territorial and jurisdictional gains which made them the dominant political figures north of the Forth. The rise of the guardian's family and allies in the north, and the associated destruction of the earl of Buchan's central Highland lordship, generated most of the spectacular political violence which afflicted Moray and Angus in the early 1390s. In the long term, the collapse of the Wolf's lordship after 1388, while a notable personal triumph for the guardian, served only to exacerbate the long-standing problems of the central Highlands, and contributed to the advance of the forces of the lordship of the Isles into the Great Glen, Ross and Moray.

By 1393, then, when the first Albany guardianship came to an end, the royal Stewart line was faced by two magnates, Albany and Archibald, 3rd earl of Douglas, who had established a pivotal role for themselves in the political structure of the kingdom and who discharged many of the functions of royal government within their own spheres of influence. Both men presided over wide-ranging and entrenched aristocratic affinities, and both wielded a regional authority which had been secured partly through their successful political opposition to the senior branch of the royal dynasty during and after 1388. The lordship of the Albany Stewarts, bolstered by the acquisition of the northern justiciarship in 1389, held sway over much of central and northern Scotland, and offered the only coordinated response to the long-term difficulties posed by the political situation in the central Highlands. In the south, the earls of Douglas headed a political, judicial and military lordship which played a critical role in Anglo-Scottish warfare and diplomacy.

The politics of Robert's reign were thus inevitably dominated by the interplay between these two great magnatial houses and the royal line. After 1390, the attempts to recover royal power and influence were spearheaded by the king's dynamic eldest son David, duke of Rothesay. David's household swiftly became an active element in the royal administration, and the duke established his credentials as a young and vigorous prince, personally involved in both Anglo-Scottish diplomacy and the leadership of military/judicial expeditions into the north and central Highlands. Unfortunately for Robert III, the first major victim of Rothesay's personal political ambition, and the resurgence in active royal lordship which he had promoted, was the old king himself. In some ways the setting aside of King Robert, and Rothesay's advance to the position of lieutenant in January 1399, served merely to confirm the political importance of Albany and Douglas, for the change in regime was effectively decided during a meeting between these men and Prince David at Falkland late in 1398. Moreover, the heir to the throne's political independence as lieutenant was limited by the council assigned to him in 1399, a body dominated by Albany, Douglas and their allies.

In late 1401 Rothesay abandoned the policy of co-operation with his uncle and attempted to establish an independent and less restricted authority based on the aggressive exploitation and assertion of royal rights, provoking a major political crisis. The portrayal of Rothesay as a hormone-crazed tyrant, whose activities earned him universal un-popularity, is clearly the product of contemporary political propaganda. The prince's aggression consisted simply of a determination to achieve freedom of action in what appear to be core areas of royal government: finance, diplomacy, and the treatment of forfeited estates. Thus the events of 1401–2 do not reveal Rothesay's unsuitability as a ruler, but rather the fact that the range of interests which Albany and the new earl of Douglas held to be within their legitimate sphere of influence had expanded to the extent that an assertive royal prince was regarded as a political threat which had to be addressed. Albany's coup against the royal lieutenant late in 1401 was accepted by Archibald, 4th earl of Douglas, in return for major concessions in areas in which Douglas ambitions and interests were at stake, and where Rothesay's policies, foreign and domestic, had begun to diverge from those required or desired by the earl. In the wake of Rothesay's arrest, it became clear that Earl Archibald had assumed control of Scottish foreign policy, and had set the kingdom on the road to military confrontation with the exiled earl of March and his English backers, a policy which would culminate in the disaster of Humbleton.

The political support necessary for the establishment of Rothesay's ill-fated lieutenancy had been secured at the meeting between the prince, Albany and the 3rd earl of Douglas at Falkland in 1398. The heir to the throne's own personal and political doom was sealed in a similar fashion, by an informal council between Albany and the 4th earl of Douglas at Culross late in 1401. The two episodes illustrate that Albany Stewart and Douglas power, acting in concert, had the capacity to make or break royal regimes which were manifestly inadequate, or which threatened or ignored Albany and Douglas interests. The relative ease with which Albany and Douglas overwhelmed the prince and his adherents says much about the status and power of the two men. Describing the governance of Scotland after the death of Robert III and the capture of James I in 1406, the English chronicler John Shirley observed: 'the duke of Albanye governyd and tuke uppone hym the reule of Scotland beyonde the Scottissche See (i.e. north of the Forth). And in the same wyesse dydde the erlle Douglas bothe governe and reule alle over this side the Scottische see'.[13] The picture of a kingdom in which effective power and the functions of government were divided between two great magnatial power-blocs was undoubtedly more sharply defined in the absence of a king after 1406, but the political foundations for just such a division had been in place for most of Robert III's reign, if not beforehand, for the triumph of Douglas and Albany power and the downfall of Robert III's kingship surely had deeper roots than Robert's personal failings and the disruption caused by the 2nd earl of Douglas's death in 1388.

In the long term, many of Robert III's difficulties are held to have originated in his father's political and territorial settlement of the kingdom after 1371. Robert was certainly the heir to a style of kingship which had, since its inception in 1371, displayed few of the menacing qualities extolled by Bower and Wyntoun in its dealings with its greatest subjects. In the years after his accession to the throne, Robert II had secured the new royal dynasty's political hold on the kingdom largely through the promotion of his five legitimate sons as major regional lords, usually in areas in which they were already active, wielding extensive delegated powers. The web of royal family influence was extended further by the conclusion of marriage alliances and territorial and jurisdictional deals which recognised, confirmed and augmented the established local or regional status of great aristocratic lineages such as the earls of Douglas. Robert II's approach to the consolidation of his dynasty's position had employed the resources and techniques of a great magnate, creating political loyalty and support through marriage treaties and mutually beneficial compromises. John, earl of Carrick, the future Robert III, had himself played an important part in this process, carefully constructing a regional lordship south of the Forth which harnessed established magnatial power in that area to the Stewart cause. All of Carrick's children who survived into adulthood, with the exception of James I, were married into various branches of the Douglas kindred which dominated the south of Scotland.

The long-established view of the loosely-bound and informal network of personal power which underpinned Robert II's rule was that it provided his successor with a dangerous and awkward political legacy, producing a feeble royal line which was barely differentiated, in terms of prestige and power, from its greatest aristocratic subjects.[14] Robert III has thus been seen as a king whose personal authority was at first inevitably circumscribed, and then eventually totally overwhelmed, by the ambitions and entrenched regional power of his aggressive and capable brothers, most notably the duke of Albany, who collectively and consistently refused to behave simply as loyal vassals of the crown. Besides the problems of political control allegedly presented by the coterie of quasi-royal Stewart aristocrats surrounding the throne, the successful exercise of royal power in the late fourteenth century is seen to have been further challenged by the appearance of a number of 'overmighty' magnates, chiefly the earls of Douglas and the lords of the Isles, whose burgeoning regional power and ambitions undermined and threatened royal authority.

The disturbed political, military, economic and social conditions of the fourteenth century had undoubtedly encouraged a growth and intensification of aristocratic power in certain localities. When Robert II came to the throne, the great Douglas lordship south of the Forth and the MacDonald lordship of the Isles in the west were established political and territorial realities with which the new royal dynasty had to deal. The origins, growth and consolidation of these regional supremacies lay in the early decades of the fourteenth century, when war (civil and national), the absence of royal lordship, famine and plague combined to disrupt and transform local society. In the south, the conversion of those areas of the kingdom bordering England into a zone dominated by the demands and opportunities of national and local warfare produced a need for effective regional military and political leadership, and encouraged the concentration of jurisdictional, military and territorial resources in the hands of active local lords. On both sides of the Anglo-Scottish border great magnates emerged to exercise lordship over a militarised society increasingly organised around male descent lineages, kin-groups which mobilised the region for war and raid, and offered their members some measure of physical, economic and political security. The creation of William Douglas as 1st earl of Douglas in 1357 confirmed that the head of the powerful and widely ramified Douglas kin-group had attained a territorial, political and social status at the forefront of this bellicose society which placed him alongside the kingdom's older 'provincial' earls.[15]

Gaelic Scotland experienced similar political and social dislocation in the early fourteenth century. As royal influence in the north and west waned, and the great edifice of Comyn power in the central Highlands collapsed, the Gaelic lords of the west took advantage of this situation to expand their territorial and political empires. In the vanguard of this process was John of Islay, lord of the Isles. Already dominant in the Isles by 1350, John and his successors extended their political and territorial interests eastwards, deep into Moray and Ross, helping to instill a profound sense of political and cultural crisis in the English-speaking elites, noble, ecclesiastical and burghal, of the north-eastern earldoms. The inexorable advance of Clan Donald was accompanied by wider social and political changes within Gaelic Scotland, particularly in the earldoms and lordships of the central Highlands. Prolonged political and territorial disruption in this area allowed effective local power to fragment and devolve into the hands of lesser Gaelic aristocrats, the leaders of durable male descent kindreds such as the *Clann Donnchaidh* in Atholl and northern Perthshire, who rode out, or positively prospered in, the turbulence of civil war. The great stramash in the central Highlands accentuated and consolidated the most militaristic features of Gaelic lordship, and throughout the region there seems to have been a general extension of the system of employing native mercenary troops.

The long-term strategic problems posed by the tumultuous situation in the central Highlands encouraged the delegation of extensive royal rights into the hands of local agents of the crown. From the early fourteenth century onwards, a succession of northern magnates appeared as royal lieutenants in the north, notably the Randolph earls of Moray, William earl of Ross, and Alexander Stewart, earl of Buchan.[16] After the destruction of Buchan's lordship in 1388–92, the most important figures in the north were the Albany Stewarts, who acquired the justiciarship north of the Forth and attempted to police the entire region from their own powerbase in the south-western Highlands. The 'judicial' expeditions of the northern lieutenants into the west and central Highlands were intimidating military progresses, a version of the coercive lordship with which the kindreds of the region were familiar. Thus the chroniclers of lowland Scotland found much to praise in the foray of Thomas Randolph's coroner into Wester Ross, which ended with the heads of fifty 'mysdoaris' adorning the walls of Eilean Donan castle.[17]

By the second half of the fourteenth century, the Douglas earldom in the south, the lordship of the Isles, and a major regional lord discharging many of the functions of royal government in the north, had become established features of the political landscape of the Scottish kingdom. However, the view that these lordships in themselves represented a dangerous build-up of aristocratic power which threatened royal authority is now hotly disputed. Most recent historical analysis has emphasised the role of these regional lords as agents and upholders of royal government, and has stressed the validity, indeed the necessity, of Robert II's style of governance through aristocratic coalition in the context of the medieval Scottish kingdom. The enduring or increasing territorial and jurisdictional power of local earls, lords and kindreds is no longer automatically regarded as a threat to the crown's control of the realm or the political balance of the kingdom; instead 'successful kingship' (in the very limited sense of kingship which provokes little political opposition) is seen as being dependent 'upon the capacity to harness the energies of a limited group of noble families and to provide them with a focal point around which their ambitions could play'.[18] Thus, it is suggested, the cultivation of a patchwork of magnate lordships and affinities linked to the royal court by kinship ties and marriage alliance was both a natural and sensible policy and 'should not be regarded as a failure to pursue an alternative programme of a more bureaucratic sort'.[19]

Robert II had certainly managed to exploit his kinship and marriage links with the great aristocrats of the realm as a means of establishing and preserving his own political authority. In doing so, the king accepted that royal power would be mediated through established aristocratic structures. As part of this process, royal territorial, jurisdictional and fiscal resources tended to become absorbed within the regional lordships of the king's sons, allies or one-time political enemies. Most notably, after 1371, the justiciarships north and south of the Forth became the preserve of the politically dominant families in each region: Douglas in the south, the Lindsays, Buchan and finally the Albany Stewarts in the north. This had not been the case during David II's personal rule, for David's justiciars had been relatively minor figures whose power and position rested on their personal and political dependence on the king. Robert II's justiciars were important men, who claimed and discharged their duties on the basis of their power in local society, rather than as agents of the royal administration whose effectiveness was guaranteed by the 'radure' of an active and aggressive king. The fate of the justiciarships and other local offices inevitably lessened the crown's direct political and jurisdictional influence in many areas, although this fact scarcely seemed to matter while the relationship between the royal line and the aristocratic officeholders remained amicable.

As the events of 1388–90 were to prove, however, a royal authority dependent on the manipulation of aristocratic alliance could be brought to ruin by unexpected shifts within the balance of magnatial power and fortune in the kingdom. The political circumstances and policies of Robert II's reign had established a legacy of royal authority mediated through entrenched regional lordships; personal infirmity and the political accidents of 1388 ensured that Robert III had no hope of 'harnessing' this magnatial power to his own ends. In fact, for much of the period after 1390, the relationship seems to have been reversed, with Albany and Douglas successfully exploiting and manipulating royal authority to advance their own political and territorial ambitions. The duke of Rothesay's attempt to prise control of royal government away from Albany and Douglas was emphatically defeated, and ended in the prince's death in the dungeons of Falkland in 1402.

After Rothesay's death, the senior line of the Stewart dynasty appeared to be on the edge of the abyss. The frail old king and his depleted court disappeared into the Stewartry and ceased to function as a source of active lordship or patronage. The manifest political vulnerability of the king and his remaining son encouraged wild speculation on the continent where, in 1404, French diplomats talked, with some interest and considerable ignorance, of the likelihood of the earl of Douglas succeeding to the Scottish throne.[20] The collapse of royal power during 1402 promoted a further dismemberment of the crown establishment. The mighty fortress of Dumbarton fell into the hands of Albany's ally Walter Buchanan, so that by 1406 two of the kingdom's three principal royal castles had been absorbed into the political lordship of the royal duke, the heritable keepership of Stirling castle having been granted to the Albany Stewarts in 1373.[21] The third major royal stronghold, Edinburgh castle, had also fallen under the effective control of a regional lord, with a life grant of the constabulary of the castle to Archibald, 4th earl of Douglas, in 1401.

Despite a brief and fragile revival in royal influence south of the Forth, spearheaded by Robert's councillors, Fleming, Orkney and Bishop Wardlaw, the king's reign ended in a crisis which fully illustrated the collapse of the royal dynasty's prestige and power. The death of one of the king's principal councillors, Sir David Fleming, in open battle at Long Hermiston Moor, and the desperate flight of the refugee Prince James from his own kingdom emphasised the forlorn position of the senior Stewart line.

As he lay dying in Bute in the dark and cheerless weeks before the spring of 1406, it must have seemed to King Robert that a long and wearisome career was spinning towards an ignominious close. The king's final political decision had ended in a predictable and cruel débâcle, with the capture of the heir to the throne, the last of the king's sons, in the stormy waters of the North Sea. The hopes of youth and the accomplishments of his middle years had turned to dust in Robert's hands, and Bower may well be right in assigning to the king overwhelming feelings of despair and resignation. But we may hope that the chronicler's depiction of Robert was correct in another regard, and that in his last hours the old king was blessed with a steady and peaceful heart, his soul ready 'to be saved in the day of the Lord'.[22]

Even with death as his guide and companion Robert III failed to escape from the physical and political restrictions which had bound and marginalised his kingship, for the final sombre royal progress from Bute to Paisley abbey was confined, appropriately, to the Stewart lordships clustered around the Firth of Clyde. The choice of Paisley rather than the prestigious royal burial and coronation centre at Scone seems to chime in well with the humility of Robert III's reply to his wife's enquiry as to the arrangements to be made for a memorial to mark his final resting place. But there was another, and more pragmatic, consideration which may have weighed against King Robert being laid to rest at Scone: the co-ordinated burial of the old king and the coronation of the new was impossible, because the king's son and heir James languished as a prisoner of the English crown.

To those attending Robert III's funeral, the political future of the kingdom must have seemed reassuringly familiar. Effective power, if not the royal title, belonged to the duke of Albany, who was duly confirmed as governor of the kingdom in James's absence in July 1406.[23] It seems unlikely that many of the magnates gathered in Paisley in the spring of 1406 could have envisaged the bloody political triumph of King Robert's son on his return to Scotland, after eighteen years of exile, in 1424. Yet many of the foundations for James I's aggressive and ruthless kingship had perhaps already been laid. In the last years of King Robert's reign the young prince had been raised on a heady and bitter mix of political insecurity, humiliation and impotence. The deaths of James's charismatic elder brother in 1402, and of his own guardian, Sir

David Fleming, in 1406, gave the heir to the throne an early and brutal schooling in the exercise of power. It was a lesson which James did not forget. It is ironic, although understandable, that the enduring legacy of the reign of Robert III, the pious and kindly king, should be the harsh and intimidatory rule of his son.

NOTES

1. *Chron. Bower* (Watt), viii, 63.
2. *Ibid.*, viii, 63.
3. *Chron. Wyntoun*, vi, 234–5.
4. *APS*, i, 555–6, 572; A. A. M. Duncan, 'Councils General', 132–143.
5. J. F. Campbell, *Popular Tales of the West Highlands* (London, 1890), ii, 379–80; J. W. M. Bannerman, *The Beatons: a medical kindred in the classical Gaelic tradition* (Edinburgh, 1986), 62. Although the king in question is identified as Robert II, the circumstances — treatment by Farquhar the Leech of a crippling leg injury — seem to fit Robert III's reign.
6. *Chron. Bower* (Watt), viii, 65.
7. *Ibid.*, 64–5.
8. *Ibid.*, 3–7.
9. G. Buchanan, *The History of Scotland*, translated by J. Aikman (Glasgow and Edinburgh, 1827–9), ii, 52, 76.
10. Sir Walter Scott, *The Fair Maid of Perth* (Edinburgh, 1828).
11. P. F. Tytler, *History of Scotland* (Edinburgh, 1839–1870), iii, 135.
12. G. Donaldson, *Scottish Kings* (London, 1967), 36.
13. M. Connolly, 'The Dethe of the Kynge of Scotis: A New Edition', *SHR*, lxxi 1992, 49–50.
14. R. Nicholson, *Later Middle Ages*, 184–5, 203–5.
15. R. Frame, *The Political Development of the British Isles, 1100–1400* (Oxford, 1990), 190–1, 201–3. A. Grant, 'The Development of the Scottish Peerage', *SHR*, lvii 1978, 4–7: for a general examination of the changes in the Scottish nobility and, in particular, for an argument which stresses the declining importance of provincial earls as the political and military leaders of local society.
16. See A. Grant, 'Thanes and Thanages', 69–70, where it is suggested that the alienation of royal thanages in the north contributed to the rise of the northern lieutenancies.
17. *Chron. Wyntoun* (Amours), v, 392–95.
18. R. Frame, *Political Development*, 190–193. Frame's summary is inspired by A. Grant's reinterpretation of the political and social structures of fourteenth- and fifteenth-century Scotland, particularly crown-magnate relationships. See A. Grant, *Independence and Nationhood*, esp. Chps. 6 and 7.

19. R. Frame, *Political Development*, 192.
20. *Letters Henry IV*, i, 205.
21. *RMS*, i, no. 554.
22. *Chron. Bower* (Watt), viii, 65.
23. *Chron. Wyntoun* (Laing), iii, 99.

Bibliography

I UNPUBLISHED PRIMARY SOURCES

Scottish Record Office, H.M. General Register House, Edinburgh

Deposited Collections:
Ailsa Muniments GD 25.
Airlie Muniments GD 16.
J. and F. Anderson Collection GD 297.
Breadalbane Collection GD 112.
Brown–Pullarton Documents GD 1/19.
Bruce and Kerr W.S. GD 240.
Cardross Writs GD 15.
Craigans Writs GD 148.
Calendar of Craigmillar Writs GD 122.
Cromartie Muniments GD 305.
Drummond Castle Writs GD 160.
Dunbeath Muniments GD 97.
Eglinton Muniments GD 3.
Lord Forbes Collection GD 52.
Inventory of Fraser Charters GD 86.
Fraser–MacKintosh Collection GD 128.
Glencairn Muniments GD 39.
Guthrie of Guthrie Manuscripts GD 188.
Haldane of Gleneagles Muniments GD 198.
Henderson of Fordell GD 172.
Lothian Muniments GD 40.
Maitland Thomson Notebooks GD 212.
Mar and Kellie Muniments GD 124.
Morton Papers GD 150.
Munro of Foulis Writs GD 93.
Murthly Castle Muniments GD 121.
Paterson of Denmuir Writs GD 1/34.
Rose of Kilravock Muniments GD 125.
Rothes Cartulary GD 204.

Seafield Muniments GD 248.
Sempill of Craigievar Muniments GD 250.
Stair Muniments GD 135.
Swinton Charters GD 12.
Torphichen Writs GD 119.
Inventory of Whitehill Papers GD 143.
Yule Collection GD 90.
Acts of Parliament PA5.
Burgh Records B30 (Haddington).
Crown Office Writs AD1.
Register House Charters RH6.
Register House Transcripts RH1–2.
State Papers SP7.

National Library of Scotland, Edinburgh
Adv.MSS., 33.3.28.;Adv.MSS., 34.3.25.
Ch. A8.
Ch. no. 47.
Ch. no. 698.
Crawford and Balcarres Collection.
Fleming of Wigtown Collection.
Morton Chartulary MS.72.

National Register of Archives (Scotland).
Buccleuch Muniments.
Fyvie Castle Muniments.
Lauderdale Muniments.
Earl of Strathmore Muniments.

Perth Museum and Art Gallery.

Edinburgh University Library
Catalogue of Manuscripts.
John Maitland Thomson Collection of Photographic Negatives.

Perth and Kinross District Archives
Perth Burgh Records B59.

Strathclyde Regional Archives
Shaw Stewarts of Ardgowan T-Ard.

Private Archives
Argyll Transcripts
Duke of Atholl's Muniments, Blair Castle, Blair Atholl.

Archives Nationales, Paris.
K 57 no. 9/12.

British Library, London
Campbell Charters.
Cotton MSS. Vespasian.
Harleian MSS. no. 4694.

Public Record Office, London.
Exchequer Scots Documents E39.

II PUBLISHED PRIMARY SOURCES

a *Record Sources*

Ane Account of the Families of Innes, Spalding Club (Aberdeen, 1864).
The Acts of the Lords of the Isles, eds. J. and R. W. Munro, Scottish History Society (Edinburgh, 1986).
The Acts of the Parliaments of Scotland, eds. T. Thomson and C. Innes, 12 vols. (Edinburgh, 1814–75).
The Book of the Thanes of Cawdor, ed. C. Innes, Spalding Club (Aberdeen, 1859).
Calendar of Close Rolls, 1354–1360 (London, 1908).
Calendar of Documents Relating to Scotland, ed. J. Bain, 5 vols. (Edinburgh, 1881–8).
Calendar of Entries in the Papal Registers relating to Great Britain and Ireland: Papal Letters, eds. W. H. Bliss and others, 16 vols. (London, 1893).
Calendar of Entries in the Papal Registers relating to Great Britain and Ireland: Petitions to the Pope, vol. i, ed. W. H. Bliss (London, 1896).
The Calendar of Fearn: text and additions, 1471–1667, ed. R. J. Adam, Scottish History Society (Edinburgh, 1991).
Calendar of the Laing Charters, 854–1837, ed. J. Anderson (Edinburgh, 1899).
Calendar of Papal Letters to Scotland of Benedict XIII of Avignon, 1394–1419, ed. F. McGurk, Scottish History Society (Edinburgh, 1976).
Calendar of Papal Letters to Scotland of Clement VII of Avignon, 1378–1394, ed. C. Burns, Scottish History Society (Edinburgh, 1976).
Calendar of Patent Rolls, 1399–1441, 8 vols. (London, 1903–7).
Cartularium Comitatus de Levenax, Maitland Club (Glasgow, 1833).
Charters, Bulls and other Documents relating to the Abbey of Inchaffray, eds. W. A. Lindsay, J. Dowden and J. M. Thomson, Scottish History Society (Edinburgh, 1908).
Charter Chest of the Earldom of Wigtown, Scottish Record Society (Edinburgh, 1910).

Charters and Documents Relating to the City of Edinburgh, 1143–1540, ed. J. D. Marwick, Scottish Burgh Record Society (Edinburgh, 1871).

Charters of the Friars Preachers of Ayr, ed. R. W. Cochran-Patrick, Ayrshire and Galloway Archaeological Association (Edinburgh, 1881).

Comptes de Trésor, ed. R. Fawtier (Paris, 1930).

Charters, Writs and Public Documents of the Royal Burgh of Dundee, ed. W. Hay (Dundee, 1880).

The Correspondence, Inventories, Account Rolls and Law Proceedings of the Priory of Coldingham, ed. J. Raine, Surtees Society (London, 1841).

Descriptive Catalogue of Impressions from Ancient Scottish Seals, ed. H. Laing, Bannatyne Club (Edinburgh, 1850).

The Exchequer Rolls of Scotland, ed. J. Stuart and others, 23 vols. (Edinburgh, 1878–1908).

Facsimilies of the National Manuscripts of Scotland, 2 vols. (London, 1867–71).

The Family of Lauder, ed. J. Young (Glasgow, 1884).

Foedera, Conventiones, Litterae et Cuiuscunque Generis Acta Publica, ed. T. Rymer, 20 vols. (London, 1704–35).

Fraser, W., ed., *The Book of Caerlaverock*, 2 vols. (Edinburgh, 1873).

Fraser, W., ed., *The Earls of Cromartie*, 2 vols. (Edinburgh, 1876).

Fraser, W., ed., *The Douglas Book*, 4 vols. (Edinburgh, 1885).

Fraser, W., ed., *History of the Carnegies, Earls of Southesk, and of their Kindred*, 2 vols. (Edinburgh, 1867).

Fraser, W., ed., *The Lennox*, 2 vols. (Edinburgh, 1874).

Fraser, W., ed., *The Melvilles, Earls of Melville and Leslies, Earls of Leven*, 3 vols. (Edinburgh, 1890).

Fraser, W., ed., *Memoirs of the Maxwells of Pollock*, 2 vols. (Edinburgh, 1863).

Fraser, W., ed., *Memorials of the Earls of Haddington*, 2 vols. (Edinburgh, 1889).

Fraser, W., ed., *Memorials of the Family of Wemyss of Wemyss*, 3 vols. (Edinburgh, 1888).

Fraser, W., ed., *The Red Book of Grandtully*, 2 vols. (Edinburgh, 1868).

Fraser, W., ed., *The Red Book of Menteith*, 2 vols. (Edinburgh, 1880).

Fraser, W., ed., *The Stirlings of Keir* (Edinburgh, 1858).

Fraser, W., ed., *The Sutherland Book*, 3 vols. (Edinburgh, 1892).

The Frasers of Philorth, ed. A. Fraser, Lord Saltoun, 3 vols. (Edinburgh, 1879).

A Genealogical Deduction of the Family of Rose of Kilravock, ed. C. Innes, Spalding Club (Aberdeen, 1898).

Highland Papers, ed. J. R. N. MacPhail, Scottish History Society, 4 vols. (Edinburgh, 1914–34).

The History and Antiquities of North Durham, ed. J. Raine (London, 1852).

A History of Northumberland, 15 vols. (Newcastle-upon-Tyne, 1893–1940).

A History of the Family of Seton during Eight Centuries, ed. G. Seton (Edinburgh, 1896).

Illustrations of the Topography and Antiquities of the Shires of Aberdeen and Banff, eds. J. Robertson and G. Grut, 4 vols., Spalding Club (Aberdeen, 1847–69).

An Index, drawn up about the year 1629, of many Records of Charters, ed. W. Robertson (Edinburgh, 1798).

John of Gaunt's Register, eds. E. C. Lodge and R. Somerville, 2 vols., Camden Society, 3rd Series (London, 1937).

Liber Carta Prioratus Sancti Andree in Scotia, Bannatyne Club (Edinburgh, 1841).

Liber S. Marie de Calchou, Bannatyne Club, 2 vols. (Edinburgh, 1846).

Liber Sancte Marie de Melros, Bannatyne Club, 2 vols. (Edinburgh, 1837).

The Miscellany of the Maitland Club, Maitland Club, 4 vols. (Glasgow, 1833–47).

The Miscellany of the Scottish History Society, Scottish History Society (Edinburgh, 1893–).

The Miscellany of the Spalding Club, Spalding Club, 5 vols. (Aberdeen, 1841–52).

Notices et extraits des Manuscrits de la Bibliothèque Nationale et autres Bibliothèques, 42 vols. (Paris, 1787–1933).

Origines Parochiales Scotiae, Bannatyne Club, 2 vols. (Edinburgh, 1851–5).

Proceedings of the Privy Council, ed. H. Nicholas, Records Commission, 7 vols. (London, 1834–7).

Proceedings of the Society of Antiquaries of Scotland (Edinburgh, 1851–).

The Records of Elgin, New Spalding Club, 2 vols. (Aberdeen, 1903–8).

Records of the Earldom of Orkney, Scottish History Society (Edinburgh, 1914).

Regesta Regum Scotorum: David II, ed. B. Webster (Edinburgh, 1982).

Regesta Regum Scotorum: Robert I, ed. A. A. M. Duncan (Edinburgh, 1986).

Registrum Episcopatus Aberdonensis, Spalding and Maitland Clubs, 2 vols. (Edinburgh, 1845).

Registrum Episcopatus Moraviensis, Bannatyne Club (Edinburgh, 1837).

Registrum Honoris de Morton, Bannatyne Club, 2 vols. (Edinburgh, 1853).

Registrum Magni Sigilii Regum Scotorum, eds. J. M. Thomson and J. B. Paul, 11 vols. (Edinburgh, 1882–1914).

Registrum Monasterii de Passelet, Maitland Club (Glasgow, 1832).

Reports of the Royal Commission on Historical Manuscripts (London, 1870–).

Robertson, W., *The Parliamentary Records of Scotland* (London, 1804).

Rotuli Scotiae in Turri Londinensi et in Domo Capitulari Westmonasteriensi Asservati, ed. D. Macpherson, 2 vols. (London, 1814–19).

Royal and Historical Letters of Henry IV, ed. F. C. Hingeston, 2 vols. (London, 1860).

Vetera Monumenta Hibernorum et Scotorum Historiam Illustrantia, ed. A. Theiner (Rome, 1864).

Wills and inventories illustrative of the History, Manners, Language statistics etc., of the Northern Counties of England from the 11th century onwards, ed. J. Raine, Surtees Society (London, 1835).

b *Narrative and Literary Sources*

Barbour, J., *Barbour's Bruce*, eds. M. P. McDiarmid and J. A. C. Stevenson, Scottish Text Society, 3 vols. (Edinburgh, 1985).

The Chronicles of Scotland compiled by Hector Boece, translated into Scots by John Bellenden 1531, Scottish Text Society (Edinburgh, 1938–41).

Hectoris Boetii Murthlacensium et Aberdonensium Episcoporum Vitae, New Spalding Club (Aberdeen, 1894).

Bower, W., *Joannis de Fordun Scotichronicon cum supplementis ac Continuatione Walteri Boweri Insulae Sancti Colonbae Abbatis*, ed. W. Goodall (Edinburgh, 1759).

Bower, W., *Scotichronicon*, ed. D. E. R. Watt (Aberdeen, 1987–).

The Brut, or The Chronicles of England, ed. F. W. D. Brie, 2 vols., Early English Text Society (London, 1906–8).

Buchanan, George, *The History of Scotland*, trans. J. Aikman (Glasgow and Edinburgh, 1827–9).

Cameron, A., *Reliquiae Celticae*, eds. A. MacBain and J. Kennedy, 2 vols. (Inverness, 1892–4).

Campbell, J. F., *Popular Tales of the West Highlands*, 4 vols. (London, 1890–93).

Chronicon Adae de Usk, ed. E. M. Thompson (London, 1904).

Chronicon Henrici Knighton, ed. J. R. Lumby, 2 vols. (London, 1895).

Chronicon de Lanercost, Maitland Club (Glasgow, 1839).

Drummond, W., Viscount Strathallan, *The Genealogie of the Noble and Ancient House of Drummond* (Edinburgh, 1831).

Extracta e Variis Cronicis Scocie, Abbotsford Club (Edinburgh, 1842).

Fordun, Johannis de, *Chronica Gentis Scotorum*, ed. W. F. Skene (Edinburgh, 1871–2).

Sir John Froissart's Chronicles, trans. T. Johnes, 2 vols. (London, 1868).

Gray, Sir Thomas, *Scalacronica, by Sir Thomas Gray of Heton Knight*, Maitland Club (Glasgow, 1836).

Gray, Sir Thomas, *Scalacronica: The Reigns of Edward I, Edward II and Edward III*, trans. H. Maxwell (Glasgow, 1907).

Hume, D., of Godscroft, *The History of the Houses of Douglas and Angus*, 3 vols. (Edinburgh, 1644).

Kervyn de Lettenhove, H., Baron, *Oeuvres de Froissart publiées avec les variants des divers manuscrits*, 25 vols. (Brussels, 1867–77).

Lauder, T. D., *The Wolf of Badenoch: A Historical Romance of the Fourteenth Century*, 3 vols. (Edinburgh, 1827).

Leslie, Bishop John, *Rebus Gestis Scotorum* (Rome, 1578).

Liber Pluscardensis, ed. F. J. H. Skene (Edinburgh, 1877–80).

Maitland Folio MS., ed. W. A. Craigie, 2 vols., Scottish Text Society (Edinburgh, 1919–27).

Martene, E., and Durand, U., *Voyage littéraire de deux religieux benedictins* (Paris, 1724).

Scott, Walter, *The Fair Maid of Perth* (Edinburgh, 1828).

Scottish Verse from the Book of the Dean of Lismore, ed. W. J. Watson, Scottish Gaelic Texts Society (Edinburgh, 1937).

Stewart, A., *A Genealogical History of the Stewarts* (London, 1798).

Stewart, W., *The Buik of the Croniclis of Scotland*, ed. W. B. Turnbull, 3 vols., Rolls Series (London, 1858).

Walsingham, Thomas, *Historia Anglicana*, 2 vols. (London, 1863).

The Westminster Chronicle, 1381–1394, eds, L. C. Hector and B. Harvey (Oxford, 1982).

Wyntoun, Andrew of, *The Original Chronicle of Andrew of Wyntoun*, ed. A. Amours, Scottish Text Society, 6 vols. (Edinburgh, 1903–14).

Wyntoun, Andrew of, *The Orygynale Cronykil of Scotland*, ed. D. Laing, 3 vols. (Edinburgh, 1872–9).

III REFERENCE WORKS

Douglas, R., *Baronage of Scotland* (Edinburgh, 1798).

Paul, J. B., ed., *The Scots Peerage*, 9 vols. (Edinburgh, 1904–14).

Robinson, M., ed., *The Concise Scots Dictionary* (Aberdeen, 1987).

Watt, D. E. R., *A Biographical Dictionary of Scottish Graduates to A.D. 1410* (Oxford, 1977).

IV SECONDARY SOURCES

a *Books*

Agnew, A., *The Hereditary Sheriffs of Galloway*, 2 vols. (Edinburgh, 1893).

Aston, M., *Lollards and Reformers: Images and Literacy in late Medieval Religion* (London, 1984).

Balfour-Melville, E. W. M., *James I, King of Scots, 1406–1437* (London, 1936).

Bannerman, J. W. M., *The Beatons: a medical kindred in the classical Gaelic tradition* (Edinburgh, 1986).

Bannerman, J. W. M., *Studies in the History of Dalriada* (Edinburgh, 1974).

Barrow, G. W. S., *Robert Bruce and the Community of the Realm of Scotland*, 3rd edition (Edinburgh, 1988).

Brown, M. H., *James I* (Edinburgh, 1994).

Crawford, G., *The History of the Shire of Renfrew* (Paisley, 1782).

Dickinson, W. C., *Scotland from the Earliest Times to 1603*, revised by A. A. M. Duncan (Oxford, 1977).

Donaldson, G., *Scottish Kings* (London, 1967).

Forbes-Leslie, J., Lieut-Col., *The Irvines of Drum and Collateral Branches* (Aberdeen, 1909).

Frame, R., *Colonial Ireland, 1169–1369* (Dublin, 1981).

Frame, R., *The Political Development of the British Isles, 1100–1400* (Oxford, 1990).

Gilbert, J. M., *Hunting and Hunting Reserves in Medieval Scotland* (Edinburgh, 1979).

Goodman, A., *John of Gaunt: The Exercise of Princely Power in Fourteenth-Century Europe* (Harlow, 1992).

Grandsen, A., *Historical Writing in England c. 550 to c. 1307*, 2 vols. (London, 1974).

Grant, A., *Independence and Nationhood: Scotland 1306–1469*, New History of Scotland (London, 1984).

Grant, I. F., *The Macleods: The History of a Clan, 1200–1956* (London, 1959).

Harvey, I. M. W., *Jack Cade's Rebellion of 1450* (Oxford, 1991).

Hayes-McCoy, G. A., *Scots Mercenary Forces in Ireland (1565–1603)* (Dublin, 1937).

Hume Brown, P., *Early Travellers in Scotland* (Edinburgh, 1973).

Hume Brown, P., *History of Scotland* (Cambridge, 1911).

Leslie of Balquhain, Col. K. H., *Historical Records of the Family of Leslie*, 3 vols. (Edinburgh, 1869).

Lindsay, A., Lord Lindsay, *Lives of the Lindsays: or a Memoir of the Houses of Crawford and Balcarres*, 3 vols. (London, 1849).

de Loray, T., *Jean de Vienne* (Paris, 1877).

Lloyd, J. E., *Owen Glendower* (Oxford, 1931).

Lynch, M., *Scotland: A New History* (London, 1991).

MacFarlane, K. B., *Lancastrian Kings and Lollard Knights* (Oxford, 1972).

McGladdery, C. A., *James II* (Edinburgh, 1990).

Mackie, R. L., *A Short History of Scotland* (Oxford, 1930).

MacQuarrie, A., *Scotland and the Crusades, 1095–1560* (Edinburgh, 1985).

Neilson, J., *Trial by Combat* (Glasgow, 1890).

Nicholson, R., *Edward III and The Scots* (Oxford, 1965).

Nicholson, R., *Scotland: The Later Middle Ages*, Edinburgh History of Scotland (Edinburgh, 1974).

Palmer, J. J., *England, France and Christendom, 1377–1399* (London, 1972).

Riddell, J., *Stewartiana* (Edinburgh, 1843).

Robertson, J. A., *Comitatus de Atholia* (Perth, 1860).

Shaw, A. M., *The Clan Battle at Perth in 1396* (Wimbledon, 1874).

Simms, K., *From Kings to Warlords: The Changing Political Structure of Gaelic Ireland in the Later Middle Ages* (Woodbridge, 1987).

Sinclair, A. M., *The Clan Gillean* (Charlottetown, 1899).

Skene, W. F., *Celtic Scotland*, 3 vols. (Edinburgh, 1890).

Smart, V., *The Coins of St Andrews* (St Andrews University Library, 1991).

Steel, A., *Richard II* (Cambridge, 1962).

Steer, K. A. and Bannerman, J. W. M., *Late Medieval Monumental Sculpture in the West Highlands*, Royal Commission on the Ancient and Historical Monuments of Scotland (Edinburgh, 1977).

Stones, E. L. G., ed., *Anglo-Scottish Relations, 1174–1328: Some Selected Documents* (Oxford, 1965).

Tuck, A., *Richard II and the English Nobility* (London, 1973).

Tytler, P. F., *The History of Scotland*, 9 vols. (Edinburgh, 1828–43).

Ullmann, W., *The Origins of the Great Schism* (London, 1948).

Vaughan, R., *John the Fearless* (London, 1966).

Wormald, J., *Lords and Men in Scotland: Bonds of Manrent, 1442–1603* (Edinburgh, 1985).

Wylie, J. H., *The History of England under Henry IV*, 4 vols. (London, 1884–98).

b *Articles*

Balfour-Melville, E. W. M., 'Edward III and David II', *Historical Association Pamphlet* (London, 1954).

Bannerman, J. W. M., 'The Lordship of the Isles', in J. M. Brown, ed., *Scottish Society in the Fifteenth Century* (London, 1977), 209–240.

Barrow, G. W. S., 'The lost Gaidhealtachd of Medieval Scotland', in W. Gillies, ed., *Gaelic and Scotland: Alba Agus a'Ghaidlig* (Edinburgh, 1989), 67–88.

Bean, J. W. M., 'Henry IV and the Percies', *History*, xliv (1959), 212–227.

Brown, A. L., 'The English Campaign in Scotland, 1400', in H. Hearder and H. R. Loyn, eds., *British Government and Administration; Studies presented to S. B. Chrimes* (Cardiff, 1974), 40–54.

Brown, A. L., 'The Priory of Coldingham in the Late Fourteenth Century', *Innes Review*, xxiii (1972), 91–101.

Brown, J. M., 'The Exercise of Power', in J. M. Brown, ed., *Scottish Society in the Fifteenth Century* (London, 1977), 33–65.

Brown, M. H., "That Old Serpent and Ancient of Evil Days': Walter, Earl of Atholl and the Death of James I', *Scottish Historical Review*, lxxi (1992), 23–45.

Campbell, J., 'England, Scotland and the Hundred Years War in the Fourteenth Century', in J. R. Hale, J. R. L. Highfield and B. Smalley, eds., *Europe in the Late Middle Ages* (London, 1965), 184–216.

Connolly, M., "The Dethe of the Kynge of Scotis': A New Edition', *Scottish Historical Review*, lxxi (1992), 46–69.

Davies, R. G., 'After the Execution of Archbishop Scrope: Henry IV, The Papacy and the English Episcopate, 1405–8', *Bulletin of the John Rylands Library*, lix (1976–77), 40–74.

Donald, T. F., 'The Dennistouns of Dennistoun', *Scottish Historical Review*, xv (1917–18), 241–44.

Duncan, A. A. M., 'Councils General, 1404–1423', *Scottish Historical Review*, xxxv (1956), 132–43.

Duncan, A. A. M., 'Honi soit qui mal y pense: David II and Edward III, 1346–52', *Scottish Historical Review*, lxvii (1988), 113–141.

Duncan, A. A. M., 'The Laws of Malcolm MacKenneth', in A. Grant and K. J. Stringer, eds., *Medieval Scotland: Crown, Lordship and Community* (Edinburgh, 1993), 239–73.

Duncan, A. A. M., 'The Scots Invasion of Ireland, 1315', in R. R. Davies, ed., *The British Isles, 1100–1500* (Edinburgh, 1988), 100–117.

Ford, C. J., 'Piracy or Policy: the Crisis in the Channel, 1400–1403', *Transactions of the Royal Historical Society*, xxix (1979), 63–78.

Goodman, A., 'Introduction', in A. Goodman and A. Tuck, eds., *War and Border Societies in the Middle Ages* (London, 1992), 1–29.

Grant, A., 'The Development of the Scottish Peerage', *Scottish Historical Review*, lvii (1978), 1–27.

Grant, A., 'Earls and Earldoms in Late Medieval Scotland, c.1310–1460', in J. Bossy and P. Jupp, eds., *Essays Presented to Michael Roberts* (Belfast, 1976), 24–41.

Grant, A., 'The Otterburn War from the Scottish point of view', in A. Goodman and A. Tuck, eds., *War and Border Societies in the Middle Ages* (London, 1992), 30–65.

Grant, A., 'Scotland's "Celtic Fringe" in the Late Middle Ages: The MacDonald Lords of the Isles and the Kingdom of Scotland', in R. R. Davies, ed., *The British Isles, 1100–1500* (Edinburgh, 1988), 118–141.

Grant, A., 'Thanes and Thanages, from the Eleventh to the Fourteenth Centuries', in A. Grant and K. J. Stringer, eds., *Medieval Scotland: Crown, Lordshp and Community* (Edinburgh, 1993), 39–79.

Grant, A., 'The Wolf of Badenoch', in W. D. H. Sellar, ed., *Moray: Province and People* (The Scottish Society for Northern Studies, 1992), 143–61.

Ho Peng Yoke, 'Ancient and Medieval Observations of Comets and Novae in Chinese sources', *Vistas in Astronomy*, v (1962), 127–225.

Lewis, N. B., 'The Last Medieval Summons of the English Feudal Levy', *English Historical Review*, lxxiii (1958), 1–26.

Lyall, R. J., 'The lost literature of Medieval Scotland', in J. D. McClure and M. R. G. Spiller, eds., *Bryght Lanternis: Essays on the Language and Literature of Medieval and Renaissance Scotland* (Aberdeen, 1989), 33–47.

Lydon, J., 'The Scottish Soldier in Medieval Ireland: The Bruce Invasion and the Galloglass', in G. Simpson, ed., *The Scottish Soldier Abroad, 1247–1967* (Edinburgh, 1992), 1–15.

MacEwen, A. B. W., *Notes and Queries of the Society for West Highland & Island Historical Research*, xiv, 6–8.

McKim, A. M., 'James Douglas and Barbour's ideal of Knighthood', *Forum for Modern Language Studies*, xvii (1981), 167–180.

M'Niven, P., 'The Scottish Policy of the Percies and the strategy of the Rebellion of 1403', *Bulletin of the John Rylands Library*, lxii (1979), 498–530.

Madden, C. A., 'The royal demesne in northern Scotland during the later middle ages', *Northern Scotland*, iii (1977–8), 1–24.

Mason, R. A., 'Scotching the Brut: Politics, History and National Myth in 16th Century Britain', in R. A. Mason, ed., *Scotland and England, 1286–1815* (Edinburgh, 1987), 60–84.

Matheson, W., 'Traditions of the MacKenzies', *Transactions of the Gaelic Society of Inverness*, xlii (1953–9), 153–181.

Meek, D. E., 'The Gaelic Ballads of Medieval Scotland', *Transactions of the Gaelic Society of Inverness*, lv (1986–7), 47–72.

Nicholson, R., 'David II, the Historians and the Chroniclers', *Scottish Historical Review*, xlv (1966), 59–78.

Palmer, J. J. N., 'The Authorship, Date and Historical value of the French Chronicles of the Lancastrian Revolution', *Bulletin of the John Rylands Library*, lxi (1978–9), 145–181, 398–421.

Scott, W. W., 'John of Fordun's Description of the Western Isles', *Scottish Studies*, xxiii (1979), 1–13.

Sellar, W. D. H., 'The Earliest Campbells — Norman, Briton or Gael?', *Scottish Studies*, xvii (1973), 109–122.

Simms, K., 'The archbishops of Armagh and the O'Neills, 1347–71', *Irish Historical Studies*, xix (1974–5), 38–55.

Stewart, I., 'The Scottish Royal Mints', in R. A. G. Carson, ed., *Mints, Dies and Currency: Essays in Memory of A. E. G. Baldwin* (London, 1971), 165–273.

Stones, E. L. G., 'The Appeal to History in Anglo-Scottish relations between 1291 and 1401', *Archives*, ix (1969–70), 11–21, 80–83.

Storey, R. L., 'The Wardens of the Marches of England towards Scotland, 1377–1489', *English Historical Review*, lxxii (1957), 593–615.

Summerson, H., 'Responses to War: Carlisle and the West March in the later Fourteenth Century', in A. Goodman and A. Tuck, eds., *War and Border Societies in the Middle Ages* (London, 1992), 155–177.

Swinton, G. S. C., 'John of Swinton: A Border Fighter of the Middle Ages', *Scottish Historical Review*, xvi (1919), 261–279.

Tuck, J. A., 'Richard II and the Border Magnates', *Northern History*, iii (1968), 27–52.

Webster, B., 'David II and the Government of Fourteenth Century Scotland', *Transactions of the Royal Historical Society*, 5th series, xvi (1966), 115–130.

Webster, B., 'The English Occupations of Dumfriesshire in the Fourteenth century', *Transactions of the Dumfriesshire and Galloway Natural History and Antiquarian Society*, 3rd series, xxxv (1956–7), 64–80.

Webster, B., 'Scotland without a King, 1329–1341', in A. Grant and K. J. Stringer, eds., *Medieval Scotland: Crown, Lordship and Community* (Edinburgh, 1993), 223–238.

Wormald, J. M., 'Taming the Magnates?', in K. J. Stringer, ed., *Essays on the Nobility of Medieval Scotland* (Edinburgh, 1985), 270–280.

Young, A., 'The Earls and Earldom of Buchan in the Thirteenth Century', in A. Grant and K. J. Stringer, eds., *Medieval Scotland: Crown, Lordship and Community* (Edinburgh, 1993), 174–202.

c *Theses*

Crawford, B. E., 'The Earls of Orkney-Caithness and their relations with Norway and Scotland: 1158–1470' (unpublished Ph.D thesis, University of St Andrews, 1971).

Grant, A., 'The Higher Nobility in Scotland and their Estates, c.1371–1424' (unpublished D.Phil thesis, University of Oxford, 1975).

MacGregor, M. D. W., 'A Political History of the MacGregors before 1571' (unpublished Ph.D thesis, University of Edinburgh, 1989).

Mapstone, S., 'The Advice to Princes Tradition in Scottish Literature, 1450–1500' (unpublished D.Phil thesis, University of Oxford, 1986).

Index

Aberchirder, 47

Aberdeen, 24, 53, 132, 136, 141–2, 201–2, 234–5, 237
  Bishops of, *see* Tyningham, Adam ; Greenlaw, Gilbert

Aberfoyle, 16

Aberluthnott, 47

Abernethy, lordship of, 164, 257

Abernethy, Margaret, countess of Angus, 82

Abernethy, Sir William, 270

Abriachan, 134

Agnew, lords of Lochnaw, 199

Albany, duke of, *see* Stewart, Robert

Alexandria, 46, 77

Angus, earldom of, 62, 79, 82, 88, 94, 135, 164, 265–6, 294, 305

Angus, countesses of, *see* Abernethy, Margaret; Stewart, Margaret

Angus, earls of, *see* Stewart, Thomas; Douglas, George

Annabella (Drummond), Queen of Scotland, 56–8, 135, 195, 236
  marries John, earl of Carrick, 22
  supports her son's bid for power (1398), 212, 224–5
  her death and its political effects (1401), 232
  masses for her soul, 283

Annandale, 52, 108–9, 111, 118, 267

Appin of Dull, 12, 76, 96, 169, 171, 183

Aquitaine, 43

Ard, Alexander de, 75

Ardnamurchan, 89

Ardneil, 117, 136
  importance of as transit point, 94

Argyll, lordship of, 72, 90, 96

growing power of Clan Campbell and the duke of Albany in, 181–4, 212, 257

Arisaig, 89

Armagh, archbishops of, 85

Armorial de Gelres, 46

Arran, Isle of, 282, 286

Atholl, earldom of, 11–13, 16, 71, 78, 96, 176, 178, 309
  acquired by the Steward (1342), 7, 162–3
  raids from, on Angus (1392), 180
  given to David, duke of Rothesay, 213
  alienated to Walter Stewart, 258–9, 282

Atholl, earls of, *see* Strathbogie, David; Steward, Robert the; Stewart, John; Stewart, David; Stewart, Walter

Avignon, 144, 149, 233, 279

Ayton, March Day at, 117

Badenoch, lordship of, 52, 76, 95–6,
  advance of the Stewarts' power in, 11–3, 71–4, 265
  behaviour of Alexander Stewart's adherents in, 85–6, 132, 170–1, 175

Badenoch, lord of, *see* Comyn, John; Stewart, Alexander

Balliol, Edward, 11–2, 16, 40, 89
  claims to Scottish crown pursued by force, 4, 6, 292
  resigns claims in favour of Edward III, 42, 177
  Balliol claims used against Robert II (1371), 42–44, 58–9

Balliol, John, king of Scotland (1292–96), 176–7
Bamburgh, 240
Bangor (Ireland), canons of, 139
Bannockburn, battle of (1314), 271
Barbour, John, author, 58–61
Barclay, Sir David, of Brechin, 15, 53
Barclay, John, of Kippo, 255–6
Barclay, Margaret, heiress of Brechin, 53–4
Bardolph, Thomas, lord Bardolph
rebels against Henry IV, 281, 286–88, 290
Barnbougle, 16
Barra, 89
Bass Rock, Prince James on, 293–96
Beaton, Michael, 13
Beatons, the, 134
Beaumont, lord, 166
Bedrule, 162
Belhelvie, 131
Benedict XIII, pope, 203, 233
Berwick, 10, 16, 117,
burgh of, 19, 110, 287 burned by earl of Orkney (1405)
castle of, 108, 116, 281
treaty of, 16
Berwickshire, 109, 111–13, 115, 142
Birse, 86
Bisset, Sir Thomas, of Upsetlington, 14–5, 25
Blanche, mother of Henry IV, king of England, 43
Boece, Hector, chronicler, 57, 85–6
Bolfracks, 170
Bona, castle of, 134, 184, 202
Borthwick, Sir William, 150, 163, 204, 270, 279
Boulogne, 120
Bourtrie, battle at, 199
Bower, Walter, chronicler, abbot of Inchcolm, 17, 20, 23, 54, 111, 122, 124, 180, 202–3, 212, 224, 227–8, 230–1, 256, 265, 307, 312
description of resistance to Robert II's accession, 40–2
his account of the Otterburn campaign (1388), 144–149

his account of the fall of the duke of Rothesay (1401–2), 232–36, 238, 242–44
his account of the Cocklaws campaign (1403), 267–73
his account of Prince James' departure for France, 291–6
estimation of Robert III's kingship, 302–4
Brechin, bishop of, 15, 200
Brechin, lordship of, 89
Brodick castle, 286
Bruce, Edward (d.1318), 3
Bruce, Margaret, sister of David II, 8–9
Bruce, Marjory, daughter of Robert I, mother of Robert II, 3
Bruges, 139
Brutus, mythical king of Britain, 59, 229
Buchan, earldom of, 46, 77, 81, 133, 199
Buchan, earls of, see Comyn, earls of; Stewart, Alexander
Buchanan, George, chronicler, 304
Buchanan, Walter, of that Ilk, 257–8, 311
Buittle, 162–3, 204
Bunkle, 164
Bur, Alexander, bishop of Moray, 72, 77
disputes with Alexander, earl of Buchan, 84–86, 132, 134–5, 170–1, 175–6
dead, 211
Burgh, Elizabeth de, wife of Robert I, 3
Bute, 120, 136, 141, 207, 231, 282, 297, 312
threatened by David of Strathbogie, 3–6
importance of for Robert II, 94–5

Caithness, earldom of, 74–6, 78, 185
Caithness, earls of, see Stewart, David; Stewart, Walter
Calder, 137
Calder Moor, 231
Cambuskenneth, parliament at (1326), 3

Campbell, Arthur, of Menstrie, 212
Campbell, Sir Arthur, of Strachur, 5
Campbell, Celestine, 136
Campbell, Sir Colin, lord of Loch Awe
  claims lordship of Argyll, 181–2,
  208, 212
Campbell, Dougall, of Loch Awe, 5
Campbell, Duncan, lord of Loch Awe,
  181, 183
Campbell, Iwar, of Strachur, 5
Campbells of Loch Awe, 16
Candia (Crete), 76
Canterbury, 81
Carcary, 263
Cardeny and Foss, lord of, 95
Cardeny, Mariota, mistress of Robert
  II, 95
Carham, battle at, 116
Carlisle, 138, 143 (attacked by Scots)
Carmichael, 162
Carrick, earldom of, 57, 198–9, 279,
  282, 294–5
  granted by David II to John Stewart
  (1368), 22
Carrick, earls of, see David II; Robert
  III; James I
Caterans (ceatharn), 13
  maintenance of, arouses opposition,
  83–88, 170, 132–4
  underpin military power of Gaelic
  kindreds, 180–1
Cavers, barony of, 204, 266, 283
  dispute over, 288–90, 295
Chalmers, William, 170, 262–4
Chamberlain Newton, 115, 117
Charles V, king of France, 112
  concludes treaty with Robert II
  (1371), 43, 109–10
Charles VI, king of France
  concludes treaty with Robert II
  (1383), 118
Cheshire, 270
Chester, 270
Chisholm, Sir Robert, 134, 178
Chisholm, Thomas, constable of
  Urquhart, 178, 201–2
Clan Donald, 182, 209, 212, 266, 309
Clan Dugall, 182

Clan 'Kay', in fight on North Inch
  (1396), 202
Clan Kennedy, 198–9
Clan 'Qwhele', in fight on North Inch,
  202
Clan Ruari, 182
Clann Donnchaidh, 7, 169, 180, 309
Claxton, Robert, English prior of
  Coldingham, 112
Clement VII, pope, 112, 179, 197
Cockburn, Alexander, 142
Cockermouth, Scots raid on (1385), 145
Cocklaws Tower, near Ormiston
  besieged by Henry Percy, relieved
  by duke of Albany, 268–73
Coldingham, priory of, 287
  dispute over 112–3
Colonsay, 90
Colville, Sir Robert, 121, 140
Colville, Thomas, 121
Comyn earls of Buchan, 21, 40, 42–44
Comyn, John, lord of Badenoch
  (d.1306), 6, 12, 77
Comyn, Sir Richard, 52, 73, 77, 163,
  179
Constance, daughter of Peter I, king of
  Castile, 43
Cornhill, 138
Corunna Bay, 240
Coull, barony of, 225
Cowal, 4–5, 182, 207, 209, 282
Crail, Adam, Scottish prior of
  Coldingham, 112
Crawford, earl of, see Lindsay, David
Crawford, William, 270
Creton, Jean de, French knight, 241
Crossraguel, abbey of, 283
Culross, council at (1401–2), 238, 241,
  307
Cumberland, 138, 246
Cumbraes, the, 282
Cunningham, lordship of, 3, 8, 282
Cunningham, Sir William, of
  Kilmaurs, 119, 139

Dairsie, parliament at (April 1335), 6
Dalziel, William, 224
Danielston, Sir John, 44

Danielston, Sir Robert, sheriff of
　　Dumbarton, 141, 183, 212
Danielston, Walter, 280
　seizes Dumbarton castle, 212–3
　made bishop of St. Andrews, dies,
　　256–8
Danielston, Sir William, 195
Danzig, 293
Dardanus, lord of Frigia, 59
Darnaway, 52
David II, king of Scotland (1329–1371),
　　12, 16, 17, 39–40, 42–3, 44–45, 51,
　　53–4, 56–8, 61, 76, 79, 90, 112,
　　118, 135, 145, 172, 178, 242
　birth, 3
　flees to exile in France (1334), 4–6,
　　292
　returns, captured at Neville's Cross
　　(October 1346), 7–8
　his captivity and release (1357), 9–11
　dispute with the Steward over Fife,
　　Menteith and Strathearn, 13–17
　faces and defeats baronial rebellion
　　(1363), 17–19
　proposes changes to succession
　　(1363), 19–22
　plans to marry Agnes Dunbar, 22–25
　death (22/2/1371), 1, 25
　intimidates William, earl of Ross,
　　46–7, 73
　style of kingship, 48–9, 91, 94, 310
　relationship with Edward III, 109–
　　110
Deer, monastery of, 283
Delny, 75
Denum, 115
Deskford, 78
Dingwall, castle and thanage, 77–78,
　　180, 258–9, 288
Dischington, Thomas, of Ardross, 256
Dischington, Sir William, of Ardross,
　　15, 48
Donald, earl of Mar, 262
Douglas, earldom of, 82, 267
Douglas, earls of, see Douglas, William;
　　Douglas James; Douglas, Archibald
　　(3rd earl); Douglas, Archibald (4th
　　earl)

Douglas, Archibald, 3rd earl of Douglas
　　(1389–1400), lord of Galloway, 'the
　　Grim', 49, 113–4, 117, 122, 137–8,
　　140–1, 174, 177, 237
　on embassy to France (1371), 109–10
　recovers Lochmaben castle (1384), 118
　chronicle treatment of his
　　involvement in Otterburn
　　campaign (1388), 143–5, 147–9
　struggle for control of earldom of
　　Douglas, 147–53, 159–61
　secures title and lands of earldom
　　(April 1389), 162–8
　hostility between Archibald and
　　royal house, 185–6, 196, 198–9,
　　205
　involved in duke of Rothesay's coup
　　against Robert III (1398), 214–5,
　　224–6
　daughter marries Rothesay, 227
　dies, 232
　importance of Douglas lordship,
　　305–11
Douglas, Archibald, 4th earl of Douglas
　　(1400–1424), 231, 234, 236, 281
　raids England, 226
　seizes Dunbar castle, 228–9
　his part in the duke of Rothesay's
　　arrest, imprisonment and death,
　　237–246, 306–7, 311
　captured at Humbleton (September
　　1402), 246, 267, 280
　his part in Percy rebellion against
　　Henry IV (1403), 269–73
　negotiations over his release, 278–9,
　　286
　ruined by David Fleming, 288, 290
Douglas, Archibald, of Cavers,
　　illegitimate son of 2nd earl of
　　Douglas, 289
Douglas, Eleanor, sister of 1st earl of
　　Douglas, 289
Douglas, George, earl of Angus, 240,
　　294–5
　illegitimate son of William, earl of
　　Douglas and Margaret Stewart,
　　countess of Mar and Angus, 82,
　　150

secures title of earl of Angus, 163–4
marries Robert III's daughter, made
  heir to Isabella, countess of Mar,
  204–6, 289
feud with Douglas of Dalkeith, 206,
  214
captured at Humbleton (September
  1402), 246
dies in captivity, 280
Douglas, Sir Henry, 140–1, 152
Douglas, Hugh, 151
Douglas, Isabella, countess of Mar,
  daughter of 1st earl of Douglas,
  150, 204, 225, 288–90
marriage to Malcolm Drummond,
  57
marriage (1404) to Alexander
  Stewart provokes political crisis,
  237, 261–5
Douglas, James, of Balvenie (later 7th
  earl of Douglas), 281–2, 287–8,
  290–1
attacks and kills Sir David Fleming
  (1406), 124, 294–6
Douglas, Sir James, of Dalkeith (I),
  109, 114, 140, 142
favourite of David II, 24–5, 49
involvement in dispute over Douglas
  inheritance (1388–9), 151–3, 160,
  167
obtains lordship of Liddesdale, 162–4
feud with George, earl of Angus,
  205–6, 214
Douglas, Sir James, of Dalkeith (II),
  267, 279
Douglas, James, 2nd earl of Douglas
  (d.1388), lord of Liddesdale, 53,
  57–8, 81, 124, 132, 195–6, 289
marries Robert II's daughter, 45
prominent role in border warfare,
  113, 115–7, 119–22, 136–9,
chronicle accounts of his role in
  Otterburn campaign, 143–9
his death sparks disputes over
  Douglas lands, 144, 148–53, 159–
  62, 304–5, 307
Douglas, Sir James, 'the Good'
  (d.1329), 60, 151, 162

Douglas, Mary, daughter of 3rd earl of
  Douglas
marries David, duke of Rothesay,
  226, 237
Douglas, Mary, daughter of William
  Douglas of Liddesdale, 163
Douglas, William, earl of Angus, 289,
  294–5
Douglas, William, 1st earl of Douglas
  (1357–84), 53, 61, 88, 110, 115,
  116, 131, 150–1, 163, 204–5, 289
leads 1363 rebellion against David II,
  17–20
opposes Robert II's claim to the
  throne in 1371, 40–5,
his opposition bought off, 45, 47, 49
close relationship with earl of
  Carrick, 55, 81–2
opposes entailing of the crown
  (1373), 57–8
role in Anglo-Scottish warfare, 113–
  4, 117–8
dies, 119
role of Douglas lordship, 309
Douglas, Sir William, of Drumlanrig,
  196
Douglas, Sir William, the 'knight of
  Liddesdale' (d.1353), 7, 151, 162–3
Douglas, William, lord of Nithsdale
  (d.1392), 198
role in Anglo-Scottish warfare, 122–
  3, 140–1, 145
Douglasdale, 162
Douglases, 282
Doune Castle, 71–2
Drumlanrig, 204
Drummond, John (d.c.1360), 16, 55
Drummond, Sir John, of Cargill, 283
Drummond, Sir Malcolm, 15
Drummond, Sir Malcolm, lord of Mar
  (d.1401/2), 176, 196, 201, 204, 246,
  283
marries Isabella Douglas, daughter of
  1st earl of Douglas, 57
pursues claim to earldom of Douglas
  (1388–9), 150–53, 159–61
loses claim (April 1389), 162, 164
negotiates with Richard II, 166–7

supports creation of Rothesay
lieutenancy (1398–9), 225
imprisoned and dies, 236–7, 261–2,
265
Drummond, Maurice, 16–7
Drummond, William, 195
Dryburgh, 138
Dublin Bay, 286
Dumbarton, 120–1, 135, 208,
castle of, 5, 44, 183
besieged by Robert III (1398), 212–3
Walter Buchanan made constable of
(1403), 256–9, 311
Dumfries, 198
Dunbar, 136, 227
castle of, 227–8
besieged by Robert III (1396), 203
seized by Archibald Douglas, 228–9
lordship of, created for Archibald
Douglas (1401), 237–9
Dunbar, dean of, 203
Dunbar, Agnes, mistress of David II,
23–5
Dunbar, Elizabeth, wife ? of David,
duke of Rothesay, 206, 229, 231
marries David (1395), 200
validity of marriage attacked (1396),
203–4
set aside by Rothesay in favour of
Mary Douglas, 226
Dunbar, George, earl of March, 61,
110, 164, 168, 176, 239, 241, 246–7
favourite of David II, 23–5, 39
supports Robert II's claim to the
throne (1371), 43–4
agreement with king over earldom
of Fife, 50–2
attacks Roxburgh (1377), 111–2
role in Anglo-Scottish warfare, 113–
18, 142, 144
his daughter marries David, heir of
Robert II, 200
marriage arrangements attacked by
king (1396), 203–4
his reaction to dissolution of
Elizabeth's marriage (1400), 226–7
loses Dunbar castle, forced into exile,
228–32, 267–9, 273

leads English raids and attacks former
adherents, 237–8
Dunbar, George, son of earl of March,
226
Dunbar, John, earl of Moray (d.1391–
2), 61, 88, 96, 164, 184
favourite of David II, made lord of
Fife, 23–5, 39
supports Robert II's accession (1371),
43–4
dispute with king's son Robert over
Fife and its resolution, 50–2, 55, 74
dispute with bishop of Moray, 84,
170
role in Anglo-Scottish warfare, 113,
120, 124, 136–7, 144, 200
dispute with Alexander Stewart, earl
of Buchan, 132–5, 153, 175–6
Dunbar, Sir Patrick (d.1357), 24
Dunbar, Patrick, earl of March
(d.c.1368–9), 15, 16, 73
flight from Neville's Cross, 7–8
rebels against David II (1363), 15–8
Dunbar, Sir Patrick, 227
Dunbar, Thomas, earl of Moray, 195,
200, 203, 205, 224
protection agreement with
Alexander, lord of Lochaber
(1394), 84, 184, 201, 209
dispute with Alexander, earl of
Buchan, 170–1
captured at Humbleton (September
1402), 246, 258, 260–1, 267
Duncan, earl of Fife, 7, 12, 50, 169
Duncan, earl of Lennox (d.1425), 141,
183–4, 208, 257
daughter marries Murdoch Stewart
(1392), 170, 179, 181
Dundee, 131, 141, 234–5
St. Saviour's kirk in, 283
Dundonald castle, 95, 139, 290, 294
death of Robert II at, 171
Dunfermline, 168–70, 297
abbey of, 112
Dunfermline, abbot of, John, 113
Dunkeld, bishop of, 15, 95, 123, 136
Dunoon, 5
Dunrobin, 75

Duns, 116
Dupplin, battle of (1332), 4
Durham, priory of, 112, 116
Durham, bishop of, 111–2, 147, 149,
    196

Eassie, kirkton of, 263
Ebchester, 117
Eden, river of, 235
Edinburgh, 6, 91, 115, 117, 119–21,
    123, 125, 136–7, 140–2, 151, 229,
    234–5, 273, 282–3
  burnt (1385), 138
  castle of, 44, 53, 55, 59, 62, 114, 125,
    228, 231, 270, 279, 290, 293–5, 311
  councils in, 77 (June 1382), 152
    (December 1388), 245 (May 1402)
  death of David II in, 1, 25
  tournament in (1398), 212
Edmonston, Sir John, 150, 270, 279
Ednam, 45, 53, 58
Edrystone, 117
Edward I, king of England (1272–
    1307), 59
Edward II, king of England (1307–
    1327), 286
Edward III, king of England (1327–
    1377), 7, 16, 39, 42–3, 109, 177
  campaigns in Scotland (1333–5), 4, 6,
    292
  proposes changes to Scottish
    succession, 9–10, 17, 19–21
  dies, 111–2
'Edybredschelis', near Selkirk, 117
Eglinton, Sir Hugh, 48
Eigg, 89
Eilean Donan, 310
Elcho, monastery of, 12
Elgin, 132
  burgh and cathedral burned by earl
    of Buchan (1390), 175–6, 302
  burgh burned by lord of Lochaber
    (1402), 246, 260
Elilaw, in Northumberland, 121
Erskine, 288
Erskine, Alan, sheriff of Fife, 170
Erskine, John, of Dun, 263
Erskine, Nicholas, 119

Erskine, Sir Robert (I),
  diplomat and court favourite in
    David II's reign, 14–5, 23–5, 39
  supports Robert II in 1371 and
    reconciled with new regime, 43–5,
    48–9
  compensated for loss of royal offices,
    52–3, 55
Erskine, Robert (II), pursues claims to
    earldom of Mar (1404), 261–4
Erskine, Sir Thomas, 176, 204
  David II favourite, 24, 39
  his role in 1371, 43–4
  his loss of office and land after 1371,
    53–4
  service in earl of Carrick's retinue,
    119, 121, 139, 142
  captured at Humbleton (September
    1402), 246
  dispute with Alexander Stewart over
    earldom of Mar (1404), 261–2
Erskine, Sir William, 121
Eskdale, 162, 267
Essich, 184
Ettrick, forest of, 267, 287
Euphemia, Queen, 2nd wife of Robert
    II, sister of William, earl of Ross,
    72
  marries Robert the Steward (Robert
    II), 11
  her influence after 1371, 75, 88–9
Euthacius Rothay, 208

Falkirk, 166
Falkland, 278
  meeting at (1398) organises coup
    against Robert III, 214–5, 224,
    306–7
  duke of Rothesay warded and dies
    in, 236, 241, 244, 311
  council at (May–June 1403), 270–3
Faslane, Walter of, lord of Lennox, 120
Felton, Sir William, 13
Fettercairn, thanage of, 47
Fife, earldom of, 94, 135, 235, 237
  David II and the Steward clash over,
    13–7
  acquired by John Dunbar (1370), 25

dispute between John Dunbar and
Robert, earl of Menteith, over
(1371–2), 50–2, 71, 74
Fife, earls and lords of, *see* Duncan, earl
of; Ramsay, William; Bisset,
Thomas; Dunbar, John; Stewart,
Robert
Fitkill, barony of, 224
Flamborough Head, 296
Flanders, 120
Fleming, Sir David (d. 1406), 200, 205
involved in coup against Robert II
(1384), 124–5
his growing power after Humbleton,
247
his role as royal favourite, 278–9,
281–3, 287
involved in dispute over barony of
Cavers, 288–90
leads royal expedition into Lothian
(1406), 293–6
killed at battle of Long Hermiston
Moor (February, 1406), 294–6,
311–13
Fleming, Sir Malcolm, 5, 53, 125, 278–
9
Forbes, Alexander, 262
Forbes, Duncan, 262
Forbes, Sir John, 262
Ford, 138
Fordun, John of, chronicler, 16, 18
his negative view of Robert the
Steward, 4, 6–8, 21
his view of the Scottish Gael, 86–8
Forres, 132
burned by Alexander, earl of Buchan
(1390), 175–6, 302
Forrester, Adam, 121
Forrester, Thomas, custumar of
Edinburgh, 136
Forrester, Walter, royal secretary, 291
Fortingall, 169–70
France, 113, 123
Anglo-French truce (18 June 1389),
167
attempt to send prince James to
(1406), 291–6
Fraser, Hugh, lord of Lovat, 260–1

Froissart, Jean, chronicler, 121–2
his negative view of Robert II's
kingship, 95, 108, 123–4, 137–8,
142
his account of Anglo-Scottish
warfare of 1384, 119–20
his account of the French expedition
of 1385, 136–9
his account of Otterburn (1388) and
death of 2nd earl of Douglas a
reflection of political propaganda,
143–50
Fyvie castle, 199

Galloway, lordship of, 78, 198, 267, 282
Garioch, lordship of, 261–2, 264
Garmoran, 90
Garth, 170
Gaunt, John of, duke of Lancaster, earl
of Richmond, 12–3, 226
plans to make him David II's heir, 9,
20–1, 42–3
role in Anglo-Scottish warfare and
diplomacy, 115–6, 119, 121, 138,
206–7, 230
forced into short exile by peasants'
revolt (1381), 117
General councils,
Glasgow (September 1384), 122–3;
Holyrood (November 1384), 124,
132; Edinburgh (April 1385), 132–
3, 135–6; Linlithgow (August
1388), 150; Edinburgh (December
1388), 152; Edinburgh (April
1389), 161, 164; Perth (April
1398), 206–7, 209–11; Perth
(January 1399), 215, 223, 225;
Edinburgh (May 1402), 244–5;
Linlithgow (April 1404), 278;
unknown location (March 1392),
181
Geneva, Robert of (pope Clement VII),
112
Gerson, Jean, 244
Glamis, 131
Glasclune, barony of, 15
Glasgow, 20, 112, council at (1384),
122–3

Glasgow, bishop of, *see* Wardlaw,
    Walter; Glendinning, Mathew
Glen Almond, 95
Glenatnay, castle of, 263
Glen Brerachan (Glasclune), battle of
    (January 1392), 180, 263, 302
Glendinning, Mathew, bishop of
    Glasgow, 162, 179, 205, 279
Glen Dochart, 71, 96, 169–70, 183, 271
Glendowachy, 78
Glenelg, 73
Glen Finglas, 95
Glengarry, 73
Glen Lyon, 76, 169
Glen Prosen, 94
Glen Shee, 95
Glen Tilt, 7
Gordon, Adam, 267
Gordon, Sir John, 116
Govàn, Laurence of, 117
Graham, John, earl of Menteith, 7
Graham, Margaret, countess of
    Menteith, 16
Graham, Sir Patrick, of Kincardine,
    185, 211, 224
Grant, John, 61
Grant, Thomas, 52, 61
Gray, Sir Patrick, wounded at Glen
    Brerachan, 180
Gray, Sir Thomas, chronicler, 13
Gray, Thomas, 264
Great Glen, 133–4, 178, 184, 201–2,
    209, 211, 305
Great Schism, 112
Great Yarmouth, 296
Greenlaw, Gilbert, bishop of Aberdeen,
    203, 214, 280
    becomes chancellor, 206
Grey, Sir Thomas, 226
Greystoke, baron of, 116
Grymslaw, John of, captain of
    Cocklaws, 268
Guelders, dukes of, 60

Haddenstank, 279
Haddington, 24, 115, 141–203, 230
    burned (1384), 119, 121
Hailes, lands and castle, 237

Hailey (Ayrshire), 121
Haliburton, Sir Alexander, 142
Haliburton, Sir John, 166, 196, 204
Haliburton, Sir Walter, 142
    takes part in battle at Long
        Hermiston (1406), 295
Haliburton, William, 166
Haliburtons, of Dirleton, 280
Halidon Hill, battle of (1333), 4
Hamilton, Sir Alexander, 164
Hamilton, Sir John, of Fingalton, 198,
    235
Hamilton, Walter, 198, 235
Hangangside, Richard, 150
Harding, John, writer, 213
Harfleur, 240, 246
Harlaw, battle of (1411), 259, 265
Hay, Sir John, 170
Hay, Sir William, 270
Hector, son of Tearlach, 202
Henry IV, king of England (1399–
    1415), 42, 267, 278–9, 297
    deposes Richard II (1399), 226
    his invasion of Scotland sparked by
        defection of earl of March (1400),
        227–32
    Scots use Richard II impostor
        against, 240–1, 246
    faces and defeats Percy rebellion
        (1403), 268–73
    crushes rebellion of Northumberland
        and Bardolph (1405), 281, 286–8,
        290
Hepburn, Sir Patrick, of Hailes (I), 142,
    227, 229, 237
Hepburn, Sir Patrick, of Hailes (II),
    killed at Nisbet Muir (June 1402),
    246, 267
Holyrood, abbey of, 112
    David II buried in (1371), 40
    John of Gaunt lodges in (1381), 117,
        230
    general council at (November 1384),
        124
Humbleton, battle of (14 September
    1402), 258, 262, 281, 307
    political effects of, 246–7, 255, 260,
        267–73, 280

Inchmurdoch (Fife), 18
Innerwick, 164, 271–2, 282
Innes, Sir Robert, 77
Inverkeithing, 18, 140
Inverness, 74, 77, 90, 134, 170–1, 184, 261, 266
Ireland, 6, 143
  Bruce campaign in (1315–18), 3
Irvine, Alexander, of Drum, 262–3
Isabella, countess of Fife,
  makes good her claim to Fife, marries Walter Stewart, 13–4
  marries Thomas Bisset, 14–5
  forced to resign Fife to John Dunbar, 25
  resigns Fife to Robert Stewart (1371), 50–1
  resigns Perthshire lands to Robert (1389), 169–70
Islay, 89
Isles, Alexander of the, lord of Lochaber,
  agreement with Thomas Dunbar, earl of Moray (1394), 84, 184
  his growing power after the collapse of Buchan's lordship, 184, 201–2
  complaints against, 207, 209–11
  raids Elgin (1402), 246, 260
Isles, Anna of the, daughter of Donald, lord of the Isles, 209
Isles, Donald of the, lord of the Isles, 223, 228, 240, 265
  Robert the Steward's grandson, 90–1
  royal expedition against (1398), 206–8, 212–3
  his ambitions in Ross, 259–60, 288
Isles, John of the, lord of the Isles, 6, 13, 52, 134
  marries Margaret Stewart, daughter of Robert the Steward (1350), 12
  nature of his lordship, 84, 182, 309
  amicable relationship with Robert II, 89–91
Isles, John of the, lord of Dunivaig and the Glens, 207, 228
Isles, Mary of the, wife of William, earl of Ross, 75, 78

James I, king of Scotland (1406–37), 89, 245, 247, 255, 308
  in safe-keeping of bishop Henry Wardlaw, 280–1, 287
  granted the Stewartry in regality (1404), 282
  defeat of Lothian expedition of 1406 precipitates attempted flight to France, 291–6, 312
  captured at sea, 292, 296–7, 307
  effect of events of 1402–6 on James' kingship, 312–3
  his assassination (1437), 54, 242
Jedburgh castle, 108
Jedworth, forest of, 204, 206, 261
Joan, Queen, wife of David II, 15
John, King of England, 16
John II, king of France (1350–64), 176
John, abbot of Newbattle, 197
Johnstone, laird of, 116

Keith, Alexander, of Grandon, 258
Keith, Janet, 53, 262
Keith, Robert, 199
Keith, William, the Marischal, 176, 199, 224
  ambitions in earldom of Mar, 261–3
Kelso, 226–7; abbot of, 203
Kennedy, Alexander, 199
Kennedy, James, 294
Kennedy, John, 136, 139
Kilblean, battle of (November 1335), 6
Kildrummy castle, 82, 237
  resolution of debate over earldom of Mar at, 261–5, 281
Kilwinning, 94
Kincardine, thanage of, 47
Kindrochit (Braemar), 94–5
Kingairloch, 202
Kingedward, barony of, 77, 199–200, 258
Kinghorn, 131
Kintyre, lordship of, 3, 5, 12, 89–90, 207
Kirk Yetholm, 239–40
Knapdale, 89–90, 207, 282
Knoydart, 89
Kyle-Stewart, barony of, 282

Kylquhous, Alexander, bishop of Ross, 171

Lammermuir Hills, 108
Lamont, Duncan, 136
Lamont, Robert Duncanson, 209
Lanark, 195, 197
Landallis, William of, bishop of St. Andrews, 14–5, 112
Lauder, Alan, constable of Tantallon, 150–1, 160, 164
Lauder, Sir Robert, 227
Lauderdale, 162, 267, 287
Leech, Farquhar the, 134
Leeds castle (Kent), 242
Leith, 136, 230–1, 293, 296
Lennox, earldom of, 72, 135, 141, 170, 181–4, 212, 257–8
Lennox, earls of, see Duncan, earl of
Lennox, Isabella of, daughter of Duncan, earl of Lennox, wife of Murdoch Stewart, 181
Leon, Bartholomew, 16, 39, 56
Leslie, Alexander, earl of Ross, 149, 200, 224
reaction to mother's marriage to Alexander Stewart, 78–82
dispute over control of Ross, 171, 179–80
dies (1402), 246, 258–60
Leslie, Sir Andrew, of Sydie, 262, 264
Leslie, Sir George, lord of Rothes, 170–1, 179, 224
Leslie, Euphemia, heiress to Ross, 258
Leslie, Mariota, wife of Donald of the Isles, 259
Leslie, Norman, 46, 77
Leslie, Walter, lord of Ross and Philorth, 73, 75–6, 79, 82, 88, 179
favourite of David II, 25
marriage to heiress of Ross, 45–8
dies (1382), 77
Letham, Sir Edward, 113
Leulighem, treaty of, 118, 196–7
Lewis, lordship of, 78, 89–90
Liddell, barony of (Cumberland), 116
Liddesdale, lordship of, 7, 115, 267
disputes over, 151–2, 162–4, 204–5

Lilburn, Sir John, 116
Lindores, abbey of, 244, 283
Lindsay, Alexander, of Baltrody, 170
Lindsay, Alexander, of the Byres?, 119
Lindsay, Sir Alexander, of Glen Esk, 82, 89, 113
favourite of David II, 45
reconciliation with Robert II (1371), 47–9
his death and its effect (1382), 76–9
Lindsay, David, 1st earl of Crawford, lord of Glen Esk, 79, 81, 96, 149, 168, 175, 204–5, 224, 279, 282
marries Elizabeth, daughter of Robert II, 47
dispute with Alexander, earl of Buchan, 89, 131–3, 135, 170–1, 178
wounded at Glen Brerachan (1392), 180
in service of David, duke of Rothesay, earl of Carrick, 195, 198, 200–1, 203, 214
created earl of Crawford (1398), 207–8
abandons duke of Rothesay (1401), 235–6
in France (1401–2), 240–1, 246
role in dispute over Mar (1404), 261–4
Lindsay, Euphemia, mistress of David, duke of Rothesay, earl of Carrick, 198
Lindsay, Sir James, of Crawford, 55, 113, 119, 131, 140, 168, 207
role in political settlement of 1371, 47–9
kills Sir John Lyon (1382), 78–81, 151
role in Anglo-Scottish warfare and diplomacy, 117, 121, 124
claims to lordship of Buchan, 132–3
captured by the English (1388), 149
his influence in household of David, earl of Carrick, 196–200, 294
his death (1395–6), 200–1
Lindsay, John, of Wauchope, 170, 204
Lindsay, Sir William, of the Byres, 47, 77, 113, 117, 150, 195, 204–5

Lindsay, Sir William, of Rossie, 196
  member of duke of Rothesay's
    household, 198, 200
  his part in Rothesay's arrest, 235–6
Linlithgow, 141, 174, 273, 282, 286–8
  Douglas demonstration against
    Robert II's accession at, 40, 43–5,
    49
  general councils at (1388), 150,
    (1404), 278–9
Lithuania, 46
Little Swinton, 112–4
Livingstone, Robert, 170
Lochaber, lordship of, 52, 73, 84, 89–
    90, 134, 184
Locharkaig, 74
Loch Fyne, 257
Lochindorb castle, 73
Loch Leven castle, 23, 73
Loch Linnhe, 183
Lochmaben castle, 108, 118
Loch Ness, 131, 133–4, 184, 201
Locrinus, son of Brutus, 229
Logie, 135, 185
Logie, Sir John (I), of that Ilk, husband
    of Margaret Drummond, 15, 135
Logie, John (II), son of Margaret
    Drummond, 22, 71, 135, 141, 185
Logie, John, 195
Logie, Margaret, see Margaret, Queen
Logierait, 176
London, 44, Richard II's tournament in
    (1390), 175–6, Tower of, 242
Long Hermiston Moor, battle of
    (February 1406), 295–6, 312
Lorn, lordship of, 182–3
Lothian, 16, 45, 53, 55, 94, 111, 139,
    142
Lovell, Richard, 264
Lyon Herald, 121
Lyon, Sir John (I), 131
  his assassination (November 1382),
    79–81, 96
Lyon, John (II), 151

Macculloch, Thomas, 286
Macdougall, Isobel, 182
Macdougall, John, of Lorn, 76, 182

Macillechoan, Hector More, 84
MacKenzies, 259
Mackintosh, Farquhar, 86
MacLean, Hector, of Lochbuie, 202
MacLeans of Lochbuie, 202
MacNaughton, Alexander, of Argyll,
    95
MacNaughton, Donald, 95
MacRuari, Amy, first wife of John,
    lord of the Isles, 90
MacRuari, Ewen, 7
MacRuari, Ranald, of Garmoran, 7, 89
  assassinated by William, earl of Ross
    (1346), 12, 90, 182
Mairead, daughter of Eachann, 171
Maitland, John, 142
Maitland, Robert (I), 23
Maitland, Sir Robert (II), 227–9
Malise, earl of Strathearn, 11, 75
Mamore, 73
Man, Isle of, 52
Mar, earldom of, 62, 88, 96, 135, 247,
    258
  acquired by William, earl of Douglas
    (1377), 81–2
  dispute over (1404), 260–6, 281
Mar, earls of, see Thomas, earl of;
    Douglas, William; Douglas, James;
    Drummond, Malcolm; Stewart,
    Alexander
March, earldom of, 237
  dismembered (1402), 239–41
March, earl of, see Dunbar, Patrick;
    Dunbar, George
Margaret, Queen, wife of David II, 58,
    71, 135
  political opposition to her marriage
    to David II (1363), 15–8
  her divorce from the king (1369),
    22–3
Markle, 237
Maryenknecht, picks up prince James
    from the Bass (1406), 293, 296
Mathesons, 259
Maybole, St. Mary's kirk in, 139
Mearns, 265–6
Meikle Swinton, 113–4
Melrose, 138

Menteith, earldom of, 96, 135, 170,
   185
   disputes over, involving Robert
      Stewart, 16–7
   Robert Stewart's regional lordship
      based around, 71–2, 181–3
Menteith, earls of, see Allan, earl of;
   Stewart, Robert
Menteiths of Rusky, 16
Menzies, Janet, 170
Mercer, Sir Andrew, 136
Merton, John, 279
Methven, 3, 11–2, 71, 94
Minto, 117
Moidart, 89
Montfort, Henry de, 286
Montgomery, Sir John, of Eaglesham,
   195
Montrose, 202, 234–5, 237
Monycabo, 290
Morar, 89
Moray, bishop of, see Bur, Alexander;
   Spynie, William
Moray, earldom of, 51–2, 62, 73–4, 84,
   88, 134, 184, 209, 247, 260, 266,
   288, 305, 309
Moray, earls of, see Randolph,
   Thomas; Randolph, John; Dunbar,
   John; Dunbar, Thomas
Moray, Sir Andrew, 6
Moray, Maurice, earl of Strathearn, 7,
   11, 17
Moray, Walter, of Tullibardine, 16–7
Mortimer, Katherine, mistress of David
   II, her assassination, 14–5
Morvern, 202
Mowbray, Philippa, 16
Mowbray, Roger, 3
Mowbray, Thomas, earl of
   Nottingham, raids Scotland, 119,
   166–7
Mull, 89
Munro, Hugh, 77
Murdach, of Glassary, 39
Mure, Adam, of Rowallan, 8
Mure, Elizabeth, 1st wife of Robert II,
   8, 20, 283
Murehede, Sir William, 278–9

Musgrave, Sir Thomas, 116
Mykery, in barony of Strathord, 113

Nairn, 135, 259
Nesbit Muir, battle at (June 1402), 246,
   273
Nether Glen App, 139
Neville, Ralph, lord Neville, 118, 137,
   166
Neville's Cross, near Durham, battle at
   (October 1346), 11, 17, 21, 24, 51,
   72
   David II captured at, 7–8
Newbattle, monastery of, 138, 197
Newbigging, William of, 205
Newcastle, 229
   agreement at, 10
   attacked by Scots (1388), 143–4, 147
Nithsdale, lordship of, 198
North Berwick, 58, 150
   dispute over barony after death of
      2nd earl of Douglas (1388–9),
      160–4
   prince James' flight to the Bass from
      (1406), 294–5
North Inch of Perth, Clan fight on
   (1396), 202–3
Northumberland, 116, 122, 246
Northumberland, earl of, see Percy,
   Henry
Nottingham, earl of, see Mowbray,
   Thomas
Nydie, ford of, 235

Ogilvy, Sir Alexander, of Auchterhouse,
   sheriff of Angus, 263
Ogilvy, Sir Walter, sheriff of Angus,
   killed at Glen Brerachan (1392), 180–
   1, 263, 302
Ogilvy, Walter, of Carcary, 263–4
O'Neill, barony of, 225
O'Neills, 85
Orkney, 280
Orkney, earls of, see Sinclair, Henry (I);
   Sinclair, Henry (II)
Orléans, Louis, duke of, 240
Otterburn, battle of (August 1388),
   159, 161, 173, 196, 215, 280, 304

political importance and divergent
chronicle accounts of, 142–51

Paisley, abbey of, Robert III buried at,
297, 312
Paris, 240
Penrith, 116
Pentland Firth, 74, 76
Percy, Henry, earl of Northumberland,
116, 118–9, 121, 137, 144, 196,
237, 246
1403 rebellion against Henry IV,
267–73
1405/6 rebellion against Henry IV,
281, 286–90
Percy, Sir Henry, 'Hotspur', 237, 304
captured at Otterburn, 144, 146, 196
role in siege of Cocklaws and 1403
rebellion against Henry IV, 268–73
killed at Shrewsbury, 278
Percy, Sir Ralph, captured at
Otterburn, 144, 196
Perth, 6, 40, 50, 52, 55, 136, 176, 224,
260–1, 263–4, 281, 288, 290, 296
importance of for Robert II, 94
Clan fight in (1396), 202
general councils at (1398), 206–7;
(1401), 232
grant to burgesses of, 283
Peter I, king of Cyprus, 46
Petyt, Duncan, chancellor, 206
Poitiers, battle of (1356), 16, 24, 109
Pontefract, 228, 242, 279
Portencross, 1, 94
Preston, 163

Ramornie, Sir John, 170, 224
his part in the arrest of duke of
Rothesay, 235–6
Ramsay, Robert, sheriff of Angus, 18
Ramsay, William, of Colluthie, 25, 39
involved in dispute over earldom of
Fife, 13–5
Randolph earls of Moray, 111, 309
Randolph, John, earl of Moray
(d.1346), 11, 17, 72–3
dispute with the Steward, 4–6
killed at Neville's Cross, 7, 51

Randolph, Thomas, earl of Moray, 51,
60–1, 72, 310
Rannoch, 76
Ratho, barony of, 282
Redesdale, 144, 149, 304
Redman, Sir Mathew, 196
Reid, Simon, constable of Edinburgh,
39, 43, 73
Renfrew, 4, 94, 282
Reres castle, 233, 243
Rhum, 89
Richard II, king of England (1377–99),
111, 116, 118, 203, 244
his dealings with the Scots in 1384,
120–3
expedition against Scotland (1385),
138–9
issues safe-conduct to Malcolm
Drummond (1389), 166–7
holds tournament in London, 175
deposed (1399), 226, 242
impostor used by Scots, 240–1, 246
Rìgh Airir Goidel, 182–3, 208, 212
Rìgh Innes Gall, 182, 208
Robert I, king of Scotland (1306–
1329), 1, 9, 39, 50–1, 72, 77, 89,
134
his death, 3–4
his posthumous reputation, 58–61,
108, 145, 147, 177, 271
his granting out of the right to bear
the royal tressure, 91
Robert II, king of Scotland (1371–
1390), 135, 139–42, 145, 150–1,
160–1, 162, 164, 170, 194, 283
his birth and early life, 1–3
divergent chronicle accounts of his
political role in the 1330s, 4–8
his behaviour during and after
Neville's Cross, 8–11
becomes earl of Strathearn, 11
clashes with David II over earldom
of Fife, 13–5
opposes David II's marriage to
Margaret Drummond, 15–17
involved in rebellion against king
David (1363), 17–9
his place in the succession threatened

in Anglo-Scottish negotiations, 19–22

apparent reconciliation with David II, 22–3

clashes with David II and John Dunbar, 23–5

his accession to the throne challenged after David II's death (1371), 39–45

his reconciliation with his opponents, 45–8

his coronation, 49

supports his son's acquisition of Fife, 50–2

promotion of the king's sons, 53–5

opposition to his entailing of the crown (1373), 56–9

his use of propaganda, 59–61

estimation of his early years as king, 61–2

promotion of his family in the north of the kingdom, 71–5, 88–9

supports Alexander Stewart's marriage to the countess of Ross (1382), 77–8

opposition to his patronage and policies in the Highlands, 79, 82, 83, 85–6, 131–3

his relationship with John, lord of the Isles, 89–91

the geographical and political orientation of Robert's kingship, 91–6

image of the king as derived from Froissart, 108–9, 136–8

supports Scottish war effort of 1370s and 1380s, 110–18

disagrees with Carrick over response to English raids of 1384, 119–22

ousted from power by Carrick (1384), 123–5

criticised in general council (November 1384), 131–2

views of the king heavily influenced by contemporary propaganda, 148–9, 168

his death (1390) and estimation of his kingship, 171–3

burial delayed, 176

his style of governance and political legacy to Robert III, 307–8

Robert III, king of Scotland (1390–1406), 72–3, 130, 159, 161, 172, 180–3, 194, 199, 226–7, 229, 234, 238, 245, 247, 259, 278, 288

rebels against David II (1363), 17

marries Annabella Drummond and made earl of Carrick (1367), 22

right in succession confirmed (1371), 49

becomes custodian of Edinburgh castle, 53

role in Stewart government of the kingdom after 1371, 55–6, 71

opposes Robert II's entailing of the crown (1373), 56–9

growing power in south of the kingdom, 62

his court increasingly regarded as a focus for political opposition to the king's policies, 81–3, 96

his role in Anglo-Scottish warfare and diplomacy, 111–17, 137

disagrees with king over response to English raids of 1384, 119–22

mounts coup against his father and becomes guardian of the kingdom (1384), 123–5

his guardianship fails to curb power of Alexander, earl of Buchan, 131–5

supports John Logie in dispute with earl of Fife, 135–6

growing control of royal patronage, 139–42

collapse of his affinity after Otterburn (1388), replaced as guardian by his brother Fife, 148–53

his coronation delayed, takes name Robert III (1390), restrictions on his power, 173–7

recovers some power through activities of his son David, 195–6

takes action against his son's marriage to Elizabeth Dunbar, besieges Dunbar (1396), 200–1, 203–4

unable to deal with problems in the north, 201–2, 206–7

his marriage agreement with Margaret, countess of Angus (1397) and its effects, 204–6

growing discontent with his rule, criticised by general council of 1398, 209–11

unsuccessful siege of Dumbarton castle (1398), 212–3

removed from power by Rothesay, Douglas and Albany, Rothesay made lieutenant, 214–5, 223–5

confined to Stewartry estates (1402–4), 255–7

intervenes in dispute over Mar (1404), 263–6

recovery of influence associated with changes in his privy council, 273, 279–81

grants prince James the Stewartry in regality (1404), 282

encourages growth of image of Rothesay as a martyr, 283–6

supports rebellion of Northumberland and Bardolph against Henry IV (1405–6), 286–7

supports David Fleming's acquisition of Cavers, 289–91

decides to send prince James to France (1406), 291–6

his death at Rothesay and burial at Paisley (1406), 297, 312–3

his posthumous reputation, 302–7

long-term factors affecting standing of his kingship, 307–11

Rosneath, 5

Ross, bishops of, see Kylquhous, Alexander; Waghorn, Alexander

Ross, earldom of, 74–6, 82, 88, 96, 184, 247, 264–5, 288, 305, 309

Alexander Stewart obtains liferent of (1382), 77–8, 83

disputes over between Alexander Stewart and countess Euphemia, 171, 178–80

disputes over between duke of Albany and the lord of the Isles, 258–9, 266

Ross, earls and lords of, see Ross, William; Leslie, Walter; Stewart, Alexander; Leslie, Alexander

Ross, Euphemia, countess of Ross, daughter of William, earl of Ross

marries Walter Leslie, 46–7

marries Alexander Stewart, earl of Buchan (1382), 77–8, 81

divorces Alexander Stewart, 171, 175, 179–80, 200

Ross, Hugh, brother of William, earl of Ross, 46, 265

Ross, William, earl of Ross, 11, 13, 24–5, 46, 75, 78–9, 264–5, 309

assassinates Ranald MacRuari (1346), 12, 90

his death in 1371, 48

Ross, William, of Balnagowan, nephew of William, earl of Ross, 46–7

Rosses of Balnagowan, 259

Rothesay castle, 4, 25, 120, 207, mythical origin of name, 208

gives rise to David Stewart's ducal title, 209

death of Robert III at (1406), 296–7

Roxburgh, burgh, castle and sheriffdom, 16, 109, 113, 115–18, 122, 138–9, 204

burgh burned in 1377, 111–12

sheriffship of, in dispute after death of 2nd earl of Douglas, 163–4

sheriffship claimed by Sir David Fleming, 288–90

Rutherglen, fermes of, 162

burgesses of, 141

Ruthven, 72

Ruthven, William, sheriff of burgh of Perth, 283

St. Andrews, 15, 241

castle of, besieged by duke of Rothesay (1401), 233–6

Rothesay briefly imprisoned in, 238

dispute over bishopric of, 256–7,
279–80
prince James in, 280, 287, 292–3
St. Andrews, bishops of, see Landallis,
William; Trail, Walter; Danielston,
Walter; Wardlaw, Henry
St. Brendan, 94
St. Brioc, 94
St. Fillan, 271
St. Giles' kirk, 120, 138
Sandilands, Sir James (I), of Calder,
131, 137, 151, 160, 166, 196
grants rights in Douglas inheritance
to George, earl of Angus (1397),
204–5, 289
Sandilands, James (II), of Calder,
dispute over Cavers, 289
Saracens, 46
Scone, 1, 17, 40, 56, 81, 90, 94, 117,
141, 206, 209, 232, 297, 312
coronation of Robert II at (1371),
49, 51
coronation of Robert III at (1390),
176
Scott, Sir Walter, novelist, 202, 304
Scrope, Richard, archbishop of York,
in rebellion against Henry IV and
executed, 286–7
Selkirk, 150, 162, 204
Semples of Eliotston, 255
Seton, Sir John, 270
Seton, Sir William, 120–1, 142
Shaw, John, 121, 211
Shrewsbury, battle of (July 1403), 268–
70, 272–3, 278
Shirley, John, English chronicler (1366–
1456), 292, 307
his account of Rothesay's arrest and
death, 242–4
Sibbald, Thomas, of Balgonie, 170
Simon Brek, 208
Sinclair, Henry (I), earl of Orkney,
142, 205
dies in 1400, 280
Sinclair, Henry (II), earl of Orkney,
246–7, 311
emerges as a royal councillor (1404),
280–3

supports Northumberland's rebellion
against Henry IV (1405), 286–7,
290–1
involved in prince James' ill-fated
Lothian expedition (1406), 293–6
Sinclair, Sir James, 163
Sinclair, Sir John, of Herdmanston,
142, 161, 163
Sinclair, Sir Walter, 163
Sinclair, Sir William, of Herdmanston,
289, 294–5
Sinclairs of Herdmanston, 150, 280
Siol Eachainn, 202
Skye, 46–7, 78, 89
Sluys, 136
Smith, Henry, 202
Solway, 116
Somerled, Rìgh Innes Gall (d.1164),
182, 208
Soules, William, 3
Southannan, 255–6
South Queensferry, 119, 121
Spalding, Richard, Dundee burgess,
234
Spynie, William, bishop of Moray, 211,
260
Stable Gorton, 151–2, 162
Steward, Robert the, see Robert II
Steward, Walter the, father of Robert
II
marries Marjory Bruce, 3
dies (1327), 6
Stewart, Alexander, son of Robert II,
earl of Buchan, lord of Badenoch,
'the Wolf', 48, 56, 81, 96, 141,
153, 159, 237, 247
imprisoned by David II (1368–9), 23
ambitions in Moray thwarted, 52, 74
build-up of his power as royal
lieutenant after 1371, 72–6
marries Euphemia, countess of Ross
(1382), 77–9
long-term factors explaining the
unpopularity of his lordship, 83–9
complaints against, 124–5, 172
failure of the assault on his position
by his political enemies during
1385, 131–5

his position in the north attacked by
the guardian of Fife (1388–90),
168–70

divorced from Euphemia, countess of
Ross, 179

opposes renewal of Fife guardianship
and attacks Elgin and Forres
(1390), 175–7

loses control of Urquhart and Ross,
178–9

his sons involved in Glen Brerachan
raid (1392), 180–1, 302

effects of collapse of his lordship,
184, 201–2, 209, 305, 309

disputes over title of Buchan, 199–
200

recovery of power after 1402, 260–66

dies in July 1405, 288

his poor historical reputation, 54

Stewart, Alexander, earl of Mar, son of
Alexander, earl of Buchan, 281,
288, 290

incorrectly blamed for death of Sir
Malcolm Drummond, 237

marries Isabella, countess of Mar, and
acquires the earldom against
wishes of duke of Albany, 247,
260–66

Stewart, David, son of Robert II, earl
of Strathearn and Caithness, 52,
56, 81, 141, 178

promotion in earldoms of Caithness
and Strathearn, 75–6, 88–9

grant of Urquhart to (1371), 74

disputes with elder brother,
Alexander, over Urquhart, 88–9

his death (1385X1389), 133–5

Stewart, David, son of Robert III,
duke of Rothesay, earl of Carrick
and Atholl, 140–1, 149, 281–2, 294

his birth (1378), 57

his precocious political career helps
to bring Fife guardianship to an
end, 194–7

his relationship with the Lindsays,
198

his household a threat to Archibald,
3rd earl of Douglas, 198–9

his marriage to Elizabeth Dunbar
and ensuing disputes, 200–1, 203–
4, 226–7

his growing role in royal
government and diplomacy, 201–
3, 205–6

created duke of Rothesay (April
1398), significance of title, 206–8

his knighting (1398), 212

granted earldom of Atholl (1398),
213

involved in coup against his father
and becomes lieutenant, 214–5

power as lieutenant restricted by
council, 223–5

faces English invasion of 1400, 228–
31

chronicle accounts of his character,
232

forceful action in bishopric of St.
Andrews (1401), 232–4

rejects council assigned to him, 234–5

arrested by his own adherents, held
in St. Andrews, 235–6

his supporters eliminated or bought
off, 236–7

moved from St. Andrews to
Falkland, 238–9

chronicle accounts of his life and
death, 239–46

his death (March 1402), 244, 255–6,
259–60

posthumous image as a martyr,
283–4

summary of his career, 306–7, 311

Stewart, Duncan, son of Alexander,
earl of Buchan, 180

Stewart, Egidia, daughter of Robert II,
141

Stewart, Elizabeth, daughter of Robert
II, marries David Lindsay, 48

Stewart, Elizabeth, daughter of earl of
Carrick (Robert III), marries
Douglas of Dalkeith, 56, 114

Stewart, Elizabeth, daughter of
Thomas, earl of Angus, 164

Stewart, Euphemia, countess of
Strathearn, 178–9, 185

Stewart, Isabel, daughter of Robert II, marries Sir James Douglas (2nd earl of Douglas), 45, 58, 150

Stewart, Isobel, daughter of Robert, duke of Albany, 180

Stewart, James, of Durisdeer, 3

Stewart, Johanna, daughter of Robert II, 79, 131

Stewart, Johanna, daughter of Robert, duke of Albany, 183

Stewart, John, of Auchingowan, 174

Stewart, John, of Innermeath, 182–3, 279

Stewart, John, son of Robert, duke of Albany, 225

Stewart, Margaret, daughter of Robert II, marries John, lord of the Isles (1350), 12, 90–1

Stewart, Margaret, daughter of Robert III, marries Archibald, 4th earl of Douglas, 56, 114, 123

Stewart, Margaret, countess of Mar and Angus, 150
mistress of William, 1st earl of Douglas, 82
secures position of her son as earl of Angus, 160–64, 166–7
marriage alliance with Robert III (1397), 204
dispute with Sir David Fleming over Cavers, 294–5

Stewart, Marjory, daughter of Robert II, marries John Dunbar, 24, 52

Stewart, Marjory, marries Duncan Campbell, 181

Stewart, Marjory, niece of Robert II, marries Alexander Lindsay, 47

Stewart, Mary, daughter of Robert III, widow of George, earl of Angus, marries James Kennedy, 294–5

Stewart, Murdoch, son of Robert, duke of Albany, 56, 179, 196–7, 214, 223, 225
appointed justiciar north of the Forth (1389), 168–9, 177
marries heiress to Lennox, 170, 181, 183–5
his captivity after Humbleton, 246, 257–8, 267, 278–9, 286, 288, 305

Stewart, Robert, duke of Albany, earl of Fife and Menteith, 49, 59, 81, 194, 280–2
marries Margaret Graham, countess of Menteith (1361), 16
in rebellion against David II (1363), 17
lays claim to Fife (1371–2), 50–2, 55–6, 73–4
the major promoter of Robert II's entailing of the crown in 1373, 56–7
his territorial advances after 1371, 71–2
role in Anglo-Scottish warfare and diplomacy, 111–14
feud with John Logie over Strath Gartney, 135–6, 141, 185
leads army into England (1388), 143
chronicle accounts of his role in 1385–88, 144–9
replaces his brother as guardian of the kingdom, 148–53, 305
as guardian supports claims of Archibald the Grim to bulk of Douglas inheritance (1389), 159–66
negotiates truce with English, 166–8
attacks position of Alexander Stewart, earl of Buchan, 168–71, 176–9, 180
his guardianship continues after Robert II's death, challenged by Alexander Stewart, 173–6
his political advances in Lennox and Argyll, 181–5
made duke of Albany (1398), significance of title, 185, 205–9, 211
removed from guardianship (1393), 195–7
disputes with Sir James Lindsay, 199–200
leads army against the lord of the Isles (1398), 213
co-ordinates coup against Robert III (1398–9), 214–5, 223–5
raises army to resist English invasion (1400), 231

his growing animosity towards
    Rothesay, 232–4
arranges the arrest of Rothesay and his
    principal supporters (1401), 235–7
makes deal with Archibald 4th earl
    of Douglas, 237–41
supervises Rothesay's imprisonment
    and death, 242–6
made lieutenant of the kingdom
    (May 1402), 246
his power shaken by events of 1402,
    247
dominates Robert III's court after
    1402, 255–6
arranges Walter Danielston's
    promotion to bishopric of St.
    Andrews (1402), 256–7
his influence in the south-western
    Highlands, 257–8
contests control of Ross with
    Donald, lord of the Isles, 258–9
his plans for Mar wrecked by
    Alexander Stewart, 260–6
his role in the Cocklaws campaign
    (1403), 267–73
Wyntoun's estimation of the duke's
    career and character, 272
his lieutenancy renewed in 1404, 278
fear of his behaviour as potential
    guardian to prince James (1406),
    292, 296
importance of the Albany lordship in
    the governance of the kingdom,
    306–11
made governor of the kingdom (July
    1406), 312
Stewart, Robert, son of Robert III,
    149, 194, 197
Stewart, Robert, of Innermeath, 140, 183
Stewart, Thomas, earl of Angus
    (d.1361), 16, 82, 150
Stewart, Thomas, archdeacon of St.
    Andrews, son of Robert II, 233–4,
    256–7
Stewart, Walter, son of Robert II,
    (d.1362), 51
    marries Isabella, countess of Fife,
        dies, 14–5, 25

Stewart, Walter, son of Robert II
    (d. 1437), earl of Atholl and
    Caithness, 56, 224, 279
his execution (1437), 54
marries heiress to lordship of
    Brechin, 89
role in Highland campaigns (1389–92),
    178, 185
involved in Rothesay's death, 255–6
given grant of earldom of Atholl
    (1404), 259, 282
Stewart, Sir Walter, of Railston, 77,
    81, 89, 178
Stewart, Sir William, of Jedworth, 195,
    267
Stewartry, 183, 255–6, 263, 279, 282, 311
Stirling, 136, general council in (1397),
    223, 225
    castle, 23, 44, 52–3, 56, 59, 62, 72,
        179, 183, 200, 258, 311
Strathbogie, David, earl of Atholl
    (d.1335), 21
    restores his inheritance, 4–5
    dies at battle of Kilblean (November
        1335), 6
Strath Braan, 12, 95, 169–70
Strathclyde, 59
Strathearn, earldom of, 12, 16–7, 24,
    71, 88–9, 96, 185
Strathearn, earls of, see Moray,
    Maurice; Robert II; Stewart,
    David
Strath Gartney, 71, 96, 135, 185
Strath Nairn, 131–33
Strathnaver, 134
Strathord, 12, 151, 169–70
Strathspey, 72, 86, 132, 170–1, 175
Strath Tay, 12, 169–70
Strath Tummel, 76, 170
Strathtyrum, 235
Sutherland, earldom of, 74–5, 78, 83
Sutherland, earls of, see Sutherland,
    William; Sutherland, Robert
Sutherland, John, nephew of David II,
    8–9, 39
    dies in 1361, 16
Sutherland, Robert, son of William,
    earl of Sutherland, 74

Sutherland, William, earl of
   Sutherland, 8, 74
Swinton, 113
Swinton, Sir Henry, 113
Swinton, Sir John, 170, 230, 240
   his career as John of Gaunt's retainer,
      112–4
   dies at Humbleton (September 1402),
      267

Tantallon castle, 82, 289
   possession of, disputed after death of
      2nd earl of Douglas, 150–1, 160–6,
      295
   prince James attempting to gain
      possession of (1406), 293–4
Tarbert, 5
Tay, bridge over at Perth, 283
Teviotdale, 108–9, 115, 118–9, 138,
      267–9, 271, 287
Thomas, bishop of Durham, see
   Durham, bishop of
Thomas, earl of Mar (d.1377), 17–8,
      49, 81
Thomas, 3rd Marquis of Saluzzo,
      194
Tibbers, 23
Towers, Sir John, 121
Trail, Walter, bishop of St. Andrews,
      176, 179, 200, 203, 209, 214
   chronicle estimation of his character,
      224
   effect of his death on political
      stability of the kingdom (1401),
      232–3, 236, 256
Traprain, 237
Tulliallan, 270
Tullicurran, in Strathardle, 263
Tulloch, Walter, 170, 234
Tweeddale, 108
Tyndale, John, 234
Tynemouth, 166
Tyningham, Adam, bishop of
   Aberdeen, 179
   as dean of Aberdeen, 57–8
   disputes with Alexander, earl of
      Buchan, 85–6, 132–3, 135
Tytler, P.F., 304

Uist, 89
Ulster, 286
Urban VI, pope, 112
Urquhart, castle and barony of, 52, 74,
      76, 83, 96
   Alexander, earl of Buchan and
      David, earl of Strathearn dispute
      possession of, 88–9, 131, 133–4
   removed from earl of Buchan's
      control (1390–1), 178, 180, 184–5
   advance of lordship of the Isles into,
      201–2, 211

Vienne, Jean, French admiral, his
   campaign in England (1385), 136,
      138–9

Waghorn, Alexander, bishop of Ross,
      262, 264
Wales, 273, 290
Walsingham, Thomas, English
   chronicler, 287–8, 296
Wardlaw, Henry, bishop of St.
   Andrews
   appointment to bishopric and
      appearance as councillor to Robert
      III, 279–83, 286–7, 311
   prince James' guardian, 291, 293
Wardlaw, Walter, cardinal and bishop
   of Glasgow, 120, 123, 280
Warenne, Sir John, 11
Wark castle, 117, 138, 226
Weddale, Henry, 164
Wemyss, Sir John, of Reres, 236
   patron of Andrew of Wyntoun, 144,
      272
   forfeit and his castle besieged by
      duke of Rothesay, 233
   at Robert III's court (1402), 255–6
Westerkirk, 151–2
Wester Ross, 310
Westmorland, 246
Westmorland, earl of, 227, 267, 273
Whitechester, 117
Whithorn, 286
Wigtown, 198
Wilton, 117
Wylyngton, Henry, 286

Wyntoun, Andrew, prior of St. Serf's,
chronicler, 14, 16, 20, 40, 43, 111,
115, 180, 199, 202, 205–6, 212,
237, 257, 279
his view of Robert the Steward, 4–8
estimation of Robert II's character,
95–6, 307
his account of Otterburn campaign
influenced by contemporary
propaganda, 144–5
sympathetic towards George Dunbar,
earl of March, 228–9, 231
his account of the Cocklaws
campaign (1403), 268–70
his estimation of the duke of Albany,
272
his account of prince James' flight
from Scotland (1406), 291–6
death of Robert III and estimation of
his kingship, 297, 302–4

York, 228, 230